HOSTILE CLIMATE

report on anti-gay activity

2000

PEOPLE FOR THE
AMERICAN WAY
FOUNDATION

CONTENTS

President's Letter 4

Introduction 6

Essays 17

    Tony Kushner 18
    Pat and Wally Kutteles 22
    James Dale 25
    Keith Boykin 28
    Samantha Gellar 30
    Rev. Jimmy Creech 33
    Rev. Irene Monroe 36
    Pam McMichael 39
    Walt Boulden 42
    Dana Rivers 45
    Katherine Triantafillou 49

Incidents 53

    National 55
    Alabama 72
    Alaska 73
    Arizona 76
    Arkansas 85
    California 87
    Colorado 115
    Connecticut 127
    Delaware 133
    District of Columbia 133
    Florida 136
    Georgia 147
    Hawaii 154
    Idaho 157
    Illinois 164
    Indiana 176
    Iowa 182
    Kansas 187

Kentucky 188
Louisiana 196
Maine 197
Maryland 200
Massachusetts 206
Michigan 211
Minnesota 219
Mississippi 220
Missouri 221
Montana 227
Nebraska 229
Nevada 234
New Hampshire 236
New Jersey 238
New Mexico 239
New York 243
North Carolina 257
North Dakota 263
Ohio 264
Oklahoma 271
Oregon 273
Pennsylvania 278
Rhode Island 287
South Carolina 289
Tennessee 290
Texas 291
Utah 310
Vermont 313
Virginia 315
Washington 322
West Virginia 328
Wisconsin 329
Wyoming 333

Appendix I: Incidents Listed by Category 337

Appendix II: Glossary of Organizations 351

Credits 358

PRESIDENT'S LETTER

Throughout our history, Americans have witnessed epic struggles over basic civil rights for women, for African Americans, for people with disabilities and for older Americans. As a nation of laws and as a people, we have made tremendous progress toward ensuring equality for all our citizens. But for gay men and lesbians across the United States, rights and freedoms that for most people are fundamental, even ordinary, are still out of reach: The ability to have their families recognized by law. To marry. To be free from harassment and violence. To visit your life partner in the hospital. To love whom you please without fear of losing your job.

Consider one fact: In 39 states, it somehow remains perfectly legal to fire an employee simply because he or she is not heterosexual. In this day and age, that's not just unacceptable — that's absurd. How could such stark inequalities continue? In part, they persist because of a strong political movement that funds itself by portraying gay men and lesbians as less than human. Every day, Religious Right broadcasters, publishers, politicians and grassroots organizers spread the myth that if you're gay, it is a 'special right' to be able to hold a job, or rent an apartment, or adopt a child. On their television shows, they talk about families, trying hard to sound reasonable. Meanwhile, in their direct-mail appeals, they warn that gay men and lesbians are roaming the streets and schools of your town, preying upon children. That is how the Religious Right has perpetuated itself financially for decades: by fomenting hatred.

The results are seen in the intense discrimination that persists in our society. They are seen in statehouse committee rooms, in local ballot initiatives, in the violence visited upon men and women almost every day.

This edition of Hostile Climate, much like our previous reports, gives a sobering sampling of that rhetoric. But this book has become much more than a catalog of right-wing attacks. Because advocates, legislators, cities, colleges and employers have applied widening pressure to recognize the civil rights of lesbians, gay men, bisexuals and transgendered people, the number of resulting disputes has risen almost geometrically. And our proliferating media are reporting them as never before. Today this book has a tremendous amount of terrain to cover, more battles won and lost. When Hostile Climate was first published six years ago, it contained 134 incidents and 83 pages. Today it takes 350 pages to tell the story of the struggle for equality for gay men and lesbians and the obstacles they face.

Among the 364 incidents in this book, there is much about which to be discouraged. In California, millions of right-wing dollars funded a mean-spirited and completely unnecessary ballot measure, the Knight Initiative that denied legal recognition of same-sex marriages, which were already unrecognized under state law. Utah prohibited gays from adopting children or becoming foster parents — even though the state has twice as many children without homes as couples willing to take them. When Mobil Corporation merged with Exxon, the resulting company abandoned Mobil's policy of providing benefits for its employees' domestic partners. And despite the hate-motivated killings of Matthew Shepard, James Byrd, Jr., and Billy Jack Gaither, the U.S. Senate's right-wing leadership once again blocked a federal hate crimes bill. The same fate befell a strong hate crimes bill in Texas — even though Texans were still reeling from the shocking brutality of Byrd's murder.

The opponents of such laws often argue that to recognize a hate crime for what it is somehow punishes thoughts. But that's simply false. As Tony Kushner writes in his essay on p. 18, "Hate crimes legislation criminalizes deeds, not thoughts; it expresses society's just revulsion and special opprobrium for such deeds.... In precisely the same way that society has always condemned calculated murder more harshly than spontaneous, unthinking violence." I cannot fathom the relentless opposition to such laws. Nor can I fathom how a common-sense measure like the Employment Non-Discrimination Act (ENDA), which would prohibit employment discrimination based on sexual orientation, remains stalled in Congress. I helped to write that bill, so I take its annual entrapment personally.

But then I turn to a page in the California section of Hostile Climate, and I see how the Legislature passed an excellent bill protecting gay and lesbian students. In Orange County, a courageous teenager named Anthony Colin succeeded in establishing a Gay-Straight Alliance at his high school — though he had to sue a hostile school board that was determined to thwart him. And in Vermont, the state's Supreme Court ruled that same-sex couples are entitled to all the rights and privileges enjoyed by married couples — an epochal shift, hopefully, in our society's view of gay men and lesbians. While the battle for full equality in this country is far from over, I believe that we gain more ground every year.

Because Hostile Climate has become such an imposing mass of data, we've tried to make our findings easier to understand and use. The introduction includes a detailed breakdown of the trend lines in individual categories. Within those categories, every incident is indexed by page in an appendix. In a new feature this year, all the right-wing organizations and individuals that appear consistently throughout the report are described in a glossary. And because last year's essayists were such a success with readers, we've invited a new group for this book. Once again, their personal stories are often heartbreaking, often uplifting, always enlightening.

On behalf of People For the American Way Foundation, I thank you for your interest in these issues. I hope that within your own community, you'll get involved in the important work described in this book. There will be an end to bigotry in this country if we commit ourselves to the task, teach ourselves about the opposition, and take action.

Ralph G. Neas
President
People For the American Way Foundation

INTRODUCTION

Throughout their struggle for equality, gays have encountered significant, often vicious, opposition. The year chronicled in this 2000 edition of Hostile Climate is no exception to this larger trend.* But several factors also distinguish 1999 from previous years in important ways. By both quantitative and qualitative measures, there are several noteworthy trends.

Hostility by the Numbers

There were more incidents reported this year than in any other year since 1993, when People For the American Way Foundation first began this annual report on the incidents that define the climate in which the battle for equality is being waged. This edition reports on 374 incidents, 242 more than the first edition reported in 1993 and 82 more than last year's edition. This increase in the number of reported anti-gay incidents may or may not reflect a rise in the total of anti-gay incidents across the United States. But, this report, like previous ones, is not a report on all anti-gay activity, but of anti-gay activity that is reported by the media.

The Youth Factor

The most notable trend this year is the rise in gay rights activism among young people. This report recounts efforts by high school students in six schools in Arizona, California, Colorado, New Hampshire, and Wisconsin to establish gay-straight alliance clubs at their schools and to persuade their school districts to bar harassment based on sexual orientation. The growing number of young people who have come out of the closet and are demanding acknowledgment and acceptance is a clear signal of the overall progress the gay rights movement has made toward equality.

At the same time, the opposition that these young people faced is a stark signal of how determined the Religious Right and other anti-gay forces are to thwart advances of gays toward legal and social equality. The anti-gay Right demonizes efforts to promote healthy, accepting environments for gay adolescents as sinister; its readiness to equate such efforts with child molestation indicates the lengths to which it will go to stop what it dubs the "homosexual agenda." Public schools are particularly vulnerable to anti-gay pressure tactics not just because they are public institutions designed to encourage a free flow of ideas, but also because they are subject to the dictates of local communities.

There Oughta Be a Law

This year was distinguished from previous ones by an unprecedented amount of legislative activity focused on protecting the rights of gay, lesbian, bisexual, and transgendered people. In 1999, 25 states considered statewide legislation, whether hate crime bills or anti-discrimination measures. Hate crimes bills that included sexual orientation, propos-

*The incidents in this book occurred in 1999, though their status was updated throughout much of 1999. New incidents from 1999 will appear in next year's edition.

als to outlaw anti-gay discrimination, and domestic partner benefit programs formed the core of these legislative proposals in Congress and the states. The National Gay and Lesbian Task Force's "Equality Begins at Home" initiative mobilized gay, lesbian, bisexual, and transgendered activists for lobbying that helped produce a diverse slate of bills.

Invisible No More

Another emerging trend this year was a growing assertiveness among transgendered activists, long an invisible minority within the gay rights movement, who began this year to take a more public stand as they campaigned to prohibit discrimination on the basis of sexual orientation or gender identity. Anti-gay activists calling themselves "pro-family" seized on this development to exploit public fears and misunderstanding. The lack of legal protections for transgendered people came into sharp focus in several 1999 incidents in which judges denied petitions for name changes and medical professionals refused to honor previously prescribed hormone treatments.

As California Goes ...

In the struggle for gay equality, California presents the nation in microcosm, with battles in the legislature, schools, communities and courts, and anti-gay Religious Right leaders weighing in. In the same year that the legislature passed and Gov. Gray Davis signed three landmark bills to protect gay rights, a statewide campaign to prohibit the legal recognition of same-sex marriage gained widespread support. The campaigns to defeat the gay rights bills and to pass the anti-gay Knight Initiative were bitter and vitriolic. In Orange County, students attending a school board meeting to show their support for creation of a gay-straight alliance club at El Modena High School had to make their way past a sign reading "Grades Not AIDS!" With the help of a legal team led by People For the American Way Foundation, Lambda Legal Defense and Education Fund, and the Los Angeles law firm of Irell and Manella, the students won an important and groundbreaking court victory that ultimately persuaded the school board to drop its opposition to the club. But the victory came only after a rancorous and divisive battle that subjected the students to significant stress and harassment.

On California's legislative front, anti-gay leader Lou Sheldon (see p. 90) gave a satanic twist to a statewide anti-discrimination in schools bill when he called it "AB 666." Award-winning transgendered teacher Dana Rivers was driven out of her Antelope, California, teaching position after announcing her intention to undergo gender reassignment surgery. In suburban San Diego, a school board trustee assailed a non-discrimination proposal for the district, saying it was "not about protection" but "about promoting a homosexual agenda." Anti-gay activists attempted to derail local and statewide policy proposals that would have protected students from discrimination and harassment based on their sexual orientation. These bitter campaigns, compounded by a general culture war against gays, made California typical of the hostility directed against them throughout the nation in 1999.

Opponents of Equality

At almost every turn, gay rights activists and their allies around the nation encountered fierce and organized resistance from the Religious Right, anti-gay organized actions and right wing residents. Although 1999 established a new high-water mark for the introduction of favorable legislation and policy proposals, the fierce opposition these proposals faced serves as a reminder of the struggles likely to continue.

The Year in Numbers and Examples

Overall. The total number of incidents described in this edition grew by nearly 30 percent over last year's, from 292 in 1998 to 374 this year. That increase is, at least in part, the result of greater willingness among the media to cover stories regarding gay men, lesbians, bisexuals and transgenders. It also reflects greater assertiveness by activists and everyday people alike in pursuit of gay and lesbian equality and the entrenched opposition by the Religious Right activists determined to prevent gays from achieving it.

The "Culture War" and the Religious Right's anti-gay crusade. The largest increase occurred in the "Culture War" category, which includes incidents reflecting general intolerance of gays, seen in response to pride parades, speeches, or artistic expressions. Last year's edition reported 36 such incidents, while this year's includes 87. A number of these incidents reflect another recent trend, as gay men and lesbians became commercially "mainstream" to an extent never before seen. Carmakers, brewers, and airlines discovered gay and lesbian consumers and marketed to them through television commercials and print ads, often sparking a backlash by the Religious Right.

To combat the growing inclusion of gays in public and private life, the Religious Right became better organized in 1999. Its leaders and grassroots participants engaged in systematic campaigns to oppose the legal protections sought by gay men and lesbians. In states like Wisconsin and Michigan, the Right organized city-by-city campaigns to defeat proposed and existing non-discrimination ordinances and domestic partner benefit programs in government. In 1999, the Religious Right built on earlier successes in using gay and lesbian issues in its fundraising efforts. Citing the controversy surrounding Terrence McNally's gay-themed play, "Corpus Christi," Concerned Women for America appealed to its members for money, claiming, "[I]t's so incredibly blasphemous it turns my stomach to write about it." CWA claimed that pressure from "radical homosexual activists, the so-called 'arts community,' and even the militant atheists" forced the New York City theater that had originally scheduled and then cancelled production of the play to reverse course again and reinstate the production after all. Religious Right groups also organized against growing efforts to establish anti-harassment policies in local school districts. The Religious Right has continued its efforts to ban any public discussion of homosexuality and to force gay men and lesbians back into the closet.

At the same time, the Right used the media to build public support for its anti-gay views. Through its "Truth in Love" television and print media campaign, the Right attempted to persuade the public that gay men and lesbians can and should change their sexual orientation through Christian devotion. This year's effort was marked by greater emphasis on broadcast media than in previous years. The Religious Right advertising strategy was to paint a kinder, gentler image of its view of homosexuality. Although the Right has had some success in interjecting the "ex-gay" issue into public debates, more and more television stations have declined to air the ads. In either case, the Religious Right continues to play a significant role in shaping public perceptions of homosexuality.

During the past year, many pundits declared that the Religious Right is, if not dead, certainly on life support. But for those who have watched the Religious Right and its institutions over time, those assessments are both overblown and premature. No issue proves the continuing influence of the Religious Right more than opposition to gay rights. The Family Research Council proved that, when its cultural analyst, Robert Knight, was invited to testify before the Senate Judiciary Committee against the 1999 Hate Crimes Prevention Act. All across the nation, the Religious Right continues to be a formidable foe to gay rights.

▌In Idaho, the Christian Coalition was joined by several state and local politicians in calling on Idaho Public Television to drop plans to air "It's Elementary: Talking About Gay Issues in the Classroom." The Coalition's executive director called the decision to air the film a "misuse of taxpayer money" and labeled it part of "the radical left's pro-homosexual agenda." Their criticism escalated when elected officials contemplated cutting the station's funding.

▌In California, members of La Amistad, a coalition of anti-gay, predominantly Latino evangelical Christian churches affiliated with Lou Sheldon's Traditional Values Coalition, held a prayer vigil in front of the district offices of state Sen. Hilda Solis. Their purpose was to demand that she drop support for two bills that would protect gay men and lesbians from discrimination in housing, employment, and public accommodations. Throughout Southern California, they participated in workshops, prayer breakfasts, and political advocacy with the Traditional Values Coalition. Sheldon joined them at the July vigil.

▌In Illinois, the Family Research Council succeeded in convincing a circuit court judge to try to invalidate a higher court's order granting adoptions to two lesbian couples. The circuit court judge attempted to award the Family Research Council second guardianship of one couple's child and illegally disclosed the parent's names to that group. When the presiding judge removed her from the cases and assigned her to traffic court, she sought to circumvent her superior's authority by declaring the adoptions still invalid and voiding her own removal from the case.

▌In Missouri and Virginia, the American Family Association and the Family Policy Network denounced brewer Anheuser-Busch for a gay marketing strategy and for sponsoring gay pride events. Both groups flew banners from a plane above an Anheuser-Busch sponsored auto racing event saying, "Anheuser-Busch: Stop promoting homosexuality." The AFA staged a press conference in which it showed reporters video clips of a gay pride festival that it said revealed acts of "human degradation."

Marriage and family. Incidents of this type rose 55 percent, from 40 last year to 62 this year, as more gays sought the right to create their own families and the anti-gay right wing sought to block those efforts. Two high-profile battles, the successful fight in Hawaii against same-sex marriage and the prospect of legal recognition for same-sex marriage in Vermont, kept the issue alive in many Americans' minds. Many individual struggles over such issues as child custody are also recorded here.

▊ In Arizona, two state legislators tried to eliminate funding for the placement of children with unmarried couples, single parents, or openly gay parents. State foster care officials were concerned because almost one-third of all children currently in the system reside with single parents, regardless of their orientation. The measure failed and the state's Republican governor, Jane Hull, reasserted the state's policy of placing foster children in suitable homes regardless of the sexual orientation or marital status of parents.

▊ In Petaluma, California, some area religious leaders and residents voiced hostility toward a proposal to extend employee benefits to the domestic partners of city employees and to create a domestic partner registry for city residents. Opponents said that marriage should be between a man and woman and that redefining the institution would morally bankrupt society and hurt the family. "We should try to emphasize marriage rather than try to destroy it," said Wayne Bigelow, pastor of the Petaluma Christian Church. After the proposals were adopted by the city council, a group called Citizens for Traditional Marriage attempted unsuccessfully to place a referendum on the ballot allowing residents to vote on the registry.

▊ Connecticut's House of Representatives approved a "poison pill" amendment, thus sinking a bill to allow unmarried couples to adopt children. Previously the bill had enough support to pass. Commenting on the adoption bill, one state representative said, "I quite frankly don't know why we have to denigrate the lifestyle I have chosen [heterosexual] and that most people in this world choose [in order] to achieve the means of gay adoption."

▊ For the second year in a row, U.S. Rep. Steve Largent (R-Oklahoma) introduced a last-minute amendment to the District of Columbia appropriations bill that would have prohibited unmarried couples from jointly adopting children. The bill was aimed at gay and lesbian parents, though it made no reference to them. The bill not only would have prevented the District from using federal monies but would have made federal grants contingent upon the District's not using its own funds for adoptions by gay men and lesbians. Opponents pointed to more than 3,000 children awaiting adoption in Washington and argued that Largent's amendment would greatly hinder their placement. The House narrowly rejected the amendment by a vote of 215-213.

▊ The Indiana Legislature considered a bill that would have prohibited gays from serving as foster parents or adopting children who were in the state's custody. Conservative Republicans and Religious Right activists united in support of the measure, which failed in a state Senate committee. Rep. Woody Burton (R), author of the House bill, said, "A person's lifestyle is their own business, it is not my job to judge that, but my concern is that it puts children who are already at risk at an even higher risk because of discrimination." He claimed that children adopted by gay men and lesbians face social chastisement because of the discrimination against their adoptive parents. Eric Miller, head of Advance America, a coalition of 3,400 conservative churches in the state, said, "We believe it is in the best interest of children to be raised in a traditional family setting." Rep. Burton said he would continue his crusade to outlaw adoptions by gays and would reintroduce the measure in a future legislative session.

∎ In Wichita Falls, Texas, a district court judge upheld a divorce agreement that he construed as prohibiting a lesbian mother from taking her daughter to worship at a predominantly gay church. The judge said that "[I]t was the intent of the parties...that mainline churches would be utilized by the parties for the religious training of the child...and that such mainline churches would include the Catholic church, churches of the Protestant church such as Presbyterian, Methodist, Baptist...and the like, as well as the Jewish synagogue would be included." He continued, "The Court finds that the Metropolitan Community Church at Wichita Falls does not fall within this category." Rich Tafel, head of the Log Cabin Republicans, a gay political group, said, "This ruling is an appalling and unconstitutional overreach of the government, and a clear violation of the separation of church and state." He added, "It is time for anti-gay organizations like the Christian Coalition, the Family Research Council and the Traditional Values Coalition, all whom have claimed that they are only concerned with religious freedom, to immediately join in condemning this ruling and demanding it be reversed." The Texas Court of Appeals upheld the trial court's ruling. An attorney for the mother said that the mother had no plans for further appeals.

∎ In the Nebraska Legislature, right-wing members sponsored a bill that would have prohibited the state from recognizing same-sex marriages regardless of where they were performed. At a committee hearing, several of the state's right-wing activists registered their support for the bill. Jeff Johnson, a professor at the University of Nebraska and a representative of Pilots for Christ International, asked, "If we cannot draw the line in what is morally acceptable, where can we draw the line anywhere?" Claiming that homosexuality is a choice, Johnson maintained that the state would be "doing what is right" by passing the bill. Gordon Opp, a self-proclaimed "ex-gay," also testified in favor of the bill, saying, "If the state of Nebraska put a stamp of approval on anything other than marriage between a man and a woman, I might have been tempted [to be in a homosexual relationship]." Jones' bill died in committee, just as a similar bill did in the previous session.

∎ In Utah, gays were barred from adopting children or becoming foster parents. The Board of Trustees of Utah's Division of Child and Family Services (DCFS) voted twice to disqualify same-sex partners from adoption and foster care, even though the agency's own director opposed the policy change. As of September 1999, there were 2,308 children in state care, but only 1,014 families prepared to care for them. After the board's actions, the Child Welfare League of America ordered the DCFS to remove its endorsement from the agency's policy manual. Child advocacy groups in Utah have filed suit against the new policy.

Politics & government. Incidents in this category rose by 13 to a high of 57 in 1999. The targets of these incidents include the growing number of openly gay and lesbian elected officials and gay rights activists' campaigns like "Equality Begins at Home." Opposition to anti-discrimination ordinances accounted for 33 incidents, one more than in 1998. (See also "Hate Crimes Legislation," a new category in this year's edition, discussed below.)

The vitriol directed at many progressive and openly gay politicians was especially apparent in 1999. In states like California, Michigan, and Wisconsin where the Religious Right is well-organized, anti-gay campaigns took a front seat.

▌ Openly lesbian California Assemblywoman Sheila Kuehl had her seat in the legislative chamber literally prayed over by a Religious Right activist who had been invited to the Assembly as part of a religious group by Assemblyman Bill Leonard. Kuehl said of the incident, "It made me feel like someone had scrawled 'fag' on my desk."

▌ Arizona state Representatives Linda Gray and Karen Johnson took what amounted to a tag team approach to deprive gays of equality and their right to pursue happiness. Together, they introduced or sponsored bills to prohibit gay student groups in public schools and eliminate funding for local governments' domestic partner benefits programs. "Homosexuality is at the lower end of the behavioral spectrum," Johnson said. Gray added, "We don't allow Playboy clubs on campus to promote heterosexuality. Why should we have gay clubs to promote homosexuality?"

▌ New York City (Queens) school board incumbent Frank Borzellieri mounted a viciously anti-gay campaign against his openly gay challenger, Wayne Mahlke. He accused Mahlke of running "to further the radical homosexual agenda." He added, "His views are an abomination to this district, to this community...He is sick." The district still forbids discussions of homosexuality in classrooms. A newspaper columnist also criticized Mahlke, saying his campaign "worries the living hell out of me." Mahlke lost his bid.

▌ In Pennsylvania, openly gay candidate Gerry Hansen faced harsh opposition to his run for a seat on a county commission. During his Democratic primary bid, opponents posted a sign across the street from a polling place saying, "Just Say No to Queers." After Hansen won the primary, his campaign signs were defaced, and a bus shelter was vandalized, both with homophobic epithets. Hansen, however, won the race.

▌ In Michigan, fights over proposed non-discrimination ordinances in two Detroit suburbs, Ferndale and Royal Oak, mirrored each other. The same religious activist was involved with both campaigns to defeat the proposed ordinances. Robert Paczkowski called homosexuality an "unnatural union" and said the Ferndale ordinance was "a smoke-screen to promote homosexual lifestyles." Ferndale adopted its ordinance only to have it repealed by a local ballot initiative. The American Family Association did its part to defeat the proposal in Royal Oak, its leaders denouncing the proposal as "special rights." The proposed ordinance never made it to a vote.

Hate Crimes Bills. The brutal 1998 murders of openly gay Wyoming college student Matthew Shepard and of an African American Texan, James Byrd Jr., and the slaying of openly gay Alabama resident Billy Jack Gaither in early 1999 added urgency to efforts by gay rights activists and their allies to push for state and federal hate crimes laws that included sexual orientation. This category of legislation, new to this edition, includes 23 incidents.

Although opponents claimed such measures would punish thought, most of the bills that either won adoption or came close to passage increase the punishments for existing crimes in specific categories if they are motivated by bias. The Right's strategy of characterizing the proposals as an attack on free speech and thought has proved immensely successful at all levels of government. The Religious Right, conservatives, and right-wing groups have not stopped there, however. Debate over hate crimes bills often sinks into discussions about the alleged sinfulness of homosexuality and the varied reasons why opponents believe gays do not deserve protection from bias-motivated crimes. The states where some of the most notorious hate crimes have taken place failed to pass hate crimes legislation.

▌In Wyoming, where Matthew Shepard was murdered, both the state legislature and the town of Laramie, where Shepard attended college, rejected proposed hate crimes measures that included sexual orientation. One state senator claimed the current statutes were sufficient for dealing with anti-gay crimes. The mayor of Laramie said he did not want the issue to become the media's reason to focus on the town, while local residents balked at the idea that the town's environment might be in any way accountable for Shepard's death.

▌Alabama's state legislature also failed to enact a hate crimes law inclusive of sexual orientation despite a massive lobbying effort by gays and their allies. Several legislators questioned the bill's merit, one reciting a familiar refrain among anti-gay activists: "Every crime is a hate crime." The bill never made it to the House floor.

▌Despite the support of Texas Gov. George W. Bush's own pastor, the state legislature refused to pass an expanded hate crimes bill that would have expressly added add sexual orientation to the state's existing hate crimes law. Supporters said the bill, named after James Byrd Jr., came under attack specifically because it included sexual orientation. Gov. Bush said he objected for that reason.

▌In Michigan, the Religious Right targeted a hate crimes bill because it would have added sexual orientation to an existing hate crimes law. Representatives from the Family Research Council and the Pro-Family Network claimed the bill would punish attitudes and beliefs and that existing laws prevent bias-related crimes anyway. One of them argued that homosexuality is a matter of choice and that, therefore, gay men and lesbians did not need the bill. They were "not born to do what they do," he said.

Struggling for Equality at Work. There are hopeful signs in the area of employment, as the number of reported incidents dropped by almost half, from 36 in 1998 to 20 in 1999.

The incidents detailed in this report suggest that activity in this category has shifted away from hiring discrimination and firings toward conflicts over requests for domestic partner benefit policies. While gays continue to struggle against discrimination to get or keep a job, an additional battleground has formed.

Opposition to domestic partner benefits focuses most strongly on public employment, with right-wing groups waging campaigns across the nation against domestic partner benefits for government employees. Anti-gay forces have often succeeded in convincing lawmakers that such policies promote homosexuality and destroy "traditional" families. Although the Human Rights Campaign recently reported that more than 3,000 private companies, colleges and universities and state and local governments nationwide offer some type of domestic partner benefits program or anti-discrimination policy that includes sexual orientation, the Religious Right and other anti-gay groups have continued their efforts to prevent or undermine equality in the workplace.

▌ In Georgia, an auto plant worker said that he endured repeated anti-gay harassment from co-workers for three years. He said his job was being sabotaged and that one of his supervisors suggested he kill himself because he was gay. Co-workers called him "homo," "sissy," and "faggot," he maintained.

▌ In Indiana, a police officer sued two county judges for allegedly failing to promote her because she was a lesbian. When a senior probation officer position opened up, the officer applied but the job was awarded to an applicant with no prior probation experience. The lesbian officer claimed one of the judges had told her that the court was embarrassed by her dating women.

▌ In California, a local Boy Scout employee sued that group for violating his privacy and firing him because he is gay. He contends the Scouts used private investigators to question his friends, associates, and co-workers about his sexual orientation and that once they discovered he was gay, they fired him. Although his former supervisor admitted that the Boy Scouts do not hire openly gay people, he denied that sexual orientation was the basis for the dismissal.

Prejudice and Censorship in Schools. Consistently one of the hottest spots in Hostile Climate, this category accounts for the second-highest number of incidents this year. We report 76 incidents in this edition, the same as last year. Gay youth have become more courageous, coming out at younger ages, and the Right considers their children susceptible to what they deem pernicious influences of the so-called "gay agenda."

The need both to protect gay and lesbian youth from harassment in schools and to expose them to affirming depictions of gay and lesbian life has become more urgent. Young people, both gay and straight, and their parents, have begun making these demands on schools across the nation. While many important gains in acceptance have been won and many schools bravely support those endeavors, proponents of tolerance in the schools have met fierce resistance from the right wing.

▍In Arizona, parents took their complaints to several legislative bodies in an attempt to disband Gays, Lesbians, and Straight Supporters (GLASS), a support group for gay and allied students, which students at Gilbert High School had formed. The school's student council also tried to eliminate it only weeks after it was organized. The Gilbert school board conducted its own review in questioning the legality of the group after parents complained it was part of the "homosexual agenda."

▍In Wisconsin, vandalism and verbal harassment were directed at students trying to organize a gay and straight student group, Pride and Respect for Youth in Sexual Minorities (PRYSM). Signs put up around the school by PRYSM members were torn down so often that they had to be posted in a locked display case. The group's faculty adviser even endured homophobic comments from fellow faculty members.

▍In Idaho, conservative citizens and Religious Right activists called upon a public library to remove children's books that dealt with homosexuality. Two residents requested that the library move two children's books,"Daddy's Roommate" and "Heather Has Two Mommies," from the children's section to the adult section. One complainant filed a petition with almost 600 signatures and organized an ad hoc group asking the library to move the books.

▍In Maryland, Peter LaBarbera, president of a far-right group called Americans for Truth About Homosexuality, showed how far the right-wing will go to mischaracterize the discussion of gay and lesbian issues in schools in his reporting on a Montgomery County private schools conference where allegations were made that children were being indoctrinated with pro-gay propaganda. A teacher who discussed the way she approaches homosexuality in the classroom came under sharp criticism and the president of one school's PTA became particularly distraught over the idea of discussing gay and lesbian issues with school-age children. One right-wing academic and the head of a national "ex-gay" group offered harsh opinions of discussing homosexuality with children in a local newspaper story on the conference.

Religion: the Power of the Pulpit. Within faith communities, 1999 was particularly noteworthy because of the greater urgency with which gay men and lesbians pressed their pleas for respect and acceptance. There were 51 such incidents in this year's report, compared to the 32 in 1998. Controversies over how to define the place of gay men and lesbians and their relationships within several Protestant denominations helped contribute to that rise.

Several mainline Protestant denominations faced significant internal battles over the role of gay men and lesbians in their ministries and their policies on same-sex marriage. The Methodists, in particular, engaged in several highly publicized confrontations, one ending with the termination of a popular clergyman's ministerial privileges. Radical leaders in the Southern Baptist Convention unsuccessfully sought to move the group's convention from Orlando in protest of that city's welcoming of gay men and lesbians during "Gay Days." The SBC continues to spearhead a nationwide boycott of the Disney Company for its equal employment policies regarding gays.

The struggle within other religions has not been less dramatic. While each faith and each congregation must reach its own conclusion as to how these issues will be resolved in keeping with its own theology, we include these incidents to give the complete picture of the climate in which gays live.

▌In Maryland, a Catholic outreach ministry to gay men and lesbians was ordered, with the Pope's blessing, to permanently cease. A right-wing, religiously affiliated group disparaged the gay outreach ministry as "clearly misguided and patently unjust."

▌The American Baptist Convention ousted four member churches in California, while the Georgia Baptist Convention expelled two Georgia churches, because of their inclusion of gay men and lesbians. One of the Georgia churches was targeted specifically both for having an openly gay assistant pastor and for using its sanctuary for same-sex unions.

▌A major publisher of Sunday School books for the Southern Baptist Convention devised a lesson teaching that homosexuality was sinful. Selling well over one million copies, the lesson also maintained that gays could change their sexual orientation through acceptance of and devotion to Jesus Christ.

▌The head of the Lutheran Church-Missouri Synod condemned President Clinton for proclaiming June Gay and Lesbian Pride Month. He said he took particular offense at the use of "pride" in the proclamation because being gay or lesbian is nothing to be proud of.

This report is not an exhaustive examination of anti-gay activity across the 50 states and the District of Columbia. It specifically does not include anti-gay hate crimes as such, but does refer to them when the response they generate from local communities or law enforcement reveals hostility directed at gay men and lesbians. Research for Hostile Climate relies primarily on press reports with additional interviews providing necessary follow-up to reported incidents.

People For the American Way Foundation has consistently sought to protect the constitutionally guaranteed rights to freedom of expression and free exercise of religion for individuals and organizations. No incident in this report should be construed as an endorsement of, or advocacy for, an abridgement of those rights. It is the opposition to the exercise of those and other rights that gay men and lesbians faced that is the subject of this report. Institutional bigotry detailed in this report continues to serve as a barrier to the rights and privileges gay men and lesbians seek to secure.

Eleven voices from
across the country reflect
on discrimination and
its consequences

ESSAYS

TONY KUSHNER

Democracy is a bloody business, demanding blood sacrifice. Every advance American democracy has made toward fulfilling the social contract, toward justice and equality and true liberty, every step forward has required offerings of pain and death. The American people demand this: we need to see the burnt bodies of the four little black girls, or their sad small coffins; we need to see the battered, disfigured face of the beaten housewife; we need to see the gay man literally crucified on a fence.

We see the carnage and think, Oh, I guess things are still tough out there, for those people. We daydream a little: What does that feel like, to burn? To have your face smashed by your husband's fist? To be raped? To be dragged behind a truck till your body falls to pieces? To freeze, tied to a fence on the Wyoming prairie, for 18 hours, with the back of your head staved in? Americans perfected the horror film, let's not kid ourselves: these acts of butchery titillate, they're good for a goose pimple or two. We glean the news to savor the unsavory details.

And then, after we've drawn a few skin-prickling breaths of the aromas of torture and agony and madness, we shift a little in our comfortable chairs, a little embarrassed to have caught ourselves in the act of prurient sadism, a little worried that God has seen us also, a little worried that we have lazily misplaced our humanity, a little sad for the victims: Oh gee, I guess I sort of think that shouldn't happen out there to those people and something should be done. As long as I don't have to do it.

And having thought as much, having, in fact, been edified, changed a very little bit by the suffering we have seen — our humanity as well as our skin having been pricked — we turn our back on Matthew Shepard's crucifixion and return to our legitimate entertainments. When next the enfranchisement of homosexuals is discussed, Matthew Shepard's name will probably be invoked, and the murder of gay people will be deplored by decent people, straight and gay; and when the Religious Right shrills viciously about how the

Tony Kushner is the Pulitzer Prize-winning playwright of "Angels in America," "Slavs!" and other plays. He adapted and updated this essay for *Hostile Climate* from two columns he wrote for *The Nation*.

murder doesn't matter, decent people everywhere will find the Religious Right lacking human kindness, will find these Gary Bauers and Paul Weyrichs and Pat Robertsons un-Christian, repulsive, in fact. And a very minute increment toward decency will have been secured. But poor Matthew Shepard. What a price!

A lot of people worry these days about the death of civil discourse. But I worry a lot less about the death of civil discourse than I worry about being killed if, visiting the wrong town with my boyfriend, we forget ourselves so much as to betray, at the wrong moment in front of the wrong people, that we love one another. I worry much more about the death in 1998 of the Maine anti-discrimination law, and about New York state's hate crimes bill, which finally passed in June after years of stalling by the state Senate.

> When a person publicly endorses discrimination, that person becomes morally responsible for the mayhem visited upon the targets of discrimination.

I worry more about the death of civil rights than civil discourse. I worry much more about the irreversible soul-deaths of lesbian, gay, bisexual, transgendered children growing up deliberately, malevolently isolated by the likes of Trent Lott and Newt Gingrich. I mourn Matthew Shepard's actual death, caused by the unimpeachably civil "we hate the sin, not the sinner" hypocrisy of the Religious Right. I mourn that cruel death more than the chance to be civil with those who sit idly by while theocrats, bullies, panderers and hatemongers, and their crazed murderous children, destroy democracy and our civic life. Civic, not civil discourse is what matters, and civic discourse mandates the assigning of blame.

This is why I hold public figures accountable for violence. Angry speech doesn't kill. Angry writing doesn't kill. But speech or writing, when it is in support of discrimination, can lead to murder, regardless of whether the words are angry or calm, because discrimination kills. When a person publicly endorses discrimination, that person becomes morally, though not legally, responsible for the mayhem visited upon the targets of discrimination. Discrimination against any group or type of people is not an indulgence in moderate distaste, no matter how moderately it may be expressed; it is not a theological scruple, or a political poker chip. It's an extremely bloody business and no one ought to tolerate it, much less promote it.

The implication of this argument, which is neither original nor new nor anything other than glaringly evident to anyone who's been awake at any point in the last 200 years, is discomfiting only to those who need scapegoats and demons to bolster their politics of fear and resentment. Citizens of a pluralist democracy have to surrender their prejudices, at least in public. The Bill of Rights protects the privately held fantasies of bigots and majoritarian tyrant wanna-bes, but the 14th Amendment — especially when interpreted, enacted and acted upon by intelligent, large-spirited adults — prevents these repellent fantasies from becoming law or terrorism.

Unprotected minorities are prey to violence, random or organized, against which society has effective ameliorative powers, if only it chooses to exercise them. I support governmental intervention in the insidious contemporary workings of oppression, and hate crimes legislation is a legitimate part of that intervention. Since our laws have always drawn distinctions between differing motivations for the same criminal act — for example, the many shadings and gradations of fatal violence, from premeditated murder to negligent homicide — why falter when it comes to identifying bigotry as a motivation?

Such faltering normalizes bigotry: it places prejudice outside the bounds of political and legislative discourse, and that ought not to be the case. A democracy can recognize historical realities such as systematic prejudice and violence; it can act to eradicate their consequences, and still remain a free and open society. The notion that government cannot address complex cultural and political realities without sliding into totalitarian injustice is a cherished lie of bigots, deregulators and mad profiteers alike. Freedom purchased at the cost of oversimplification and amnesia will prove to be illusory at best, and at worst a prelude to new forms of oppression.

Hate crimes are not thought crimes. A thought crimes law would criminalize thinking, which is of course, unthinkable. Hate crimes legislation criminalizes the acting-out of bigotry as violence. It criminalizes deeds, not thoughts; and it expresses society's just revulsion and special opprobrium for such deeds, for bigots who act on their hatred, in precisely the same way that society has always condemned calculated murder more harshly than spontaneous, unthinking violence.

The same standards of proof should apply to hate crimes as to any other criminal investigation, and determining whether acts of violence were motivated by bigotry will be as complex for juries as determinations of motivations and states-of-mind have always been. I believe rape is a hate crime. And I think getting sexual orientation included in hate crimes legislation is a more winnable objective at this point in history than same-sex marriages, which gay men and lesbians will achieve only after we have established our claim to protection under the 14th Amendment.

Here's something I recently read in Charles Davis' and Henry Louis Gates' "The Slave's Narrative": An African visitor to London in the 18th century, John Henry Naimbanna, appalled by the racism he heard during a House of Commons debate on the slave trade, made the following speech outside the House immediately afterward: "If a man should try to kill me, or should sell my family for slaves, he would do an injury to as many as he might kill or sell, but if anyone takes away the character of black people, that man injures black people all over the world; and when once he has taken away their character, there is nothing he may not do to black people ever after." Hence, Naimbanna concludes, disparaging the character of an entire people is the one unforgivable act.

Forgiveness is a vexed business, and homophobia is not interchangeable with the slave trade, but Mr. Naimbanna's point is essentially my own: Discrimination is deadly; it sets the scene for holocausts.

An account of the campaign against a production of Kushner's "Angels in America" in Kilgore, Texas, appears on p. 304.

PAT AND WALLY KUTTELES

PHOTO: KANSAS CITY STAR

A year ago, we were living peacefully and quietly in Kansas City, Missouri. We had three wonderful sons. Our son Barry was a bright young man with a promising career in the United States Army. Barry was a good kid, and he had become a good, kind and honest man.

By the Army's own measures, Barry was an outstanding soldier. Already, the Army had awarded him a number of medals. He was the best .50-caliber gunner in his company and his fellow soldiers called him "Top Gun." Barry's goal was to become the best helicopter pilot in the Army. We grieve that we will never get to see Barry fulfill the promise of his youth.

In the early morning hours of July 5, 1999, while he slept in his barracks at Fort Campbell, Kentucky, Barry was viciously attacked and killed by a fellow soldier. This soldier, who was supported and encouraged in this crime by another soldier, beat Barry to death with a baseball bat. They killed him, in part, because they thought he was gay.

We both have military connections, including Wally's service in the Korean War. We encouraged Barry's interest in a military career. We were proud that Barry wanted to serve our country. Barry had struggled in school because of a learning disability. We were happy that, in the Army, he had found something in which he excelled.

What we did not know at the time was that the Army our son served so well and so proudly was fostering an atmosphere of hatred that would lead to his murder. A year ago, we did not know our son was being harassed daily by his leaders and fellow soldiers.

Barry knew we loved him. Our children's happiness, not their sexual orientation, is all that matters to us. If Barry was discovering that he was gay, we know he would have told

Pat and Wally Kutteles are the parents of Pfc. Barry Winchell, who was slain in his Army barracks in 1999. Since then they have advocated for reform of the military's policies toward gay men and lesbians through the Servicemembers Legal Defense Network, which has a website at www.SLDN.org.

us when the time was right for him. We have both mentored kids in the past and Pat has worked with troubled teenagers, including gay kids who have been rejected by their parents. This rejection is heartbreaking, and we shared this with all three of our sons as they were growing up. We wanted our sons to know that our love for them is unconditional. If you love your child, whether gay or not, you're going to fight for him. We loved our son very, very much. And we want the world to know how much we loved him and were proud of him.

Although the men who murdered Barry have been tried and sentenced, justice has not been served. Yes, we hold those two men responsible for Barry's death. But we hold the U.S. Army responsible, as well. The Army allowed — and even promoted — an atmosphere of hatred toward gay men, lesbians and bisexuals. The Army allowed our son to be murdered. Following Barry's death, it took months for the Army to acknowledge that his murder was motivated by hate. Even in the wake of Barry's murder, the Army has allowed anti-gay harassment to continue.

> The Army allowed an atmosphere of hatred toward gay men, lesbians and bisexuals. The Army allowed our son to be murdered.

We are in touch with many soldiers, and they tell us they must endure slurs and threats every day as a condition of serving our country. They are scared, very scared, that they will be the next one who is attacked.

Because Army leaders have not taken responsibility to change this dangerous climate, our family has been forced to take legal action against the Army. We do this reluctantly, as a last resort, because we are afraid that someone else's child is going to be hurt.

We have done this in the hope that it will help change the hostile climate that exists in the military. We want to see leaders set the example. We want leaders to hold those who harass and assault their fellow soldiers accountable for their actions, rather than letting them act with impunity. We want to see the military truly look out for the well-being of all our nation's men and women in uniform.

We have recently begun to accept invitations to speak at public events, including last summer's Millennium March on Washington and PrideFest America in Philadelphia. We have decided to accept these invitations, despite having never spoken publicly before, because we wanted to pay tribute to Barry's memory. We wanted to honor him.

We never thought that we would become activists, but we want to do all that we can to ensure that other parents and children don't suffer the pain that we have suffered. We believe that we must work in Barry's memory to repeal the "Don't Ask, Don't Tell, Don't Pursue, Don't Harass" policy. This destructive law does nothing more than foster prejudice and hatred. It must end. Openly gay men, lesbians and bisexuals must be permitted to serve our country. The policy is a failure and it contributed in no small measure to our son's death.

In the meantime, we will continue to do whatever we can to stop the harassment and violence that continues in the military. It's an uphill battle, but we have seen progress. Recently, as a result of Barry's murder, the Department of Defense began to tell all service members that harassment will not be tolerated. The department conducted a survey that revealed that 80 percent of service members had heard anti-gay speech within the past year. It should not have taken the death of our son for harassment to be addressed. The Servicemembers Legal Defense Network, the legal aid organization that has supported our family since Barry's death, has reported a constant rise in anti-gay harassment in the military for the past six years. While the Department of Defense's acknowledgment of harassment is a positive step, we wait to see whether military leaders take the issue seriously.

This has been a devastating year for our family. We miss our son terribly, but we have found solace in the kind words of condolence we have received from thousands of caring people. We truly believe that Barry would want us to continue on the path we have chosen. Every day that we work to protect other parents' children, we honor the memory of our child.

An account of continuing anti-gay hostility at Fort Campbell appears on p. 190.

JAMES DALE

Scouting taught me everything a young kid should know — self-reliance, leadership and honesty. For more than half my life I happily worked and volunteered in the Boy Scouts. Things changed in July 1990, when a letter arrived from the Scouts. "We have decided that your membership with the Boy Scouts of America should be revoked," it read. We "forbid membership to homosexuals," a second letter detailed.

I was overwhelmed by feelings of shock and betrayal. I was 19 and I had never experienced such painful and blatant discrimination. How could the same people who had taught me to respect myself now reject me for being gay? After a 10-year legal battle that traveled to the U.S. Supreme Court, the answer still eludes me.

By the Scouts' own standards, I was more than qualified. At 15 I was elected to Scouting's honor society, the Order of the Arrow. At 17, I earned the Eagle Scout Badge, and on my 18th birthday I volunteered as an Assistant Scoutmaster. My commitment and dedication seemed not to matter, though. This discrimination was about identity. The Scouts value honesty and sincerity — but not if you're gay.

Before my dismissal from Scouting, things had gone well with my coming out. At Rutgers University, I found a welcoming, accepting environment. It was a community of diverse individuals. At first my parents' reactions were far from perfect, but over time they worked hard to unpack their fears and prejudices. Today they march in gay pride parades and speak at meetings of Parents, Families and Friends of Lesbians and Gays.

When I began to accept being gay — when I could say it to myself — I stopped hiding. This was back 1989, light years ago in terms of gay and lesbian civil rights. But even then,

James Dale's lawsuit against the Boy Scouts, described here, became a historic, decade-long fight against discrimination. The U.S. Supreme Court ruled on his case in June 2000. Dale, who lives in New York City, continues to work to raise awareness of gay civil rights issues. For more information on his case, visit www.LambdaLegal.org.

I was fortunate to enjoy the work of the many who came before me, both at Rutgers and across the country.

Over the course of 11 months, I came out: first to my college friends, and a bit later to my parents. At that time an article in the Newark Star-Ledger quoted me speaking at a seminar on the needs of gay teens. Someone in the Boy Scouts saw the story and began the process that led to my expulsion. It's sad and ironic that my attempt to educate others prompted such a reaction from the Scouts. For so many years, Scouting had taught me to be honest, to be a leader, to give back to my community — and that's what I was trying to do. But if you're gay, the Scouts punish you for living by those values.

> If a boy is gay, the Scouts teach him to hate the part of himself that makes him worthless in their eyes.

Initially I viewed my expulsion from Scouting as an act of discrimination to me personally, wondering, "How could they do this to me?" But the past decade has given me perspective on this case. Discrimination doesn't just harm an individual — it destroys the very fabric of our society.

When the Scouts suggest to a boy that he is better than a gay kid, they do two things. First, if that boy is gay, they teach him to dislike a part of himself — to hate the part that makes him worthless in their eyes. Secondly, they teach a non-gay child that he only needs to deal with people who are just like him. They rob him of the important lessons that come from working with a diverse group of people. As a Scout, I learned the value of belonging to a community that provides skills and guidance for boys; that's an experience that gay youth deserve to benefit from as well.

The Boy Scouts' lawyers argued that a gay man cannot be a fit role model or be "morally straight," which is stated in the Scout Oath. But the Boy Scout Handbook defines "morally straight" as being a person "of strong character [and to] guide your life with honesty, purity and justice. Your relationships with others should be honest and open." The handbook further implores Scouts to "respect and defend the rights of all people."

So, with the help of Lambda Legal Defense and Education Fund, I challenged the Boy Scouts' policy, arguing that it was based on discrimination and prejudice. In the summer of 1999, the New Jersey Supreme Court unanimously agreed that Scouting is not about discrimination, and that gay men are perfectly qualified to be leaders and members. The Boy Scouts appealed to the U.S. Supreme Court.

In June, a narrow 5-4 majority of Justices decided they understood New Jersey's anti-discrimination law better than the state's own high court. They ruled that the Boy Scouts have a First Amendment right to discriminate against me. In his dissenting opinion,

Justice John Paul Stevens declared, "[U]ntil today, we have never once found a claimed right to associate in the selection of members to prevail in the face of a State's anti-discrimination law."

Despite this ruling, the optimist in me realizes that this case has already done a great deal of good. I'm proud that I stood up for my rights and beliefs. And the positive education that has taken place in America over the course of this 10-year battle cannot be undone. Many people have been motivated to speak out and discuss civil rights. People continue to learn from this story and others like it. Whether the conversation is about same-sex marriage or hate crimes legislation, more Americans have come to accept and understand lesbian, gay, bisexual and transgendered people and the prejudice they confront.

I'm thankful to have witnessed and enjoyed many of these benefits. The work is far from over, but we've come a long way. I can only hope the Boy Scouts of America will be returned to its core principles, because I wouldn't be the person I am without them. Scouting encouraged me to be a leader, and to stand up for what is right. In the end, those lessons taught me to stand up to the Scouts themselves.

KEITH BOYKIN

PHOTO: LEE ENOCH

In the spring of 1980, my uncle, a black gay man, was shot down in the bedroom of his home in St. Louis. The murderer was never apprehended. I learned from that experience that some lives are more dispensable than others.

A few years later, a woman at a Dartmouth College fraternity party asked me if I was gay. I denied it, but her question sent me into weeks of self-reflection and doubt about my sexual orientation. What was I "doing wrong," I wondered, to have sent that message?

After graduating in 1987, I worked nearly two years for the presidential campaign of Massachusetts Gov. Michael Dukakis, who virtually never addressed gay issues and had a mixed record on the topic.

Finally in law school in 1991, I came out of the closet. I told my family, one by one, but was told not to tell my grandmother. Eventually she found out, and she made it known to my boyfriend at my law school graduation ceremony that she did not approve of my "lifestyle." She even asked him to provide his mother's telephone number so she could contact her. My grandmother and I argued and left the issue unresolved.

By 1992, gay issues were central to the presidential campaign, with all the Democratic candidates taking a pledge to lift the ban on gays in the military. Only a year and a half after I came out, I was working in the early days of the Clinton White House when I overheard a senior staff member joke about the issue of "fags in the foxhole." That was enough to prod me even farther out of the closet. Later, Surgeon General Joycelyn Elders was fired because she had the temerity to discuss masturbation as a sexual abstinence tool to reduce the spread of HIV and AIDS. The message again — some lives are apparently more dispensable than others.

Keith Boykin served in the White House as a special assistant to President Clinton, and later helped lead the National Black Gay and Lesbian Forum. He is the author of *One More River to Cross: Black and Gay in America* and *Respecting the Soul: Daily Reflections for Black Lesbians and Gays*. For more information, see his website at www.KeithBoykin.com.

Much to the dismay of my family, I left the White House in 1995 to write my first book, a nonfiction piece about being black and gay in America. Before I finished writing, I found myself on the front lines of another debate as I led an openly gay contingent of 200 African American men in the Million Man March. "We're black! We're gay! We wouldn't have it any other way!" we chanted, as we marched through the streets of Washington. As our group connected with the larger assembly on the Washington Mall, we kept marching and chanting into the throng of hundreds of thousands of men until the crowd separated to make room for us. A member of our contingent observed that it was almost like watching the parting of the seas.

A few days later I was in South Central Los Angeles looking for a barbershop. I decided on a place on La Brea Avenue, although some friends had warned me the barbers were homophobic. The barber who cut my hair asked where I lived; I told him I lived in Washington but worked in Los Angeles. "Really," he said. "Where do you work?" I told him: "The National Black Gay and Lesbian Leadership Forum." He put down his clippers and I could almost feel the wheels turning in his brain. "The National Black what?" I told him once more. Nothing happened.

> When we have the courage to be honest about who we are, many people will not only accept us, they will respect us more.

When my book was published the following year, I went on a nationwide book tour to 20 cities, including my hometown, St. Louis, where my grandmother lives. My grandmother and several people from her church showed up. I asked one of them afterward why he attended and how he heard about it. He told me that my grandmother, without my knowledge, printed invitations to the book signing and gave one to him. In fact, she gave them to all her friends at church and even asked that the church announcer read the invitation during the announcements.

I learned from that incident, and from the barbershop and Million Man March episodes, that when we have the courage to be open and honest about who we are, many people will not only accept us, they will respect us more. Nevertheless, many of my brothers and sisters are suffering each week in the closets of homophobic workplaces and places of worship.

Unfortunately, self-empowerment is important but it's not a panacea. I've seen that many times recently. Tyra Hunter, a black transgendered woman, died after a Washington, D.C. emergency technician stopped treating her at the scene of an accident once he discovered her male genitalia. Lynn Vines, a black gay man in Baltimore, was shot six times by a group of people who yelled anti-gay slurs. Being out and proud was not enough to protect them. All of us share the responsibility to prevent these crimes from happening.

No one's life is dispensable.

SAMANTHA GELLAR

In my first 18 years, I have come to learn that very few people realize that they can become as powerful as the heroes they worship. Any normal person can become a legend, but humans don't naturally assume they're worthy of the deeds that accompany someone great.

When I was 16, living in Charlotte, North Carolina, I did not think of myself as a decent person, much less an individual capable of goodness. Challenged with coming out in a world that kills, insults, slurs, and generally despises homosexuals, I decided to stand back. When I heard a slur, I ignored the speaker; when I sensed danger, I walked the other way.

Like almost every other gay teenager I met, I had my stories of brushes with death via suicide attempts and a sense of alienation from anything normal. The one escape I did have was my imagination. Ever since I was a kid, I'd make up stories to entertain myself; fantasies and fears expressed themselves in these tales. It was only a matter of time before I wrote them down.

My stories had always come out in prose. But a recent interest in theater had me testing out playwriting. "Life Versus the Paperback Romance" flew out while I was in the midst of a much more mundane script. It was almost subconscious how I tapped out those pages over a few days. And in a way, the play did express exactly what I was keeping in the closet of my mind: A simple romance with humor and sappy happiness; nothing complex, only minor hurdles — the only difference was that the characters involved were two women. My hopes for romance, my fears of rejection and hatred, and my personal feelings about life and love infiltrated the script. I saw in it a replica of myself. I didn't think of myself as controversial or upsetting (my self-image at the time was truly mundane and unassuming), and I entered it in the Charlotte Young Playwrights Festival.

Samantha Gellar, 18, is a freshman at Hollins University. When a one-act play she wrote won a regional contest last year but was not performed with the contest's other winners, she began to speak out against censorship. The theater community rallied to her cause, and her play was staged in June 1999 at New York's Public Theatre. She can be reached via Charlotte's Time Out Youth at www.TimeOutYouth.org.

Ultimately it was one of five plays to win awards. I watched as the other four plays were then staged by The Children's Theatre in Charlotte — but not mine. They said its content was "not appropriate for middle to high school audiences." Yet when I wrote it, I was traversing from middle to high school.

That a lesbian would be considered any more upsetting than, say, a blind woman is proof that our society is diseased. Both are born different, both live differently, yet we hate one and pity the other. Hatred and pity are the two punishments we hand out to what we fear; I got the hatred.

Banned from staging the play, thrust into the spotlight, and still quite shy — I made a choice. So many of my friends tried speaking out but were never heard. Here I was with the opportunity, but an untested voice. Unable to avoid something new, I tested it. I began to let people know what was on my mind. I told them how young people suffer, hating their very beings. I spoke about the huge barriers that young people face in schools and out, the bigots and ignoramuses who censor everything from school reports to simple plays entered in ordinary contests.

> Hatred and pity are the two punishments we hand out to what we fear. I got the hatred.

I wasn't the first; my message had been spoken before. But this time people were listening — not because of me or the play, but because they were ready to hear it. At the start, my talents as a speaker were pretty modest; I said what I knew and learned along the way. I began to watch my situation grow into something much bigger: a giant forum of media, political figures, and normal people exchanging their views on censorship of gay youth and youth in general.

But becoming a figure for the media, having my play performed in New York, and winning the support of so many wonderful people: these were not superhuman feats. They were merely side dishes to the entrée I was passing out: the fact that that we are suffering. Gays, lesbians, transgenders and bisexuals are dying by the voice of society — the voice that tells others that we are not worth living and are dangerous enough to murder; the same voice that tells us we're better off dead.

The devices used to kill gays, lesbians, bisexuals and transgendered people may be held by their own hands, but are driven by the highly publicized message that we are downright evil. I tried to give our youth a new message: We are good and capable of even greater goodness.

I wasn't born in a magical cycle of the moon. My family tree is not dotted with revolutionary heroes. I just told the truth; anyone is capable of that. We just don't realize the greatness within. Oppression, hatred, pity and fear all fade, but an act of heroism never dies — it builds a better world. Find in yourself the legends that lie dormant. Whether you're shy, angry, tired, or scared: You are a human being, capable of immense beauty. Don't let that brilliance go to waste.

An account of Samantha Gellar's experience also appears on p. 260.

REV. JIMMY CREECH

In a church trial that took place in Grand Island, Nebraska, on November 17, 1999, a jury composed of United Methodist clergy found me guilty of "disobedience to the Order and Discipline of the United Methodist Church" and, as punishment, withdrew my credentials of ordination. My crime was the celebration of a holy union for two men, Larry Ellis and Jim Raymer.

This was the second trial I had experienced, as a United Methodist pastor, for honoring and celebrating same-sex unions. The first was in March 1998. In that trial, I was narrowly acquitted by a minority of the jurors. The jury in the second trial, however, voted unanimously for my conviction. While I was the one charged and tried, each trial was an act of violence against lesbian, bisexual and gay people.

The trial brought to an end a 29-year relationship that I have had with the United Methodist Church as an ordained minister. The ordination that was taken from me by the jury was given to me by the United Methodist Church. It belongs to the church and the church had a right to take it back. It was not mine to claim; it is not an entitlement. This is my understanding of the meaning of ordained ministry.

This is not to say that what the church revoked was unimportant to me. I can no longer serve the church as a pastor. There is nothing I love more than being a pastor of a congregation. I know that I cannot be a United Methodist pastor now. I will not dwell on it, but be assured that I grieve for what has been taken from me.

However, the ordination that preceded it and cannot be reclaimed by the church is the one that came with my baptism, and the one confirmed by my call to ministry. These belong to me still, and no institution, jury or person has the authority or power to take them away. I will continue to honor and live out this ordination in all that I do.

After a trial in 1999, Jimmy Creech was defrocked by the United Methodist Church for presiding at a union between two gay men. He continues to speak around the country and writes about the Church's struggle to welcome gay and lesbian people, and he is active in Soulforce, an interreligious movement with a similar mission.

While I grieve for my loss, I grieve more for those who are being rejected, oppressed and persecuted by the church because of who they are and because of whom they love. The ordination that has been taken from me is one that the United Methodist Church has routinely denied and withdrawn from gay people. Many gifted people called by God have been denied ordination because of their sexual orientation. Others have been denied fellowship, if not membership in the UMC. Many have been spiritually and psychologically abused by vicious judgment and condemnation. I am only a casualty of the church's bigotry against bisexual, lesbian, gay and transgendered people. They are the true victims and martyrs. I have been punished only for what I've done. They are punished for who they are and whom they love. The difference is profound. My loss and pain trifle in comparison.

> While I grieve for my loss, I grieve more for those who are rejected and persecuted by the church because of who they are and whom they love.

Since 1972, the United Methodist Church has officially condemned and discriminated against lesbian, gay, transgendered and bisexual people, doing them great spiritual harm and contributing to a pervasive hostility toward them in our society. Almost all other mainline and evangelical denominations, as well as the Eastern Orthodox and the Roman Catholic churches, share in this bigotry. It is a bigotry very much like the racial injustice I observed and experienced in the 1950s and '60s. Then, the church rationalized and supported a segregated society, misusing Scripture, tradition and social custom to dehumanize people of color and to deny them full fellowship in the church.

The celebration of love and commitment between two people is a profound and particular embodiment of the gospel of Jesus Christ. It is arrogance on the part of the church to elevate some people's relationship with God, while denigrating others' on the basis of innate sexuality. This arrogance is evil — comparable to racism. The consequences of this arrogance are spiritual, psychological, social and physical violence against gay, lesbian, and bisexual people, their families and friends, and a profaned witness to the gospel of Jesus Christ. We have repented of our racism, although we have much work to do to remove it from our souls and institutions. Now, we must also repent of our unjust treatment of bisexual, transgendered, lesbian and gay people.

The policies and teachings of the United Methodist Church also contribute to the breakup of families. They encourage mothers and fathers, sisters and brothers, daughters and sons not to accept and love their children or siblings or parents whom they discover to be lesbian, gay, bisexual or transgendered. Families who do accept and love their gay members are given no public and official support, forcing them to live in isolation with their "family secret" because of the inhospitality of our church.

This injustice and persecution must end — not only for the sake of the victims of our prejudice, but for the integrity of the church, as well as other Christian communities. Those committed to be followers of Jesus Christ, who spoke of God's realm in which all are welcomed, respected and loved, cannot, with integrity, continue to persecute people because of their sexual orientation and because they love another of their gender. To continue this persecution is to follow fear and ignorance, not grace and truth.

The good news is that the official policies and teachings of the United Methodist Church are not supported by all its members. There is a strong and growing movement among gay and non-gay members to end the bigotry. Lesbian, gay, bisexual and transgendered people within the church constitute a redemptive presence that will ultimately change the church and society through God's grace. This movement toward justice, community and compassion is of God and cannot be resisted, not even by the church. Whether or not the church changes and becomes faithful to the witness of Jesus, God will use this movement to create something new that respects and honors all people as children of God, with undeniable dignity and integrity.

An account of Jimmy Creech's trial appears on p. 230.

REV. IRENE MONROE

PHOTO: MARILYN HUMPHRIES

As a public theologian, one of my outreach ministries is writing a biweekly column called "The Religion Thang" for *In Newsweekly*, a newspaper for the lesbian, gay, bisexual and transgendered (LGBT) community that circulates widely throughout New England. Because the Bible functions as an authoritative text in this society as a means of social and political control toward certain groups of people, I see my ministry as spreading the good news that the Bible is an inclusive text.

Religion has played a salient role in discrimination against all people at different times in this country. Religious intolerance and fundamentalism not only shatter the goal of American democracy, they also foster a climate of spiritual abuse that leaves many people in spiritual exile for the rest of their lives. At present, its excommunicated population is lesbian, gay, bisexual and transgendered people.

Until the 4th century A.D., when the Emperor Constantine converted to Christianity, Christians were despised as much in those days as LGBT people are today. As a matter of fact, to be called a Christian was considered a religious epithet, and it subjected Christians to ridicule and hate crimes in much of the same way as we queers are today.

Just as LGBT people have transformed the pejorative term "queer" into a positive word of self-reference, Christians transformed the word "Christian" into one of self-reverence. Having known this history, I found calling myself a queer Christian neither blasphemous nor oxymoronic. Both are tied to the unending struggle for human acceptance.

Religion has become a peculiar institution in the theater of human life. Although the Latin root of "religion" means to bind, it has served as a legitimate power in binding people's shared hatred.

Irene Monroe is a doctoral candidate at Harvard Divinity School in Cambridge, Mass. A columnist and Ford Foundation fellow, she served on the board of the Millennium March on Washington.

For example, I come from a black religious tradition born of struggle for human accept-ance. When slave masters gave my ancestors the Bible, their intent was not to make us better Christians, but better slaves. The Bible, at least according to slavers, provided the legitimate sanction for American slavery. But my ancestors turned this authoritative text, which was meant to aid them in acclimating to their life of servitude, into an incendiary text that first birthed slave revolts and abolitionist movements — and later the nation's civil rights movements. The Bible told us how to do what must be done. And, in so doing, Nat Turner revolted against slavery, and Harriet Tubman conducted a railroad out of it. My ancestors expanded not only the understanding of what it meant to be human, but also the parameters of what it meant to be a Christian.

Knowing this history, I found that calling myself a queer African American Christian made me no less black nor less Christian. Once again, all are tied to the struggle for human acceptance — just at different times along the human timeline. Jesus' birth came at a difficult point along that timeline. As a Jew who lived during the Roman occupation of Israel, Jesus' life was monitored and shaped by this oppressive reign from his birth to his crucifixion.

Many of those who engage in queer-bashing say they are doing God's will as they interpret the Bible. However, doing God's will is a prodigious task and unmistakably a human enterprise. As a human enterprise, "doing God's will" is invariably subject to error because it is fraught with both humble intent and righteous indignation. Its anchor and its impetus are found in the human act of interpreting "the Word of God." Interpreting Scripture as the Word of God is always subjective, and is always suspect in intent, whether it is done in the ivy towers of seminaries or within the holy walls of sanctuaries. Interpreting Scripture with menacing messages and litanies of "do's and don'ts" is not about embracing and empowering all people; it's about authority and power over certain groups of people. The authority of Scripture does not lie in what God said. It lies in the hands of those in power who determine what God ought to say.

> The authority of Scripture does not lie in what God said. It lies in the hands of those in power who determine what God ought to say.

The Bible is replete with messages that are contradictory and damning to all people. Determining which messages are discarded and which are upheld is not a battle about bib-lical inerrancy or God's will. It is an unmitigated battle of *human* will. For example, there are two creationist myths in the Bible (Genesis 1:27 and Genesis 2:22). The first myth says that God made woman and man simultaneously. The second creation myth is our "rib story," in which Eve is born from a rib of Adam. Undoubtedly this story has ribbed and poked at Christian women throughout the centuries, since it is the authoritative text for substantiating gender inequity in society. The Curse of Ham (Genesis 9:18-27) and the

Apostle Paul's edict to slaves (Ephesians 6:5-8) served as the scientific and Christian legitimation for the enslavement of people of African ancestry. The Sodom and Gomorrah narrative (Genesis 19:1-29) is one of the most quoted Scriptures to argue for compulsory heterosexuality and queer-bashing.

Is it the will of God to devalue and to dehumanize the lives of women, people of African ancestry, and queers? On the question of race, Americans — both Christians and non-Christians — clearly see the answer as no. However, on the question of sexual orientation, many of us are religiously challenged.

As LGBT people enter the new millennium, I can't help but feel a "queer imperative" — a call for our prophetic voices, in the same way that the civil rights movement in this country called for the prophetic voices of African Americans. Our queerness is a prophetic call for social justice, not only here in the United States but throughout the world.

PAM McMICHAEL

I'm sitting outdoors at a Mexican restaurant with my good friend Ben Guess, a main mover of the effort to pass fairness legislation in Henderson, Kentucky. Henderson was the third of four Kentucky communities that passed legislation in 1999 to ban discrimination based on sexual orientation. The ordinances in Louisville, Lexington, and Jefferson County also include gender identity.

Henderson is a somewhat idyllic community of 30,000 sitting peacefully on the banks of the Ohio River across from Evansville, Indiana, where director Penny Marshall filmed "A League of Their Own." Ben is in a league of his own — growing up, coming out and now pastoring a church in the community where he was born, where he played as a child, organized for the Young Democrats, and now lives as an openly gay United Church of Christ minister and social justice activist.

So the effort in Henderson was very personal to Ben and his family, and very personal *about* Ben and his family. The people who have made discrimination their mission — I call them the "Anti's" — often lead their bigoted statements with, "Now I know Ben, but ... I went to school with Ben, but ... I love you, Ben, but ... [fill in the blank]. But....You are wrong. You are immoral. You are a sinner. You do not deserve to live."

Bigotry in smaller towns has a different flavor. As Maria Price with Kentucky Fairness Alliance said, "We know who the extremists are in Louisville, but Frank Simon is not standing next to me on the treadmill at the Y. He's not the one who cut my meat for 10 years and now stands with the Anti's holding hurtful signs."

Over chips, salsa and chicken burritos, Ben is telling me about exploring out-of-town jobs, partly because of what the effort to pass fairness laws took out of him and left on him. That's the trouble with living in a hostile climate. Even when you win, it can break your heart.

Pam McMichael is a writer, activist and co-director of Southerners on New Ground. Led by lesbian, gay, bisexual and transgendered people of color, SONG is a Louisville, Kentucky-based organization that helps people do their social change work in multi-issue and anti-racist ways.

I'm mostly a "glass half-full" kind of person when it comes to the long haul of working for social change, and I know Ben is, too. Nothing is more energizing than work that comes out of and gives back love, nothing more moving than to see the efforts of everyday folk move us all inch by inch closer to fairness and justice. We celebrate the big wins and draw hope from the small ones. So I'm listening closely, because these are not words he is saying lightly.

I've heard longtime civil rights activist Anne Braden say that when she left her white world of privilege to cast her lot in the fight against racism, she thought she might be called upon to give up her life. ("The Wall Between," an incredible book Braden wrote in the 1950s, has recently been re-released.) But, she says, she came to realize that being committed to social change calls on you to give up your life in little ways. "Dying for the movement" is often by degrees, with sacrifices made daily.

> Homophobia does not exist in a vacuum. There's a lot of hostile climate out there based on race, gender and class.

For most of us, heroic efforts for social change are things like licking stamps, or passing out leaflets, or writing letters, or making phone calls, or spending hours in conversation to expose who benefits and who loses from the countless myths and stereotypes that we all learn.

Anne's comments make me think of the similarities between the fight-back against oppression and the effects of it. For most of us, it's the little things that add up to big ones, that daily hostile climate that constantly wears on us.

I'm not ignoring the reality of murder, torture and other forms of physical violence. The threat of violence is key to fostering and maintaining oppression, and too many names can easily roll off our tongues of those who met that ultimate hostile climate.

What I am saying is this: When Matthew Shepard was killed, some people lamented to me how horrible it was, but some of those same people have never really understood the countless ways that homophobia expresses itself in daily life, that form the fertile ground of the hostile climate that killed Matthew.

I missed the Matthew Shepard vigil in my home of Louisville. I was an hour away, caring for my father, who had terminal cancer. His sister and I were his primary caretakers 24 hours a day, seven days a week. I watched the news coverage alone, thinking about Matthew and my activist friends who were at the vigil. My family had to take priority — but of course, I don't know anything about family values. I am a lesbian.

At the time of my mother's death, I was the lobbyist for the Kentucky Fairness Alliance. One week after her funeral, a constitutional amendment to recriminalize adult consensual sodomy passed out of committee. The chairman had promised me he wouldn't hear the bill. While I wanted to curl up in a ball, I had to be in Frankfort, the state capital — on my toes, thinking strategically, organizing other lobbyists and convincing state legislators that we are human beings. I know what Ben is talking about.

For six and a half years now I have worked with Southerners On New Ground, launched by black and white Southern lesbians to form a unified front against prejudice based on race, class, gender and sexual orientation. Through that work, we have seen a hostile climate much closer to home than what comes at us from the other side. On one hand, too much organizing done by the lesbian, gay, bisexual and transgendered (LGBT) community is single-issue identity focused, leaving progressive LGBT people isolated from that organizing. We've also seen another version of "don't ask, don't tell," in which LGBT employees of otherwise progressive social change groups are silenced for fear of alienating a constituency, or found their long-trusted reputations doubted when they come out.

There are also great changes. The four wins in Kentucky were situated in the multi-issue context of building allies, connecting issues and broadening the "we." Our victories came out of 15 years of creative, committed Fairness organizing that rightfully stands in the proud tradition of work for civil and human rights.

Homophobia does not exist in a vacuum. There's a lot of hostile climate out there based on race, gender and class. Our fight-back has to take it all on. We are all part of one another. As LGBT people, we are multiple identities. When we create holes in that hostile climate, we must all walk through together.

What gives me hope is the growing activism that crosses those difficult divides of race, class, gender and sexuality to build an anti-racist, justice-seeking majority in this country. It is, I believe, our only hope to save our lives.

WALT BOULDEN

In October 1998, my friend Matthew Shepard was kidnapped, tortured, beaten and left tied to a fence to die in the cold Wyoming wind. He had made the mistake of admitting he was gay to two bullies. He was only 21 years old. His murderers were also in their early 20s. They had all grown up in Wyoming, a state with pristine landscapes and friendly neighbors often referred to as "a small town with long streets." But that friendliness depends on "fitting in" and being accepted as an "insider."

Wyoming reflects the epitome of the "don't ask, don't tell" mentality, which requires turning a blind eye not only to the very existence of gays and lesbians, but also to the systematic discrimination, harassment, and violence used to "keep them in their place." It's an attitude that says: if gays become visible, or "flaunt it," they are legitimate targets for harassment and violence.

I was also raised in Wyoming, where anti-gay hatred is such a part of the culture that every child knows the most dangerous thing you could ever discover about yourself is that you are gay. It's common for adults to use slurs like "abomination," and to perpetuate rumors and jokes that portray gays as perverts, predators and derelicts. In elementary school, children play "smear the queer" on the playground and bullies taunt, harass and assault the "sissy boys," while the other kids laugh and the teachers and adults look the other way.

As an adult gay man, I lived with the constant unspoken threat of anti-gay hatred and violence hanging over my head. I knew breaking the "don't ask, don't tell" rule could mean losing my job, friends, family, and acceptance as an insider. As a gay father, the fear that I could lose access to my own children haunted me for years.

Though we lived in this suffocating atmosphere, some of us were bringing the topic out of the closet. I had conducted workshops on issues facing gay men and lesbians through-

Walt Boulden completed his doctorate in social work in October 1999. He is currently converting his doctoral dissertation, "How Can You Be Gay and Live in Wyoming?," into book form. He lives in Kansas City, Mo.

out Wyoming since 1994, and concerned people were participating. We established a Safe Zone project at the University of Wyoming to help educate faculty, staff, administration, and other students about the issues facing lesbian, gay, bisexual and transgendered college students. I was "out" to my colleagues, some of my family, and students in my classes. We provided access to accurate information, presented positive gay and lesbian role models, and tried to counter destructive stereotypes. We challenged the "don't ask, don't tell" rule and were trying to make a difference.

Then Matt was murdered. Nothing could have prepared me for the horror, the grief, or the onslaught of the media, as the community and world awoke to the reality that Matt had been so brutally attacked. I was inundated with demands for media interviews and information, and I found myself in front of national TV cameras, my name in newspapers across the country. My friends and family tried to be supportive even while they feared for my safety. And all the while, I struggled not to completely break down with grief and, yes, guilt. After all, I had encouraged Matt to move back home to Wyoming and go to school in Laramie, where he would be safer than in the big city.

By the end of October 1998, I packed my bags, sold my house and left Wyoming. I had no idea where I should go. I just knew I could not stay where everything I saw triggered memories of Matt and images of the horror he went through out on that fence. I was 46 years old and had never lived outside of Wyoming. But I got into my car and headed east on Interstate 70. I felt like the notorious tumbleweed that had just been ripped from its roots by a savage gust of Wyoming wind and blown out across the prairies of Kansas.

> I felt like a tumbleweed, ripped from its roots by a savage gust of Wyoming wind and blown out across the prairies.

Two years later, I live in a self-imposed exile. I do not envision ever living in Wyoming again. Not so much because Matt was murdered there, but because of how Wyoming has responded to his murder.

The good-old-boy conservatives in Wyoming have traditionally maintained their control of the state by playing on the myth of self-reliance, casting suspicion on all outsiders. When Matt was killed, they circled the wagons and brought out "spin doctors" to work on image control. They branded the national media and national gay and lesbian organizations as "outsiders with their own agendas" in an attempt to take the spotlight off their own anti-gay hatred.

Sadly, distrust of outsiders is such a part of the fabric of life in Wyoming that the general population jumped on the bandwagon to defend their state's reputation against the "evil outsiders." Today, some in Wyoming still respond to the name "Matthew Shepard" as if they had just heard a curse word. They blame him for bringing outside media attention to Wyoming, for tarnishing their image.

At the same time, the political bullies in the Wyoming legislature continue to defeat hate crimes legislation. They kill bill after bill without even having to go on record with their anti-gay hatred. To justify their opposition, all they have to do is invoke the state's fear of outside influence with statements like, "we must not yield to the external pressure that could be out there."

I don't see myself ever living in Wyoming again. I will not have my tax dollars support the tyranny of a state government that sanctions anti-gay hatred, discrimination, harassment and violence. Nor will I cower before the bullies, or turn a blind eye to their tactics. I am more dedicated than ever to breaking the "don't ask, don't tell" edict, and adding my voice to the chorus demanding social justice and equal treatment for everyone — not just those who are accepted members of the privileged classes. Matt's memory deserves no less.

DANA RIVERS

I was born David Warfield on February 16, 1955, in Chicago. My parents tell me that they were proud of their first child. They moved us out to California two years later, and rented apartments until a modest three-bedroom home could be purchased for the princely sum of $12,500. Over the next five years, another son and two daughters were added to the brood. Our family fit right into the rest of the blue-collar neighborhood, except for one important, unseen difference. I had a condition known as Gender Identity Disorder, and would grow up as a male-to-female transsexual. My life would be anything but normal.

From the age of 4, I became a loner on the streets and playgrounds. I sought refuge in the Boy Scouts, where the boys had to include me. But soon I distanced myself from them, too. By the time I reached puberty, gender confusion set in and I had my first suicidal thought. My teenage years saw me turn ever more distant. I turned to drugs and alcohol, and barely earned my high school diploma. A month after graduating in 1973, I joined the Navy on a whim. Here, too, I was lost and ostracized by my peers. The last fitness report I received before my discharge read that I was an intense young man who had not found his place in the Navy. The same could be said for the rest of my life.

After the Navy, I quickly married a high school friend. Almost immediately, we fought about my propensity for wearing her clothes, and for wanting to be treated like a woman during intimate moments. We stayed together just long enough to have my only child, Gwendolyn. There, in the delivery room, I knew that something was wrong with me, and I felt more alone than ever. I will never forget wanting to be my wife, as she cursed my

Dana Rivers, an award-winning teacher, was forced to resign from her Sacramento, Calif., high school when the school board refused to support her transition into a female gender role. The ensuing controversy made her a national advocate, lecturer and consultant on discrimination and transgender issues. She spoke at the Millennium March on Washington. She can be reached at: info@lectureliterary.com.

fatherhood during the throes of labor. We divorced months later. My wife said that my gender confusion was too much for her, and she wanted to raise our daughter with a real man.

My second marriage was a variation on the theme of my first. We fought over my gender weirdness. Outwardly, I earned three college degrees and achieved political and financial success. But inside I suffered, so much so that I contemplated ending my life in earnest by drinking myself to death. With my stomach burning with ulcers as I descended into an alcoholic abyss, I stumbled across a twelve-step program and got sober. My life began to turn around from that day, November 16, 1988.

Five years later, after a second divorce, I moved to the foothills of Northern California to be near the wild Sierra rivers that I had grown to love. Whitewater rafting had become a passion, and it was along the banks of the American River near the spot that Marshall discovered gold that I met my third wife. We fell hard for each other, and our love boiled over from river trip to river trip. We were married outdoors, surrounded by family, friends and majestic redwoods. At last, everything seemed right, and I vowed to keep my gender issues at bay for good.

> When I exclaimed that I had finally discovered my true self, I looked down to see my friend and partner in tears.

However, being transsexual is not a choice. You cannot will it into being nor can you erase it from your psyche. And so, my erratic gender behavior crept into this new relationship. My wife tried to understand, more than anyone else had. She encouraged me to seek therapy. I did, and when I came home triumphant and exclaimed that I had finally discovered my true self, I looked down to see my friend and partner in tears. Her man was a fraud. She had instead married a woman who only appeared male. When I explained that the treatment included a transformation to correct the ambiguity, she nodded in hollow acceptance.

Professionally, I was peaking. My career as a teacher at Sacramento's Center High School was in full bloom. I won awards for my ability to connect with students who had difficulty with school. I saw in their young eyes reflections of me, back then, when I was lost and confused also. My colleagues and I built a program for these students, and the effort paid off. I found myself staying at school later and later to accommodate these kids who wanted to stay to work on projects. I even slept overnight in the lab a few times, rather than drive home for just a couple of hours before returning to teach the next day. As my students said, it was all good.

My therapy was also reaching a peak. The hormones I had begun taking were coursing through my body. I felt alive as never before. The chronic depression I had held at bay for so long left me, and the sparkle in my eyes danced with newfound joy. My body was changing to finally align itself with how I felt inside.

It was time to tell my employer that I would return to school in the fall as the woman I was always intended to be. Initially, it went well. First my principal, then department colleagues, then the entire school staff learned about me, and almost to a person indicated support. The district administration told the school board, and after a meeting with their attorney, the word came down that my transition would be supported by three of the five board members. I left school in June 1999, officially changed my name to Dana Lee Rivers, and told my caregivers that I was on track. During the summer, I worked with colleagues and prepared myself for a smooth transition. I learned to walk and talk and dress professionally. Makeup became less a mystery and more a morning ritual. I overcame shyness and worked hard to feminize my voice.

During this same time, the two school board members that opposed me hatched a plot to dismiss me. They found a third vote among my three supporters and enlisted the help of the ultraconservative Pacific Justice Institute, which had successfully harassed other transsexual teachers around the country. Just prior to the start of school last fall, I was summoned, along with my union-sponsored attorney, to a board meeting where I was put on leave pending dismissal. The charge was that I was suddenly unfit for service. My limited communication with students in the spring was seen as improper. In fact, it would not have mattered what I did or didn't do. These men wanted me gone. I never set foot in a Center High classroom to teach again.

The media picked up my story. Students rallied to my side. They spoke at board meetings, held demonstrations, enlisted a local radio station to help organize a rally on the steps of the state Capitol, and demanded that the school board live up to its claims of tolerance and support for diversity. Parents and community members did the same. I found myself in front of cameras at ABC-TV's Times Square studios with Diane Sawyer. Articles about me ran in *People* and *Time* magazine, as well as the *New York Times* and almost every other major paper in the country. My case was debated on the cable TV shout-fest talk shows, and I was inundated with requests to appear on almost every daytime talk program. I had to enlist the help of an agent and friends just to handle the phone calls.

The crescendo of media attention reached its zenith around Thanksgiving 1999. My attorney said my case would be dragged through the system for at least a year, maybe more. I was exhausted from the pressures of martyrdom and I missed teaching. My wife had long since departed our home. My daughter had decided to forgo her freshman year at UC-Berkeley, claiming stress from all the craziness I had brought into our home. Who could blame her? When the district offered me a negotiated buyout settlement, I accepted. In exchange for three years' salary and the elimination of all charges from my personnel file, I would agree never to teach at Center High School again.

Since then, I have become a spokeswoman on behalf of gender rights. I have appeared on "Oprah." "20/20" did a segment about my struggle. I speak at universities and conferences. The message is clear no matter where I talk: gender rights are human rights, and this country must face the fact that discrimination against people like me is wrong.

My divorce is pending. My daughter has yet to attend a day in college. I am about to put our beloved country home on the market to pay bills. I share a rental across the street from a busy freeway with two other women. My savings account bleeds each month I do not teach as I wait while my credential is reviewed by the state. My gender-related medical expenses mount, since they are not covered by insurance. And in spite of all of this, I have never been more at peace with who I am.

An account of Dana Rivers' dispute also appears on p. 91.

KATHERINE TRIANTAFILLOU

My stepdaughter describes herself as bisexual, as do a number of her friends. Quite frankly, I was surprised; I'd thought she was avowedly heterosexual, given the number of crushes on boys through the years. My partner chided me — where have you been, haven't you noticed? I didn't notice. Maybe that's progress. A new generation of women who feel comfortable with expressing their sexuality in a multiplicity of ways. With men. With women. I think I like it.

When I came out, it was in two stages. First the sexual stage, the act of having a sexual experience with another woman. That was when I was 14. Then there was the political coming-out. That was in my twenties when I had graduated from law school. I took the label lesbian because it seemed like the only way to claim my space in the world: I love women, so get used to it. It also helped me define who I was politically — a feminist intent on changing much of the world of law and politics. I was sick of the patriarchy and the limitations it put on me as a woman, and angry. Being a lesbian meant there was no room for confusion or gray areas. My life was woman-centered. I even constructed a law practice on those principles.

But I digress. Being lesbian or gay or bisexual or transgendered means being different. I always felt different as a child, but coming out does it in a way that is hard to describe. Being black is different too, but black parents do not disown their children for being black. (Sometimes they do if they are gay.) When I used to lecture about gay rights, this is the point I always wanted to make. When you come out you not only can lose your job, you can lose your family.

When I was a teenager, my family suspected that I was having a relationship with an older woman in my home town. Rather than deal with it gently, I was herded into the kitchen and interrogated about what I did in bed with this woman. I was sitting on a chair

Katherine Triantafillou is an attorney specializing in human rights and family law. She is also an author, international consultant and professor of law. She was the first open lesbian elected to the Cambridge City Council in Massachusetts, where she served for three terms.

with my father, mother, sisters and brother arrayed in front of me. At one point I remember being yelled at and hearing the word "queer!" I thought I was going to die from the indignity of it all, but mostly I went numb with grief as I was forbidden to have contact with this woman ever again.

It took years of therapy to undo the damage of that confrontation about my sexuality. In the meantime, I learned to channel my anger into defending lesbians and gay men from the ravages of institutionalized homophobia. It is of course no accident that I became a lawyer or that I used to have an exclusively lesbian and gay practice. My first case involved two women discharged from the Army for being gay who were found out in a "witch-hunt" that was common before "don't ask, don't tell" became the norm. My last case established the right of lesbians and gay men to jointly adopt children in Massachusetts, to become "co-parents." The first time I saw the form from the registry after we won the case, I cried, remembering the long road to freedom and acceptance.

> I thought I was going to die from the indignity of it all, but mostly I went numb with grief as I was forbidden to have contact with this woman ever again..

So I'm glad my daughter calls herself a bisexual. In reality, I probably am too. But I feel like she has choices about her sexuality that I never had. And I want her to explore all the facets of her life, be it with a man or a woman. I want her to learn to love well. And you can only do that when you can love freely and without fear of reprisal. Coming out means you will stand firm for who you are. I care less now about the label. Happy will do. (Is this the inevitable consequence of aging? Have I lost my edge as a lesbian feminist? Or is this what happens when you've been whacked about for six years as a result of being a politician?) I have also reconciled with my family.

Twenty-five years ago when I first started practicing law, People for the American Way Foundation would never have published this book, much less asked someone like me to write something for it. Lesbians barely retained custody of their children, let alone thought about the right to marry. Gay men were routinely harassed and entrapped at rest stops for "lewd and lascivious" behavior, a favorite law enforcement tool. We had no gay judges, no gay politicians, no dyke doctors, or gay social workers' associations. It was a very different world.

I like to think my standing up and saying the words "I am a lesbian" helped bring about these changes. At least it challenged others to reconsider the notion of what a lesbian is. Looking forward, I like to think it paved the way for young people to feel comfortable being bisexual or transgendered. But most of all I like to think it made it possible for others less able, less strong, less sure, to have the courage to love whomever they wanted to with dignity.

Or, as Olga Broumas writes in her poem "Four Beginnings":

"I love. You are the memory

of each desire that ran, dead-end, into a mind

programmed to misconstrue it. A mind inventing

neurosis, anxiety, phobia, a mind expertly camouflaged

from the thought of love

for a woman, its native

love."

My life's work has been to teach the world and myself that love should never be misconstrued. Only accepted and revered... wherever you can find it.

INCIDENTS

Proposed Hate Crimes Prevention Act fails

For the second year in a row, Congress failed to pass a federal hate crimes law that included sexual orientation. The Hate Crimes Prevention Act (HCPA) would have authorized local law enforcement officials to enlist federal assistance in investigating and prosecuting hate crimes. The 1998 bill had failed when neither house of Congress took action. But attention to the 1999 bill was heightened by the brutal murder of Billie Jack Gaither in Alabama in February and the murders of James Byrd and Matthew Shepard in late 1998. Judy and Dennis Shepard, Matthew's parents, personally urged members of Congress to pass the bill. The Laramie, Wyoming, police department joined the lobbying effort. Laramie Police Commander David O'Malley said, "I once thought all crimes were hate crimes. I have changed my mind after working on the Shepard case because I have never seen a clearer example of hate-motivated crimes and the negative ramifications it has on our society."

Although the Senate passed the 1999 version as an amendment to a bill funding the Departments of Commerce, Justice, and State, the bill failed in the House largely due to the efforts of conservative Republicans and national right-wing organizations.

Religious Right groups launched direct mail and media campaigns to defeat the bill. In a news release, the Traditional Values Coalition (see p. 357) called the push for the bill a "masquerade" and accused supporters of "riding the emotional outrage of several tragic incidents." It continued, "[T]he legislation is literally a Pandora's box for families, churches, schools, state courts, and the Constitution." Matt Kaufman, with Focus on the Family (see p. 355), wrote, "[P]oliticians jumped on the rhetorical bandwagon. President Clinton led the

> "Apparently, the GOP leadership learned nothing from the recent wave of hate crimes that have rocked our nation."
>
> — Human Rights Campaign President Elizabeth Birch, on the removal of the Hate Crimes Prevention Act from a year-end bill in Congress.

charge." One of that group's other press releases echoed similar statements from opponents nationwide: "Hate-crime laws are unneeded. Every crime they cover is already illegal under existing state and local laws." Concerned Women for America (see p. 354) maintained that "Hate crimes laws undermine civil rights" and "infringe on free speech." CWA and the Family Research Council (see p. 355) developed and distributed a list of talking points to better prepare opponents of the bill to confront supporters.

Robert Knight, director of cultural studies at the FRC, testified before the Senate Judiciary Committee in May. He told the committee that the bill established "special classes of victims, who are afforded a higher level of government protection than others" and claimed that it "would politicize criminal prosecutions." He also said, "[I]t would have a chilling effect on free speech by making unpopular ideas a basis for harsher treatment in criminal proceedings." Knight told the committee that gay and lesbian activists have said that anti-gay comments incited violence, claiming, "In effect, the HCPA creates thought crime," after which he touted the benefits of so-called "ex-gay" ministries. Despite such testimony, the Senate passed the bill in July with bipartisan support.

During House Judiciary Committee hearings on the bill in August, California Rep. Mary Bono questioned the merits of testimony given by two gay men who had been victims of a hate crime. Tony Orr and his partner, Tim Beauchamp, described an attack on them in Tulsa, Oklahoma in 1997, when Beauchamp withdrew money from an ATM machine. The assailants asked Orr if he was a "[expletive] faggot," to which he responded yes. Orr said they knocked him down and kicked him severely. When Beauchamp tried to help Orr, the attackers beat him. After they were arrested, the assailants reportedly told police they were only "rolling a couple of fags." Orr said they all received minimum sentences, two of them getting 40 hours of community service and a suspended jail term. Orr and Beauchamp told the committee that they disagreed with the Tulsa district attorney's handling of their case. Rep. Bono, however, confronted them, saying information from the Tulsa district attorney's office suggested the two were "less than cooperative" with the prosecutor. After the committee heard all the testimony from the witnesses, Rep. Bono singled out Orr again as being less than truthful. Orr denied that characterization and reiterated his position that justice was not served. Observers claimed Rep. Bono had not been as skeptical concerning the testimony of other victims of hate crimes. One of those also testifying before the committee, Daniel Troy of the American Enterprise Institute, said Rep. Bono was "the only Republican to direct hostile questions to any Democratic witness." Writing in the conservative American Spectator, he criticized the way Republicans had conducted the hearings, saying Bono looked "as if she were further victimizing the already victimized."

The FRC later urged House-Senate conferees on the bill to drop the hate crimes provision. Its spokesperson, Janet Parshall, wrote a critical op-ed piece that appeared in newspapers nationwide. "Instead of pulling us together as a united people, hate crimes divide and categorize by declaring one man's death more heinous than another." Republican House members were largely opposed to the inclusion of sexual orientation in the amendment; their version of the funding bill had not included the hate-crimes rider. Opposition within the Senate continued. John Czwartacki, spokesman for Majority Leader Trent Lott, asked, "What crime isn't a hate crime?"

Republican conferees ultimately dropped the amendment from the compromise bill in October. Sen. Judd Gregg said, "That was one elephant too much for this boa constrictor." Elizabeth Birch, head of the Human Rights Campaign, said, "Apparently, the GOP leadership learned nothing from the recent wave of hate crimes that have rocked our nation." Although the FRC was delighted with Republican leaders, Congress's inaction did not stop the head of the American Family Association (see p. 352) from calling on Congress to continue opposing hate crimes legislation that included sexual orientation. Don Wildmon, that group's president, said, "President Clinton and the homosexual movement are willing to sacrifice the First Amendment of the Constitution in an effort to normalize homosexuality...Obviously the president places a higher priority on the homosexuality movement's agenda than on protection of the general public from crime in America."

President Clinton vetoed the appropriations bill for not including the hate crimes amendment, among other reasons. During White House negotiations on a revised spending bill, the amendment was again dropped and the president signed the bill. Birch criticized the administration and the Republican leadership for missing an "historic opportunity" to pass the measure.

ExxonMobil's employment policies

Employment policy choices for the former Exxon Corporation and the newly formed ExxonMobil Corporation outraged investors and gay and lesbian activists. At a May stockholders meeting, a group of Exxon's gay and lesbian stockholders put forward an initiative to include sexual orientation in the company's non-discrimination policy. Stockholders defeated that proposal with 94 percent of the vote. Several months later, Exxon merged with Mobil Corporation to create ExxonMobil. The new company announced in November that it would not offer domestic partner benefits to its newly-hired employees and would not include sexual orientation in its written non-discrimination policy. Mobil had offered domestic partner benefits to its employees and had included sexual orientation in its non-discrimination policy. Right-wing organizations applauded ExxonMobil's employment policy decisions, while gay and lesbian groups denounced them.

Groups that had for a year been trying to get Mobil to eliminate its domestic partner benefits policy cheered ExxonMobil's announcement. The American Family Association, the Family Research Council, and Concerned Women for America (see p. 352) had written a letter in 1998 to Mobil executives asking them to end the company's domestic partner benefits program. Janet Parshall, spokesperson for the FRC, praised the new company's decision, saying, "Think of the energy ExxonMobil can now channel towards delivering gas instead of pumping the homosexual agenda."

In response to criticism from the Human Rights Campaign and gay and lesbian activists across the country, the new company, which employs approximately 121,000 people, staunchly defended its decisions. Tom Cirigliano, a company spokesperson, said that ExxonMobil would only offer spousal benefits to employees in legally valid relationships, including legally valid common law marriages. He also said that former Mobil employees who remained with the new company would continue to receive domestic partner benefits, but that newly hired employees would not. When asked about the new company's refusal to offer domestic partner benefits to employees who do not have the option of obtaining legal recognition of their family relationships, Cirigliano responded, "We need some criteria to establish a relationship." When he was asked about the refusal to include sexual orientation in the new company's non-discrimination policy, Cirigliano claimed that existing policies cover all people. Pressed further, he asked, "Where do you stop?"

ExxonMobil further defended its refusal to cover sexual orientation discrimination explicitly in its non-discrimination policies by claiming that the company itself denounces anti-gay employment discrimination. Cirigliano provided the Gay Financial Network, a gay news service, a copy of Exxon's proxy statement that had been given to shareholders in advance of the May vote on the non-discrimination proposal. In that statement, Exxon condemned discrimination based on sexual orientation, but it also stated, "[I]t is Exxon's practice to list as forms of harassment in its policies only those which are specifically prohibited by federal law." Employment discrimination based on sexual orientation is not prohibited by federal law. According to Shelley Alpern, an ExxonMobil stockholder and supporter of the non-discrimination policy proposal offered in May, ExxonMobil's human resources director Lynn Reed claimed that the vagueness of the new company's non-discrimination policy proves that it prohibits sexual orientation discrimination. According to Alpern, Reed made that claim during a November meeting the two had during which they discussed the concerns that gay and lesbian investors had with ExxonMobil's refusal to adopt a domestic partner benefits policy or to include sexual orientation specifically in its non-discrimination policy.

> "For...sexual behavior there are now rights. That's what I'm worried about, with the pedophilia and the bestiality and the sadomasochism and the cross-dressing. Is this going to be 'rights' too?"
>
> — Radio host "Doctor Laura" Schlessinger, responding to two lawmakers' attempts secure passage of gay rights legislation in the California Assembly.

Wired Strategies, an Internet-based gay news source, reported that ExxonMobil sent an e-mail to customers saying, "Recent news reports stating that ExxonMobil has rescinded non-discrimination policies...are simply not true." Wayne Besen, spokesperson for the Human Rights Campaign, claimed that this statement misrepresented what the new company has done, saying, "They flat-out lied to people about their non-discrimination policy." He added, "They are at the bottom of the barrel of all the major oil companies."

Schlessinger's month of rants

Syndicated columnist and radio talk show host Dr. Laura Schlessinger, whose audience includes 18 million listeners, singled out gay men and lesbians for condemnation several times in June on her radio show. She criticized everything from pro-gay bills in state legislatures to gay video programs and lesbian parenting. In early June, she shared excerpts from a report published by the right-wing U.S. Justice Foundation with listeners. The report claimed that a proposed bill in the California legislature would require public schools to hire gay men and lesbians and that "having openly homosexual, bisexual, and cross-dressing teachers could have a substantially negative impact on impressionable elementary and/or junior high school children."

Days later Schlessinger criticized on the air an editorial in the Los Angeles Times favorable to gay civil rights. "Rights? For sexual deviant...sexual behavior there are now rights. That's what I'm worried about with the pedophilia and the bestiality and the sado-masochism and the cross-dressing. Is this going to be 'rights' too?" Schlessinger asked. The editorial concerned two lesbian lawmakers' efforts to pass gay rights legislation in the California Assembly.

Schlessinger later criticized the documentary "It's Elementary: Talking About Gay Issues in Schools," by award-winning filmmaker Debra Chasnoff, on air, claiming that it brainwashed children. She had previously disparaged the documentary in a May syndicated column. Schlessinger said to her listeners that the film, which was airing across the country on PBS stations, told children, "Everything your parents tell you is wrong about homosexuality. We're all phobic. We're going to tell you the truth," she said. "When you're trying to establish a world order that is deviancy becomes the norm and everything is OK and there should be no judgment, the first thing you have to do is either remove kids from their homes to brainwash them...or the second thing is dissolve, weaken the relationship between parents and children so there's a lack of respect and sense of authority..."

After she condemned President Clinton's proclamation of June as Gay Pride Month, Schlessinger launched into an on-air tirade about lesbian parents, targeting Human Rights Campaign Executive Director Elizabeth Birch and her partner: "Is there not the most voluminous amount of material which indicates that fatherless homes hurt children? I don't give a damn about what these two women want! It hurts children!" Referring to plans the couple said they had to enlist a nanny's help in raising their children, Schlessinger asked, "[H]ow can any adoption agency give twins to two lesbians who don't even want to raise the kids?" She claimed that although not all gay men were pedophiles, "it's a greater percentage, much greater."

The Gay and Lesbian Alliance Against Defamation soundly criticized Schlessinger and began a campaign to educate the public about the effects that her comments have on gay men and lesbians. The group's efforts accelerated when Paramount's UPN television network announced it was developing a show for Schlessinger.

Right-wing groups assail "It's Elementary"

In addition to creating local controversies across the country (see incidents in Idaho, Illinois, Kentucky, Maine, North Carolina, Texas and Washington), "It's Elementary: Talking About Gay Issues in School" drew the ire of several national right-wing groups when it was broadcast on affiliates of the Public Broadcasting System (PBS). Religious Right leaders claimed the documentary, which was designed to help educators and other adults discuss homosexuality in age-appropriate ways with young children, was everything from gay propaganda to an attempt to get kids to "embrace the homosexual lifestyle." They attacked PBS for using public funds to broadcast a film on gay and lesbian subject matter. On one edition of his national radio show, James Dobson, President of Focus on the Family (see p. 355), urged listeners to contact Congress and tell legislators that they should not use public funds for gay and lesbian programming. He also called on them to contact their local PBS affiliate and demand that it not broadcast the program or to protest if the station did. The Center for Reclaiming America (see p. 353) sent out its own fundraising letter condemning the film, which it called an "innocently named homosexual propaganda video" and "child abuse." Asking for contributions, its president, D. James Kennedy, said, "God help us not to turn America's children over to homosexual propaganda!" Kennedy added that donations would fund the center's own video refuting "It's Elementary." Don Wildmon, President of the American Family Association (see p. 353), called the film, "a pro-homosexuality bombshell that has been fired into our children's elementary schools."

Other Religious Right groups warned their members of the film's homosexual content. The AFA sent out an Action Alert in February claimed that the film tells children not to listen to their parents when it comes to homosexuality. Wildmon asked supporters for donations to distribute the AFA's video "Suffer the Children," which it claims refutes "It's Elementary." He called the AFA video "factually and biblically sound," though most PBS affiliates refused to air it. The Capital Research Center (see p. 353) and the Family Research Council (see p. 355) also disparaged director Debra Chasnoff's work. Christopher Yablonski of the CRC said, "These private foundations are essentially subsidizing — with tax-exempt dollars — an aggressive campaign to browbeat taxpayer-funded television stations into airing this controversial program." Janet Parshall, spokesperson for the FRC, said, "It's not a video. It's a tutorial done by lesbian activists whose purpose is to normalize deviancy...It's important that our children not be used as pawns in a chess game to change the culture."

Debra Chasnoff contributed an essay about the campaign against "It's Elementary" to the 1999 edition of Hostile Climate.

Anti-gay remarks during presidential campaigns

Opposition to gay rights and hostility toward gay men and lesbians was standard fare during the fall campaign for the GOP presidential nomination. Candidates made anti-gay comments in a variety of forums around the country.

Several times during his quest for the nomination, U.S. Sen. Orrin Hatch expressed less-than-tolerant views of homosexuality. Hatch, who had previously said that Democrats were "the party of homosexuals," told the Utah Republican Party's state convention that they should be proud of the party because "we don't have the gays and lesbians with us." He said, "It's a religious belief to me that homosexuality flies in the face of biblical teachings...[T]hough in contradistinction to people of color, people of color can't do anything about their color. But I do believe gay people have a choice to live within the legal rules or not." Hatch also said that being gay is "scripturally wrong."

Conservative radio host Alan Keyes also made hostile comments about gay men and lesbians during his campaign. In an interview with the Arizona Republic, Keyes rejected a comparison between civil rights based on race and those based on sexual orientation. When the reporter asked if he thought gays were evil, Keyes responded, "Gays are immoral...I can tell you that [their] conduct and the persistent engagement in that conduct is immoral. I can only say that gays are evil if they engage in that persistent immoral conduct as a result of a conscious determination against God." In other venues he called homosexuality an "abomination" and claimed that hate-crime laws inappropriately punish attitudes and would be used to punish anti-gay opinions.

During publishing magnate Malcolm "Steve" Forbes Jr.'s campaign, Forbes said he opposed several gay rights measures. When asked if he would employ gay staff, he said, "I will hire people who are qualified for the job, people who can do the work at hand, people who are there to get something done: not to make a political statement about a lifestyle." In December, however, Forbes said, "Homosexuality is a lifestyle that I personally do not approve of." He also said that he opposed same-sex marriage and agreed with the military's "don't ask, don't tell" policy barring openly gay and lesbian service members. "The military is not an institution for social engineering," he said.

Gary Bauer, former director of the Family Research Council (see p. 355), made opposition to gay rights one of the focal points of his campaign. Before the Vermont Supreme Court ruled that gay and lesbian citizens had a constitutional right to all the benefits and privileges of marriage, Bauer criticized the court for even taking up the matter. He told a crowd in Montpelier, "I don't think Vermont wants to be known as...the same-sex marriage state. It's known for a lot better things than that." Saying that the issue should be decided by voters, Bauer called the state supreme court ruling "profoundly radical," "a cave-in to the gay rights movement," and "the goofiest thing I ever heard in my life." He went on to denounce same-sex marriage during a stop at a Nebraska high school. His criticism of homosexuality carried on into New Hampshire in November, where he told a college crowd that "Corpus Christi," a play by award-winning playwright Terrence McNally, was "repulsive" because it depicts a Christ-like figure as gay. Bauer also said that another play was "about homosexual relationships flourishing under the brutal repression of the Catholic Church," although he failed to specify which one. Rich Tafel, Executive Director of the Log Cabin Republicans, a gay Republican group, called Bauer the "most hostile" of all the candidates. Tafel said, "Bauer's work when he headed the Family Research Council made it seem as if the chief objective was being anti-gay."

Questioned by anti-gay activist Bill Horn, Texas Gov. George W. Bush said he opposed same-sex marriage and a New Jersey Supreme Court ruling in which that court held that the Boy Scouts' prohibition on openly gay members violated state law. Bush's campaign sent Horn a letter elaborating on his position: "Governor Bush believes marriage is between a man and a woman and therefore, does not believe in gay marriages." It also said he opposed adoptions by gay men and lesbians. After attending a closed-door meeting with Bush and leaders from several conservative organizations, columnist Cal Thomas reported that Bush said he would not "knowingly" appoint people who were open advocates of homosexuality to positions within his administration.

> "The fact that he carries a magic bag doesn't make him gay...It's a children's show, folks."
>
> — Steve Rice, spokesman for Itsy Bitsy Entertainment Co., U.S. licenser of "The Teletubbies." Jerry Falwell had asserted that the show's "Tinky Winky" character was gay.

When weeks later Bush named several openly gay members to his campaign steering committee, Christian conservatives were dismayed. Michael Farris, president of the Home School Legal Defense Association and an organizer of the earlier meeting with Religious Right leaders, defended Bush, saying the appointment of openly gay people was "not happy news for me," but that appointments to the campaign were different than those to a Bush administration. "He was not going to appoint a person who is flamboyantly not only promoting his lifestyle as a homosexual, but advocating his position as well," Farris said.

Falwell and Tinky Winky

In the February edition of his National Liberty Journal, televangelist Jerry Falwell claimed that a preschool television character was gay and cautioned parents against watching the British-made children's television program "The Teletubbies," which airs on PBS affiliates nationwide. While Falwell initially said that the sexual orientation of the character Tinky Winky was a matter of dispute, his column identified the show as having explicitly gay themes. "As a Christian, I believe that role-modeling the gay lifestyle is damaging to the moral lives of children," Falwell said. "I find the flat denials of such a portrayal by Teletubbies producers to be disingenuous and insufficient in answering the questions that have been raised about the Tinky Winky character..." Falwell said he drew his conclusions because Tinky Winky often carries "a red purse," his purple color is also a symbol of gay pride and his antenna is shaped like a triangle, also a symbol of gay pride. These subtle depictions, Falwell contended, were intentional. He also referred to a lighthearted Washington Post feature that cast Tinky Winky opposite openly lesbian actress Ellen Degeneres-Degeneres in the "out" column, and Tinky Winky in the "in" column. In a "Parents Alert" in the National Liberty Journal, Falwell told readers, "[P]arents are warned to be alert to these elements of the series."

Steve Rice, a spokesperson for Itsy Bitsy Entertainment Co., which licenses "The Teletubbies" in the United States, disputed Falwell's assessment of the show. According to Rice, the red purse is actually the character's magic bag. Rice said, "The fact that he carries a magic bag doesn't make him gay...It's a children's show, folks. To think we would be putting sexual innuendo in a children's show is kind of outlandish...I really find it absurd and kind of offensive."

Falwell's claims turned out to have quite the opposite effect from what he intended. Although Tinky Winky had been somewhat popular within gay and lesbian communities, he was adopted as an unofficial mascot soon after Falwell's pronouncements. He has been featured in gay pride parades and other functions since his "outing." A department store in Boston reported that sales of Tinky Winky dolls shot up after Falwell's pronouncement appeared. Several newspapers lampooned Falwell's characterization, which became a national joke.

Americans for Truth About Homosexuality (see p. 352), however, tried to turn the matter back on the heads of gay and lesbian activists. Its president, Peter LaBarbera, claimed that America's pundits were missing the central point about how gay and lesbian activists were targeting school children, "even kindergartners," with "inappropriate pro-homosexual lessons." He added, "Instead of ridiculing Rev. Jerry Falwell...the media should be exposing the aggressive homosexual 'kiddie agenda.' " He accused groups such as the Gay, Lesbian and Straight Education Network of pushing "pro-homosexual programs" on schoolchildren to "redefine the next generation's attitude toward homosexuality, bisexuality, and transgenderism."

Right-wing response to "Just the Facts"

Right-wing organizations attacked a report issued in November on gay and lesbian students. An unprecedented coalition of education, health, and mental health organizations — among them the National Education Association, the American Psychiatric Association, the National Association of Social Workers, and the American Association of School

Administrators — developed "Just the Facts About Sexual Orientation and Youth" as a primer for principals, educators and school personnel across the country. Endorsed by leading gay and lesbian youth-oriented organizations including the Gay, Lesbian, and Straight Education Network (GLSEN) and Parents, Families and Friends of Lesbians and Gays, the primer is designed to better acquaint educators with the issues and needs facing gay and lesbians students. "Just the Facts" includes a discussion of how children develop their sexual orientation, the negative effects of "reparative therapies" that use psychiatric techniques in an attempt to change sexual orientation, religious ministries that try to do the same thing through spiritual devotion, and relevant laws regarding schools' use of both "conversion" techniques. Opponents, however, assailed the report as a piece of gay propaganda and a tool of gay and lesbian activists.

Notice of the report's publication prompted negative comments from syndicated columnist and radio talk show host Dr. Laura Schlessinger. After advising listeners about the misuse of the term "tolerance," arguing that heterosexuality is the "biological norm" for humans, and supporting reparative therapy for gay men and lesbians to change their sexual orientation, Schlessinger claimed that the book was part of "the gay agenda" and had "nothing whatsoever to do with tolerance."

The nation's leading conservative organizations joined Schlessinger in assailing the report. Janet Parshall, spokesperson for the Family Research Council (see p. 355), said, "We're all for the facts about homosexuality getting out, but you won't find them in this publication...This is another attempt by the homosexual lobby to silence any views on homosexuality but its own." She added, "If they're going to talk about 'the facts,' here's a fact: All the major religions of the world consider homosexuality wrong." John Paulk, self-proclaimed "ex-gay" and analyst with Focus on the Family (see p. 355), said, "They're saying they want to present factual information on homosexuality, but we believe that they're presenting propaganda." He also criticized the book for not affirmatively addressing reparative therapies. He said organizations that have debunked the technique, which seeks to change sexual orientation, acted "on the basis of political motives, not scientific evidence." Peter LaBarbera, head of Americans for Truth About Homosexuality (see p. 352), described the report as an "intimidating document" and said, "It seems to me that this is a thinly veiled attempt to intimidate principals from talking about the other side of homosexuality, that healthy change is possible...If you're going to have gay activists in schools, then the other side should be told, too."

The Family Research Council went so far in its response to "Just the Facts" as to issue its own guides to schools in November. "Top 10 Strategies Used by Homosexual Activists in Schools" and "How to Protect Your Children from Pro-Homosexuality Propaganda in Schools," both written by LaBarbera, include instructions to parents and school officials on how to counteract what the FRC describes as predatory behavior by gay and lesbian activists.

"Just the Facts" was reportedly distributed across the nation to the country's more than 15,000 school district superintendents.

Log Cabin Republicans controversy

The subject of homosexuality entered the Republicans' fall presidential primary campaign as partisans and pundits debated whether the contenders should meet with the nation's largest gay Republican group, the Log Cabin Republicans. Proposed and actual meetings with the group and the two party frontrunners, Texas Gov. George Bush and Arizona Sen. John McCain, caused a stir within the party's right-wing elements.

Although Bush earlier said that he was "someone who is a uniter, not a divider," on a November edition of "Meet the Press," he said that he would not meet with the group. Explaining why, he said, I don't believe in group thought, pitting one group of people against another. And all that does is create a huge political nightmare for people." A campaign spokesperson added, "Gov. Bush doesn't want to politicize this issue and their agenda."

Meanwhile, McCain faced sharp criticism for having met with the Log Cabin Republicans in November. Members of that group said McCain told them, "I am unashamed, unembarrassed, and proud to work with you." McCain supporters in South Carolina, a state holding a pivotal position in the primary calendar, said they had received anonymous mailings of a gay news-paper story about the McCain-Log Cabin meeting. When McCain said that an openly gay person could be elected president, having not served in the military, party officials criticized him. "If McCain's saying it's OK to be the leader, but not a member of the armed forces, that's preposterous," said Cindy Costa, a South Carolina member of the Republican National Committee. She called it "a bit of a turnoff" to conservative Christian voters. Another party official criticized McCain, saying that support from the Religious Right is crucial to winning the South Carolina primary. Another national Republican leader, Dr. Buddy Witherspoon, said, "Sounds like he's talking out of both sides of his mouth." Peter LaBarbera, head of Americans for Truth About Homosexuality (see p. 352), disparaged McCain's acceptance of donations from the Log Cabin Republicans. "Apparently money matters more to these politicians than faith or principles," LaBarbera said. "They can embrace the homosexual cause, but they shouldn't also try and sell themselves as pro-Christian or pro-family."

Bush's elaboration of his anti-gay positions continued during a meeting with the leaders of several major right-wing organizations — including longtime Religious Right activist Tim LaHaye, D. James Kennedy of Coral Ridge Ministries (see p. 354), and President of the Heritage Foundation (see p. 354) Paul Weyrich. Bush reportedly said he would not "knowingly" appoint openly gay or lesbian staff to his administration. After he was criticized for appointing openly gay men to his campaign staff, the Log Cabin Republicans called on Bush to clarify his position. Bush said that he did not say that he would not appoint gay men and lesbians, but that he would not fire them.

In April 2000, Bush did meet with a handpicked group of gay Republicans, but they were not affiliated with the Log Cabin Republicans.

GOP leader faulted for meeting with gay group

A major right-wing organization and far-right Republicans sharply criticized a congressional leader for meeting with a gay Republican group. In February, the Family Research Council (see p. 355) denounced U.S. Rep. Thomas Davis III for meeting with the Log Cabin Republicans in January. Davis met with the Log Cabin Republican Club of Northern Virginia to discuss ways the group could work with the party on the 2000 elections. Davis told them, "If we are to be a majority party...if we are to step ahead, we need to be a party of inclusion." His appearance made him the first high-ranking Republican member of Congress to address the group. Davis is chairman of the National Republican Congressional Committee, which supports House candidates.

The Family Research Council, opposed to Davis' selection as head of the fundraising committee in 1998, objected to his meeting with the Log Cabin group and criticized him for giving "legitimacy to radical homosexual groups." Robert Knight, a spokesperson for the group, said, "If I were in the [Republican] leadership, I would ask Mr. Davis whether he is really interested in alienating pro-family voters...to acquire the endorsement of the fringe of a splinter group totally at odds with the majority of people in the party." A February newsletter from the Council called on readers to contact the Republican National Committee and Davis and register their objections.

Davis, considered a moderate on social issues among House Republicans, differs from many within his party on gay and lesbian issues. Mike Neal, a party activist who opposed Davis' bid for the leadership position, was not surprised by the Log Cabin meeting, saying, "I believe he has sold us out plenty of times. But this is not a big deal." Others like Arthur Purves, a Republican candidate for local office in Davis' district, simply said that the Log Cabin Republicans' policies do not mesh with the "time-tested values" of the party. "My concern about homosexuality is that in a sense it is anti-choice...because it says that you really have no choice about your lifestyle...It subordinates morals to feelings."

Pro baseball player's tirade

Atlanta Braves pitcher John Rocker launched into a xenophobic and anti-gay tirade during an interview published in Sports Illustrated in December. Rocker reportedly had been given a hostile reception at an October game in New York against the Mets. During the interview, he criticized life in New York City, telling a reporter, "Imagine having to take the 7 train to [Shea Stadium] looking like you're [in] Beirut next to some kid with purple hair, next to some queer with AIDS, right next to some dude who got out of jail for the fourth time, right next to some 20-year-old mom with four kids. It's depressing." He had previously called New York fans "stupid." Referring to Mets fans, he said, "Nowhere else in the country do people spit at you, throw bottles at you, throw quarters at you." Rocker said he would retire before he would play for a New York team, adding, "The biggest thing I don't like about New York are the foreigners... How the hell did they get in this country?" While driving in a limousine during the interview, he reportedly spit on a toll booth and mocked an Asian woman. Rocker issued a statement soon after the interview was published in which he said his remarks "went way too far."

Some members of the baseball community quickly distanced themselves from Rocker's remarks. Major League Baseball Commissioner Bud Selig called the remarks "inappropriate and offensive" and said, "We will take appropriate action." Braves General Manager John Schuerholz said, "The viewpoints attributed to John Rocker in no way reflect the views of the Atlanta Braves organization." Rocker's teammate, Brian Jordan, said, "You can't respect a guy that makes comments like that publicly..." Baseball legend and former Brave Hank Aaron said he was "very sick and disgusted about the whole situation" and questioned how Rocker could continue in baseball.

Gay, lesbian, and other minority activists across the nation condemned Rocker's remarks. Days after the story ran, a diverse group of protesters gathered outside the Braves' offices at Tuner Field in Atlanta to demand Rocker's immediate dismissal. Michael Langford, head of the United Youth-Adult Conference, said, "There may be some room for redemption, but not as an Atlanta Brave. We encourage him to enter his resignation right now and go into an early retirement." Civic groups and the Atlanta City Council sent a letter to Braves owner Ted Turner and the general manager asking for Rocker to be fired. City Council member Derrick Boazman said, "This was more than just rhetoric. This was hate."

However, there were many who came to Rocker's defense. Among them was former teammate Ryan Klesko, who said, "He's not a bad guy. He's not one of those guys who hates everyone like everybody thinks. He's young. He's a good guy."

Rocker was initially banned from all of spring training and the first 28 days of the 2000 regular season and fined $20,000. An independent arbitrator cut his spring training suspension to 13 days, cut his regular season suspension to 14 days and reduced the fine to $500. Rocker was cheered in Atlanta during his return to the pitcher's mound.

Call for gay content warning

The Christian Action Network (see p. 353) announced in February that it would launch a grassroots campaign to have an "HC" warning label placed on all television programming with "homosexual content." CAN claimed that more than two dozen gay or lesbian characters were being portrayed weekly on prime-time television alone. Its President, Martin Mawyer, said, "Members of our organization have become increasingly disgusted with the amount of homosexuality in television programming." The group called on the Federal

Communications Commission to add the label to network and cable television programming in order to warn parents. Mawyer said he sent a letter to FCC Chairman William Kennard asking for a meeting to discuss the request. Mawyer said, "There are parents across the country that are sick and tired of having their living rooms invaded by homosexual characters and activities on their television." Mawyer pointed to two programs whose gay content he found objectionable — HBO's "The Sissy Duckling" and Fox's "That '70s Show." He also claimed that gay content has even become part of television advertising. FCC spokesperson David Fiske said that the Commission had not seen the letter. He also noted that the existing programming labels, which denote levels of violence, sexual situations and adult language, are voluntary.

The television industry largely disagreed with CAN's claims and ignored his request. Jack Valenti, head of the Motion Picture Association of America, said, "It's an inhumane proposal that should be ignored." Prompted by the CAN request and a recent court decision against one investigative television program, NBC President Robert Wright reiterated that network's opposition to government-imposed television ratings. The producers of the television show "Frasier" said, "The whole thing is absurd, insane, and frightening...The first show to get the HC will be 'Teletubbies.' " Max Mutchnick, producer of "Will and Grace," the only show in 1999 with an openly gay leading character, said that the HC label is "totally offensive, but it adds up to nothing. The numbers are telling us everything," referring to the fact that that show has consistently garnered top ratings. "Clearly, no one is having a problem with it." The Gay and Lesbian Alliance Against Defamation denounced the CAN campaign, saying it would "serve to stigmatize members of the lesbian, gay, bisexual and transgender community by suggesting that something is inherently wrong with them."

Helms tries to have Clinton order voided

Sen. Jesse Helms introduced a bill that would have effectively voided President Clinton's 1998 executive order prohibiting discrimination based on sexual orientation in the federal workforce. The "Freedom of Speech Act" would have prohibited the government from establishing new classes of people protected from discrimination. Helms said his bill would make sure "that federal employees are not forced to check their moral beliefs at the door when they arrive at the federal work place." He also contended that the White House had exceeded its authority with the executive order: "This bill attempts to make sure that President Clinton is not allowed to do by executive order what Congress declined to enact in the past two congressional sessions." The bill languished in committee without action. Religious Right groups, including the Family Research Council (see p. 355) and Concerned Women for America (see p. 354), had condemned the executive order when the president initially signed it and supported a failed 1998 attempt by Rep. Joel Helfey to overturn the order.

Lutheran official condemns gay pride decree

Rev. A.L. Barry, president of the Lutheran Church-Missouri Synod, the second largest Lutheran denomination in the country encompassing major portions of the midwest, condemned President Clinton's proclamation of June as Gay and Lesbian Pride Month. "I think it's the president's use of the word 'pride,' more than anything else, that gives me pause," said Barry. "It suggests to me that Mr. Clinton is no longer limiting himself to talking about tolerance of, or civil rights for, gays. In invoking the notion of 'pride,' he is publicly advocating homosexuality as an appropriate, even a commendable, orientation for one's life." Jeff Wunrow, director of the Privacy Rights Education Project, a gay and lesbian St. Louis advocacy organization, said "We are not going to allow religious leaders to make us ashamed of who we are."

Baptist Sunday School lesson

In January, a major publisher of Sunday School lessons for member churches in the Southern Baptist Convention distributed a specific lesson denouncing homosexuality. Entitled "Offering Hope to Homosexuals," the lesson characterizes homosexuality as sinful, urges gay men and lesbians to change their sexual orientation and asks Christians to help them. The lesson is part of the "Life and Work" series focusing on social issues. Some of the lessons in that series identified additional readings on "healing" homosexuals and referred readers to so-called "ex-gay" groups like Kerusso Ministries (see p. 355) and Exodus International (see p. 354). Ross McClaren, a specialist at Lifeway Christian Resources in Nashville and author of some of the "Life and Word" lessons including "Offering Hope to Homosexuals," said, "I hope through this lesson that people would see an open door for all sinners and come and have a changed life through Jesus Christ." Lifeway is the publishing arm of the 15.6 million-member Convention.

McClaren said it would be the first time that one of the lessons has focused solely on homosexuality. Lifeway said it had sold about 1.5 million Southern Baptist handbooks, and McClaren said a majority of member churches would be using them.

Gay and lesbian advocates were outraged. Bill Turner, co-chair of the Lesbian and Gay Coalition for Justice in Tennessee, said, "I know plenty of lesbian and gay Christians who are quite convinced that they have a perfectly adequate relationship with God and are still gay...The problem is imposing that doctrine [that gays should change] on the rest of the culture." Rev. Mark Caldwell of Glendale Baptist Church, said, "When you put questions to the Bible that the Bible knows little or nothing about, you don't get legitimate biblical answers." Victor Anderson, a Christian ethics professor at Vanderbilt University, said, "The issue is whether homosexuality ought to be rightly understood as a spiritual perversion. On that point I simply disagree."

Congressman panders to anti-gay group

U.S. Rep. Tom Coburn (R-Oklahoma) reiterated his opposition to homosexuality after a right-wing organization criticized the fact that he had given a speech to a gay Republican group. Coburn raised concerns among members of the Family Research Council (see p. 355) after he met with the Log Cabin Republicans, a gay partisan organization, in April. That group had praised him for his work to increase funding for AIDS research. However, Coburn later told the Family Research Council's Culture Facts newsletter, "The Bible is prejudicial against all kinds of sin — including homosexuality. No one stands harder against homosexuality than I do...Homosexuals are caught in a desperate situation, and they are trying to defy it any way they can." He stood by his support for AIDS research funding, saying, "[W]e have an obligation to do what we can to help people with AIDS."

Wrestling characters

Turner Network Television's World Championship Wrestling (WCW) introduced a character, Lenny, who wore pink trunks, ribboned pigtails and body glitter. Lenny reportedly entered the wrestling arena by skipping through the crowd, usually paired with his fellow wrestler Lodi, who wore similar outfits. The pair was referred to as "The West Hollywood Blondes." The audience usually responded with "Faggot! Faggot! Faggot!" when Lenny was in the ring. As Lenny got beaten up, the crowd responded again with the same taunts. The Gay and Lesbian Alliance Against Defamation contacted the WCW to complain about how the depictions incite hostility toward gay men. GLAAD media director Scott Seomin wrote that the episodes were "shocking in its promotion of homophobia and, literally, gay-bashing," and said that the Lenny character was presented to incite homophobic behavior from the crowd. "Such programming gives license to viewers to ridicule and harass all gay people," Seomin said. Although GLAAD received written assurances in August that the character would be dropped, Lenny appeared again in September. The WCW said it wanted to complete the Lenny "storyline." In October, the WCW and TNT issued a statement saying they had discontinued the character.

Kia television commercial pulled

The Kia Motors America car company developed a television commercial that referred to a transgendered character as a "freak of nature." In the commercial, a man drives his Kia car across the country, encountering adverse conditions on the way. At the end of the trip, he passes a man wearing a dress who blows him a kiss. The bottom of the screen read, "57 acts of nature...and one freak of nature." The Gay and Lesbian Alliance Against Defamation complained that the commercial was offensive to gay men and lesbians. Joan Garry, GLAAD's executive director, wrote a letter to company officials, saying, "It seems pretty clear that labeling someone a 'freak' does more than just make a joke: it passes judgment, it perpetuates stereotypes, and in this case, it stigmatizes an entire group of people...Transgendered persons are among the most frequent victims of bias-motivated crimes." Kia promptly pulled the commercial.

Derisive terms in online thesaurus

Until mid-January, an online thesaurus listed several insensitive and anti-gay terms as synonyms for "homosexual" and "bisexual." The thesaurus for America Online, licensed from Merriam-Webster, listed "dyke," "fruit," "faggot," "homo," "sodomite" and "pederast" as alternative words for homosexual. It listed synonyms for bisexual as "androgynous," "hermaphrodite," and "hermaphroditic." Several gay and lesbian rights groups complained that the alternative terms needed to be labeled as derogatory. America Online chose to take the site down instead. Merriam-Webster apologized for the situation, noting its long-standing policy against identifying derogatory synonyms for racial and ethnic groups as such. America Online later put the site back online but without the objectionable terms.

ALABAMA

Statewide: Hate crimes bill debated

The February murder of Sylacauga's Billy Jack Gaither, who was targeted because he was gay, spurred legislators to propose a bill expanding the state's existing hate crimes law to include sexual orientation. The bill faced bipartisan opposition.

Activists from across the state converged on the Capitol building in March to lobby for the bill as part of a larger campaign for gay and lesbian rights. David White, with the Gay and Lesbian Alliance of Alabama, said, "We want to be able to let Alabama legislators and officials in the state know that we're important...We want to convince the legislators of Alabama we like living here and we want to make living in Alabama better."

Several legislators questioned the bill's merit. Rep. Neal Morrison said, "Every crime is a hate crime." Rep. Blaine Galliher took issue with assertions that all of the amendment's opponents were anti-gay, saying, "not all churches support homosexuality, and not all churches are hatemongers because they don't support that lifestyle." Despite these reservations, the House Judiciary Committee passed the bill in May with a 6-5 vote. Supporters had waited weeks for committee chair Bill Fuller to bring up the measure and finally forced the vote. Although Gov. Don Siegelman indicated his support in a state newspaper, further consideration of the bill was postponed indefinitely and the bill did not make it to the House floor for a vote before the end of the 1999 session.

Birmingham: Phelps protests Gaither service

Rev. Fred Phelps and members of his Westboro Baptist Church (see p. 356) protested at a memorial service for Billy Jack Gaither, who was murdered in February by two men who said they had killed Gaither because he was gay. While 17 speakers and more than 200 mourners remembered Gaither inside the Covenant Metropolitan Community Church, Phelps and his church members protested outside and across the street. Phelps said, "We are outraged at this violent crime, but the issue is the homosexuals are exploiting it...It is no longer merely an event for the family and friends to grieve." He also attacked the service for being held in a predominantly gay and lesbian church. "That's not a church, that's a dog kennel...It's a wonder to me that God doesn't snuff [out] that center of abomination of desolation...for it's evil. It's great evil." One of his fellow protesters carried a sign reading, "Billy Jack Gaither Burns in hell." Phelps and his followers frequently picket at funerals of gays.

Another group stood near the church carrying signs affirming gay men and lesbians. One member of that crowd, 9-year-old Max Griffies, said, "It makes me feel disgusted because everybody is created equal and all people are created by God." Max made his own sign that read, "God loves all people."

ALASKA

Statewide: Domestic partners lawsuit

Right-wing state legislators condemned a lawsuit filed by eight gay and lesbian state employees and the Alaska Civil Liberties Union against the state of Alaska and the city of Anchorage in state court. The employees, all of whom have same-sex partners, claimed that the state discriminated against them by not offering them family benefits similar to the benefits that married heterosexual employees receive. The suit did not seek to invalidate the state's refusal to recognize same-sex marriages, but it did charge that Alaska uses the ability to marry as a litmus test in awarding employee benefits to public employees. Jennifer Rudinger, head of the AKCLU, said, "The government can't refuse equal treatment to an employee simply because of the gender of that employee's life partner...Alaskans may not agree on the issue of marriage, but I hope we can all agree that employees deserve to be treated fairly." The plaintiffs wanted the government to begin offering the benefits to unmarried couples who work for the government.

Sen. Loren Leman, who was instrumental in the legislature's passage of the 1998 law that prohibited the state from recognizing same-sex marriages, was the most vocal detractor of the lawsuit. "Why should I pay 1 to 5 percent more for my insurance so Dan Carter and Al Incontro [the two male plaintiffs] can have their homosexual relationship and feel secure in their economic situation?" he asked. "I don't see why I should pay more so they have some benefit they think they should have." State officials estimated the cost for annual health insurance premiums would eventually rise if the state offered domestic partner benefits. Leman also claimed that providing the benefits only to heterosexual couples was a social benefit. "[Heterosexual marriage] provides some measure of stability. We've made as a society a conscious judgment to confer that preferred status to married couples."

The plaintiffs took issue with Leman's characterization. Shirley Dean, a plaintiff, pointed out that gay and lesbian employees pay into the same state health benefits fund as heterosexual employees but are not able to receive any of the benefits for their domestic partners that heterosexual employees do for their spouses. "I have been with the state almost 16 years. So I am eligible to share full medical costs with my spouse [if she were married to a man]. Over a lifetime, that would be a considerable sum. It's not only medical; if I were to die, I couldn't leave a death benefit to [my partner] Carla," Dean said. "We are not asking for anything special — just the exact same thing my co-workers get," she added. Maureen Longworth, another plaintiff, said that she had $20,000 worth of necessary dental work performed. Although her insurance did not cover the work, her partner's insurance with the state Department of Labor would have.

In November, Chris Goinet, a 12th-grade teacher at Grace Christian School in Anchorage, had his government class submit letters to the editor of the Anchorage Daily News denouncing the lawsuit. One student wrote, "I find it quite ridiculous that 'domestic partners' are seeking benefits from the state and believe that they should have the same benefits as a man and woman with a marriage license. What if a man and his horse want these same benefits?" Another wrote, "Why does it always seem like homosexuals want to rip out the straight long nails that hold what's left of our society just to fill them with their silly putty? Gays shouldn't get marriage benefits (the key word there being 'marriage')!" And a third wrote, "I read your article...about the same-sex marriage lawsuit and was appalled. These people need to give up. The gays have fought and fought, and they haven't heard the public's response. We don't care. We don't care if they want pension benefits equal to married couples; they aren't married so they shouldn't get the benefits." Yet another wrote, "[H]omosexuals are taking away the real marriage criteria, or the meaning of marriage." The lawsuit is still pending.

Statewide: Housing discrimination lawsuit

In January, a panel of the U.S. Court of Appeals for the 9th Circuit ruled that landlords may legally refuse to rent to unmarried couples if the landlords object on religious grounds. Two Anchorage landlords originally filed the case in 1995. They were not the subject of a discrimination complaint, but rather preemptively tried to defeat non-discrimination laws in housing that included provisions prohibiting discrimination based on marital status. Kevin Thomas and Joyce Baker, the plaintiffs, argued that they were being forced to choose between their religious beliefs and "facilitating" sin. Several anti-gay organizations filed *amicus* briefs on the plaintiffs' behalf.

A three-judge panel of the court ruled 2-1 that the laws in question prohibiting discrimination based on marital status unconstitutionally infringed upon the landlords' right to free exercise of religion. The dissenting judge argued that the ruling set a dangerous precedent. He wrote that the "potential for harm will be seen when a landlord in this circuit refuses, on the basis of religious beliefs...to rent or sell housing to divorced individuals, interracial couples, victims of domestic abuse seeking shelter, or single men or women living together simply because they cannot afford to do otherwise."

Some observers thought the ruling would have a broad impact. Steven T. McFarland with the Center for Law and Religious Freedom (see p. 353) said, "I'm happy for religious citizens who now have a stronger handhold when they want to bring their religious convictions into the marketplace...The school district that doesn't want to allow parents to opt out of a religiously objectionable curriculum, now they've got to listen to that parent." Religious Right groups, such as Focus on the Family (see p. 355) and the American Center for Law and Justice (see p. 352), filed briefs on behalf of the plaintiffs.

Legal experts concerned with protecting the rights of gay men and lesbians voiced concern with the court's ruling. Clyde Wadsworth, with Lambda Legal Defense and Education

Fund, said, "Lesbian and gay couples will be swallowed up by that exception by landlords who claim a religious exemption." He added, "I think it has the potential for gutting civil rights laws in many cities and states." Los Angeles City Attorney James Hahn voiced the same fears: "This ruling...would allow discrimination against unmarried couples, gay men, lesbians, people with AIDS, HIV, and other disabilities. It opens the door to other forms of discrimination, which theoretically could be justified on religious grounds." Other attorneys noted that the ruling might allow landlords to pry into the private lives of their tenants. Because the 9th Circuit encompasses nine of the westernmost states, the ruling could have had an impact far beyond Alaska.

However, in October, the court granted a request by the state of Alaska and the city of Anchorage to rehear the case. The court set aside the January decision and ordered a new hearing before an 11-judge panel in March 2000. On Aug. 4, the full 9th U.S. Circuit Court of Appeals dismissed the landlords' suit, saying their challenge to Alaska laws prohibiting housing discrimination based on marital status was not ripe for judicial review. Judge M. Margaret McKeown, writing for the majority in *Thomas v. Anchorage Equal Rights Commission,* said that "at this stage the dispute is purely hypothetical and the injury is speculative."

Anchorage: Gay book targeted in middle school

A book containing a gay-themed story was nearly removed from a middle school's library in February. Parent Sue Frances complained to school officials at Goldenview Middle School that a story in "Athletic Shorts" by Chris Crutcher "has lots of foul language in it...is disrespectful to parents and authority" and "makes [homosexuality] sound like a normal thing." She specifically targeted the story, "A Brief Moment in the Life of Angus Bethune." The award-winning book is a collection of stories about difficult issues facing teenagers, including sexual orientation. In Crutcher's story, Angus has gay parents, both of whom have same-sex partners. Frances wanted the book available to students only through the principal's office. A teacher countered that the story was about overcoming prejudice and stereotyping. He said he used the story to spark a class discussion about empathy and human emotions.

"Why should I pay 1 to 5 percent more for my insurance so [two male plaintiffs] can have their homosexual relationship and feel secure in their economic situation?"

— Alaska state Sen. Loren Leman, criticizing a lawsuit by several gay and lesbian state employees seeking domestic partner benefits.

The matter was referred to the school board's Controversial Issues Review Committee, which voted unanimously to keep the book on the shelves. Frances was disappointed with the decision and brought the matter before the full Anchorage school board. The board voted 6-0 to keep the book in the middle school library; however, it was pulled from elementary school libraries.

Palmer: Student mural defaced

Students defaced a mural painted by an openly gay high school student in May. Frank Asay III painted a mural at Colony High School as part of an art class project shortly before graduating. Asay said he had confronted homophobia head-on throughout his years at Colony. His painting consisted of a poem called "Peers" that did not have a gay theme, but it was done with rainbow lettering and illustrated with a fence, meant to signify murdered college student Matthew Shepard. Several students reportedly questioned whether it was a "gay mural," and many in the school community objected.

Some parents complained to school officials. One educator reportedly told the art teacher, Melody Mann, that the mural was offensive because "it was a memorial to a martyr for homosexuals." Although he was somewhat disappointed with Mann's suggestion that he paint over parts of it, Asay reluctantly obliged just days before the school board meeting where he had heard it was to be discussed. Some of the old paint bled through the new layers, making it hard to cover up.

In the meantime, a sociology class in school developed a project in which some students repainted the original words while other assessed the responses of the student body. They discovered that a number of students resented those who had helped restore the original mural. Vandals smeared gel over the mural, blurring the words until they were illegible.

Mann said, "When Frank was painting the mural, it woke me up to the fact that it's not always that safe or protected out there." Asay said he felt that most students had sided with him in the matter after they witnessed the depth of opposition he faced, saying, "I feel I painted more on the memories and minds of the people that saw it."

ARIZONA

Statewide: Ban on gay foster parents

In what opponents called a thinly veiled attempt to keep gay men and lesbians from serving as foster parents, Republican State Reps. Karen Johnson and Barbara Blewster added language to a bill covering the agency in charge of the state's foster children that eliminated funding for the placement of children with unmarried couples, single parents, or openly gay and lesbian parents. Johnson and Blewster introduced the measure late in the legislative session after they had faced considerable opposition to earlier anti-gay legislative initiatives.

State foster care system administrators worried about the proposal because almost one-third of all children currently in the system reside with single parents, regardless of their sexual orientation. The Arizona Human Rights Fund called the directive "utterly irresponsible." Johnson and Blewster used a parliamentary maneuver to shield the budget directive from the line-item veto power the governor could have exercised.

The measure never made it to a floor vote. In fact, Republican governor Jane Hull reasserted the state's policy of placing foster children in suitable homes regardless of the sexual orientation or marital status of the parents. Reports referred to this as a "Don't Ask, Don't Tell" policy similar to the military's policy of not inquiring into the sexual orientation of recruits and the enlisted. Although Johnson expressed dismay and surprise over the governor's action, an earlier internal review ordered by Gov. Hull concluded the current policy was sound and beneficial. Mary Ault, head of the government division in charge of foster care and adoption, said, "Quite honestly, we're not asking about marital status...We're asking about whether it's a stable relationship."

Statewide: Bill to prohibit gay student groups

Several Republican state legislators in Arizona tried to prohibit gay student groups in the state's public schools. The bill would have prohibited any student group that promotes any kind of sexual orientation, sexual activity, or criminal behavior. Objectors to the bill said associating homosexuality with criminal behavior labeled gays and lesbians as deviant and dangerous.

The bill's chief supporters made several anti-gay remarks during its consideration. State Rep. Linda Gray argued that Arizona should stop using government funds to support these types of student groups. "We don't allow Playboy clubs on campus to promote heterosexuality," she said. "Why should we have gay clubs to promote homosexuality?" Saying that the clubs were "part support group, part recruitment," she claimed gay and lesbian students would really be trying to convert straight students into gay men and lesbians. Three other state representatives joined Gray in sponsoring the bill, including one who had promoted similar legislation two years earlier.

In a letter to the editor of the Arizona Daily Star, one Arizonan said, "The last thing they [teens] need is to be told that a deviant perversion like homosexuality is nothing more than an 'alternative lifestyle.'...A student organization that promotes immoral, perverse behavior such as homosexuality has no place on a school campus." The letter writer echoed Rep. Gray's assertion that gays seek to convert other people to homosexuality. One local school official, disgusted with lawmakers' efforts to ban gay student groups, said, "I can't believe this stuff. These people have nothing better to do with their lives." He went on to note that a gay-straight alliance at a high school in Sunnyside helped educate students and faculty about discrimination.

State and local elected officials feared a replay of Utah's experience, in which a school board ultimately eliminated all non-curriculum-related student groups rather than allow a gay-straight club to meet. Under the federal Equal Access Act, a secondary school that receives public funds and that allows at least one non-curriculum-related student group to meet cannot discriminate against any other student group. Rep. Gray eventually pulled the bill, allegedly heeding persistent warnings that it would have violated the Equal Access Act. She reportedly considered offering an amended version of the previous bill requiring students to get written consent from their parents to join any school organization. The revised bill would have also required all student organizations to promote abstinence and would have prohibited schools from advertising or promoting any student clubs. She never submitted that bill, however. Trying to resuscitate the measure, Republican Rep. Debra Brimhall made a last-minute threat to attach a ban on gay student clubs as an amendment on another bill. However, the amendment was never submitted.

> "A student organization that promotes immoral, perverse behavior such as homosexuality has no place on a school campus."
>
> — From a letter to the editor in the Arizona Daily Star, supporting a bill to prohibit student groups from discussing homosexuality.

In the end, criticism of the bill outweighed its support. Opponents feared that because most of the students in gay student clubs are not "out" to their parents or peers, Gray's proposal would have paralyzed most gay student groups. Openly gay Democratic Rep. Ken Cheuvront said, "The Republicans in this state are trying to micromanage all levels of life, from the bedroom, and now to the schools."

Statewide: Domestic partner benefits

Republican state Rep. Karen Johnson introduced a bill that would have prohibited state municipalities from offering domestic partner benefits to their employees. Prompted by recent trends in Pima County and the city of Tucson, which extend family benefits to the domestic partners of municipal employees, Johnson and her co-sponsors sought to eliminate those policies and halt the movement before it spread elsewhere. At the time of the proposed legislation, about 70 municipalities around the nation were extending some form of benefits to the domestics partners of their employees.

Johnson is well known for opposing state policies and legislation intended to eliminate discrimination against non-heterosexual Arizonans. Arguing that domestic partner policies are themselves discriminatory, Johnson concluded that because gay men and lesbians do not have families in need of care, they do not deserve benefits such as insurance. According to Johnson, gay men and lesbians do not need health or life insurance because "They can afford it," referring to the myth that all gay men and lesbians have high incomes.

Johnson maintained that homosexuality and domestic partner benefits were detrimental to society. "On the law books of our state is a law against cohabitation, and we're going to reward people [who cohabit] with our tax dollars by giving them insurance benefits?" Johnson said. "I certainly wouldn't think it is incumbent on the state to reward that type of behavior." Defending her attempt to exclude gays from state benefits, she claimed that "Homosexuality is at the lower end of the behavioral spectrum." Johnson linked gays to diseases such as AIDS, gonorrhea, anal carcinoma and something she called "gay bowel disease." She said, "Public policy must be established by which promiscuous heterosexual and homosexual activity is firmly resisted...Unlike laws, morals are carved in stone and therefore immutable." During committee hearings on her bill, Johnson called gay men and lesbians, "a threat to society" and declared they were "undermining the natural family."

The bill's co-sponsor, Republican Barbara Blewster, went further. In a letter to a constituent, she compared homosexuality to "bestiality, human sacrifice and cannibalism." Blewster claimed that ancient civilizations that embraced homosexuals also practiced sex acts with animals and human sacrifice. She wrote that homosexuality "is a high sign of the downfall of the nation." Blewster said, "[Homosexuality] is a progression of perversion, as I know it" and added that there is "no joy in life without taking on the responsibility of a wife and children."

Support for the bill also came from the Arizona Religious Right. Frank Meliti of the Arizona Tradition Values Coalition (see p. 357) testified at the committee hearing: "Homosexuals are known for telling lies and twisting the truth and attacking and calling names those who would stand up and not go along with their agenda." Rev. Andrew Cosentino of the Interfaith League of Sound Government added, "God made Adam and Eve, not Adam and Steve."

Johnson's opponents said that her calling gay men and lesbians promiscuous was hypocritical. Johnson has divorced four times and has seven children by four different fathers. Openly gay state Rep. Steve May said of Johnson, "My tax dollars are supporting her fifth relationship...She's been using my tax dollars to support five husbands."

Subsequently, the Pima County human resources manager said that the costs of providing partner benefits are relatively low and that most of the couples who have taken advantage of the program are heterosexual.

The bill's success early in the legislative session seemed imminent. It cleared the GOP-majority Government Reform Committee on a solid party-line vote. However, further debate over Johnson's bill became so rancorous that the legislature tabled the measure for further consideration during the next legislative session.

Statewide: No to same-sex marriage

When the Vermont Supreme Court in December ruled that gay men and lesbians are entitled to all the benefits of marriage heterosexuals enjoy, even progressive lawmakers in Arizona's legislature said there was no chance it would happen there. Conservative voices across the state confirmed their opinion. Democratic state Rep. Ken Cheuvront, who earlier voted against a ban on same-sex marriage, said, "With the current Republican leadership in the House and Senate, I doubt it would be something that would pass or even get very far." Republican Gov. Jane Hull also joined those opposing same-sex marriage.

Conservative columnist Betsy Hart wrote an editorial in a state newspaper outlining her view that same-sex marriage would hurt the country. She claimed that government has continually undermined the strength of American families. The Vermont Supreme Court judges maintained that tradition, she wrote. She suspected that allowing same-sex marriage would result in legalizing polygamy or incestuous marital unions. Granting any semblance of same-sex marriage "erodes one of the strongest and most stabilizing, restraining building blocks on which the structure of our culture rests."

Statewide: Sodomy repeal fails

A few right-wing state legislators obstructed the repeal of Arizona's sodomy and cohabitation statutes. Backers of the repeal had initially mustered enough votes for a bill repealing both laws, but Republican House Speaker Jeff Groscost used parliamentary maneuvers to kill it. Groscost held the vote on the bill on a day he had discovered that openly gay Rep. Steve May would be absent. May and his cosponsor, openly gay Rep. Ken Cheuvront, had secured just enough votes to pass the repeal, but May's absence allowed the bill to fail by one vote. Republican Rep. Linda Gray, an opponent of the repeal, moved to reconsider the bill, which would have prevented supporters from revisiting the issue because House rules permit only one attempt to reconsider a bill. The move to reconsider was defeated, as Gray reportedly expected. Laws outlawing sodomy and cohabitation have regularly been cited by some right-wing legislators to justify denying civil and legal rights from gay men and lesbians.

Statewide: Women's studies threatened

Republican State Rep. Linda Gray introduced a bill that would have terminated funding for women's studies programs at the state's three public universities because they included discussions of homosexuality. Stage plays and courses dealing with homosexuality at Arizona State University, the University of Arizona, and Northern Arizona University alarmed Gray and several of her co-sponsors.

Gray's objections ranged from stage plays to course content and assigned texts. She deplored a production of the award-winning off-Broadway hit, "The Vagina Monologues," sponsored by the Department of Women's Studies at Arizona State University. Gray objected to a requirement in a University of Arizona women's studies course that students purchase a book from a store catering to lesbians. Students had to purchase Jeanette Winterson's "Oranges Are Not the Only Fruit," a novel about coming out of the closet in a religious family, from Antigone Books. Gray's bill would have required that all course materials be made available at on-campus facilities. Ignoring appeals from faculty and students, who focused on the merits of diverse educational opportunities, Gray considered having the three university presidents address her concerns about gay and lesbian content in the courses.

Gray did not stand alone. Fellow Republican State Rep. Jean McGrath joined Gray in her concerns about the departments. After questioning the merit of an undergraduate degree in women's studies, McGrath pondered, "I don't know why they would delve into homosexuality...How many people do you think we have in this country that are homosexual?"

Gray, who sits on the House subcommittee in charge of university funding, later retreated from her demands just before the proposal went to a vote, saying she just wanted to focus attention on the teaching of homosexuality in public colleges and that she never intended for her concerns to become public. Rep. Gray sponsored or co-sponsored several other bills hostile to gay men and lesbians in the 1999 legislative session.

> "Homosexuals are known for telling lies and twisting the truth and attacking and calling names those who would stand up and not go along with their agenda."
>
> — Frank Meliti of the Arizona Traditional Values Coalition, testifying in favor of a bill to prohibit cities from offering domestic partner benefits.

Gilbert: Gay-straight club opposed

When about 20 students at Gilbert High School formed the Gays, Lesbians, and Straight Supporters (GLASS) Club in January, several parents reacted with outrage. The parents took their complaints to the Gilbert Legislative Network Committee, where they were rebuffed and sent back to the local school board. Other opponents of the club joined their attempts to have the group disbanded.

Two months after the club was founded, opposition had grown throughout the state. Gilbert High School's student council tried but failed to dissolve GLASS a few weeks after the club started. Meanwhile, the local school board began investigating whether the group could lawfully exist. In mid-March, parents dissatisfied with the pace of those deliberations took their cause to the state legislature's Gilbert Legislative Network Committee, but the parents were told the committee did not have jurisdiction over the matter. That body, which typically deals with matters such as school construction, referred them back to the school board.

During a school board meeting in late March, parents opposed to GLASS said they feared that the organization might recruit other students into the "homosexual lifestyle." They claimed a gay and lesbian club would lead teens into sexual experimentation, changing them into homosexuals. "I don't think high school is an appropriate place to be determining one's sexuality," one parent said.

Those voices did not go unchallenged. One mother of a gay son countered, "You don't have to love my gay child. You don't even have to like him. I just ask that he be given equal opportunity to be class president...just like my straight children." Two editorials in a local newspaper criticized the intolerance shown toward GLASS and said the club would benefit a variety of students. Leaders of GLASS said the organization would provide urgently needed peer support for students struggling with their sexual orientation. Reportedly half the members of GLASS are gay or lesbian, many not openly so. Although other area schools have gay and lesbian support groups, Gilbert High School was the only one with a club that sought official recognition.

> "[Homosexuality is] a death style, not a lifestyle."
>
> — State Rep. Karen Johnson, in an e-mail to a student leader explaining her opposition to a gay-straight student club at Gilbert High School.

GLASS members endured several direct, verbal attacks. State Rep. Karen Johnson fired off an e-mail to one student leader calling homosexuality "a death style, not a lifestyle." Even during meetings before the school board and state legislature, several hostile parents told club members that GLASS's campaign was completely inappropriate. Johnson had also co-sponsored a bill to prohibit cities from offering domestic partner benefits and opposed another measure that would have repealed the state's sodomy laws. She also co-sponsored bills in the state legislature to bar discussions of homosexuality and gay-related student clubs from public schools.

The school board avoided taking sides. Fearing costly legal challenges, the board officially recognized GLASS. However, several board members echoed fellow board member Elaine Morrison's measure of acceptance of gay and lesbian students. Morrison said, "We should leave the kids alone...Let's see what happens next year."

Phoenix: Gay vets barred from parade

Phoenix's Veterans Day Parade prevented a group of gay veterans from participating, organizers claimed, because in the 1998 parade, one member marched in drag. The Phoenix gay veterans group maintains that its exclusion from the parade, which is partly sponsored by the city, involved discrimination by an organization funded with public money. Parade officials also removed the president of the Phoenix chapter of Gay, Lesbian, and Bisexual Veterans of America from the parade's organizing board after having personally invited him to join. Planners maintained that in the 1998 parade, the gay group was the only contingent to receive any backlash. One organizing board member said that some organizations chose not to participate because the gay veterans group was present.

An e-mail to the gay group from parade organizers read, "[T]he committee felt it would not enhance the mission of the parade if you or your group participated in the 1999 parade." An official later said, "They came to the parade as cross-dressers in drag attire. None of them came in patriotic clothing." Organizers maintained, therefore, that the gay veterans were barred because of their appearance, not their sexual orientation.

The president of the gay veterans group said and parade organizers confirmed that he was excluded from what he called "secret meetings" of the parade's planning committee. A parade organizer said that the parade has never notified other groups of parade policy changes or screening criteria. She said that 1998 participants were informed that uniforms or other patriotic attire were required although there has never been a written dress code. Gay veterans claim they were never informed about a dress code and noted that several non-military contingents, among them beauty queens and veterans' mothers, participated in 1998 in civilian clothing. The person whom organizers described as a cross-dresser was in fact a male-to-female transgendered veteran who always wears traditional women's clothing.

Phoenix: Lesbian officer alleges discrimination

Claiming she endured abuse, retaliation, and discrimination because she is a woman and a lesbian, Phoenix Police Lt. Sharon Patches filed a civil rights lawsuit against the police department in Phoenix. Her suit claims she suffered undue emotional, physical, and professional stress because of harassment and discrimination based on gender and sexual orientation.

One gay rights advocate was surprised that a Police Department she felt was gay-friendly would subject an employee to the alleged behavior, but Beth Verity, of Arizona Central Pride, also said that Arizona law does permit employees like Patches to be fired because they are gay or lesbian.

In her lawsuit, Patches alleges that the Police Department began an investigation into a personal relationship she formed with a another female officer. Patches also alleges that the department does not investigate male officers alleged to have committed domestic violence and other criminal acts. Patches, who had been a member of the Phoenix police force for 16 years, further asserts that in their final report to police officials, internal investigators ignored evidence that would have exonerated her, leading command staff to reach inaccurate conclusions about her conduct. After an additional investigation by the department's Professional Standards Bureau, three of the original five charges remained. Although her initial punishment involved 60 hours of suspension, that amount was later reduced to 40 hours. The Phoenix Police Department reportedly refused to comment on the lawsuit.

Phoenix: Military investigates gay legislator

Army officials contemplated expelling openly gay reservist Steve May, a state representative, for violating the armed forces' policy on gays in the military. In February, May became embroiled in a public dispute when, during a legislative committee hearing, he condemned state Rep. Karen Johnson for her remarks on a bill prohibiting towns and cities from offering domestic partner benefits. He objected to Johnson's remark, "If cohabitating and homosexual behavior is detrimental to the individual and to society, besides breaking the law, then society has the responsibility to resist it." Though he publicly affirmed his homosexuality at that legislative hearing, he was not on active duty at the time. The media never made May's sexual orientation a substantive issue when he ran for office as an openly gay candidate. May was charged with violating the military's "Don't Ask, Don't Tell" policy on gays in the armed forces. Public attention to May's case drew Rev. Fred Phelps (see p. 356) to the state Capitol.

May, First Lieutenant and second-in-command of the 348th Transportation Company for the Army Reserve, has condemned the Army's investigation for being unsubstantiated and detrimental to his command. The investigation began with an anonymous complaint. When the Army formally notified May in August of its intent to charge him, it asked him to waive his right to counsel. May refused and solicited military defense counsel. In a November letter explaining the Army's evidence against May, Maj. Patricia Maddox claimed that May's orientation made him "engage in, attempt to engage in, or have a propensity or intent to engage in homosexual acts." In that same letter, Maddox insisted that May provide private information about his sex life to refute the charges that he was gay and warned him that discharge was imminent if he failed to comply.

May's attorneys claimed that Army investigators repeatedly violated state and federal law and Army guidelines. May, they contend, was a civilian at the time the remarks were made. As a state representative, his remarks were made in an official capacity as a legislator. He was fulfilling constitutional obligations to his constituents. The attorneys also said the Army should not have demanded that May provide them with information regarding his sex life.

May's attorneys pointed to his performance reviews and distinguished record as a basis for having the charges against him dropped. After years of outstanding service by May and an honorable discharge, the Army even called him back to active duty in April to serve in Kosovo. In December, while he was training with the reserves, Army officials delivered to May a report recommending his discharge. Several of May's military colleagues wrote letters of support attesting that his sexual orientation did not disrupt morale. One rationale military and congressional supporters of "Don't Ask, Don't Tell" offered for adopting the policy was that openly gay servicemembers hinder unit cohesion and troop morale. May's attorneys contended that his record of performance and support proved that a discharge would not be in the Army's best interests.

Through the entire ordeal, Amy officials ignored opportunities to end the discharge proceedings. U.S. Reps. Tom Campbell and Barney Frank issued a letter to the president and the Pentagon signed by over 100 members of Congress urging them to stop the discharge procedures. The Department of Defense Public Affairs Office said it never received the letter. One of May's attorneys advised his battalion commander, Maj. Eileen Norton, that military guidelines permit officials to overlook the allegations if doing so would best benefit the Army and that the letters of support and performance reviews said as much.

Military officials were not the only ones targeting May. In September, the rabidly anti-gay Rev. Fred Phelps of Topeka, Kansas (see p. 356) directed a protest against May at the Arizona state Capitol. Phelps failed to follow through with his threat to burn the state flag, but he and several of his fellow church members did bring their infamous "God Hates Fags" placards. "A burning everlasting hell — a lake burning with fire and brimstone — awaits homosexuals," Phelps said after condemning the state for promoting a homosexual agenda.

Although he has been officially charged with violating the guidelines on gays in the military, Steve May has not been discharged from the Army. Charges are still pending.

Phoenix: Phelps protests pride parade

Fred Phelps, the anti-gay preacher from Topeka, Kansas (see p. 356), made his way to Phoenix to protest an April gay pride parade. He said he would make special signs just for his targets in Phoenix. Phelps and members of his congregation from Westboro Baptist Church carried signs saying "No Special Laws for Fags," "AIDS Cures Fags," and "Fags Doom Nations." They also brought their usual stock "God Hates Fags" placards.

Phelps tried to enter a particularly offensive float in the parade but found the parade's requirements intolerable. Parade organizers said he had to sign a declaration supporting gay rights. The float, entitled "Piece of Americana," featured pictures of slain Wyoming college student Matthew Shepard with the flames of hell surrounding him. It also had an ad for the church's Internet web address.

ARKANSAS

Statewide: Hate crimes bill fails to pass

A bill that would have increased penalties for hate crimes, including those motivated by anti-gay bias, died in the state legislature. Supporters said it failed largely because opponents objected to the inclusion of sexual orientation. State Rep. Ted Thomas questioned whether the bill protected some classes of people more than others. During testimony before the House Judiciary Committee, Larry Page, head of the Christian Civic Foundation of Arkansas, said that protecting some groups and not other creates an unequal justice system. He maintained that hate crimes legislation is used to promote homosexuality. Citing the murder of Wyoming college student Matthew Shepard, Page said the killers should be punished "because they killed a human being in the most vicious, barbaric way...not because of who it was." Page said the bill would punish speech by requiring "juries to be thought police." State Rep. Michael Booker disputed that, saying juries already are required to determine intent in the commission of crimes.

The bill did have the support of the state attorney general.

The House Judiciary Committee voted 12-4 against the bill in February. The bill's two sponsors, state Reps. Booker and Joe Harris, vowed to bring it back up for a vote. Harris said, "With more understanding and more education about the bill, I think the bill will fly."

Statewide: Sodomy repeal challenged

The state's prosecutors offered various legal strategies to dismiss a lawsuit challenging the state law prohibiting homosexual sodomy. The Arkansas sodomy law, passed in 1977, only criminalizes sex between members of the same sex. The controversy began in January 1998 when seven gay and lesbian plaintiffs, represented by Lambda Legal Defense and Education Fund, filed a lawsuit in state court arguing that the sodomy statute violates the plaintiffs' right to equal treatment and privacy guaranteed under the state and U.S. constitutions. The plaintiffs sought a permanent injunction to stop enforcement of the sodomy statute. The state attorney general and the Pulaski county prosecuting attorney sought to have the lawsuit dismissed on three separate occasions — once immediately after it was filed, again in the spring of 1998 as an appeal to the state supreme court prompted by Chancery Court Judge Collins Kilgore's denial of their first motion, and another in June 1999, in which they cited new legal grounds. In his ruling denying the attorney general and county prosecutor's first motion to dismiss, Judge Kilgore wrote that the plaintiffs "live and suffer harms associated with continuing threats of criminal prosecution under a constitutionally suspect scheme."

As part of their appeal to the state supreme court, the state attorney general and Pulaski County prosecuting attorney argued that because none of the plaintiffs had been arrested, their case should be dismissed. When the state supreme court ruled on that appeal in June 1999, it refused to dismiss the case and ordered that the state circuit court should hear the matter. Suzanne Goldberg of Lambda Legal noted, "Two Arkansas courts, including the highest in the state, have recognized that people who are injured by a law can seek judicial relief without having to be arrested."

Along with the Pulaski County prosecuting attorney, state Attorney General Mary Pryor, who had taken office in January 1999, filed another motion to dismiss the case in the fall of 1999. They claimed the plaintiffs had sued the wrong defendants. Because Arkansas state laws forbid lawsuits against the state, the plaintiffs sued the attorney general and county prosecutor as law enforcement officials. The attorney general had also argued that because the plaintiffs had not been charged with crimes, their suit had no basis. The Pulaski County Circuit Court heard oral arguments on that motion in November.

The circuit court ruled in February 2000 against the attorney general and county prosecuting attorney's motion to dismiss, agreeing that the plaintiffs had sued the appropriate officials. Beatrice Dohrn, legal director at Lambda Legal, said, "We are thrilled that at long last we will be able to argue the merits of this case...Three Arkansas courts...have rejected these desperate attempts to keep our challenge out of court."

CALIFORNIA

Statewide: Domestic partnership bill opposed

AB 26, a bill that would extend a variety of benefits to state employees and codify rights for unmarried couples met stiff resistance throughout California. As passed, the Domestic Partners Act created a statewide registry for same-sex couples, required hospitals to permit the domestic partners of their patients to visit the patients unless no visitors were allowed, and authorized municipalities that participate in the state employee benefits system to extend employee benefits to the domestic partners of their employees.

Legislators opposed to the bill claimed it was an indirect attempt to legalize same-sex marriage. As part of his campaign against all gay-friendly legislation in this session, state Sen. Pete Knight labeled the bill part of a decline of society. He said, "I maintain same-sex is abominable...The state should not promote a new definition of marriage." State Assembly member Steve Baldwin said, "It's quite clear what is going on. This is the proverbial camel's nose in the tent for gay marriage."

Opponents also attacked the bill outside of the legislative chambers. Protesters held a candlelight vigil at the Capitol to influence the Assembly's vote. The Capitol Resource Institute (see p. 353) claimed that it feared the bill would infringe upon religious rights. Its president, Mark Washburn, said that if enacted, the bill "will make our centrist governor a radical." The Traditional Values Coalition (see p. 357), Focus on the Family (see p. 355), and the California Southern Baptist Convention, among other Religious Right groups, launched a statewide campaign against this and other bills concerning gay men and lesbians.

The bill passed both houses in September. The Senate vote was 22-14, and the Assembly vote was 41-38. Gov. Gray Davis signed it into law in October.

Statewide: Initiative to limit marriage

The effort to pass a ballot initiative that would effectively prohibit the state from recognizing same-sex marriages turned into a bitter campaign against gay civil rights. Although the state had not previously recognized same-sex marriages, the proposed initiative defined marriage as a union between one man and one woman. State Sen. Pete Knight, the initiative's sponsor, garnered the support of disparate religious and social interest groups for a crusade that produced heated rhetoric against gay men and lesbians. The state legislature had previously rebuffed Knight's attempts to prohibit recognition of same-sex marriage through a series of bills.

In a fundraising letter for the initiative, Knight characterized the effort to obtain legal recognition of same-sex marriages as an assault on fundamental American values. He claimed gay men and lesbians are trying to ruin the institution of marriage and destroy a cornerstone of American society. He referred to a television commercial opposing the initiative by the cast of the television show "Will and Grace" as a slick attack against those who want to defend "traditional marriage" and said, "a defeat for Prop. 22 [the initiative's number on the April 2000 ballot] in California would open the floodgates for 'same-sex marriages' not only here but all across our country."

Churches supporting the proposed prohibition mobilized their membership. Catholic bishops referred to same-sex relationships as "growing trends which represent a serious threat to the future of the family and of society itself." Mormon officials sent letters to hundreds of thousands of their California members in an effort to rally their support for the initiative. The California Southern Baptist Convention also backed the initiative.

Support from some organized religious groups sparked fundraising controversies. Reports surfaced in late summer that California's Catholic Dioceses and the Mormon Church had each donated more than $100,000 in support of the initiative; along with Knight's other allies, they raised considerably more money than organizations opposing the measure. Mormon and Catholic officials also lobbied state legislators. Knight, along with these church leaders, enlisted the aid of major Religious Right contributors. The Capitol Resource Institute (see p. 353) and the Chalcedon Foundation (see p. 353), whose leaders together donated nearly half a million dollars, regularly finance other Religious Right and anti-gay causes.

In October, the San Francisco Board of Supervisors called on the Internal Revenue Service to investigate the Mormon Church's fundraising activity. Because the Mormon Church is based in Utah, the supervisors also questioned the legality of the church's interstate fundraising and political activity. In response to this challenge, Mormon and Catholic leaders quickly condemned the Board of Supervisors. U.S. Sen. Orrin Hatch (R-Utah), who is a Mormon, called the resolution "bigoted and prejudiced."

In a surprising turn, Pete Knight's son, David, admonished his father in a Los Angeles Times op-ed reprinted in several other newspapers throughout the nation. David Knight said when he revealed his homosexuality to his father, their relationship ended. His column also said that Pete Knight had a gay brother who died of AIDS-related illnesses. Sen. Knight responded days after his son's piece appeared in the press, calling David's comments unfair and inaccurate.

Supporters of the initiative denounced a successful pre-election challenge to its title. In response to a complaint lodged by gay rights groups that the original title of the initiative— "Definition of Marriage" — would have deceived voters, the state attorney general, Bill Lockyer, ruled that the name should be changed to the "Limit on Marriage" initiative. The complainants had alleged that the true function of the initiative was to change California's policy of honoring marriages performed in other states. The initiative's sponsors criticized Lockyer's ruling and unsuccessfully tried to challenge it in a state court. "This political maneuver shows that he is plainly unqualified to make a fair and impartial judgment on this issue," said Robert Glazier, spokesman for the Protection of Marriage Initiative campaign.

Child-care experts predicted that passage of the initiative would be harmful to children raised in gay and lesbian families. A Stanford University family law expert issued a report finding that passage of the initiative would stigmatize same-sex couples and their children. The report also said that passage would also damage the emotional well-being of their children and destabilize the financial security of their families. Ironically, the initiative's supporters characterized their drive as one to save families.

In March 2000, Californians voted overwhelmingly in favor of the initiative, which passed with more than 60 percent of the vote. Only in five counties clustered around San Francisco did a majority of the voters reject the initiative.

Statewide:
Bill to move anti-discrimination provisions

The state Assembly considered bill that would move the state's prohibition of discrimination based on sexual orientation in housing and employment, placing those provisions under the state's Fairing Employment and Housing Act. Existing state law prohibits sexual orientation discrimination in housing and employment. The bill would only move those provisions to a different place in the state code and shift enforcement powers for those provisions to the state Department of Fair Employment and Housing, which has more expertise in addressing complaints of discrimination. The bill would not have, as many of its opponents claimed, prohibited any new forms of discrimination against gay men and lesbians not covered under existing state laws.

"[Homosexuality is] a sickness... an uncontrolled passion similar to that which would cause someone to rape."

— State Sen. Richard Mountjoy, explaining his opposition to a bill updating existing provisions prohibiting anti-gay discrimination.

Nevertheless, legislators hostile to the bill misrepresented what it effectively would do. Members of the Assembly Committee on Moral Concerns claimed the bill granted "more than equal protection" to gay men and lesbians, while other legislators made more outrageous claims. After asking, "What about fat people?" Assembly member Pat Bates claimed that the bill granted "special rights" to gay men and lesbians. In arguing against the bill, state Sen. Richard Mountjoy claimed that homosexuality is "a sickness...an uncontrolled passion similar to that which would cause someone to rape." Other legislators said that the bill was unnecessary because gay men and lesbians do not suffer the same types of discrimination that other minority groups do.

Critics challenged legislators who supported the bill at the Capitol and in their home districts. Protesters targeted state Assembly member Lou Correa's Santa Ana office because he supported the bill. Carrying signs with "Protect Family Values," they gave speeches and marched. The ad hoc group Orange County Families Against Homosexuality helped to organize the demonstration.

After the legislature had passed the bill in September, opponents flooded Gov. Gray Davis' office with phone calls demanding his veto. They also took to radio and television to encourage opposition. In October, after Gov. Davis had signed the bill, hundreds gathered in Riverside at a rally organized by the Campaign for California Families. Protesters denounced those legislators who support gay and lesbian rights and called for the governor to be recalled. Along with writing "Evil Man" and "Doom for California" on their placards, they tarred and feathered an effigy of the governor. Cherri Gardner, the group's Southern California director, said, "This [demonstration] is about the voters. Not the 2 percent of homosexual voters. The voters." As part of its statewide effort, the Campaign for California Families organized this event as well as similar ones in Sacramento, Fresno, and Los Angeles to criticize the governor's signing of two other bills concerning the rights of gay men and lesbians.

Statewide: School safety bill opposed

Critics assailed two bills intended to protect gay and lesbian students from discrimination and harassment based on their sexual orientation. They targeted the initial Dignity for All Students Act from its introduction through its failure in the state Assembly. That bill would have added sexual orientation to the existing provisions of the California Educational Code prohibiting various forms of discrimination. Opponents then went after the bill proposing the California Student Safety and Violence Prevention Act, which eventually passed the legislature and was signed by the governor. That bill would amend sections of the state educational code prohibiting discrimination in and guaranteeing equal access to educational programming and activities in any public or private school or post-secondary institution that receives public funds, so that they include sexual orientation as a prohibited category. Effective campaigning against the first bill forced supporters to scale back the scope of the second bill to assure its passage.

Rev. Lou Sheldon, head of the Traditional Values Coalition (see p. 357), launched a radio campaign calling on listeners to fight for the defeat of the Dignity for All Students bill. Sheldon claimed that the bill would prohibit schools from discussing or promoting heterosexuality and would require hiring quotas for gay and lesbian teachers in public, private, and parochial schools. He further claimed that the bill amounted to "special rights" for gay men and lesbians. At a rally outside the Capitol, Sheldon said, "This should not be called AB 222. It should be called AB 666." Several churches joined him at the rally.

James Dobson, head of Focus on the Family (see p. 355), sent a letter to several California churches urging them to help defeat the bills. In it he claimed, "The California State

Legislature is considering several bills which would put at risk the freedom to express biblically-grounded convictions about homosexuality and force homosexual views upon children, families, and employers." He, too, claimed the Dignity for All Students bill would "allow the state to mandate the teaching of homosexual curricula and the promotion of homosexual 'marriage' to students in K-12 public schools, colleges and universities."

Capitalizing on the growing population of Latinos in California, the campaign to defeat the Dignity for All Students Act reached out across racial and ethnic lines. Latinos Por La Familia, an organization of fundamentalist Christian Latinos, distributed fliers that depicted an interracial male couple kissing. The caption read in Spanish, "Protect the Children Against Homosexual Assault." It claimed the bill would promote homosexuality in public schools. That campaign extended to radio and print media ads. The Capital Resource Institute (see p. 353) and Campaign for California Families, two Religious Right organizations, helped to fund and organize the campaign by Latinos Por La Familia.

> "This should not be called AB 222. It should be called AB 666."
>
> — Traditional Values Coalition Chairman Lou Sheldon, at a rally against a bill in the Assembly that would protect gay and lesbian students from harassment.

Opponents also attacked assembly members who supported the bills. When Speaker Antonio Villaragiosa addressed a Latino group, an unidentified group distributed fliers asserting that Villaragiosa was part of "the homosexual agenda." State Assembly member Sheila Kuehl, who sponsored both bills, said that Christian conservatives had bombarded her office and those of several freshman representatives with faxes and telephone calls threatening political retaliation should the legislature pass the bill. Because of her sponsorship of the bills, Kuehl said that one legislator accused her of supporting bestiality.

After the Assembly defeated the Dignity for All Students Act in June, supporters reintroduced the California Student Safety and Violence Prevention bill in September as another piece of legislation. The legislature approved the latter bill, and Gov. Gray Davis signed it.

Antelope: Transgendered teacher ousted

Before the summer 1999 recess, teacher David Warfield began a process for gender reassignment surgery to become Dana Rivers and drew the ire of parents and officials at Center High School and the local school board. Soon after Rivers, an award-winning journalism and history teacher, notified officials of her intention, the board distributed a letter about her decision to all of the district's parents, four of whom wrote back to complain.

Led by the Pacific Justice Institute (see p. 356), religious conservatives united in their demands that the Center Unified School District fire Rivers. The Institute filed an administrative complaint on behalf of one parent seeking Rivers' removal. Brad Dacus of the Pacific Justice Institute said, "One student had to be pulled from school, and two children have had to be put in counseling." Rivers disputed that claim, saying it had never been substantiated. Dacus reportedly offered the school board his organization's legal assistance in removing Rivers or in fighting a lawsuit by her against the district, should she file one. A parent stood up at a board meeting to describe how the issue had traumatized her daughter. However, her daughter followed her to the microphone and rejected her mother's assertion. Board member Raymond Bender said of his colleagues, "They'll say things about parental rights and all that, but what this amounts to is: No way will they allow a transgender teacher to teach in the Center district."

Citing what it said was her "Evident unfitness for service," the school board voted 3-2 in June to fire Rivers, withholding its official announcement to her until September. The board members who voted for Rivers' dismissal claimed her firing had nothing to do with her being transgendered. They said, as Bender predicted, it was about parents' rights. The school board also placed Rivers on administrative leave shortly before fall classes started in August. After she was notified in September, Rivers filed a complaint with the state labor commissioner seeking to be reinstated to her teaching position.

Several media outlets added insult to injury by improperly addressing Rivers. The Conservative News Service referred to Rivers as a "he/she." On a program on the cable network MSNBC, host John Gibson also referred to Rivers both as "he/she" and "he." Gibson scolded a student who insisted that he use gender-appropriate pronouns. He asked the student, "Who is it that can make a woman? God or a surgeon?" Rivers said that other people in the media interviewing her or reporting on her story, however, used appropriate pronouns.

Rivers later dropped the complaint she made to the state labor commissioner as part of a settlement with the school board in which she also agreed to resign. The school board agreed to pay her $150,000 in compensation, purge all reference to the incident from her employment files, and support her search for another teaching job. Rivers is currently a spokesperson for basic human rights for transgendered people. She said, "I am going to teach again in a place where I am judged for my abilities, not for the shape of my body."

Rivers' students were strongly supportive of her throughout the ordeal. One of them said, "If anything, she'll be a better teacher now because she won't have to hide this."

A personal essay by Dana Rivers appears on p. 45.

Cabazon: Anti-gay comment at Esprit store

A woman who was fired by Esprit for denigrating gay men and lesbians tried to start a boycott against the company. "I am not going to support queers," Esprit employee Janet Landry admitted to saying at a staff meeting. She said she made the remark to explain why she refused to sell bracelets at the store to raise money for AIDS service organizations. The store promptly fired her for violating its anti-harassment policy. To protest her termination, Landry and her husband placed signs on their truck at the Cabazon mall where the store is located accusing Esprit of opposing family values and badgering employees because of their religious beliefs. In a letter to the store, the couple claimed, "Our religious and moral upbringing and belief in the Bible turns us against other than normal lifestyles. Our opinion is that lifestyles other than hetersexual [sic] relationships are both unethical and immoral." Though the couple contacted the news media and asked church groups to help, their boycott appeared to have little effect.

Contra Costa County: Catholic outreach to schools assailed

Opponents assailed a Catholic community organization's decision to fund a tolerance program that includes discussion of sexual orientation. The John Muir/Mount Diablo Community Health Benefit Corporation voted 7-2 to provide $45,000 to aid Catholic Charities of the East Bay, which regularly sponsors gay and lesbian programs. The grant will fund a program designed to educate teachers about harassment of gay and lesbian students.

Opponents made several arguments against the program. Camille Giglio, an anti-abortion activist, led a group of about 15 protesters at the corporation's meeting. She claimed the program was inappropriate for public schools and violated the separation of church and state. Grace Ellis, a Community Health Benefit board member who voted against the grant, said, "They're asking us to accept a different lifestyle, a lifestyle that has been proven to be very dangerous healthwise." She added, "This program doesn't teach anger control. It promotes homosexuality." Staff in several schools who had completed the tolerance training felt otherwise.

Advocates pointed to the pressing need to teach tolerance in Bay area public schools. The district had to clean anti-gay graffiti off of school walls twice in as many years. Several teenagers also reported suffering harassment because they were gay or lesbian. Teachers are already instructed on how to deal with these and other forms of intolerance and bigotry among students.

Opponents promised to continue their fight against the program. "This is not a done deal," said Giglio.

Costa Mesa: Rich Agozino's anti-gay radio show

Christian radio talk-show host Rich Agozino made several anti-gay remarks on his program in May. He regularly invites anti-gay activists to speak on his program, and his fiery attacks against gay men and lesbians have in the past reportedly advocated genocide.

During one of Agozino's programs in May, Scott Lively, head of Orange County Families Against Homosexuality, said, "The homosexuals are at war with the family." He also spoke about how what he called a "gay agenda" was infiltrating schools and targeting children. Lively is the co-author of "The Pink Swastika," a book that claims gays created the Nazi regime and sponsored the Holocaust. He also worked with the Oregon Citizens Alliance (see p. 356), which makes opposing gay and lesbian civil rights a top priority. Agozino's program was followed with a show titled "Recruit-Proof Your Children." Referring to gay men and lesbians on another program that month, Agozino said, "Their lifestyle is a death style."

Ed Personius, the station manager, has defended Agozino in the past, saying he was simply insisting his listeners follow the "word of God." The Orange County Human Relations Commission found Agozino's program so objectionable that it passed a resolution urging residents to write the radio station to tell the manager of the harm the show inflicts on gays men and lesbians and to also write a letter to the Federal Communications Commission.

El Monte: Campaign against pro-gay legislator

Members of La Amistad, a coalition of anti-gay, predominantly Latino evangelical Christian churches affiliated with Rev. Lou Sheldon's Traditional Values Coalition (see p. 357), held a prayer vigil in front of the district offices of state Sen. Hilda Solis demanding that she drop her support for AB 1001, a bill that would move the state's prohibition of discrimination based on sexual orientation in housing and employment, placing those provisions under the state's Fairing Employment and Housing Act. Throughout Southern California, they participated in workshops, prayer breakfasts, and political advocacy with the Traditional Values Coalition. Sheldon joined them at the July vigil.

La Amistad said it based its opposition to the bills on religious and moral grounds. Rev. Martin Garcia added that gay men and lesbians do not deserve minority status for that reason: "They want to give homosexuals minority status and they are going to change the whole system in our state." He also argued that the bills would force landlords to rent to people they deem immoral. Garcia said that if he were a landlord, he would never rent to gay men or lesbians. "To me, that person is immoral. I wouldn't want them in my house or my apartment," Garcia said. Solis, who heads the committee that considered the bills, was in Sacramento during the vigil and was surprised by it.

La Amistad fell short of influencing Solis or defeating the bill. When Solis learned of the vigil, she reaffirmed her opposition to all forms of discrimination. "Having gone through situations where I was discriminated against for my sex, ethnicity, and my age, I feel there should be no discrimination against any group," she said. Enough of her colleagues in the legislature agreed. Both houses of the state legislature approved AB 1001 and Gov. Gray Davis signed it.

With the help of the TVC, La Amistad sponsored a breakfast in September to generate support for continued anti-gay political work. They said their goal was to protect Latino families from what they called a "homosexual agenda." Conservative groups had some fence-mending to do with Latinos because of the Republican Party's support for a state ballot measure banning state services to undocumented aliens. At the breakfast, members of La Amistad expressed their fears of the anti-discrimination bills. Republicans hoped these

Latinos would become a potent force to defeat what conservatives called "special rights" for gay men and lesbians.

The Religious Right's organizing in Latino communities went beyond La Amistad. Carlos Mendez, the leader of the Hispanic Christian Council of Churches, said, "I've seen schools deteriorate as we've been compelled by law to accept certain lifestyles" and also said he believed gays wanted "special rights." Sheldon praised Mendez and La Amistad, whose offices are housed at the TVC headquarters, for their support.

Grossmont: Safe schools proposition

"Recall! Recall!" several attendees at a school board meeting shouted as the trustees of Grossmont Union High School District voted in June to adopt a policy proposal prohibiting discrimination on the basis of sexual orientation. The controversy began when the student representative to the local school board proposed adding actual or perceived sexual orientation to the school district's anti-discrimination policy. The school district's Race-Human Relations Task Force also recommended adding sexual orientation to the district's non-discrimination and anti-harassment policies. The proposal needed preliminary approval from the district's Board of Trustees before it could be formally adopted.

In May, the trustees held a meeting to vote on preliminary approval, during which critics of the proposal mounted a feverish opposition campaign. During the meeting, which was attended by approximately 1,200 people, opponents of the proposal accused the trustees of participating in what they called a conspiracy by the "gay lobby" to legitimize its lifestyle and recruit impressionable youth. Others objected to the one-hour limit on testimony from the public. One student brought a petition against the measure, which he said was signed by 500 students from two district high schools. Before the final vote, trustees amended the proposal so that it prohibited the district from promoting of a "gay lifestyle" and so that it would not apply to the district's curricula and multicultural policy. The trustees voted 3-2 to give preliminary approval of the amended proposal, but the changes failed to mollify the protesters.

Opponents carried their campaign to the meeting at which a final vote would be made. Fliers distributed at school encouraged students to stay home from school to protest the proposal. On the day before that meeting, about 14 percent of students boycotted classes in opposition to proposed policy. Outside the meeting, people carried signs opposing gay and lesbian student rights. Parent Priscilla Schreiber said the school board was acting against the wishes of the majority of residents by "enabling this [gay] agenda to infiltrate the schools."

The trustees voted 3-2 in favor of the proposal. After casting his vote against the proposal, trustee Gary Cass said, "This is not about protection. This is about promoting a homosexual agenda." Grossmont High senior Amanda Batz was disappointed by the vote. "If you could take a student vote, it would show you how many students are against this," she said. One man was removed from the trustees' meeting because he repeatedly inter-jected his opposition to the policy.

Immediately after the trustees voted, attorney Steve Knoblock submitted to school board president Ted Crooks a copy of a petition to recall him. Knoblock had been gathering sig-natures for his petition in the belief that a majority of the trustees would vote for the pro-posal. Although Knoblock and an ad hoc recall committee canvassed the school district for supporters, mostly in church parking lots, they never gathered the amount required for the issue to be put before voters on a ballot. A signature-by-signature count revealed the recall petition had failed by almost 3,000 signatures; almost 1,000 people who signed the petition did not live within the school district. Independent Business PAC, a political action committee created by conservative businessman and Religious Right activist Howard Ahmanson, contributed to the $86,000 the recall committee raised. Priscilla Schreiber, spokesperson for the recall committee, said her group would shift its focus to passing a statewide ballot initiative prohibiting legal recognition of same-sex marriages. Committee members still vowed to defeat Crooks and the other two members of the board who had voted for the amended policies in the next election.

Hemet: Student removed from lesbian teacher's class

A lesbian high school teacher filed a complaint in February with the California Labor Commission against the Hemet Unified School District charging that administrators had discriminated against her when they removed a female student from her class. The stu-dent's parents objected to their daughter's being taught by a lesbian. Janiece Betrand said she requested that her child be removed from Alta Kavanaugh's class because homosex-uality is against her religious beliefs. "I believe she was teaching tolerance in the class-room, and she was being sneaky about it," Betrand said. Kavanaugh had assigned stu-dents to talk about an important person in their lives, and she voluntarily discussed her same-sex partner as an example. Kavanaugh's complaint charged that the school district had violated the terms of her employment contract and state labor laws against discrimi-nation by not first holding meetings with both herself and Bertrand to discuss the matter. The school district claimed the mother feared the child's ability to learn was impaired. In January 2000, the California Labor Commission ruled in favor of Kavanaugh. The school board appealed that decision. At press time, that appeal was pending.

Los Angeles: Radio station's billboards

Talk radio station KFI in Los Angeles put up billboards in several Los Angeles area loca-tions, including the San Fernando Valley, Van Nuys, and North Hollywood that read, "Is your son's coach gay?" The radio station created the advertisements for the purposes of publicity. Station marketing director Stuart Turner said the billboards were designed to elicit discussion on a controversial topic and get people to listen to the station's programs. Los Angeles area gay and lesbian activists feared the billboards might provoke homophobic responses. Although their stations did not put up anti-gay billboards, other talk radio hosts in suburban Los Angeles encouraged their listeners to join local anti-gay campaigns. Christian radio talk-show host Rich Agozino, for instance, had anti-gay activist and author Scott Lively on in May (see Costa Mesa incident, p. 93). After several telephone complaints, KFI took down the billboards.

Los Angeles: UCLA Coming Out Day protest

A group of protesters, most of them affiliated with religious right-wing organizations, arrived on the campus of the University of California-Los Angeles to oppose National Coming Out Day festivities. "We're here to tell them the truth: that if they don't repent of their sins, they'll wind up in hell," a member of the Christian Anti-Defamation League (see p. 353) proclaimed. Beginning at noon, the protesters argued with students for several hours at a campus plaza. Another carried a banner that read, "AIDS, the homosexual contribution to the world." Undergraduate Bobby Bahremand said one of the men yelled at him, "Hey you homo, get off this campus."

After three hours of staging their own program, the protesters proceeded to another section of campus to challenge a speaker who had come to address an audience about National Coming Out Day. Keith Boykin, a noted national gay and lesbian rights leader and author, was participating in a campus program celebrating "coming out of the closet" when several of the protesters began challenging his interpretations of the Bible. Though they heckled every speaker at the program, their demonstration was not enough to distract the enthusiastic audience. At the conclusion of the program, several students walked through a makeshift closet to symbolically "come out." The protesters returned to preach their anti-gay message twice that semester. The student body largely ignored them.

A personal essay by Keith Boykin appears on p. 28.

Menifee: School harassment alleged

A Menifee Valley Middle School student filed a discrimination complaint with the U.S. Department of Education's Office of Civil Rights, claiming school officials allowed continuous harassment of him by other students. The unnamed student said that educators failed to halt the taunting and intimidation he received from classmates because he is gay. He alleged their inaction inhibited his ability learn. The boy's mother and a parent advocate also claimed that the district suspended the student 18 times to build a basis on which to expel him. His mother said he had missed more than 70 days of school, mostly because of his fear of harassment and a need for safety. Menifee officials claimed that they based the suspension on alleged lewd remarks he made to other students and faculty. At press time, the complaint was pending.

Mission Viejo:
Lesbian allegedly refused medical treatment

A Mission Viejo woman sued a physician whom she said refused to continue to treat her because she is a lesbian. Michelle Dupont sued Dr. Ronald Axtell and his medical practice for discrimination based on sexual orientation. Dupont claimed that Axtell told her to seek treatment from another doctor at Bristol Park Medical Group Inc. because of his personal objections to homosexuality. The subject of Dupont's sexual orientation arose when Dr. Axtell questioned Dupont during a routine physical examination about her method of birth control. Dupont explained that she is a lesbian and did not require any birth control. Axtell reportedly responded, "I don't approve of what you are." According to Dupont, he then recommended other doctors in the practice she should see for medical treatment. Dupont filed the suit under state law that prohibits discrimination based on subjective characteristics, which the state Supreme Court had previously held to include sexual orientation.

The parties settled the suit in August. As part of the settlement, Dupont received financial compensation and the Bristol Park Medical Group agreed to reiterate its own non-discrimination policies, sponsor sensitivity training, require employees to sign affidavits attesting to their compliance with those policies, and post signs stipulating its non-discrimination policies.

Modesto: Wal-Mart employee fired

A gay man who said he was harassed and threatened on the job and then fired filed a lawsuit in federal court against the Modesto Wal-Mart. Ty'Ger Dacosta said that fellow employees taunted him by calling him "faggot" and "queer" in addition to telling him that "God does not approve of gays." Dacosta claimed that when he told store managers about the harassment, management failed to respond and that the harassment increased. According to Dacosta, management transferred him to the health and beauty department, but the harassment escalated into physical threats. Dacosta was fired soon after he said he received those threats. He then sued Wal-Mart in July, claiming that he suffered discrimination, harassment, and emotional distress and that management fired him because he is gay. Dacosta's suit also contends that Wal-Mart's non-response to his complaints of harassment and its firing of him violated the California law prohibiting employment discrimination based on sexual orientation. Wal-Mart was unavailable for comment to the press. The case was pending at press time.

Oakland: Gay display removed from library

After several library patrons complained, librarians at an Oakland Library branch removed a Gay Pride Month display with a picture of a gay male couple kissing. The picture was part of the library's general collection and available for patrons to check out.

The reasons for the display's removal are in dispute. Julie Odofin, the interim director of library services, said she ordered the display removed and delivered to her so she could begin an investigation of the process for reviewing patron complaints. She said the picture should have been taken to her office, which is in another section of the city. The librarian who removed the display from the West Oakland Branch, however, said she understood Odofin's order as a censure of the display. That librarian dismantled the display and put the picture of the two men back into circulation. The picture was soon checked out by a patron who said he feared it would be confiscated. Odofin said she eventually received the picture but only after the Gay Pride Month display had been scheduled to be retired.

> "Who is it that can make a woman? God or a surgeon?"
>
> — MSNBC host John Gibson, after a student criticized him for not using gender-appropriate pronouns in reference to transgendered teacher Dana Rivers.

Regardless of the circumstances under which it was removed, library staff and officials agreed they needed to implement guidelines for reviewing complaints of this nature. The library's policy covering patron complaints currently pertains only to books and library materials and not displays.

Oakland:
Reported attack at Creating Change conference

Participants at the Creating Change conference, sponsored by the National Gay and Lesbian Task Force, were alarmed by the apparent response of the Oakland police to an activist who reported that she had been attacked. An African-American transgendered activist called police for aid after she said two assailants had attacked her with a broken bottle. When an Oakland police officer arrived at the scene, he allegedly blamed the activist for prompting the attack. According to the activist, the officer told her that she should not have been in that area. The activist said the officer then proceeded to complain about the paperwork involved in reporting the incident, saying, "I am tired of your shit." The reported attack took place just a few blocks from the conference hotel. More than 1,000 activists from the conference later staged a protest march.

Orange:
El Modena High School Gay-Straight Alliance

Students at El Modena High School in Orange met stiff and well-organized opposition when they created a Gay-Straight Alliance Club. Founder Anthony Colin, who said he was the victim of anti-gay harassment at El Modena High School, created the Gay-Straight Alliance to promote respect for and among gay and straight students at the school and to serve as a safe place for students to discuss topics related to sexual orientation and homophobia. Instead of following normal procedures in which the principal reviews and routinely approves applications for new student clubs, school officials subjected the application to unusual and discriminatory actions and, ultimately, to rejection. After Colin submitted an application for the group to be approved at the beginning of the school year, the principal passed the matter along to the school board. According to Colin, she later told him that the board did not think the club's name was appropriate. After delaying action on the club's application several times, the school board formally rejected it.

In November, the Board held an unprecedented "public forum" about the club for members of the community. Many Orange residents expressed their views about the club and to homosexuality in general. Saying that they feared being gay was medically dangerous and citing the Bible, opponents of the club called on the board to reject the students' application. According to press reports, Michael Fisher said, "Basically, homosexuality is physically and morally wrong ... It is counterproductive to an abstinence program and is leading our children down a dangerous path that could prove deadly." Former school board member Max Reismueller reportedly insisted the board should ignore the potential cost of litigation if members of the GSA sued the school district for rejecting their application for the club.

> "[T]he parents of these 'gay' students should be prosecuted for promoting this lifestyle."
>
> — Larry Nicholson of Placentia, in a letter to the editor opposing a gay-straight student club at El Modena High School.

According to the press, current school board member Bill Lewis stated, "The Bible says we're all sinners, but this, in my opinion, is asking us to legitimize a sin." Other opponents added that they would rather have the board ban all student groups than allow the Gay-Straight Alliance Club to meet, if the decision came to that. El Modena High has dozens of student clubs, many of which are not related to the curriculum. Outside of the "public forum," a recorded church sermon by Pastor Rick Danna in which he disparaged what he termed "the homosexual agenda" was left on several cars.

Debate spilled into other public forums. Several editorials and letters to the editor in Southern California newspapers voiced hostility toward the Gay-Straight Alliance. In one letter to the editor, a minister, who said his parishioners included many self-proclaimed "ex-gays," said, "... I refuse to support a high school group that encourages the 'gay' selves of teenagers. Such 'help' is at least premature and at most dangerous." Larry Nicholson of Placentia wrote, "[T]he parents of these 'gay' students should be prosecuted for promoting this lifestyle since all definitions of homosexuality implies [sic] sexual activity and promoting sexual activity to minors, whether it is heterosexual or homosexual, is a crime." Another resident accused Colin of being a puppet of adult gay activists and of polarizing the school. A group calling itself "Parents, Grandparents, and Other Concerned Citizens" distributed a flier throughout El Modena High's community stating in part, "The Gay Agenda is Attacking Our School District. Help Stop Them! They're After Our Kids."

In November, Anthony Colin, Heather Zetin (another Gay-Straight Alliance member), their parents and the club itself filed a lawsuit in federal court against the school board and school district officials seeking relief from the school district's unlawful refusal to allow the club to meet. The suit charged, among other things, that the defendants violated the plaintiffs' rights under the federal Equal Access Act and the First Amendment. The Equal Access Act provides that once a secondary school that receives federal funds (as does El Modena High) allows any non-curricular student club to meet, it cannot discriminate against any other student club on the basis of the content of the speech at club meetings.

Having twice delayed its decision on whether to approve the club's application, the school board held a meeting in early December at which it finally acted on the club's application. Protesters had gathered outside the board's offices the morning of the meeting to discourage board members from approving the club's application. During the meeting, members of the school board claimed that the name and purpose of the club were objectionable. Parent Donna Sigalas claimed, "The most compassionate thing we can do is discourage them from a homosexual lifestyle." She also told the board, "AIDS, that's our concern. Health. We don't want our children exposed to this." Outside of the meeting, protesters carried placards reading, "Grades not AIDS." The board voted 7-0 to reject the club's application.

In late December, the plaintiffs filed a motion for a preliminary injunction asking the court to order the school district to allow the GSA, while the lawsuit was pending, to be able to meet and have access to school facilities on the same basis as all other student clubs. In February 2000, the court granted the plaintiffs' motion. The court held that the plaintiffs had shown a likelihood of success on the merits of their claim that the school district had violated the Equal Access Act. In addition, the court stated that it found many of the arguments advanced by the board to be "pretextual." This historic decision was the first time a federal court had ordered that a gay-affirming club be permitted to meet pursuant to the Equal Access Act. In accordance with the injunction, the club met for the first time in February and continued to meet throughout the spring semester.

In August 2000, the school board voted 5-2 to enter into an agreement with the plaintiffs settling the lawsuit. The settlement agreement was a ringing victory for the students. In accordance with that agreement, the school district granted the club's application and recognized the Gay-Straight Alliance as a non-curriculum-related student club. It also agreed to accord the GSA access to school facilities equal to that given all other student clubs, including the right to meet on school premises and to broadcast announcements of club meetings over the school's intercom. In addition, the GSA kept its preferred name, and will be able to discuss the issues of concern to its members, including homophobia and discrimination based on sexual orientation. The settlement agreement took effect in September 2000, when the school board voted to adopt several new rules applicable to all student clubs.

The plaintiffs were represented in their lawsuit by attorneys with People For the American Way Foundation, Lambda Legal Defense and Education Fund, and the law firm of Irell & Manella.

Petaluma: Boy Scouts reject application for new troop

The Boy Scouts of America rejected a proposal to sponsor a new troop in Petaluma whose proposed leader advocates an end to the Scouts' refusal to permit openly gay members and leaders. When Steven Cozza, with the help of his father, Scott Cozza, enlisted a local United Church of Christ church to sponsor a troop, the application Steven submitted was turned down by the Scouts. Scott Cozza helped found Scouting for All, an organization working to end the Boy Scouts' refusal to admit gay Scouts and Scoutmasters. The Petaluma Boy Scouts had previously stripped Cozza of a leadership position reportedly because of his work with Scouting for All.

The rejection frustrated the proposed troop's supporters. Lynda Burris and Tim Talamantes, the church's pastor and co-pastor, had guaranteed the Boy Scouts that the troop would not serve as a conduit for Scott Cozza to advocate overturning the Scouts' anti-gay policy. Six other boys who reportedly planned to join the troop and the pastors were particularly eager to sponsor the troop because they planned to draw on and work with potential Scouts from a local church homeless shelter. For these reasons, U.S. Rep. Lynn Woolsey, a member of the church's congregation, was angered by the rejection. She said, "They talk about inclusion and acceptance of all, and then they pick and choose and qualify who they will include." Because the Petaluma Scouts rejected the application for a new troop, seven boys have been left without a troop.

In their rejection letter, the Boy Scouts never clarified the grounds for their rejection beyond saying that they were "not prepared to charter a troop led by Scott Cozza or adult leadership recruited by him." Burris said he believes that Cozza's past efforts to overturn the Scouts' anti-gay policy were the actual basis for denying the application for the new troop.

Petaluma: Domestic partner benefits controversy

Despite opposition from members of the local community, the Petaluma City Council voted unanimously to extend employee benefits to the domestic partners of city employees and to create a domestic partner registry for city residents. Some area religious leaders and residents voiced their hostility toward the proposed benefits and registry, claiming that marriage should be between one man and one woman and that redefining the institution would morally bankrupt society and hurt the family. "We should try to emphasize marriage rather than try to destroy it," said Wayne Bigelow, pastor of the Petaluma Christian Church.

After the proposals were adopted, a group called Citizens for Traditional Marriage attempted to place a referendum on the ballot allowing residents to vote on the registry.

They gathered only a third of the required number of signatures. After this failure, the group said it would consider an initiative campaign, which would have allowed them a longer period of time to collect signatures.

Pleasant Hill: Employee's alleged anti-gay harassment

Employees at Wherehouse Music in Pleasant Hill allegedly harassed gay employee Lou Casolari for several months before he quit. He filed a lawsuit against the chain in November arguing that employees and management at the Pleasant Hill store harassed and discriminated against him because he is gay. In his lawsuit, Casolari alleges that co-workers and management inflicted emotional distress on him and wrongfully fired him in retaliation for his complaints.

Casolari contends that co-workers and management created a hostile work environment for him. Co-workers allegedly called his clothes "faggy." He claims the district manager told other employees, "Don't leave Lou alone in the back room with another guy." When Casolari complained about the harassment, his manager allegedly demoted him, reduced his work hours, and eventually sent him to work at another store. Further complaints fell upon deaf ears, Casolari says. He added that he was the store's only openly gay employee and that the harassment persisted for almost a year.

Company officials expressed surprise at the allegations. Vice President Barbara Lewis said Wherehouse Music is "very open-minded and very progressive." She said the company employs several openly gay people in its corporate offices. The suit was pending at press time.

Redlands: Controversy over proposed commission seat

At a March meeting of the Redlands Human Relations Commission, the Rainbow Council, a local gay and lesbian rights group, recommended that the commission reflect the diversity of the community by including a seat for a gay man or lesbian and including sexual orientation in the commission's diversity statement. Don Wallace, the anti-gay pastor of Redlands Christian Center, objected, saying that the commission should remove references to sexual orientation from its bylaws and mission statement. He claimed that doing so would open up the commission to skateboarders, skinheads, and others whom he said were undesirable. Wallace had previously caused a stir among members of the commission when his church placed an anti-gay message on its marquee. Without taking action on the proposals, the commission voted to sponsor another meeting.

At the next meeting, Wallace said he would continue to publicly denounce homosexuality. Wallace also threatened to sue the commission if it resolved to condemn his church for its signs reading, "God didn't create Adam and Steve" and "Same-sex marriages; no, no, no." One commissioner, Leonora Jiminez-Sims, stormed out of the meeting, saying, "We've totally lost control." She denied accusations that she had verbally accosted a member of the Rainbow Council after the previous session. The meeting ended with no resolutions passed.

Two months later, however, the City Council took up the issue of how the commission's diversity statement should be worded. Members of the Rainbow Coalition wanted sexual orientation included in the diversity statement. During the meeting at which the council voted on the proposed additions, critics registered their opposition. Wallace said he feared that adding sexual orientation to the diversity statement would encourage other minority groups to seek special privileges from the commission. "Are we prepared to bless deviant behavior in our city law?" he asked. Most of the audience was hostile toward supporters of the addition. The council took two votes: one not to add sexual orientation to the diversity statement and another to remove references to all minority groups from the diversity statement. Mayor Bill Cunningham, who opposed the proposed additions, claimed that by not naming minority groups, the commission would recognize all minority groups. Opponents of adding sexual orientation to the diversity statement were pleased with the City Council's actions.

> "Are we prepared to bless deviant behavior in our city law?"
>
> — Rev. Don Wallace, pastor of Redlands Christian Center, opposing a gay-friendly proposal to revise the Redlands Human Relations Commission's diversity statement.

Gay and lesbian residents, however, criticized the council's votes. Juliann Anderson, a Rainbow Council member, said, "We didn't see a lot of courage here tonight." Father John Ayers, a gay Catholic priest, was disturbed: "I'm also a gay man, and these people [opponents of the proposal] frighten me."

The Human Relations Commission acted on the Rainbow Council's initial proposal and added a gay man to its panel in August.

Redlands:
Discussion of homosexuality during health class

At Cope Middle School, several parents complained about remarks made by a health teacher regarding homosexuality during health class. According to one student, the teacher said being gay or lesbian is no different than being straight. The teacher reportedly added that homosexuals should be proud of who they are. More than a dozen parents took their concerns to a June school trustee meeting. "We do have a problem with the teacher's lack of prejudgment," Sharon Yee, a parent, complained. Another parent accused the teacher of inappropriately moralizing on important social questions. Because the teacher in question was the school's only health teacher, parents requested that the school board hire another teacher so they could opt to enroll their students in another class whose instructor did not make the same statements. Several students called the parents' effort a "witch hunt." In June, school district officials yielded to the parents' demands and hired an additional health teacher who would start the following fall. Officials also revised permission slips to inform parents when abortion, contraceptives, masturbation, and sexual orientation would be discussed. Finally, they changed district policy on how teachers can address "controversial" topics, mandating that teachers should "avoid responding in a class setting when they have reason to believe the answer may contradict religious or personal beliefs."

Sacramento: "Ex-gay" youth conference

Focus on the Family (see p. 355) targeted California youth and the teachers, pastors, and medical professionals who work with them when it brought its "Love Won Out" series to Sacramento. "Love Won Out" claims to teach gay men and lesbians that they can and should change their sexual orientation through religious devotion. The Sacramento conference specifically attempted to persuade parents and teachers to oppose local school policies favorable to gay and lesbian students and teachers. Many of those in attendance sought guidance on how to reconcile their anti-gay religious beliefs with the realities of living in a pluralistic society. John Paulk, a policy specialist with Focus on the Family and self-professed "ex-gay," coordinated the event. He spoke about his personal difficulties with his sexual orientation and claimed that through faith, he learned that he could become heterosexual. Paulk encouraged the same hope in the audience.

The conference also sought to equip parents and teenagers with skills to combat what organizers see as the growing acceptance of homosexuality in schools and other areas of public life. One session presented methods of including anti-gay views in AIDS education and other programs in schools. Attendees at another session said that hearing from "ex-gays" like Paulk and his wife empowered them to assert that sexual orientation is a choice. Yet another session lambasted the instructional video, "Teaching Respect for All." That video, produced by the Gay, Lesbian, and Straight Education Network, instructs educators on methods of combating anti-gay bias in schools.

Sacramento: Fired employee sues Boy Scouts

After 22 years of employment, Chris Keener sued the Golden Empire Council of the Boy Scouts, which he claims violated his privacy and fired him because he is gay. Keener, an Eagle Scout who held the position of assistant council executive, alleged that his employers used private investigators to question his friends, associates, and co-workers about his sexual orientation. Keener maintains that once the Scouts discovered he is gay, they fired him. Keener's lawsuit, filed in state court, also contends that his supervisors repeatedly told him that known gay employees would be fired. The Boy Scouts claim that Keener was fired because he violated the organization's policy against accepting personal discounts from donors. Although Keener's former supervisor, Scott Johnson, admitted that the Boy Scouts do not hire openly gay people, he denied that sexual orientation was the basis for Keener's dismissal. Keener's attorney said the lawsuit was the first employment discrimination case brought against a California Boy Scout troop by a former employee. California labor code prohibits employment discrimination based on sexual orientation. At press time, the lawsuit was pending.

Sacramento:
Lesbian commitment ceremony divides Methodists

Opponents of same-sex marriage were outraged when Rev. Don Fado of St. Mark's United Methodist Church in Sacramento performed a commitment ceremony for a lesbian couple in front of about 1,200 supporters. Fado, the couple's minister, and other participating Methodist ministers, which various reports numbered from 90-100, were later charged with violating church doctrine against performing same-sex commitment ceremonies. Led by Rev. Micke Goodyear, members of the First United Methodist Church of Orangevale identified ministers who had participated in the ceremony. Goodyear intended to force church officials to act against Fado and his supporters by filing complaints charging that the ministers had violated the Methodist Church's ban on blessing holy unions for same-sex couples and that they had brought shame and embarrassment on the church. A variety of religious and secular forces launched a campaign to denounce the ceremony.

The Evangelical Renewal Fellowship, a Methodist group opposed to same-sex commitment ceremonies, staged a protest outside the church during the ceremony and held a news conference and candlelight vigil. The group opposed the same-sex commitment ceremony on both biblical and doctrinal grounds. Even before the ceremony, Carl Adams, an active member of the Yuba City Methodist church where the Fellowship held its protests, threatened to bring charges against the ministers who had officiated at the ceremony.

The Fellowship protesters were joined by Rev. Fred Phelps and members of his Westboro Baptist Church of Topeka, Kansas (see p. 356). Phelps denounced the ceremony as a "joyous event by two smelly old sows" with "80 backslidden Methodist preachers officiating in the name of Satan." They carried signs reading "Brides of Satan" and "Methodist Fag Church."

The California-Nevada United Methodist Church Conference brought charges against 68 of the participating pastors, targeting only those from within that conference. Although he personally disapproves of the church's prohibition against ministers performing same-sex commitment ceremonies, Bishop Melvin Talbert, the church official designated to bring charges against alleged violators, said he had to obey church law. The charges were later dropped against all those charged. Officials said, "There were not reasonable grounds to certify the charge as proper for trial."

Sacramento: Prayer said over lesbian lawmaker's desk

A prayer said over the desk of at least one openly lesbian state legislator caused a stir in February. "It made me feel like someone had scrawled 'fag' on my desk," openly lesbian state Assembly member Sheila Kuehl said after discovering that a member of a religious group had said a prayer over her desk in the California Assembly chambers. At the invitation of state Assembly member Bill Leonard (R), members of the California State Solemn Assembly, a religious group, had conducted a prayer meeting in the legislature's chambers.

One member of the group broke off during the meeting and allegedly singled out Kuehl's desk. Stephanie Steele stopped at the desk, placed a banner over it, and prayed. "I went over to one of the desks and placed my banner over that desk...and I looked at the name on the desk as I prayed and called it out..." Steele said. Witnesses reported that Steele also stopped to pray at the desk of openly lesbian state Assembly member Carole Midgen. Steele, however, claims she did not know that either Kuehl or Migden is a lesbian and that she prayed over only one desk. Migden expressed her disgust with the events: "It's an insult to the people and to us, and we just want an end to these persistent attacks." Steele later sent a letter of apology to her minister, Joe Walsh, who had organized the event. Walsh offered the apology to Migden and Kuehl on behalf of Steele.

San Bernardino County: Domestic partner policy proposal rejected

San Bernardino County supervisors rejected a proposal to extend insurance and other employee benefits to the unmarried domestic partners of county employees. Prompted by a new series of proposals from insurance carriers, the Board of Supervisors rejected the opportunity to cover the same-sex partners of county employees.

Though the measure received strong support from labor representatives and gay employees, it generated significant community opposition. "Gay marriages are not recognized as legal in the state of California. That's what this comes down to: special rights for gays and lesbians," said Rev. Stephen Anderson, pastor of a local church. He questioned whether the measure was actually supported by the union representing county employees. County officials also rejected the argument that domestic partner benefits aid recruitment efforts.

However, Ken Lutz, a sheriff's deputy supporting the benefits package, said, "They violated their own policy today. I can't discriminate against someone because of their sexual orientation or marital status, yet they can discriminate against me?"

San Francisco: Attempt to defrock Catholic priest

More than a dozen San Francisco-area Catholics petitioned Bishop John Cummins to defrock the Rev. Dan Danielson for permitting same-sex marriage ceremonies in his Pleasanton church. One of Danielson's parishioners, Mary Arnold, organized the petition. She told Cummins that Danielson should be removed "to protect the flock from error." Arnold objected to any tolerance of same-sex relationships. Danielson, the pastor at St. Augustine's Catholic Church, said he allowed the blessing of "same-sex friendships," but denied that he officiated at weddings for his gay parishioners. Cummins ignored the charges and no disciplinary action was taken against Danielson.

San Francisco:
Coalition sues city for denouncing "ex-gay" ads

A coalition of right-wing organizations sued the city and county of San Francisco and lesbian Supervisor Leslie Katz for denouncing its anti-gay "Truth In Love Campaign." The American Family Association (see p. 352), Kerusso Ministries (see p. 355), and the Family Research Council (see p. 355) targeted Katz, the city, and the county for what they characterized as a violation of their rights to free speech and free exercise of religion. In 1998, the Board of Supervisors passed a resolution denouncing the so-called "ex-gay" ministries, which claim that gay men and lesbians can and should change their sexual orientation through religious devotion, and urged local television stations not to air advertisements for them. Most area stations complied with that request, though such resolutions are not legally binding for private media outlets. Stephen Crampton, chief counsel in the American Family Association's litigation wing, said about the city's actions, "This fierce rhetoric by San Francisco is an open invitation to homosexuals to commit acts of violence against Christians." He added, "I would equate the homosexuals' use and abuse of the media with the Nazis' abuse of the media." Crampton continued to tout the merits of the ad campaign, saying, "Deep down, there is that little question, that part that knows that what he is doing is not morally correct under God's law. There is one universal truth and one universal law that is applicable to all men everywhere."

> "I would equate the homosexuals' use and abuse of the media with the Nazis' abuse of the media."
>
> — Stephen Crampton, chief counsel for the American Family Association, discussing a lawsuit several right-wing organizations brought against San Francisco for denouncing an "ex-gay" ad.

The groups allege the city violated their right to free speech and free exercise of religion by condemning the ad campaign. They also contend the board defamed them when it issued a letter connecting the widely reported murder of Wyoming college student Matthew Shepard with the ad campaign. The coalition is seeking financial compensation for what they claim was defamation as well as an order prohibiting all city employees from speaking out against the "ex-gay" movement. The case is still pending in a California federal court.

This was not the first time the Religious Right has sued the Board of Supervisors. The American Center for Law and Justice (see p. 352) lost its legal challenge to San Francisco's domestic partners ordinance in May. The ACLJ filed its challenge in U.S. District Court on behalf of an electronics manufacturer in 1997. It vowed to appeal.

San Francisco: "Coming Out of Homosexuality Day"

For the fifth year in a row, a coalition of right-wing organizations sponsored an observance of National Coming Out of Homosexuality Day. The organizations sponsoring the event claim that homosexuals can and should change their sexual orientation and become straight. Held in a San Francisco park, NCOHD featured several leaders of anti-gay organizations and self-proclaimed ex-gay speakers, all of which billed the event as an alternative to National Coming Out Day, when closeted gay men, lesbians and bisexuals are encouraged to affirmatively proclaim their sexual orientation.

Michael Johnston, of the ex-gay Kerusso Ministries (see p. 355), his family members, representatives from the Family Research Council (see p. 355), and American Family Association (see p. 352), and Rev. Eugene Lumpkin, a former member of the San Francisco Human Rights Commission, all addressed the crowd of about 60. Former San Francisco Mayor Frank Jordan removed Lumpkin in 1993 after he said, "the homosexual lifestyle is an abomination against God." At the NCOHD rally, Lumpkin reportedly claimed that murdering gay men is justified in the Bible. Johnston followed up on those remarks by denouncing what he called the "homosexual agenda" and criticizing several national gay and lesbian rights organizations. Rev. Jerry Falwell, who spoke via satellite, said, "Just as people can come out of the closet, so can people choose to come out against a sinful lifestyle." Gay and lesbian activists criticized the timing of the event, which took place on the eve of the anniversary of the much-publicized murder of Wyoming college student Matthew Shepard.

San Francisco: Four Baptist churches ousted

The American Baptist Churches in the USA expelled four San Francisco-area churches because they embraced openly gay and lesbian members. The membership of the First Baptist Church of Berkeley, Lakeshore Avenue Baptist Church of Oakland, San Leandro Community Church, and San Jose's New Community of Faith membership in the denomination was revoked. All four are members of the Association of Welcoming and Affirming Baptists, a national organization that urges congregations to embrace gay and lesbian members. Leaders of these congregations were surprised by the ouster. Rev. Esther Hargis, pastor of First Baptist, said, "It's unprecedented...They set aside Baptist principles to do this." Baptist denominational doctrine maintains that individual congregations operate autonomously. The American Baptist Churches says it objects to gays' and lesbians' sexual activity outside of marriage, not their sexual orientation. The denomination has no official policy allowing same-sex marriage or commitments.

San Francisco: Lesbian mural defaced

A mural by student artist Sun Yom, which depicted her embraced in a kiss with a former girlfriend, was defaced in March. Yom and other students painted the mural embracing multiculturalism on the front wall of the student center at the City College of San Francisco. Students conceived the mural as part of a protest of Proposition 209, the ballot initiative prohibiting affirmative action, and worked on the mural for more than two years. They finally began painting in March. Using paint thinner, a vandal marred the faces of the two women, obscuring the kiss. Neither school officials nor city police were able to identify a perpetrator. Mayor Willie Brown and Supervisor Tom Ammiano joined more than 30 students at a rally in front of the mural to denounce the vandalism. Yom was able to repaint the scene.

San Francisco: Library books defaced

A vandal repeatedly damaged books in the gay and lesbian collection of the San Francisco Public Library. The unidentified assailants ripped bar codes from several books, effectively taking them out of circulation. They tore complete pages from books as well. Library officials said the problem became so bad they had to solicit help in catching the vandals. Hundreds of books have been damaged; many were repaired only to be destroyed again. The collection, housed in the library's James Hormel Gay and Lesbian Center, was the only collection to be targeted. "[T]his is somebody who has really got an agenda and is pretty savvy about carrying it out," said Jim Van Buskirk, program manager for the center.

The center gained prominence when Hormel was nominated to become the U.S. ambassador to Luxemborg. Several right-wing groups sent copies of coloring books owned by the library to all 100 members of the U.S. Senate.

San Francisco: Mass same-sex wedding protested

Rev. Fred Phelps (see p. 356) traveled half-way across the country to San Francisco to picket a mass same-sex wedding ceremony officiated by Mayor Willie Brown. One hundred and ninety couples participated in the ceremony, which was organized to express the couples' opposition to the Knight Initiative, a statewide ballot initiative defining marriage as between one man and one woman, and to affirm their own relationships. Phelps and about a dozen of his fellow parishioners bellowed, "Sick, sick, sick!" from across the street. A few local residents joined them outside in hurling other anti-gay epithets at the participants and their supporters. The protesters taunted the crowd with anti-gay placards. A flier announcing the protest featured a picture of two women as pigs, possibly referring to a lesbian couple's Sacramento commitment ceremony where Phelps had protested earlier in the year. The Unitarian Universalist Church and other congregations led a counter demonstration whose participants outnumbered the Phelps supporters.

San Francisco: Principals discount "Just the Facts"

"Just the Facts," a resource guide helping educators deal with issues of sexual orientation, received mixed reviews in the San Francisco Bay area. The guide, developed by a coalition of groups including the American Academy of Pediatrics, the American Association of School Administrators, the American Federation of Teachers, and the American Psychological Association, is intended to help educators make schools more supportive of gay and lesbian students. Religious Right groups including the Family Research Council (see p. 355) and Focus on the Family (see p. 355) criticized the guide as "homosexual propaganda," and several Bay Area teachers and administrators said they would not distribute it. The booklet has been endorsed by the Gay, Lesbian, and Straight Education Network, the National Association of School Psychologists, the National Education Association and the National Association of Social Workers.

One administrator rejected the authority of the coalition that produced the guide, saying that so-called "ex-gays" who have renounced their homosexuality are better experts. Antioch schools chief Lee Jenkins said, "Probably the most reliable source is former homosexuals who have given up that lifestyle, who can refute that." He referred to the "ex-gay" ministries seeking to change the sexual orientation of gay men, lesbians, and bisexuals through faith-based conversion. Jenkins dismissed any responsibility to protect gay and lesbian students from harassment, saying, "Our responsibility is to teach math, science, history, geography, English. It is not our mission to be involved in those controversies." Others like Gary McHenry, superintendent of the Mount Diablo Unified School District, felt that combating anti-gay harassment was not a priority. "Whether we take instructional time to discuss (gay tolerance), I'm not sure I would do that."

San Francisco: Sisters of Perpetual Indulgence

When San Francisco's Sisters of Perpetual Indulgence scheduled their 20th anniversary celebration for Easter Sunday, they found themselves at the center of a firestorm of criticism, thanks in part to the city's Roman Catholic Archdiocese. The Sisters of Perpetual Indulgence is a gay, lesbian, bisexual, straight, and transgender troop whose members dress in nuns' habits to do performance art and raise money for various community charities. The Sisters of Perpetual Indulgence requested that the Department of Parking and Traffic close a street in the Castro for their celebration, angering many of the city's Catholic leaders. When the street closure request was turned down, many gay and lesbian residents asked the Board of Supervisors to overturn the Department of Parking and Traffic's decision. In response to the request, the Catholic League for Religious and Civil Rights threatened to seek a boycott by Catholic convention groups should the board permit the street closure. The Board of Supervisors voted 8-0 to overturn the Department of Parking and Traffic's decision, ordering it to allow the street closure.

Catholic officials then called on the Board of Supervisors to rescind the order for the street closure. A Diocesan spokesperson compared the street closing for the Easter celebration to an endorsement of a neo-Nazi celebration during Passover. Though he denied the Sisters were a hate group, University of San Francisco history professor Andrew Heinze claimed their "displays are flagrantly disgusting and in poor taste, demeaning and abhorrent."

The Catholic League continued its campaign to get the city to stop the street closure. But in March, the Board of Supervisors voted not to rescind its order closing the streets. So the Catholic League issued a notice to all Catholic convention groups asking them to boycott the city by hold their conventions elsewhere. The board's action sparked so much controversy that in the week before Easter Sunday two supervisors attempted to change the date for the celebration.

Santa Barbara County: Controversy over proposed registry

A proposal that Santa Barbara County create a registry for domestic partners angered many residents. The proposed registry would allow unmarried, adult, co-residents to declare a partnership and have that certified by the county government. The proposal would not require companies contracting with the city or private employers to extend family benefits to the same-sex partners of their employees. Most opponents based their opposition to the proposal on religious grounds.

Opponents said they feared the proposal would permit gay men and lesbians to ruin what they believed to be the county's heterosexual "lifestyle." Fearing what he said would be an influx of gay men and lesbians, Pat Reihle, local coordinator of the right-wing American Family Defense Coalition, said, "It would invite excessive numbers of homosexuals to Santa Barbara County." Another resident added that it would "tear at the fabric" of society. Yet another resident warned, "You will be held accountable by God" should the proposal pass. Resident Barbara Murphy added, "It would trivialize marriage at a time we need to strengthen it." When councilman Tom Urbanske registered his support for the measure, the crowd reportedly heckled him.

With only one member voting against the measure, the County Board of Supervisors in June adopted the proposal and created the registry.

Scotts Valley: Fired employees sue company

Two former employees of Westek Electronics in Scotts Valley sued the company for what they maintain was enforcement of strict gender stereotyping. Colleen Perrin and Monica Foskett allege that Westek officials fired Foskett because they perceived her to be a lesbian. Both women contend that the company routinely discriminated against effeminate men, masculine women, and sexual and religious minorities. In order to enforce traditional gender roles, the plaintiffs claim Westek prohibited women from lifting heavy objects and men from answering phones.

In the lawsuit, Perrin, a former accounting manager, asserts that a Westek official ordered her to fire Foskett, a former accounting clerk, allegedly because Foskett wore short hair and had a masculine style of dress. Foskett and Perrin contend that those traits led the company official to conclude that Foskett was a lesbian. Perrin maintains that she, herself, resigned rather than fire or demote Foskett. Foskett claims that Westek demoted her after Perrin quit and assigned her to sort mail that included journals from the anti-gay American Family Association (see p. 352). The plaintiffs claim that these practices denigrated gay men and lesbians by enforcing gender stereotypes and punishing those who do not agree with the organization's practices.

The plaintiffs also claim that several previous employees were fired because they were perceived to be gay or lesbian or because they practiced "New Age" spirituality and pagan mysticism. They maintain that the Westek's president, Kevin Larkin, objected to all sorts of "pagan" activities, including Halloween decorations.

Larkin said that he could not comment on the lawsuit. But Westek attorney Carol Freeman did say, "We reviewed the complaint, and we will vigorously contest it in the courts." At press time, the lawsuit was pending.

Simi Valley: Police officers lampoon gays

A videotape showing Simi Valley police officers ridiculing gays and other groups emerged as a lawsuit alleging discriminatory attitudes and practices was filed against the department. In the suit, two white officers claimed the department had harassed them after they filed worker's compensation claims, and a black officer alleged that he was racially harassed. Although the tape's producers claimed it was intended as a joke for a departing officer, other officers say it revealed widespread intolerance. Former police chief and current City Council member Paul Miller, who was among those featured in the video, had no comment. City Manager Mike Sedell admitted the video was done in poor taste, but said, "There may be one or two places with some inappropriate wording, but it's no worse than anything you see on 'Saturday Night Live' or 'Mad TV.' "

John Hatcher, president of the local chapter of the National Association for the Advancement of Colored People, disagreed, saying that the fact that the tape was supposed to be a joke didn't mean it was not also racist and a form of harassment. He added, "A joke like that is a violation of federal law, simple as that. The joke he calls in poor taste creates a hostile and intimidating work environment."

One scene in the video, which takes place in Miller's former office, suggests a male officer wants to return to work so that he can continue an affair with a male police investigator. In it one officer says, "A lot of people don't want to work with a coke freak." Another responds, "Or a [homosexual]." Reportedly, an anti-gay slur was used repeatedly.

Sedell reported that all those involved with the video have been verbally reprimanded for inappropriate behavior, but no additional disciplinary action was taken against them.

Simi Valley: Pride parade protested and opposed

For the second year in a row, Ventura County's gay pride festival, held in Simi Valley, encountered anti-gay hostility. Before the festival began, Roger Willis, pastor of the Valley Bible Community Church, claimed, "The [gay] lifestyle is proven to be a deadly lifestyle." He warned that young people should be aware of what he called the biblical commands against homosexuality. Other critics said the parade was a way to promote special rights. Steve Frank, president of the National Federation of Republican Assemblies, said, "It is an effort to show support to create more government programs for their special interest." A few days before the event, vandals spray painted "No pride in being gay" on banners scheduled to be displayed in the parade. In 1998, 30 protesters had denounced the parade and demonstrated outside the festival grounds.

Turlock: Alleged anti-gay treatment at Denny's

Two lesbians sued the Denny's restaurant chain, alleging that the staff at its Turlock location removed them from the establishment because they were openly affectionate. When Angelica McBride and Catrina Vargas met at Denny's on a May night, they said they welcomed each other with a hug and kiss. They claimed a waitress quickly went to them and said, "You guys can't be doing that in here, kissing and sitting that close to each other." McBride and Vargas alleged that after the waitress admonished them, the manager told them that if they chose to continue "doing that gay stuff," they would need to leave the restaurant. The two women said the manager then summoned a security officer to their table to force them outside. In their lawsuit, they claim the wait staff and management made several anti-gay remarks before throwing them out. According to McBride and Vargas, when they questioned the reason for their expulsion, the manager told them it was because they were lesbians. A spokesperson for Denny's said the chain did have a non-discrimination policy that included sexual orientation.

An attempt at arbitration in January 2000 failed. The parties settled in May 2000, the terms of which have not been made public.

COLORADO

Statewide: Same-sex marriage bill

Buoyed by a new Republican governor, the Colorado legislature attempted to pass a bill that would have prohibited the state from recognizing same-sex marriages. Both right-wing and gay activists agree that existing state law does not recognize same-sex marriages performed in Colorado even though the state never adopted a specific ban on recognizing them.

But state Sen. Ken Arnold (R) said the state should have a specific law prohibiting the recognition of same-sex marriages performed or recognized anywhere outside of the state because, he claimed, the law is unclear in that area. In 1996 and 1997, Arnold co-sponsored and the legislature voted for bills that would have prohibited the state from recognizing same-sex marriages performed in Colorado, but Democratic Gov. Roy Romer vetoed both bills. In 1999, Arnold said he hoped that the state's new Republican governor, Bill Owens, would approve the measure. Arnold said, "Let's get away from this dirty gray area, and let's make it black and let's make it white as far as our morals are concerned." Arnold's bill was part of a slate of bills dealing with controversial social issues during the 1999 legislative session.

Early attention to the bill suggested that its passage was likely. While the bill was still in the Senate Judiciary Committee, Gov. Owens signaled that he would sign the measure if passed, saying, "I think it has always been the intent of Colorado law that marriage is a union between a male and a female." Much of the testimony before the state Senate supported the proposal. A law professor from Utah's Brigham Young University urged the legislature to act quickly out of concern that other states and foreign countries might recognize same-sex marriages. Catholic Church officials also gave their support. Although the Senate Judiciary Committee passed the measure, voting along party lines, with Democrats opposed, the bill died in the House Judiciary Committee when both Republicans and Democrats voted against it.

Statewide: Same-sex marriage initiative

Anti-gay activist Gary Rogers began the process to put an initiative on the ballot that would prohibit the legal recognition of same-sex marriages. The initiative, approved by the Colorado secretary of state, would amend Colorado's constitution to prohibit the state from recognizing such unions performed in other states or foreign nations, although existing state law does not recognize such unions. Earlier in 1999, a bill to prohibit recognition of same-sex marriages regardless of where they were performed died in the state legislature.

Rogers formed Coloradans for Traditional Marriage to spearhead the drive to pass the initiative. Rogers has extensive experience in organizing for conservative causes. He is the president of the Colorado Pro-Life Alliance and pushed a successful 1998 ballot initiative restricting abortion rights. After a short period for public comment on the title, proponents needed to gather 64,000 signatures by June 2000 to put the question before voters in November of that year.

Plans for the initiative were cut short in May 2000 when the state enacted a law prohibiting the state from recognizing same-sex marriages performed in Colorado or any other state. Lori Girvan, Executive Director of the gay rights group Equality Colorado, said the initiative was pulled from the November 2000 ballot and that its backers had put their energies into supporting the Colorado Pro-Life Alliance's effort to place an anti-abortion measure on the ballot.

Statewide: Lesbians' child's birth certificate challenged

The Colorado Attorney General's Office sought to overturn a state district court's ruling allowing same-sex couples to place both partners' names on their children's birth certificates. Assistant State Attorney General Hollie Stevenson argued that the absence of appropriate statutes does not allow the court to "provide authority to establish the relationship of a child and more than one natural mother."

> "Certainly the foundations of everything this country grew up with are shaking."
>
> — State Rep. Mark Paschall, attacking a court ruling that allowed same-sex couples to place both parents' names on their children's birth certificates.

In an earlier custody ruling that preceded the birth of the twin girls, Boulder district Judge Roxanne Bailin had permitted a lesbian couple to register both of their names as parents on the birth certificates of their twin daughters. In her decision, Judge Bailin wrote that a child could have two legal and natural mothers. She based that ruling on state laws that permit non-biological parents and other unrelated people to secure parental privileges. The law has been used in the past to secure fathers' rights.

A complaint by a registrar in the Colorado Department of Public Health and Environment prompted the attorney general's legal challenge. A registrar questioned the legality of the judge's order and sent the certificate in for review. "We believe the judge gave us something outside the law," said Cynthia Honssinger, a Health Department director. The Attorney General's Office acted on behalf of the state Register of Records, who, under the Department of Public Health, maintains birth and death records for the state.

The attack on Judge Bailin's ruling did not stop at the Attorney General's Office. Republican state Rep. Mark Paschall said that the ruling would lead to the downfall of

American civilization. "Certainly the foundations of everything this country grew up with are shaking," he said. He also said that the Greek and Roman empires fell because they accepted homosexuality.

John Paulk, a self-proclaimed "ex-gay" and public policy specialist for the anti-gay Focus on the Family (see p. 355), also disparaged the ruling. "We believe children are best suited in families with a mother and a father, and that goes along with the mainstream opinion of most Americans," Paulk said. Referring to the judge's ruling, he added, "It muddies the waters because gay marriages are not legal in states, and it is a disservice to the child."

The attorney representing the lesbian parents said she would continue to file similar petitions for other gay and lesbian parents.

Statewide: Non-discrimination bill defeated

The state legislature rejected a bill that would have protected gay men and lesbians from discrimination in housing, employment, and public accommodations. It was the first time such a bill was considered on the floor of the House. Groups opposed to gay and lesbian rights proved crucial to the bill's ultimate defeat.

Colorado for Family Values (see p. 354) circulated a letter to lawmakers claiming that homosexuals "practice dangerous and potentially deadly behavior." James Dobson's Focus on the Family (see p. 355) called on Coloradans to urge their state legislators to reject the bill. In a citizen alert, Focus on the Family claimed that the bill would require public charter schools not only accept gay and lesbian students and teachers, but also to "accept and teach homosexuality as a civil right." The text of the bill made no such provision. The alert also claimed that gay men and lesbians are in no way disadvantaged because of their sexual orientation. Joined by state Religious Right leaders, Focus on the Family followed the alert up with ads on several talk radio stations.

Other right-wing groups jumped on the anti-gay bandwagon. Littleton's Family First sent a letter to legislators alleging that gays are more likely to be pedophiles than heterosexuals and should not be granted civil rights protections. The organization claimed that passing the bill would endanger the state's children. Its efforts worked.

After the bill's introduction, opponents of the measure from across the state reportedly flooded several representatives' offices with calls and letters. Many made personal attacks against those state legislators who supported the bill. State Rep. Shawn Mitchel (R) remarked, "When government takes an official opinion and enshrines it in civil rights, it discredits anyone with a contrary belief... This proposal interferes with the principle that people should be free to choose their own paths, their friends, their philosophies, and their associations." State Rep. Mark Paschall offered the most overarching critique of the bill: "I think we are going to be plowing ground that has been cause for further decline in other civilizations."

Statewide:
Proposed amendments to hate crimes law defeated

A bill that would have added protections for gay men, lesbians, and others to the state's existing hate crimes law died in the state legislature. The bill would have expanded the existing "Ethnic Intimidation Law" to include crimes against the disabled, mentally ill people, the elderly, homosexuals and bisexuals. Several organizations affiliated with the Religious Right lobbied against the bill. Although almost no one uttered the word "gay" during debate, the rhetoric of anti-gay lawmakers seemed to pander to the right wing. State Rep. Shawn Mitchell, one of the most outspoken opponents, claimed passage would signal the beginning of a larger effort towards gay and lesbian rights. "This is part of the creeping totalitarian tolerance philosophy," Mitchell said. In the previous legislative session, the Senate had approved the measure only to see it defeated in the House.

The House Committee on Appropriations passed the bill, but the full House vote in April was a 32-32 tie, one vote short of passage. The Senate version died in the Judiciary Committee. On the day of the full House vote, members unanimously approved a Holocaust Remembrance Week to honor victims of Nazi persecution in Europe and condemn anti-Semitic intolerance.

Arvada: "Hell House"

The Abundant Life Christian Center in Arvada sponsored its fifth annual Hell House for Halloween. In an effort to simulate aspects of an existence in Hell, the Rev. Keenan Roberts and his fellow church members featured a same-sex wedding as part of the event. In the hyperbolic finale to this spectacle, one "spouse" died of an AIDS-related illness, and the couple's honeymoon bed was replaced with a hospital bed. The gay male couple included one man and one woman dressed in male drag. In explaining why he did not feature two male actors, Rev. Roberts said, "They kiss at the end of the ceremony, and I'm not going to have two guys kissing." The actors were youth members of the church. The overall effort was to demonstrate activities in which teens engage that would, according to Roberts and his followers, condemn them to Hell.

The wedding was a new addition to the church's other skits, which depicted abortions, drug use and other acts church members deemed sinful. The church eliminated last year's adultery scene featuring President Clinton and Monica Lewinsky in the Oval Office. Roberts said he hoped the show would heighten media attention to his effort to "battle sin of every kind," adding that people needed "the hell scared out of them." Hell House ran for 12 days.

Boulder: Lesbian Episcopal minister fired

An Episcopal minister from Boulder filed a lawsuit against St. Aidan's Episcopal Church, accusing church officials there of firing her because she is a lesbian. Lee Ann Bryce also alleges that officials at St. Aidan's and the Episcopal Diocese of Colorado defamed her, invaded her privacy, and violated her employment contract. St. Aidan's originally hired Bryce as a part-time supervisor for its youth program. She said her job never required her to teach spiritual matters, perform religious rituals, or be a church member. Bryce, who based the lawsuit on her status as an employee of the church and not its doctrine, said she was fired shortly after she took part in a commitment ceremony with her same-sex partner. That ceremony did not take place in an Episcopal church.

Bryce contends that her firing came as a result of officials learning about her role in the same-sex wedding ceremony. She also maintains that church officials should have known or actually did know before the ceremony that she was a lesbian and that Bryce's superiors allegedly held a meeting after they learned of the commitment ceremony, after which Henderson allegedly told Bryce that she violated church doctrine requiring ministerial staff to be either married or celibate. Bryce's lawsuit claims that her privacy as an employee was violated because "remarks and insinuations" about her private life and sexual activities were made during meetings between church leaders and members of the congregation, including alleged comments by Henderson calling homosexuality a disease. At press time, the case was pending.

Boulder: Transgender ordinance

After years of efforts by local activists, the Boulder City Council voted to add gender expression to the city ordinance prohibiting discrimination in employment, housing, and public accommodations. An editorial in Boulder's Daily Camera, however, denounced the council's action, saying, "This broad definition goes too far, even for progressive Boulder." Rather than focus on the discrimination that transgendered people face, the editorial raised inflammatory issues related to how businesses and places of public accommodation might be affected by the new laws. "And what about the — admittedly rare — person who 'switches' genders from day to day, week to week?" it asked. After raising these issues, the editors encouraged opponents of the measure to voice their opinions at an upcoming council meeting. Despite the paper's attempts to drum up opposition, the City Council voted to extend protections to transgendered persons, thereby joining fewer than a dozen U.S. cities that currently do so.

Colorado Springs: Anti-gay Initiative

In January, local politicians and conservative community groups urged the City Council to amend Colorado Springs' non-discrimination employment policies so that they would not cover gay men and lesbians. The current anti-discrimination policy, passed in 1997, stipulates "zero tolerance for any form of discrimination of a racial, ethnic, sexual, or religious nature." Council members Dawson Hubert and Lionel Rivera joined Paul Jessen, chairman of Colorado for Family Values (see p. 354), seeking to redefine the policy so that the word "sexual" would not include protecting gay men and lesbians. Hubert and Rivera, who voted for the policy in 1997 but oppose it now, said they did not know that the wording could be construed to bar sexual orientation discrimination. Acting on behalf of CFV, Hubert tried to introduce legislation that would have defined "sexual" to exclude gays and lesbians. "This has never been about discrimination," Jessen said. "This is only about the affirmation and credentialing of an immoral lifestyle by public policy." After the council rejected that proposal, Hubert tried to get the council to place a charter amendment on the April ballot that would rescind employment protection for gays and lesbians in city employment. The council rejected that proposal as well. Hubert's attempts came a month after the CFV failed to collect enough signatures for an initiative to revoke the employment protections.

Mayor Mary Lou Makepeace called the proposed amendments "just plain wrong" and labeled the activities of CFV "mean-spirited." She and two council members reiterated that the policy covers everyone. The council chose not to clarify whether "sexual" specifically protects homosexuals. Gay and lesbian activists still cheered the council's bravery.

CFV vowed to press on with their attack against the protections and their supporters. Jessen suggested the organization might attempt yet another petition drive or possibly force a special election. The organization also gave council members Bill Guman and Randy Purvis its assurances that they would have CFV's support if they ran for mayor against Makepeace.

Colorado Springs: Gay student club

Officials at Palmer High School opposed the formation of a gay and lesbian student group. They contended that sanctioning the club would lead to approval of student groups of devil worshippers and Nazi sympathizers. Principal Jay Engeln twice refused to charter the Palmer Gay and Lesbian Club, calling it a "special interest club."

Students appealed the principal's decision to John Bushey, the school district's director of school leadership. Bushey rejected the appeal, saying, "[A gay club] doesn't address the issues around curriculum and instruction and what we do in schools." The school policy on which the decisions to reject the group were based states that the school district "endorses the creation of clubs and other approved school organizations for the purpose of reaching the interests of as many students as possible."

While school officials claimed that the Gay and Lesbian Club would be detrimental to the interests of the student body, club organizers and their faculty adviser said they envisioned a student organization that would discuss current events as they relate to homosexuality and offer literary criticism of famous gay and lesbian authors. Organizers rejected any notion that the club would be a "gay singles club." They opposed the association of their club with hate groups of any kind, as the school board maintained. Delores Garcia, one of the student organizers, said, "One of my friends is gay, and I'm not, and we were talking one day and we realized that there was a lot of fear and mixed messages that gay students get from straights. We thought this club would be a good thing and it was needed."

In April, the American Civil Liberties Union of Colorado sent a letter to the school board on behalf of the student organizers, informing them that the federal Equal Access Act favors the students in this dispute. Under that law, a secondary school that receives public funds and that allows at least one non-curriculum-related student group to meet cannot discriminate against any other student group on the basis of the content of the speech at club meetings. No legal action was taken, and although the school board said it forwarded the letter to its attorneys, no action has been taken to approve the club as of press time.

Colorado Springs:
Religious Right condemns City Council

PrideFest Week, a week-long celebration of gay and lesbian pride culminating in a parade and festival, sparked a round to protests by anti-gay activists in the streets and on the radio. At the end of August, the City Council and Mayor Mary Lou Makepeace issued proclamations honoring PrideFest Week. Anti-gay activists, however, held a demonstration during the parade and festival. At a city corner by which the parade passed, several demonstrators held placards that denounced the festival, while others carried crosses. A number of them also urged parade participants to repent. On the day of PrideFest, Focus on the Family (see p. 355) ran an ad in a Colorado Springs newspaper criticizing local gay and lesbian activists for condemning the organization's anti-gay activities.

In response to the proclamations from the City Council and mayor, James Dobson, president of Focus on the Family, interrupted his regular daily radio show days after PrideFest to demand that listeners call City Hall and complain. More than 200 callers besieged the council, halting its normal workday. A spokesperson for Americans United for the Separation of Church and State referred to the tactic as "telephone terrorism."

Dobson and others continued the attack on PrideFest Week by assailing several area church leaders for failing to take public stands against homosexuality. Several other anti-gay activists also took to the airwaves to condemn Mayor Makepeace and the City Council and to vilify gay men and lesbians. The local Christian Coalition (see p. 353) reprimanded the mayor for supporting a "radical homosexual agenda."

For an entire week following PrideFest, local right-wing radio talk show host Chuck Baker urged listeners to recall Makepeace. He referred to the mayor derisively as "Butch" and even allowed one caller to muse that gays should be killed. Such threats prompted local gay pride organizers to contact the Federal Bureau of Investigation and to warn parents against bringing their children to the gay pride festival. Baker later apologized for the comments.

Denver: "Corpus Christi" protested

In October, religious protesters marched and waved signs outside the Denver premiere of critically acclaimed playwright Terrence McNally's, "Corpus Christi." Members of the right-wing group Shadowgov.com, along with the Pro-Life NonViolent Action, coordinated the protest. They objected to the play's portrayal of Christ-like leading character and his disciples as gay men. The play is set in Corpus Christi, Texas, and follows the life of Joshua, a modern-day Jesus. Through the course of the play, Joshua discovers he is both the son of God and gay. Commenting on the tone of the demonstration, one protester said, "It's tough love. We're not going to baby them to repent like others do." When told by counter protesters that gays can also be Christians, she retorted, "They're deluded. There's lots of people claiming to be Christians who have no clue what the Bible says."

The Denver protest mirrored the public reaction the play received during its initial run in New York City in 1998. In that instance, threats of violence led to a temporary cancellation before the play's opening.

Denver: Domestic partners registry criticized

The Denver City Council's approval of a registry system for same-sex couples raised the ire of local anti-gay activists. The registry is largely symbolic since it confers no legal rights or privileges on same-sex couples, though it will give corporations guidance in verifying the relationships of employees seeking domestic partner benefits. Councilman Ted Hackworth called the registry unnecessary. He added that it was a "worthless piece of legislation," and, in his opinion, a waste of bureaucratic time, ripe for fraud because of the ease with which couples could register with the city clerk. Because Hackworth and another council member abstained from voting, the measure passed with no dissenting votes.

Denver: Methodist bishop targeted for same-sex ceremony

Methodist Bishop Mary Ann Swenson came under fire for allowing a Denver minister to perform a same-sex marriage ceremony. In the spring, Rev. Mel Brown brought charges against Swenson for allegedly breaking church law by permitting a Denver minister under her authority to officiate at a same-sex marriage ceremony. This marked the first instance in the Methodist Church in which a bishop had been charged for permitting a minister under his or her authority to perform marriage rites for same-sex couples. In the past, Methodists have brought charges against specific ministers but not their supervising bishops. Current Methodist law considers same-sex marriage ceremonies a "chargeable offense" that could result in a trial.

The charges stem from a wedding that Rev. Toni Cook, of St. Paul's Methodist Church in Denver, performed for a same-sex couple. Since that ceremony, the Methodist Church has ruled that there are no church laws prohibiting bishops from officiating at same-sex weddings, and has dropped the charges against Swenson. Bishop Swenson and Brown have a history of tension. Brown has criticized Swenson's pro-gay stances several times in the past.

Denver: Public schools expand discrimination policy

In January, the Denver Public School Board proposed amending its non-discrimination and anti-harassment codes, which cover both students and teachers, to include sexual orientation and gender identity as protected categories. The board's proposal made Denver only the third school district in Colorado to consider such protections. The proposal faced considerable opposition from right-wing residents.

The major concern centered on fears that the changes would lead to gender confusion among the students. One school board opponent, Bernie Miller, said the majority of the board was being "politically correct" in supporting the proposal. He questioned whether anyone ever really doubts his or her gender, saying the board should "stand for what is natural inside you." But Miller's major concern centered on his fear that the proposed changes would lead to cross-dressing among students. Arguing against cross-dressing, Miller said, "If you've got male parts, you're male." He argued that male students wearing dresses would disrupt school. Supporters of the proposed protections countered that transgendered students, regardless of their reception at school, should be protected from discrimination and harassment.

"Homosexual teachers are appreciably more apt to have sexual relations with pupils than non-homosexuals."

— Discredited psychologist Paul Cameron of the Family Research Institute, during a school board meeting on a proposal to prohibit anti-gay harassment in Denver's public schools.

During one school board hearing on the proposal, opponents of the protections called homosexuality "aberrant behavior" and added that gay men and lesbians were morally wrong. One resident threatened to sue the city's schools. Right-wing psychologist Paul Cameron of the Family Research Institute declared, "Homosexual teachers are appreciably more apt to have sexual relations with pupils than non-homosexuals...If you make this decision, you will be doing the wrong thing." Cameron, who had quit the American Psychological Association shortly before the organization moved to revoke his membership on the grounds that he had falsified data, reportedly once said that murdering gays was the only permanent way to deal with homosexuality. One gay teacher testified to the anti-gay taunts he received in Denver's high schools.

After an emotional debate and an extensive presentation of the slurs, debasement, and harassment faced by gay and lesbian students, the board voted to adopt the new protections. One board member who had previously opposed the new protections said of his former opinion, "I have a sense of embarrassment, indeed, humiliation." The Gay, Lesbian, and Straight Education Network said the new policy made the Denver Public School System a leader in protecting the rights of gay students.

Grand Junction: Lesbian school skit targeted

A high school teacher in Grand Junction who allowed students to perform a skit involving two married women contemplating a lesbian affair drew the ire of disgruntled parents. One parent said that the play signaled the moral decay of society.

Students performed the play, "Anything for You," in an introductory speech class with students of all grade levels. The play's central conflict revolved around one woman's desire for an affair. The object of her attraction was her female best friend. They both later confide that they are in love with one another, and the skit ends before the characters make any attempt at sexual romance.

Parent Donald Pacini took his opposition to the play to the local school board. Pacini read to them a letter he wrote to Virginia Settle, the school principal, in which he said, "I had had no idea the moral decay of modern society had crept so far into our own high school." Though he added that the skit would have been improper even if it featured straight people, he concluded that "the implied acceptance of homosexuality as normal behavior turns it from bad to repugnant." Settle described the play as inappropriate for the classroom, and, after a minor reprimand, the teacher apologized.

Greeley: Human rights ordinance

Greeley was the site of a bitter fight over a ballot initiative that would have prohibited discrimination in employment, housing and public accommodations on the basis of sexual orientation, race, military status, and public assistance status, among other categories. Two local groups, Second Mondays and Concerned Citizens for Human Rights, sponsored the proposal as part of a broad initiative for human rights. A local committee calling itself No Special Rights for Greeley organized opposition to what it characterized as special treatment for the city's gay and lesbian population. The initiative was soundly defeated by more than a 2-1 majority.

The result indicated that opponents had been able to define the terms of debate. "The question is, do we want people who are practicing homosexuality or who are members of a neo-Nazi group being able to fine or jail those who disagree with their behavioral practices?" asked Nanci Lamborn, a member of No Special Rights for Greeley. "It's socialistic to fine and imprison those opposed to a sexual behavior." She added, "I don't think homosexuals deserve minority status. I definitely don't believe they have a right to force people to accept their sexual choices."

Opponents mocked the broad and inclusive intent of the initiative and compared gay men and lesbians to hate groups. One resident suggested, "As a good deal of legislation nowadays goes on the books, we may see such [sic] as pedophilia, rape, stealing, adultery, slavery, lewdness and other forms of debauchery receiving such mild penalties as are to be casually acceptable." Others compared homosexuality to alcoholism, drug abuse, and smoking.

Self-professed "ex-gay" speaker Michael Johnston of Kerusso Ministries (see p. 355) made two appearances to drum up opposition. Two local churches sponsored Johnston's visit, which drew almost 100 people each night for two nights. Although he primarily spoke against what he claimed were the dangers of the "gay lifestyle," he also encouraged the crowd to reject the ballot initiative. Johnston warned residents that approval of the initiative would open the floodgates to the entire "gay agenda," protect pedophiles, and encourage bestiality. "These ordinances aren't about anti-discrimination. They're about intimidating people into silence," he said. Johnston told the crowd that if they got to know gay men and lesbians, they could more effectively minister to them. David Schachter, who attended a protest against Johnston's speech, said, "Mr. Johnston's message is a thinly veiled message of hate. He is here to teach people to loathe themselves as he loathes himself."

The Greeley Tribune, a local newspaper, editorialized against the initiative. The editors wrote that the ordinance would add an undue level of bureaucracy and burden to the local court system and, further, that the existing state and federal protections made the law unnecessary. Colorado and federal laws, however, do not prohibit or punish discrimination in employment, housing, or public accommodations based on sexual orientation. Despite their stance, the editors did obliquely criticize the rhetoric of opponents. Other opponents of the initiative argued that the ordinance would only benefit lawyers involved in costly discrimination litigation.

> "I wonder how in the name of God anyone can truly believe perversion should be acceptable to honest, upright people… Even little children try to hide deviant behavior."
>
> — From a letter to the editor opposing a ballot initiative in Greeley that would have prohibited anti-gay discrimination in employment, housing and other areas.

Local residents sounded their opposition vehemently. In a local paper, one resident opined, "I wonder how in the name of God and common decency anyone can truly believe perversion should be acceptable to honest, upright people. I do not believe they do believe such deep down in their souls." She added, "Even little children try to hide deviant behavior. We all know that legalizing wrong won't make it right."

Jefferson County: Joint custody for lesbians criticized

When a Jefferson County district judge awarded joint custody of a 9-year-old girl to two women who had separated as a couple, a conservative lawmaker fumed that the courts had overstepped its legal bounds. The history of this case is complicated. After the women separated, the non-biological parent filed for joint custody of the child they had been raising together. In 1998, District Court Judge Frank Plaut issued such a joint custody ruling. In October of that year, the biological mother married a man and moved to New

York. When she filed for sole custody of the child in March 1999 so she could take her to New York permanently, the case sparked renewed attention among right-wing opponents to non-traditional families. Opponents pounced on a ruling later in that month that required both parents to develop a custody agreement suitable to the court. "The court is definitely being activist, setting a social agenda that is antithetical to the values of this country," said Republican state legislator Mark Paschall. He insisted that biological parents must always be favored in custody disputes.

Gay and lesbian advocates, however, cheered the decision. The ruling "treats the gay family the same way as if this were a heterosexual couple breaking up at the end of the marriage," Kate Kendell, executive director of the National Center for Lesbian Rights, told the Denver Post. "My hope is that it does in fact signal that courts are going to look at the substance of our families rather than legal formulas."

A court-appointed legal counsel for the child reported that the girl is equally fond of both mothers. The final agreement awarded both women joint custody. The child will spend the school year in New York with the biological mother and the rest of the year in Colorado with the non-biological parent.

Littleton: Anti-gay high school rumors

After the initial shock of the killings at Columbine High School in Littleton, rumors began circulating that at least one of the two killers was gay. Several right-wing activists led by Rev. Fred Phelps (see p. 356), hurled accusations that Eric Harris and Dylan Klebold staged the attack because they were gay. To date, no credible evidence has established that either Klebold or Harris was gay or related their sexual orientation to the massacre.

Rumors circulated around the time of the killing spree about a posting on an Internet website that claimed Klebold and Harris were part of an underground network of gay outcasts. The site celebrated their killing spree as revenge against heterosexuals for tormenting gays. The rumor's source remained anonymous. No link between the site and the "Trench Coat Mafia," an unofficial student group to which Harris and Klebold belonged, has been established.

Referring to the two as "smirking faggots," a press release from Phelps' Westboro Baptist Church read, "Two filthy fags slaughtered 13 people at Columbine High." Decrying the media's lack of attention to these rumors, it continued, "the sodomite-controlled media and Littleton, Colorado community are engaged in a massive conspiracy of silence to cover up the fag component of the bloody crimes." On a nationally broadcast news program, Rev. Jerry Falwell referred to the two killers as gay.

Trinidad: Phelps protests against doctor

Virulently anti-gay Rev. Fred Phelps (see p. 356) carried through on his threat to protest Stanley Biber, a doctor internationally famous for sex-reassignment surgery in Trinidad.

Ten members of Phelps' Topeka, Kansas-based church protested at Mount San Rafel Hospital. Members of his congregation carried their trademark "God Hates Fags" posters and signs condemning Dr. Biber and his staff to hell. The protesters reportedly shouted anti-gay epithets at hospital staff. The group garnered little attention during the hour and a half they remained.

The protesters emerged later that day in town decrying what they claimed was complicity among local churches in Dr. Biber's medical practices. Phelps targeted three churches, saying "[they] have been silent about the manifold transgressions and mighty sins of Dr. Biber." At both the hospital and downtown Trinidad demonstrations, Phelps and his followers met little fanfare.

CONNECTICUT

Statewide: Court rules against adoption

In a 6-1 decision, the state Supreme Court ruled in January against the adoption of a 6-year-old by his biological mother's lesbian partner, which would have given both women parental rights with respect to the child. The couple sought a second-parent adoption for the non-biological mother, but the state Adoption Review Board refused to approve it, prompting the couple to file a lawsuit. Even though a Superior Court ruled that the adoption should be allowed, the Adoption Review Board refused to grant it. The parents then took the case to the state Supreme Court. During the hearing before that court, all the experts involved with the case testified that the adoption was in the child's best interest. The state Supreme Court ruled against the adoption on the grounds that its responsibility is to apply the law, and existing state laws did not permit such an adoption. The court said that the task of establishing family law policy lay with the state legislature. Current state law prohibits most second-parent adoptions, those in which a biological parent permits another individual unrelated to the child by blood to become another adult legally responsible for the child. Children are only eligible for second-parent adoption when they have no legal parent or if a step-parent seeks an adoption. In June, anti-gay state legislators derailed a bill that would have granted greater adoption rights to gay and lesbian parents.

Statewide: Adoption bill assailed

Just before the legislative session ended in June, the state House of Representatives approved a "poison pill" amendment, thus sinking a bill allowing unmarried couples to adopt children. Previously the bill had enough support to pass. Debating the anti-gay amendment in the state Senate required more time than the legislative session allowed, killing the bill's chance of passage. The amendment would have defined government-recognized marriage exclusively as a heterosexual union, replacing the state's existing definition of a union between two people. The amendment would also have punished those who officiate at same-sex marriage ceremonies. Commenting on the original bill, Republican state Rep. Peter Nystrom said, "I quite frankly don't know why we have to denigrate the lifestyle I have chosen [heterosexual] and that most people in this world choose [in order] to achieve the means of gay adoption." Evan Wolfson, an attorney with Lambda Legal Defense and Education Fund, criticized the tactic, saying, "If right-wing legislators want to have a debate on an anti-marriage measure, they should introduce it [early in the session] and hold [public] hearings. Don't use it as a poison pill."

Statewide: Partner benefits for state employees

Negotiations between a state employees' union and Governor John Rowland's administration stalled over the issue of extending health care and pension benefits to the domestic partners of gay and lesbian state employees. The State Employees Bargaining Agent Coalition, which negotiates pension and health benefits for about 43,000 state employees, said it was an issue of civil rights. "We're talking about a situation where real, live human beings can't get health care because the state doesn't recognize domestic partners," said Dan Livingston, the chief negotiator for the union. The governor rejected the proposal as too costly and ripe for abuse, thus forcing the issue before an arbitrator in October. In February 2000, the arbitrator ruled that the state must provide the benefits. Domestic partners would have to sign affidavits attesting to their relationships with state employees. Livingston said the ruling "simply recognizes that the crucial need for working families to have decent health care and pension coverage doesn't disappear just because the families are headed by same-sex couples." The ruling became binding when its opponents in the state legislature failed to muster a two-thirds majority vote to override it.

Branford: Anti-gay health worker

A federal court in Hartford dismissed a lawsuit brought by a gay couple who alleged that a state health worker made anti-gay remarks to them in their home. Attorneys for Jo Ann Knight, a nurse consultant for the Connecticut Department of Public Health, said that the ruling by U.S. District Judge Dominic Squatrito was about free speech and free expression of religion. The court ruled that Knight's remarks were protected under free expression guarantees. The American Center for Law and Justice (see p. 352) represented Knight before the court.

In 1996, Knight made a routine visit to verify that a gay patient suffering from AIDS-related illnesses was receiving adequate home care. The patient's partner was his primary care-giver. While the couple reportedly spoke about the lack of emotional support they received from friends and family, Knight allegedly told Kenneth Johnson and Byron Benton that homosexuality was against her religious views and that if they accepted Christianity and renounced their homosexuality, their lives would improve. She added that they would "burn in Hell" because they were gay and not Christian. The two men subsequently filed a federal lawsuit, alleging that Knight's comments constituted an unfair imposition of her religious views and anti-gay harassment. Knight was suspended for two weeks and later reassigned to another position following the couple's complaints.

Bristol: "Gay Day" canceled at park

A Bristol amusement park imposed so many conditions on the New Haven Gay and Lesbian Community Center's plans to host a "Gay Day" that the center ultimately canceled it. Gay Day is an event where gay men and lesbians are encouraged to attend and a portion of their admission fee goes to benefit the community center. The previous year's event had been a successful one for the community center's fundraising effort at the park. But, claiming the park had too many complaints from patrons after last year's Gay Day, Lake Compounce Marketing Director Richard Bisi forbade the center from using the same slogan and fundraiser title. Park administrators required the community center to advertise that Lake Compounce did not officially support or endorse the event, which they admitted they did not require of any other group. The park also wanted to limit the number of discounted tickets made available for the fundraiser, claiming they did not want to compete with the center in selling tickets to the public. Other groups, however, have not been subject to the same requirements and limitations.

Hartford: Gay pride flag protested

Flying the gay pride rainbow flag over the state Capitol caused an uproar among conservative legislators and an anti-gay activist. Almost as soon as the rainbow flag was raised over the state Capitol commemorating a week of lobbying for gay and lesbian rights, Shuni Plaskett charged the stage and yelled into a microphone that the Capitol would "go down" if the flag flew. He was later arrested and charged with interfering with an officer. That was the first of several attempts to take the flag down.

Several anti-gay Republican state legislators later condemned the flying of the flag. "Allowing the gay pride flag to fly over our Capitol implies that the people of Connecticut support this lifestyle," Rep. T. R. Rowe said. "Many state residents have strong moral objections to the homosexual lifestyle, and these citizens have the right to expect that the Capitol flagpole will not be used to further the gay agenda," he said, also comparing gay and lesbian rights groups to the Ku Klux Klan. Three other legislators signed on to Rowe's letter to the House speaker and Senate president pro tempore condemning the flying of the flag and demanding that it be taken down. Although he did not push to remove the flag, House Republican Leader Robert Ward called the whole controversy a series of "embarrassments."

> "Citizens have the right to expect that the Capitol flagpole will not be used to further the gay agenda."
>
> — State Rep. T. R. Rowe, who led an effort to ban the rainbow flag from being flown above the state Capitol.

Although the flag controversy occurred in March, Rev. Fred Phelps (see p. 356) kept the memory of the flag alive. He made a special stop in Hartford in late November to protest the flying of the flag. Along with members of his Westboro Baptist Church of Topeka, Kansas, Phelps led a demonstration at the state Capitol. Church members carried signs saying "God Hates Fags." They claimed that the state brought shame upon itself "by officially sanctioning that filthy sin which God has declared abomination." Their protest drew only a small crowd, and Phelps and his followers left after a short time.

Despite the calls to take it down, the flag continued to fly over the Capitol for almost an entire week, marking the first time a gay pride flag had been flown atop a state Capitol.

Storrs: Anti-gay preacher at U-Conn.

In October, the notoriously anti-gay preacher "Brother James" gave a vitriolic noontime speech on the steps of the Student Union at the University of Connecticut in Storrs. Although he verbally bashed a host of races and religions, he spoke most feverishly against gay men and lesbians. James Gilles, better known as Brother James, along with Stephen White, periodically take their message of homophobia and intolerance to college campuses throughout the United States. Based in Evansville, Indiana, Brother James has reportedly said that male smokers are gay because "A man who would put a cigarette in his mouth would stick anything in his mouth." He claimed he knew how to spot a lesbian. He told the students, "Here's how you spot a lesbian. If you run across a female at U-Conn., that she is extremely irritable 24 hours a day [sic], highly agitated, filled with venom of a viper, viciousness and maliciousness, bite your head off for the fun of it, has the personality of a viperess [sic], also you conclude from this behavior pattern of her, she is suffering from chronic PMS 30 days a month, you pretty well can conclude that she's a lesbo." He added that women who "hide out inside the women's studies department" are "lesbos" and that "nothing is worse than a lesbian, unless of course you are a communist lesbian."

> "The Constitution was written by people who loved the Bible, not by Hindus, not by Buddhists, not by homosexuals and lesbians."
>
> — "Brother Steve," a preacher who travels to college campuses, speaking at the University of Connecticut.

"Brother James" was joined by "Brother Steve" who also travels to various college campuses. Based in the Philadelphia area, "Brother Steve" reportedly tries to provoke unlawful responses by making hostile remarks to a crowd. After his opponents break the law, he reportedly files a lawsuit seeking civil damages. Neither speaker was successful in inciting the U-Conn. crowd to violence. "Brother Steve" did, however, offer the students his version of a history lesson. He said, "The Constitution was written by people who loved the

Bible, not by Hindus, not by Buddhists, not by homosexuals and lesbians. It was written by people who loved the Bible. It was written by people who love the word of God." A group of students later formed a circle around "Brother Steve" and sang "We Shall Overcome," countering his message of hate.

Storrs: Anti-gay graffiti at U-Conn.

Anti-gay graffiti littered the University of Connecticut during the fall semester. The campus awoke one October morning to anti-gay chalkings etched onto a campus sidewalk. An unidentified person wrote, "If your gay go away" [sic]. Several students who were disturbed by the graffiti, however, modified it by drawing a sad face on the letter O in the word "go" and writing the title of a gay and lesbian studies course above it. Although someone filed a formal complaint and contacted campus police, they never identified the perpetrators. During the previous week, unidentified people wrote "FAGETS GO TO HELL" [sic] adorned with a swastika on a message board in a dormitory. These two incidents punctuated the end of a series of graffiti attacks that began at the opening of the semester.

In another campus residence hall, "Eat Shit," "Die fags," "Fags must die," and "Fags are going to hell" were all written on the doors to various students' rooms earlier in the semester. A resident of another dormitory complained that vandals had destroyed gay and lesbian-themed bumper stickers on her door. The Rainbow Center, the campus office in charge of gay and lesbian student services, had its gay pride flag stolen four times. In one incident, the vandals ruined the flag with a paint ball. Rainbow Center officials reported that the meeting place for the gay, lesbian, bisexual, and transgender student group is routinely defaced. This outbreak of anti-gay activity caused several openly gay and lesbian undergraduates to search for off-campus housing.

That search may have begun prematurely. In yet another incident, a carload of people allegedly yelled homophobic epithets at a heterosexual student and his friends as they walked down a busy area boulevard. After the harassers allegedly yelled "fags" at the group, the student claimed the harassers tried to incite a fight by continuing with other homophobic insults. Fortunately, no physical violence ensued.

The university president denounced the rash of anti-gay activity in a press release. He said that the chalking, vandalism, and gay-baiting were not exercises in free speech. Police never found suspects in any of these incidents.

Stamford: Gay minister's election targeted

A second appeal to a Presbyterian judicial board by two church members prevented an openly gay minister from serving on the governing board of the First Presbyterian Church of Stamford. In May 1998, that congregation had elected Wayne Osborne to its governing board. Two members of the congregation, James McCallum and Mairi Hair, challenged Osborne's selection as a violation of church doctrine in a complaint to the Southern New

England Presbytery's Permanent Judicial Commission. After an all-day trial, however, that body ruled in March 1999 against the complainants that the congregation did not violate church law.

McCallum and Hair continued their campaign to overrule the congregation's decision by appealing this ruling. They took their complaint to the Synod of the Northeast, which hears appeals in the church. Walter Baker, their attorney, said, "We cannot pick and choose the things we like and don't like in our constitution." The Synod ruled in October 1999 that the initial Judicial Commission's hearing incorrectly validated the congregation's election by not thoroughly examining Osbourne's statements about homosexuality. It did not overturn his appointment to the church's governing board, however. But the Synod did stop Osborne's ascension in addition to ordering a new investigation of the original complaints. By this time, the appeals process initiated by McCallum and Hair had prevented First Presbyterian from implementing an election it held almost a year and a half earlier. At press time, the new investigation was still proceeding.

Presbyterian religious doctrine stipulates that married officials be in monogamous marriages or celibate, and also bars sexually active gay men and lesbians from serving on church boards or being ordained as ministers. Although the church does not maintain that homosexuality is inherently sinful, it regards homosexual sex as a sin.

West Hartford: Dispute over pool discounts

Twice the town council of West Hartford angered gay and lesbian residents by refusing to offer a family discount to all resident parents. In 1998, a gay couple complained to pool officials that their policy of excluding unmarried couples from family discounts was unfair. Town officials later ruled that only legally married couples with children could purchase discounted family memberships. Childless couples, regardless of their sexual orientation, had to purchase separate memberships for each family member. The council further angered gay and lesbian parents and unmarried heterosexual couples because childless married couples who already held discounted family memberships had been "grandfathered" in.

A group of families took their case to the Connecticut Commission on Human Rights and Opportunities. In September 1999, the commission held that West Hartford had unfairly discriminated against gay and lesbian couples with children by not offering them the same family memberships it offered to opposite-sex couples with children. The commission said it would work with both sides to develop a policy beneficial to the town's diverse families.

DELAWARE

Statewide: Anti-discrimination bill defeated

The Delaware House of Representatives defeated a bill that would have prohibited employment discrimination based on sexual orientation. Its defeat marked the fourth time that the legislature had considered such a measure. Debate on the bill was the longest that legislators held on any proposed legislation in the 1999 session. Activists, more than 80 of whom had lobbied for the bill, said this that reflected the polarizing nature of gay and lesbian rights in Delaware politics. According to one gay rights activist, Rep. Charles West told one of a group of gay citizens lobbying for the bill, "I'm not going to vote for it because I don't like the way you [gay people] recruit children to your lifestyle." According to the same activist, West went on to say, "It was one thing when you people were quiet, but now that you're coming forward, wanting your rights, that's hard to take." Activists pointed out that in the 1950s, a national newsmagazine featured West discussing his opposition to desegregation using racial epithets.

Enduring criticism from his fellow Republicans, the bill's co-sponsor, Republican William Oberle, said, "This is not about sexual preferences. It is about human rights. The right to go to work without the fear of reprisal from your employer because of your sexual beliefs." Despite such pleas from lawmakers, the bill failed by three votes.

DISTRICT OF COLUMBIA

Church rejects gay minister

In May, at the behest of his congregation, a Lutheran bishop fired a pastor supportive of gay and lesbian ministries. Rev. Don Prang, interim pastor at Georgetown Lutheran Church, claimed Bishop Theodore Schneider had fired him because of his campaign urging the church to ordain gay men and lesbians. Prang said he was also targeted because of his criticism of the church's opposition to the blessing of same-sex relationships. He said he would perform same-sex commitment ceremonies at Georgetown Lutheran. "The Church has been doing violence to gays and lesbians for generations," he said. Schneider said that Prang's activism and combative style resulted in complaints from church members. Church member David Lippe said, "It's just that it [Prang's message] was shoved down people's throats."

In February, an openly gay member suggested that an openly gay minister be selected as pastor. Prang, who had been serving as interim pastor since September 1998, supported that idea. The bishop warned against such a choice, saying the church would lose denominational affiliation because the Lutheran Church bans the ordination of openly gay men in same-sex relationships. The church committee voted in May to support the bishop's decision to remove Prang.

Gay group excluded from march

Organizers of an anti-abortion march barred a gay group sympathetic to their cause from participating. The Pro-Life Alliance of Gays and Lesbians (PLAGAL) was barred from marching in the annual March for Life in January. Organizers complained to the city's police department about the gay group's desire to participate. Police informed PLAGAL that they risked arrest if they joined the march against the will of the organizers. Instead of marching with a contingent of other groups, the Pro-Life Alliance rallied at the march's destination — the Supreme Court. They distributed pamphlets saying, "an inclusive pro-life movement will save more unborn children." The group's founder, Tom Sena, said, "PLAGAL believes that anything that endangers human life is wrong. Homophobia is one such danger. So is abortion." Spencer Epps, a member, asked, "March organizers can't tell someone, 'You're too black to be pro-life. You're too Jewish to be pro-life.' Why are they telling us, 'You're too gay to be pro-life'?"

Hostile firefighter promoted

District of Columbia Fire Chief Thomas Tippett promoted a firefighter found by a jury to have denied services to a transgendered car accident victim. The jury's finding in 1995 that Adrian Williams denied emergency medical aid to Tyra Hunter after discovering that she was biologically a male is being appealed by the city. Williams' 1999 promotion drew the ire of openly gay City Council member David Catania, who vowed to block approval of the Fire Department's budget unless Chief Tippett rescinded the promotion. Catania asked the chief during a council hearing, "You said in your testimony today that [the department] won't tolerate non-performance... Chief, how do you explain promoting an officer who withdrew care and cost the city, in part, $2.9 million [the amount the jury decided the city should pay Hunter's mother for Hunter's wrongful death]?" Tippett denied Catania's assertion that Williams did not have to be promoted, saying that he "could not put this person on administrative leave without cause." Catania went on to tell the committee chair, "I'm putting you on notice now. This budget is in peril. I will do my level best to rider this thing into oblivion until this is solved." He said that he would urge fellow council members not to approve any increases in the department's budget unless the promotion was rescinded. Catania later told a gay newspaper that most firefighters in the city are "competent and honorable." However, he added, "What we cannot accept is firefighter brutality. This is every bit the same as police brutality." In April 2000, Mayor Anthony Williams said his staff would look into the propriety of the chief's promotion and the legality of rescinding it.

Largent offers another adoption prohibition

For the second year in a row, U.S. Rep. Steve Largent (R-Oklahoma) introduced a last-minute amendment to the District of Columbia appropriations bill that would have prohibited unmarried couples from jointly adopting children. The bill was aimed at gay and lesbian parents, though it made no reference to them. The bill not only would have prevented the District from using federal monies but would have made federal grants contingent upon the District's not using its own funds for adoptions by gay men and lesbians. He drew the ire of gay and lesbian advocates from across the nation. The District's House delegate, Eleanor Holmes Norton, gave an impassioned defense of allowing gay men and lesbians to adopt. "There is no chance that unsuitable parents can adopt in the District because the courts strictly regulate these adoptions," she said. Norton and other members opposed to the amendment pointed to more than 3,000 children awaiting adoption in Washington and argued that Largent's amendment would greatly hinder their placement.

> "The right wing... [is] so blinded by its fixation on punishing gays and lesbians that it is willing to sacrifice the well-being of the most vulnerable members of society: children."
>
> — Christopher Anders of the American Civil Liberties Union, speaking against an amendment in Congress that would have prohibited gay men and lesbians in the District from adopting children.

Several organizations supporting gay and lesbian rights also spoke against the amendment. John Aravosis, head of the Internet-based Wired Strategies, called the amendment "a disgusting attack on us all" and "a legislative hate crime." Christopher Anders, of the American Civil Liberties Union, said, "The right wing of the Republican Party continues to be so blinded by its fixation on punishing gays and lesbians that it is willing to sacrifice the well-being of the most vulnerable members of society: children in the foster care system." The Child Welfare League of America and the American Psychological Association also condemned the amendment.

The House narrowly rejected the amendment by a vote of 215-213. Human Rights Campaign Political Director Winnie Stachelberg noted, "The welfare of children triumphed over anti-gay politics." National Gay and Lesbian Task Force Director Kerry Lobel said, "To defeat a same-sex adoption ban on the floor of the House is a victory for real family values."

Psychiatric conference protested

A coalition of right-wing groups that promote so-called "ex-gay" ministries staged a news conference during the American Psychiatric Association's annual meeting in May. Representatives from the Family Research Council (see p. 355), Transformation Christian

Ministries (see p. 357), Parents and Friends of Ex-Gays (see p. 357), and Americans for Truth About Homosexuality (see p. 352) urged the APA to change its policies on accepting homosexuality as a valid sexual orientation. It also sought an end to the APA's denunciation of reparative therapies that use psychiatric counseling to change gay men and lesbians' sexual orientation. The coalition specifically called on the APA to change these policies in its Diagnostic and Statistical Manual.

Robert Knight, a cultural analyst with the FRC, said, "People who are struggling against unwanted desires should have the freedom to seek counseling without institutional roadblocks. They should have the freedom to choose mental health instead of surrendering just because it has become politically fashionable to do so." He added, "As many earlier studies on homosexuality disintegrate upon closer examination, and the ranks grow of people who have overcome homosexuality, one would think the APA would reassess its actions." Knight said APA had caved in to "homosexual propaganda" about sexual orientation.

Anthony Falzarano, head of Parents and Friends of Ex-Gays (PFOX) and emcee of the news conference, claimed that many therapists are losing their licenses because of the APA's attacks on reparative therapy. His comments were challenged by Dr. Robert Spitzer, the architect of the APA's 1973 decision to remove homosexuality from its list of mental disorders. Falzarano claimed that labeling of reparative therapy as "unethical" and "destructive" interferes with insurance payments to therapists for such work.

FLORIDA

Statewide: Prohibition on adoptions challenged

Religious Right organizations across the state attacked the American Civil Liberties Union (ACLU) for challenging Florida's prohibition on adoptions by gay men and lesbians. The class-action lawsuit, filed in federal court, contends that the prohibition violates the children's and adults' constitutional rights to equal protection, privacy, intimate association, and family integrity, and deprives needy children of stable and loving families. Ironically, the state does permit gay men and lesbians to serve as foster parents The ACLU's attorneys claimed the prohibition is based on little more than ignorance and prejudice and that it excludes an entire class of qualified adults from adopting parentless children.

The Christian Coalition encouraged the state to launch a massive campaign to defend the law prohibiting these types of adoptions. John Dowless, executive director of the Florida Christian Coalition (see p. 353), said, "We think the law reflects what is best for kids... Kids need to be in a home with a mom and a dad, and the state needs to fight for what's right." A report issued by the Family Research Council (see p. 355) and based on information from discredited psychologist Paul Cameron claimed that gay and lesbian households are not fit for raising children. "Children need and deserve the best environment possible in which to learn and grow. The traditional mom-and-dad family provides this, while homosexual relationships do not."

Since 1977, when Anita Bryant led a statewide anti-gay campaign that included calls for other anti-gay laws, Florida has barred gays and lesbians from adopting children. In 1997, a lower state court allowed a lesbian couple from Fort Lauderdale to adopt a child, but the state Supreme Court later overturned that ruling and upheld the law prohibiting gay men and lesbian from adopting children. Florida became the only state with such a prohibition after New Hampshire rescinded its ban in 1999. A judge ruled in April 2000 that the case could proceed; its outcome is still pending.

Statewide: University Regents Reject Partner Benefits

Regents of the state university system denied repeated requests to extend family benefits to the domestic partners of system employees. They also turned down requests to prohibit discrimination based on sexual orientation in Florida's public colleges and universities. The Board of Regents claimed it had no legal authority to honor either of the requests. The students said that the regents asked them to investigate whether the board had any authority. In January, the regents repeated their statement denying their authority and told the students to take the issue up with state legislators. Within weeks of that meeting, the students held a rally at the state Capitol.

Student R.J. Thompson, chairperson of the University of South Florida's gay and lesbian campus group, was disappointed with the decision and said the regents did not even try to send a signal of support for the students' request. "I think there is still a role, especially for presidents, to be outspoken and to try to issue the strongest policy statements we can… " He added, "Unfortunately, it seems to most of us that instead of looking for ways they could do the right thing, the chancellor and the board chose to do nothing at all. That's unacceptable." A bill to establish a statewide domestic partner registry died in assembly committee on children and families.

Fort Lauderdale: Anti-gay conference

Coral Ridge Ministries sponsored its annual "Reclaiming America for Christ" conference in February, featuring several sessions that denounced homosexuality. The conference was designed to promote the Religious Right's agenda and fight against what its views as America's moral decay. Its efforts included countering the influence of gay and lesbian rights advocates. John and Anne Paulk, a self-described "ex-gay" couple, hosted a workshop on fighting homosexuality in the media. They claim gay men and lesbians can be cured of their homosexuality by accepting God. Other organizations affiliated with the Religious Right sent representatives. Former Family Research Council (see p. 355) President Gary Bauer, Janet Parshall of the same group, and Janet Folger of the Center for Reclaiming America (see p. 353) joined host D. James Kennedy, president of Coral Ridge Ministries (see p. 354).

The conference organizers delved directly into politics. U.S. House Majority Leader Dick Armey (R-Texas), who once referred to U.S. Rep. Barney Frank (D-Massachusetts) as "Barney Fag," addressed the conference. Referring to the support that many moderates lent to the Employment Non-Discrimination Act in the Congress, the FRC's director of cultural studies, Robert Knight, called moderate Republicans "the bane of our existence."

Elected officials' mixing of politics and religious to attack gay men and lesbians concerned many progressive activists. Winnie Stachelberg of the Human Rights Campaign pointed out how the divisive tactics of the Religious Right divided the Republican Party and fostered an atmosphere hostile to gay and lesbian equal rights legislation.

Fort Lauderdale: Board investigates Boy Scouts

In October, the Broward County Human Rights Board launched an investigation into whether the Boy Scouts of Florida are violating a county law by excluding members based upon their sexual orientation. The Boy Scouts of Florida prohibit gay males from becoming members. Jeffrie Herrmann, an executive with the Scouts' South Florida Council, said the "lifestyle of a homosexual is not compatible with what we're trying to teach young people." Randy Fleischer, a current member and former chairperson of the Human Rights Board, maintains that the Boy Scouts are a public organization and, therefore, must abide by the human rights ordinance. He said, "I'm most concerned that the Scouts are teaching bigotry."

The Boy Scouts of America have been the subject of other lawsuits across the country challenging their exclusion of gays from membership and employment. Heeding the advice of its legal counsel, the Human Rights Board voted to await the outcome of a U.S. Supreme Court case involving the Boy Scouts' denial of membership to gay males.

Fort Lauderdale:
Broward County partner benefits opposed

Opponents of Broward County's ordinance governing domestic partner benefit programs challenged them in state court. In January, Broward County adopted an ordinance which the allowed the county government to create a registry for domestic partners, to recognize jail and hospital visitation rights, to recognize the designated domestic partner authority in making health care decisions, and to offer preferential treatment to businesses contracting with the county that extend family benefits to the domestic partners of company employees. Under the ordinance, the county also began offering spousal benefits to the domestic partners of its employees. Broward County offers a broader array of benefits to and protects more rights of gay men and lesbians than any other Florida county. Critics attacked the ordinance, sought to obstruct its passage, and eventually filed a lawsuit to legally challenge it.

When the topic was first broached in 1998, Florida's Religious Right immediately assailed the proposals. John Dowless, then executive director of the Christian Coalition of Florida (see p. 353), claimed the ordinances would make the county the home of extreme leftists. "Broward just needs to start their own state," Dowless said. "They're so far from mainstream America, it's unbelievable. They seem to have no semblance of right and wrong." He added, "What I find most offensive is that they're forcing their views on others." Janet Folger, director of the Center for Reclaiming America (see p. 353), said, "This is about more than Broward County, it's about advancing the national homosexual agenda... This is a direct attack on people of faith, on families, and on the taxpayer." A week before the ordinances were adopted, a coalition of conservative religious groups called a press conference to denounce the County Commission. Northstar Legal Center (see p. 356), the Family Research Council (see p. 355), the Center for Reclaiming America, and Coral Ridge Ministries

> "Enough is enough. We will no longer sit back and have them subsidize the gay lifestyle."
>
> — Lawrence "Wally" Lowe of the right-wing Concerned Citizens for Broward, which opposed Broward County's domestic partnership ordinance, the most expansive in Florida.

(see p. 354) claimed the proposed ordinance would violate Florida's Defense of Marriage Act by creating a new definition of marriage. They vowed to sue should the proposals pass. An exasperated Lawrence "Wally" Lowe, spokesperson for the right-wing Concerned Citizens for Broward, complained, "Enough is enough. We will no longer sit back and have them subsidize the gay lifestyle." The county's Republican Party chairman, Ed Pozzuoli said, "Everybody in Broward will pay for this social engineering." In op-ed columns and letters to the editor of local newspapers, other opponents expressed their opposition to the proposals. Because of strong conservative opposition, the commissioners dropped an earlier proposal that would have required businesses contracting with the county to offer domestic partner benefits.

At the hearing at which the new ordinance was enacted, County Commissioners endured complaints, threats, and even warnings of God's wrath for approving the proposal. The right-wing group Concerned Citizens for Broward promised to fund a legal challenge to the ordinance. Resident Dee Maynard said, "I'm not a homophobe. I'm just a taxpayer who doesn't want to pay for a high-risk lifestyle choice. I shouldn't have to pay for that any more than I would pay for an abortion." Others worried about the impact the ordinance would have on young people. "If you pass this legislation, you are subsidizing people who are not married, and living together. You are giving a bad signal to our youth," said Francis Mahoney, a local resident.

In February, Concerned Citizens for Broward followed through on its pledge and began a campaign to invalidate all provisions within the ordinance. Lowe, with help from Northstar Legal Services, filed a lawsuit in state court claiming that the entire ordinance violated the state government's sole authority to regulate marital matters and would place undue financial burdens on taxpayers. Northstar has helped to successfully challenge a domestic partners policy covering Arlington County, Virginia employees. Northstar sought an injunction to prevent Broward County from implementing the contracting provision within the new ordinance. Justifying the suit, Lowe said, "they want me to subsidize and pay for it. And I don't want to."

Circuit Judge Robert Andrews did not grant the injunction, holding that the county had not created a new marital status as the lawsuit had contended. The suit was dismissed, and by July, the county's gay men and lesbians could take advantage of the new ordinances.

Fort Lauderdale: Conflict over Bally's partners discount

In November, a Bally's Total Fitness health club refused to extend family discounts to domestic partners certified by the Broward County government. When Donna Watson initially tried to sign up for a family membership for herself and her same-sex partner, she said the staff was less than cooperative. After Watson showed them her partnership card, the staff reportedly laughed at her and sent her to corporate managers. A mid-level supervisor allegedly told her, "Forget it. We don't care if she is your family. We don't honor it." According to Watson, another supervisor told her to "fight it in Congress." Watson had responded to a Bally's ad offering members a discount to sign up a spouse.

> "We will deservedly be left to our own sick demise, consumed by our chosen sexual perversion, and drug-infested, hedonistic lifestyles."
>
> — From the website of Lee County Sheriff John McDougall, which used the county police's official Internet site to denounce "Gay and Lesbian coalitions, rabid feminist groups, and United Nations one-world government radicals."

A local attorney for Bally's said the county's domestic partners ordinance does not require the company to honor couples' relationships certified by the government. At the time, though, Bally's did offer discounted memberships to domestic partners in its Washington, D.C., New York City and San Francisco locations.

Watson remained undeterred. She started to organize boycotts and protests of Bally's. Gay and lesbian press outlets across the country featured her story, and public pressure mounted. In December, the company changed its policy in all its locations to honor domestic partnerships certified by local governments. A happy Watson commented, "Sometimes, one person has to scream loud enough."

Fort Myers: Sheriff's anti-gay website

Lee County Sheriff John McDougall used government-owned computers to denounce homosexuality on the Internet. In September, Dougall used the Lee County Police website's section for crime prevention to protest against gays, feminists, and civil libertarians for what he called their "despicable conduct and agenda." The posting ignited a fierce debate about the balance between free speech and the proper use of government websites.

McDougall, who is well-known throughout the county for his right-wing beliefs, staunchly defended his website. He appeared on NBC's "Today" show saying his website discourages moral and social crimes. "What many fail to see, however, are the diabolical forces of moral corruption working feverishly, behind closed doors," he said. Among these "forces" his website listed were "... Gay and Lesbian coalitions, rabid feminist groups, United Nations one-world government radicals." McDougall claimed, "We will deservedly be left to our own sick demise; consumed by our chosen sexual perversion, and drug-infested, hedonistic lifestyles."

Donalie Benyak, a former official with the local chapter of the National Organization for Women, feared that McDougall's words prove he is not responsive to the law enforcement needs of gay men and lesbians. "... [He] would be very, very slow to respond to anyone in that group, anyone he disagrees with," Benyak alleged.

State and local officials did not take any action against the sheriff. Neither the county attorney general nor the state attorney general would comment on the postings. Lee County Commissioner John Manning stopped short of condemning McDougall, questioning only the appropriateness of the site.

Although public officials did not halt the sheriff's campaign of hate, computer users nationwide temporarily did. The computer hosting the website was not powerful enough to handle all of the "hits" the website received after news about Sheriff McDougall became nationally known in October. The sheriff was forced to remove his tirade temporarily. However, his diatribe against gays and others was back up on the website and available after a brief hiatus.

Lakeland: Church sponsors session for "ex-gays"

In October, the First United Methodist Church of Lakeland sponsored a conference on converting gay men and lesbians into heterosexuals. Rev. Jim Gentile, executive director of Transforming Congregations in Philadelphia (see p. 357), was the featured speaker. He is a so-called "ex-gay" who preaches that gay men and lesbians can and should change their sexual orientation through religious devotion. He shared his story of sexual conversion and how he had reared "100% male" children. Other "ex-gays" representing a variety of conversion ministries also addressed the congregation. They each spoke about being "healed" of homosexuality.

Lakeland: Harassment of gay neighbors

Persistent harassment by an anti-gay neighbor made two gay Lakeland residents decide to sell their home and his move in October. Gary LaRose and his partner, Raymond

Maxwell, alleged that Ronald Trim badgered them for well over a year. Trim claimed that Maxwell, who is black, had erroneously told another neighbor that Trim's dog killed that neighbor's rabbits. LaRose claimed this misunderstanding prompted the harassment. Trim, who is white, admitted to raising a Confederate flag and dangling a noose in his front yard, but he denied doing that to intimidate the couple. He also acknowledged posting a sign warning neighborhood children that "F-E-R-R-I-E-S" [sic] lived next door with an arrow pointing to LaRose and Maxwell's home. Trim denied the sign was derogatory because of the way he hyphenated "FERRIES." The sheriff's office reportedly advised LaRose to move.

The stress of the situation wore heavily on the couple. Maxwell moved away earlier in the year, and LaRose said he had to move his niece, who had been living with the couple, into a friend's home. "I can't put a 4-year-old child through this," he said. LaRose complained to the Federal Bureau of Investigation; in September, a year after the complaint had been filed, the bureau decided not to pursue the case. According to the FBI, absent any physical confrontation, it did believe it had sufficient evidence to prosecute Trim. Since then, LaRose has planned to sell his home and move out of the neighborhood.

Miami: Drive to repeal human rights law

The Florida Family Association (see p. 355) and the Christian Coalition of Florida (see p. 353) followed through on an earlier promise to fight to repeal a 1998 amendment to Dade County's existing human rights ordinance that added protections for gay men and lesbians. In December 1998, the groups began gathering signatures to put the new measure up for a referendum in the hope that voters would be less receptive to it than the Miami-Dade Commission had been. By February 1999, they were mailing letters that spread outright falsehoods about the effect of the amendment. Those efforts echoed Anita Byrant's 1977 bitter but successful campaign to pass a ballot initiative repealing an anti-discrimination ordinance that included sexual orientation that the Miami-Dade Commission had then recently passed.

The FFA and Christian Coalition criss-crossed the county with their petition drive. With the help of 250 churches and 80 civic organizations, they targeted black and Latino neighborhoods specifically and pandered to anti-gay attitudes by focusing on the gay "lifestyle." They also planned to present self-proclaimed "ex-gays" as the campaign's centerpiece. A letter on Christian Coalition letterhead characterized the amendment to the human rights ordinance as an "effort by Satan aimed at our families." Titled "The Gay Manifesto," it said, "Every Christian should be so motivated by this outbreak of sodomy that they would do everything in their power to reverse this gay rights ordinance." Several locales rejected their overtures and vowed not to cooperate with either group.

The coalition failed to get enough signatures by the April 2000 deadline, ending the chance to put the issue up for a popular vote. They were about 5,600 signatures shy of the required 4 percent of registered voters needed.

People For the American Way was part of the coalition SAVE/Dade that initially sponsored the amendment to the human rights ordinance and was active in the campaign to defeat the proposed referendum.

Miami Beach: Gay employee fired from hotel

A hotel in Miami Beach fired a gay employee in April after he took a day off to care for his partner, who was in the hospital. When Felix Garcia returned to work the next day, he said the hotel manager questioned him about the matter. Describing his reason for the absence, Garcia said he revealed that he was in a same-sex relationship. The manager reportedly said, "So you're gay," which Garcia said he confirmed. According to Garcia, the manager then fired him and told him to leave. Garcia contends the manager did so because he found out that Garcia is gay. That hotel manager no longer works there, but his replacement denied that Garcia was fired because he is gay, citing a number of gay hotel employees. Garcia, nonetheless, took his case to the Miami-Dade Equal Opportunity Board, which is currently investigating the matter. In December 1998, the Miami-Dade County Board of Commissioners outlawed discrimination in employment based on sexual orientation.

Orlando: "Gay Days" at Disney World protested

A coalition of Religious Right groups protested an annual gay and lesbian pride celebration at Disney World in Orlando. Some of them attempted to air television ads urging gay men and lesbians to change their sexual orientation through religion, but most local stations turned them down and the media attention reportedly brought them more criticism than converts.

> "Religious Americans are about to turn Cinderella into a pumpkin."
>
> — Martin Mawyer of the Christian Action Network, threatening a boycott of Disney over the "Gay Days" held at Walt Disney World.

A television ad featuring "ex-gays" was one of the focal points in the campaign against "Gay Days." Janet Folger, of the Center for Reclaiming America (see p. 353), said, "The primary motivation [behind the ads] is to provide hope for change for those who want to walk away from homosexuality. If it brings more awareness [to Gay Days], so be it." Yvette Cantu of the Family Research Council (see p. 355) vowed to continue the campaign regardless of its outcome. She remained hopeful that the "ex-gay" message would overshadow the overwhelmingly positive coverage Gay Days had received in recent years. Along with several other anti-gay organizations, both groups funded the television and radio ads featuring testimonials from "ex-gays." They criticized the network affiliates that turned down their ads.

The Florida Family Association (see p. 355) has attacked Disney for several years for not stopping Gay Days. Its president, David Caton, said, "They allow this tremendous event with lots of same-sex demonstrations and T-shirts proclaiming the homosexual lifestyle as normal," he said. "We believe it is a part of Disney's plan to impact the culture."

Because of his long-standing opposition to the celebration, Caton cheered what he perceived to be the decreased attendance at Disney World by both gay and straight tourists. He attributed this to the increased visibility of Gay Days. Attendance have reportedly spread out over more days at more theme parks. Organizers say that Gay Days have actually become increasingly successful since the celebration began. Total attendance in 1999 approached 100,000.

Opponents followed up on their attacks with a call for future boycotts. Members of the Southern Baptist Convention, which has led a boycott of Disney products since 1997, called on the organization's leaders to boycott the city of Orlando by not holding the SBC's 2000 convention there as planned. Rev. Wiley Drake, a Baptist minister and one of those calling for a convention boycott, likened Orlando to "Sodom and Gomorrah." Some of Drake's fellow Baptists soundly criticized him for making such a call, saying it would be too costly. The Christian Action Network (see p. 353) threatened its own boycott of Disney unless the company told park visitors and hotel guests about Gay Days in advance. A press conference announcing CAN's planned boycott featured a video of same-sex couples dancing together and kissing at a Disney theme park. "Religious Americans are about to turn Cinderella into a pumpkin," the group's president, Martin Mawyer, said.

Gay Days started in 1990 as an unofficial gathering of gay men and lesbians at the Walt Disney World theme park. Although the celebration has expanded to include more days and venues, none of the major theme parks in and around Orlando officially sponsors events.

Palm Beach County:
School board rejects non-discrimination policy

Palm Beach County's school board rejected an opportunity to prohibit discrimination against gay and lesbian students. Parents and anti-gay activists mobilized quickly to defeat a proposal to expand the district's policies against student harassment and discrimination to include sexual orientation.

As soon as the board announced that it would consider the proposal, anti-gay forces objected. In February, a month before the vote, opponents denounced the effort as part of an attempt to promote homosexuality as acceptable. Two-time school board candidate Sally Beach, who also has opposed many of the district's sex education proposals, said, "I think, ultimately, the motivation is to try to include that type of lifestyle as the norm." She added, "We don't include fat people in a special category. We don't include people with glasses." Chris Nick, another activist who has opposed sex education programs, added, "If we're going to listen to a homosexual activist, let's at least also listen to an ex-homosexual." Former school board candidate David Walsh added, "The schools need to stop trying to regulate morality. That should be done at home."

The board heard from gay and lesbian students and faculty. In 1998 and 1999, the Gay, Lesbian, and Straight Education Network (GLSEN), an organization dedicated to improving educational environments for gay and lesbian students and faculty, gave Palm Beach County public schools a failing grade for not instituting policies prohibiting discrimination against gay and lesbian students and staff, not supporting gay student clubs, and not providing enough staff on gay and lesbian issues. John Sickler, a former student and part of a group of 10 advocates for the protections, spoke in support of the proposal. When Sickler pondered what Jesus Christ might do in this situation, a heckler in the crowd shouted, "He would tell you not to be gay."

> "I can't put a 4-year-old child through this."
>
> — Gary LaRose of Lakeland, who alleged that he and his partner were harassed for a year by a neighbor. LaRose sent his niece to live with friends, and eventually he and his partner moved to a new neighborhood.

During the March school board meeting at which the final vote was taken, opponents quoted liberally from the Bible. Well over two dozen people spoke out against protecting gay and lesbian students. Many opponents came to the board meeting prompted by an incendiary, anti-gay flier distributed throughout the school district that warned of endorsement of homosexuality in school if the measure passed.

In the end, the board seemed unconvinced by anti-harassment appeals. A report by Cynthia Prettyman, the district's legal counsel, claimed that the measure would open the school board up to a flood of lawsuits from gay and lesbian students. The board voted 4-3 against the proposal, saying it feared the prospect of increased legal liabilities. School Board Chair Sandra Richmond said she would not hesitate to bring the issue back before the board if the question of liability were resolved.

Pierson: Dress code at the prom

Taylor High School Principal Peter Oatman initially denied a male student's request to wear a dress to his senior prom, then changed his mind. In March, Oatman told openly gay student Charles Rice that he would be denied entrance to Taylor's senior prom if he wore a dress. It "was just something I had to stand up for," Rice said. The next week, Oatman changed his mind. After Oatman and school attorneys consulted with the Bill Hall, the school district's superintendent, and reports appeared in the local media, Oatman allowed Rice to wear a dress to the prom. However, he warned that no other students would be allowed to do so during school or at special events. Since Oatman previously had allowed Rice to wear women's clothing at special school programs, Hall said that denying Rice's request for the prom would constitute a change in policy. Volusia County, of which Pierson is a part, allows principals to establish dress codes for each school, but the courts have ruled that any dress code must be consistently enforced.

Pinellas County:
School harassment and non-discrimination policies

Despite vocal opposition, the Pinellas County School Board adopted a non-discrimination policy in hiring and employment that included sexual orientation and an anti-harassment policy that included protections for gay and lesbian students. The board examined the two measures in March, and Religious Right organizations lined up to oppose both. David Caton, president of the Florida Family Association (see p. 355), said that adopting the protections in hiring and promotion would encourage teachers who "share and openly discuss their sexual preferences." He also claimed the bill would open the school district up to a flood of lawsuits. Ron Scheffler Sr., of the local chapter of the Christian Coalition (see p. 353), claimed that employees and students already enjoyed federal protections under the Constitution and to include sexual orientation would be excessive. "This is not like someone who is black or who is born Chinese. This is something where they have decided on a lifestyle." The board gave preliminary approval to the anti-harassment measure and voted against the measure outlawing discrimination in hiring and promotions.

> "We don't include fat people in a special category. We don't include people with glasses."
>
> — School Board candidate Sally Beach, at a meeting of the Palm Beach County School Board, urging the board not to adopt a non-discrimination policy to protect gay and lesbian Students. The proposal was defeated.

In May, the school board voted 4-3 to adopt the non-discrimination policy in hiring and promotions. Board member Jane Gallucci changed her earlier position to cast the deciding vote in favor of the measure. Disturbed by the vote, a district guidance counselor claimed she would be offended by a policy tolerating homosexuals. A member of the Florida Family Association pledged to challenge the policy in court.

Tallahassee: Anti-gay state agency head

Florida Gov. Jeb Bush appointed to head the state Department of Health a former state legislator known for a previous anti-gay campaign. Bob Brooks had previously criticized the Walt Disney Company for extending benefits to the domestic partners of its employees. In 1995, he authored a letter co-signed by 14 other Florida state legislators charging that domestic partner benefits belittled marriage and that offering them was "a big mistake both morally and financially." Although Brooks said during his confirmation hearing that he would not fire state employees on the basis of their sexual orientation, two Democratic legislators on the committee evaluating his candidacy remained unconvinced and voted against his confirmation. Brooks was confirmed and currently serves as the head of the Florida Department of Health.

Tampa: Transgendered student denied run for homecoming queen

The Hillsborough County School Board denied a local high school student the opportunity to compete for homecoming queen. JaVonn Hicks, a transgendered sophomore who is physically male but dresses in female clothing, wanted to compete for the title at Tampa Bay Vocational and Technical High School. Hicks stated, "I'm not ashamed of who I am. I want to set a precedent and show people no matter who you are or how you dress or look, you shouldn't be discriminated against." Although she won the support of the student body, the school principal and county school board did not allow her to compete. School spokesperson Mark Hart said, "If there wasn't a category for him to participate, then he would have the right to be homecoming queen. He has the opportunity to run, because he's a boy, for king." Although admittedly upset, Hicks found a bright side to the matter: "I sent a message and an example for the young teens who are called 'different'."

GEORGIA

Statewide: Anti-gay school amendment

In March, a bill came to the floor of the state House that would require state and local school boards to develop a "character curriculum" to help students build discipline, good habits and respect for others. Conservative state Rep. Jeff Williams tried to amend the bill to state "cultural diversity" in the curriculum "shall mean ethnic and regional differences but shall not include sexual orientation." His amendment would have protected the state's ability to teach about its increasing racial and ethnic diversity while inhibiting program choices that deal with homosexuality. Williams said, "The school system should not prescribe what values are accepted in the home, and there are those areas in our communities that are changing dramatically... Some of those changes are ethnic in nature, and some [like sexual orientation] are choices that people make, and we need to maintain that distinction." Longtime gay activist Larry Pelligrini said that he was not surprised by the move. He said, "I'm not sure they won't try again, so that's why we have to be especially vigilant [to watch out for hostile amendments] as the session draws to a close." The amendment failed by 19 votes, though the character curriculum bill passed the House by an overwhelming margin.

Atlanta: City's domestic partner law upheld

State Insurance Commissioner John Oxendine blocked implementation of Atlanta's domestic partner benefits for city employees. The city sued Oxendine in state court in March, seeking to force him to comply with a 1997 state Supreme Court ruling upholding the benefits package. State laws require insurance benefits to be approved by the state insurance commissioner. Since 1995, Oxendine has prevented employers across the state, including cities like Atlanta, from offering domestic partner benefits to their employees. "What he's doing is unconstitutional. He's going against what the court has already ruled on," said Nick Gold, spokesperson for Mayor Bill Campbell. Oxendine told the city that granting the benefits would be "unfair, inequitable, would encourage misrepresentation and is contrary to the public policy of the state." Assistant Attorney General Paul Weisbecker told Judge Wendy Shoob at a June hearing that Oxendine opposed the benefits because he believes they encourage illegal sexual relationships.

At a September hearing, Lambda Legal Defense and Education Fund successfully argued on behalf of the city and openly lesbian City Council member Cathy Woolard, who had intervened in the suit, that Oxendine's actions were unlawful and unreasonable. Judge Shoob held that Oxedine's actions were "outside the scope of his authority" and "an abuse of his discretion." Lambda attorney Stephen Scarborough said, "After years of frustrating delays, this ruling stands to provide great relief to many Georgia families. What's more, the Court adamantly rejected Commissioner Oxendine's view that non-marital relationships should be branded 'immoral.' " Lambda's attorneys hoped the ruling would encourage employers across the state to offer domestic partner benefits.

In October, Oxendine announced that he would not challenge Judge Shoob's ruling, clearing the way for the city to provide domestic partner benefits to its employees. Oxendine's spokesperson said, "We will comply with the court's ruling and decide on a case-by-case basis" whether to approve other employers' domestic partner plans. A week after Judge Shoob's ruling, supporters of the benefits package held a "Just Registered" cake-cutting ceremony at city hall, hosted by Mayor Campbell, city officials, and gay and lesbian activists. In order for city employees to receive the benefits, they must register their relationships with the city clerk.

Buoyed by this victory, Mayor Campbell announced in December that he would consider a revision to the domestic partner ordinance that would require contractors with the city also to offer domestic partners benefits to their employees, as San Francisco currently does.

Atlanta: Controversy over publication on the Holocaust

In January, references to the gay victims of Nazi persecution were deleted from a publication of the Georgia Commission on the Holocaust intended for educators. "Triangles, Badges & Stars: Remembering the Mosaic of Victims of the Holocaust" is a teachers' guide for middle and high schools around the state and was funded in part by the Atlanta office of the law firm Holland & Knight. Two paragraphs — one saying, "German male homosexuals were targeted and arrested because they would not breed for the master race: they were an affront to the Nazi macho image," and another describing the ordeal gay men faced — were removed from the original draft. Sylvia Wygoda, director and chairperson of the commission, defended the decision to publish the report without the paragraphs on gay victims, saying, "[The deleted material] wasn't even necessary to the content of the book, and... it is not our place to put sexually graphic material into the schools."

The deletions angered members of the Georgia Equality Project (GEP), a statewide gay and lesbian advocacy organization. Its director, Harry Knox, said, "Erasing persecution of gays from the history of the Holocaust repeats the tragic silence of most Germans in the Nazi years. And it's a shame that children in Georgia would be led to ignorance and silence by the Holocaust Commission out of an apparent fear that legislators will punish them for telling the truth about gays under the Nazis." GEP helped organize a protest rally in Atlanta a day after press reports of the deletions were published.

Several local and national gay and lesbian activists, including Kerry Lobel, then head of the National Gay and Lesbian Task Force, and Knox, met with members of the commission in January, hoping to develop a solution to the problem and end the controversy. Because it was too late to reprint the edition in dispute, all the parties agreed to issue an errata sheet containing the deleted paragraphs to be sent to all who had received the booklet. They also agreed that the packet would include a teachers' guide from the U.S. Holocaust Memorial Museum describing the persecution of gay men and other non-Jewish victims. GEP voluntarily agreed to pay for distribution of the extra publications. Knox said, "We were really thrilled... [W]e feel that we were heard and understood and treated with great respect today." Wygoda also agreed to have gay men and lesbians appointed to the Commission. Precisely who had ordered the deletions had been a matter of dispute that was not settled during the meeting; members of the commission, on the one hand, and attorneys at Holland & Knight, on the other, continued to blame each other.

In April, Wygoda had security guards eject Knox from a commission meeting after he questioned the composition of the commission's advisory committee. He said Wygoda's decision not to appoint gay members to the commission violated the January agreements.

Atlanta and Decatur:
Baptists oust affirming congregations

The Georgia Baptist Convention, a state affiliate of the Southern Baptist Convention, voted in November to oust two affiliated churches that welcome gay men and lesbians. In April, the Georgia Baptist Convention's executive director sent a letter to Oakhurst Baptist Church in Decatur and Virginia-Highland Baptist Church in Atlanta, asking them whether a GBC policy adopted in 1998 excluding churches that welcome gay men and lesbians applied to their congregations. Oakhurst responded by touting its successful struggle to welcome diversity, which included welcoming gay men and lesbians. "We came to believe that the biblical references to homosexual behaviors do not address the Christian commitments and loving relationships of our gay and lesbian members," the statement read. In September, the convention's executive committee voted 134-1 to recommend that the full body oust Oakhurst Baptist, making it the first church targeted under the 1998 GBC policy. Rather than saying the action was a "move against homosexuals," the Southern Baptist Convention's vice president, Bill Merrill, characterized the vote as an unambiguous message about the sinfulness of homosexuality. The committee cited Oakhurst's openly gay assistant pastor and Virginia-Highland's gay deacons and use of the sanctuary for a same-sex wedding as particularly egregious.

> "We believe the greatest act of love is to tell the truth about sin... does your church minister to homosexuals?"
>
> — J. Robert White, executive director of the Georgia Baptist Convention, discussing its decision to oust congregations that welcome gay men and lesbians.

Overwhelming majorities adopted the executive committee's recommendations at the November meeting. "Messengers," as the delegates are called, voted 2,086 to 262 to sever ties with Oakhurst Baptist and 2,111 to 228 to expel Virginia-Highland, marking the first time in the convention's 177-year history that it expelled a congregation. The churches will lose their affiliation and stop sending financial contributions to the convention, though Virginia-Highland stopped making contributions in 1993. J. Robert White, the convention's executive director, said, "We believe the greatest act of love is to tell the truth about sin... does your church minister to homosexuals... or does your church go beyond that to honor the sin of homosexuality?" He added, "We believe that honoring homosexuality in this way is an error." James Merritt, pastor of Snellville First Baptist Church and a supporter of the expulsion, told the delegates they must "draw a line in the sand."

Officials and members of both churches denounced the votes. Oakhurst pastor Rev. Lanny Peters vowed to send a letter to other churches within the convention telling them the executive committee's efforts were "un-Baptist." He added, "The ministry that lesbian and gay Christians offer so joyfully to our church is a blessing and a crucial part of the life of this congregation." Oakhurst member Amy Greene said, "We represent something that's frightening, the radical notion that Jesus came for everybody. And that stirs people up." Pastor Tim Shirley of Virginia-Highland boasted his church's "ministry and mission is to serve all who come."

News of the convention's actions spread quickly through Georgia's press. Authors of several letters to the editors of state newspapers rejoiced in the convention's vote. Carl Pyrdum wrote to the Atlanta Journal-Constitution, "While it may be admirable to aggressively pursue all avenues of inclusiveness in our society, it cannot be at all costs." Virginia Smith wrote the Macon Telegraph, "Homosexuals are living in sin... The Baptist Convention did right to throw out the churches that accepted homosexuals, because they are accepting sin in their churches."

Rev. Bill Ricketts, the new president of the GBC, supported the November vote, saying the delegates were not being judgmental or intolerant of gay men and lesbians, but rather, were disciplining rebellious congregations. He said, "I'm firmly convinced that Jesus calls us to love all people. What we do not believe is that we can condone the homosexual lifestyle," and added, "I believe you can accept a sinner without accepting a sin."

Cobb County:
Transgendered woman denied name change

In August, a Cobb County judge denied a transgendered woman's request to change her name in August. Heather Lindsay claimed that Judge Watson White had denied her petition because the name change would allow her to use women's bathrooms. In his ruling, Judge White wrote that he was denying the petition because Lindsay "has not had sex change surgery." Lindsay claimed that the judge did not deal with her argument that the name change would simply allow her to more comfortably live the life she was already living. Lindsay said that she had followed all the legal steps required under state law to change her name: petition the court, publicize the request, and prove the notice was published. "When I left [the courtroom], I was pretty much [up] in arms, but I realized it could help everybody if I pursue it through the right channels. If I broke ground, it would benefit everybody," she said.

One therapist described the potential posed by the denial of a requested name change in such circumstances. Dr. Barbara Rubin, an Atlanta psychologist, said, "It is important that we respect the new name and pronoun that people wish to be called, because that is their identity. It is what looks to us like a new gender identity, but for them it is what they feel like they have been all along." Lindsay said, "All of these years, I've been this way, but I never could express myself. Now I'm happier with myself, and I like who I am."

Transgendered activist Karen Collins noted the social and legal problems that being denied a name change presents. "Since you have to live for a full year as your target gender [before you can have surgery], it is kind of difficult to maintain that life with a name that is specific to the opposite gender," said Collins, head of Trans=Action, a transgender education and advocacy group. "This is really the baseline for your entire document change. You need the name change granted by the court, then you can get your name changed on your driver's license, which can be a point of difficulty. If you get pulled over and your license has a male name and a female picture, it can be very difficult to deal with police officers in certain areas of the state," Collins said. She added that a judge has the discretion to deny or approve a petition for a name change and called Judge White's reported bathroom rationale "totally irrational." According to Collins, other transgendered people have been denied name changes by Judge White.

Trans=Action member Dallas Denny said her organization would send a letter to the Cobb County Commission informing them of Lindsay's problem. Denny faulted the commission for creating a hostile climate toward gay, lesbian, bisexual, and transgendered people when it issued a resolution in 1993 condemning the "gay lifestyle." "I would like to give the Commission an indication of how their policies trickle down to affect citizens in negative ways... I think it all goes back to that silly anti-gay resolution. That basically serves as an instruction to all of the county's employees that it is okay to treat anyone who is gender-different or that they assume to be gay or bisexual any way they want," she said.

Gwinnett County:
Prosecutor to continue with sodomy charges

Gwinnett County Solicitor Gerald Blaney vowed to continue prosecuting gay men who solicit sex in public. Laura Brown, a reporter with the Southern Voice, a gay newspaper in Atlanta, interviewed Blaney and other area county prosecutors for an article about the legality of arresting men on charges of soliciting sex in public in the wake of a recent state Supreme Court ruling nullifying Georgia's statute criminalizing sodomy. Several county prosecutors reportedly said they would no longer prosecute men who solicit sex from other men in public given that ruling. The court, however, did not rule that the law prohibiting solicitation of sodomy in public was unconstitutional. Other county prosecutors consulted for the article reportedly said they would continue to charge gay men with violating that law.

According to the article, Blaney made several anti-gay comments during his interview. He said he would gladly prosecute people for soliciting sodomy regardless of whether the solicited acts were to take place in private. He also said he wanted to defend the solicitation of sodomy law before the state Supreme Court. Blaney also said his office has been working on a list of sexual puns and vowed to use them in his legal arguments should he appear before the court defending the solicitation statute. After suggesting a few to Brown, he said, "Honey, I make 'em roll when I go down there [to the Supreme Court]." He also made derisive comments about Cobb County Solicitor Barry Morgan, who had told Brown he would not prosecute men for soliciting sodomy. When Blaney asked Brown whether the Southern Voice was a gay and lesbian paper, she told him that it was. He asked, "Are you one of them? Or are you normal?"

Hapeville: Harassment complaints at factory

A Ford auto plant worker claimed that he endured repeated anti-gay harassment from co-workers for the past three years. Ruben Camp said that his co-workers had taunted him, disrupted his work, physically assaulted him, and even suggested he commit suicide because he is gay. According to Camp, the harassment began in 1996 when he said fellow workers on his assembly line began treating him differently. "Homophobia had a lot to do with it... I felt my job was being sabotaged," he said. He complained to his local United Auto Workers union, which filed a complaint with Ford on his behalf. According to Camp, one of his supervisors at Ford apologized, but later said to him, "Because of your lifestyle, why don't you just go and kill yourself? A lot of people think about it." Camp said he started seeing a therapist.

Within a year, Camp claims other co-workers escalated the harassment. Camp said three of them repeatedly taunted him with "homo," "faggot," "sissy" and other epithets. He maintained that most of the taunts were made in front of supervisors. According to Camp, on one occasion, a co-worker brought his son into work and had him call Camp a "sissy." Camp brought a formal complaint against that co-worker. Camp said that another worker made sexually explicit gestures to him. He said that while one friend and co-worker told him to report it, another co-worker "teased me all night," and yet another sent him dead animals. According to Camp, when one co-worker brought him pornographic magazines, Camp just "told him to leave my station." He said, "I was ignoring everything and not reporting it. I would try to talk to them, but it only escalated. They took me as a joke."

> "Because of your lifestyle, why don't you just go and kill yourself? A lot of people think about it."
>
> — Ruben Camp, a worker at a Ford plant in Hapeville, alleged that a supervisor said this to him, and that other co-workers harassed and physically assaulted him.

Camp said that his employment situation grew intolerable in January when a co-worker physically assaulted him. After Camp requested a repair on the assembly line, he claimed the repairman told him he wasn't "going to put up with no faggot shit" and that he was "gonna run [Camp's] faggot ass upstairs if I caused problems." According to Camp, the harassment continued for some time until Camp asked the man to stop yelling at him. Camp said that the repairman responded, "I'm not your faggot ass boyfriend. I'll kick your faggot ass," and finally struck Camp. Camp reported this and several other incidents to labor relations representatives with minimal results. The repairman received a two-day suspension, and the representative told Camp that he had to be "tough" to work on the assembly line. In the meantime, Camp was diagnosed with post-traumatic stress syndrome and granted medical leave.

Ford officials later said they investigated the matter but took no action. A Ford spokesperson said, "Ford doesn't tolerate harassment. Basically, the company's position is, it will take whatever steps it needs to make sure employees feel they can contribute and feel safe." She pointed to the company's efforts at diversity education and to the gay workers organization, GLOBE (Gay, Lesbian, or Bisexual Employees).

Nevertheless, Camp's attorney, Gail Mackinson, said she plans to hold Ford accountable for its "zero tolerance" policy about anti-gay harassment. She said that Ford put Camp in jeopardy by effectively ignoring his complaints, and that Camp is considering suing some of his co-workers for intentional infliction of emotional distress. "He [Camp] just wanted to go about his business," she said, "Once his co-workers see that there are no consequences for this behavior, they think it's okay, and it becomes standard."

Statewide: Anti-discrimination bill assailed

Anti-gay conservatives denounced a bill that would have prohibited discrimination based on sexual orientation in housing and public accommodations, citing religious and moral grounds. Hawaii already prohibits sexual orientation discrimination in employment, but Gov. Ben Cayetano proposed expanding those protections.

Right-wing religious and legal groups led opposition to the bill. Testifying before a legislative committee, Leon Siu of the Christian Voice of Hawaii said, "Like same-sex marriage, domestic partnership, and hate crimes, this bill seeks to require society to recognize and approve of homosexuals and bisexuals as a designated protected class." He claimed there was no evidence that gay men and lesbians suffer from discrimination. "Are we trying to fix a problem that doesn't exist?" he asked. Robert Matsumoto, director of the Hawaii chapter of the American Center for Law and Justice (see p. 352), claimed that the religious rights of landlords would be violated if they had to rent to gay and lesbian couples. He cited a 1999 federal appeals court ruling favoring the religious rights of landlords over the rights of same-sex couples to justify his opposition to the Hawaii bill. Siu said his group, which has about 500 members, shared those concerns. "Which has the overriding prerogative, sexual orientation or religious belief?" he asked.

A diverse coalition supported the measure. The state Commission on the Status of Women, the League of Women Voters, the Gay and Lesbian Community Center, and Parents, Families, and Friends of Lesbians and Gays all pushed for passage. Barry Porter of the Gay and Lesbian Community Center in Honolulu said, "It is surprising that testimony would be necessary to convince anyone that a citizen of this state should not be homeless because of who they love and reside with." Harry Yee, head of the Civil Rights Commission, said, "A person's ability to obtain food, shelter, and other necessities should not be limited by their sexual orientation."

In March, House Labor Committee Chairperson Terry Yoshinaga (D) effectively killed the bill, saying the committee would have to study the issue for another year. Her committee also gutted a bill on hate crimes. Those moves disappointed Allicyn Hikida Tasaka, who heads the state Commission on the Status of Women. "And to say this particular group can still be discriminated against, knowing that discrimination occurs is profoundly unjust," she said. Others, like Kelly Rosati, head of the Hawaii Family Forum, rejoiced. "It's a real concern the bill would have been an invitation for a lawsuit against the Boy Scouts," she said referring to a recent New Jersey Supreme Court ruling that the Boy Scouts' prohibition on gay members violated a state law prohibiting sexual orientation discrimination by places of public accommodation.

Statewide: Domestic partner benefits expire

Partners of state employees stopped receiving domestic partner benefits in June because the state legislature chose not to renew the law that authorized the government to grant them. State employees were first offered domestic partner benefits in 1997 when lawmakers sought to head off a larger attempt at having the state recognize same-sex marriage. Under the plan, state employees paid their entire premiums for domestic partners with the state contributing nothing, although the state does pay the premiums on the family benefits retired state employees receive. In January 1999, Gov. Ben Cayetano proposed a more generous benefits package, but that measure stalled in the House Judiciary Committee because legislators wanted to pair the bill with another measure defining marriage as being between opposite-sex couples only. Other legislators wanted to wait for a ruling from the Hawaii Supreme Court on the question of the state's recognition of same-sex marriage. In 1998, Hawaiians had overwhelmingly approved a state constitutional amendment allowing the legislature to prohibit the state from recognizing same-sex marriages. James Di Giambattista, partner of a University of Hawaii employee, was disappointed, saying, "In the past, we prided ourselves on providing universal coverage for working men and women. Now, because of religious prejudice, and that's really what this is, we're about to say only certain people are entitled to coverage."

Statewide: Same-sex marriage lawsuit dies in court

In December, the Hawaii Supreme Court ruled that an 8-year-old lawsuit by several same-sex couples seeking marriage licenses had been rendered "moot" by a 1998 amendment to the state Constitution that allowed the legislature to prohibit the recognition of same-sex marriages. The Court construed that amendment as retroactively validating a pre-existing law restricting marriage to opposite-sex couples.

In 1990, the Department of Health took the position that, based upon an opinion by the state attorney general, it would deny marriage licenses to same-sex couples. Three same-sex couples then sued the Department, contending that its policy violated their state constitutional right not to be discriminated against on the basis of sex. After a lower court dismissed the lawsuit, the state Supreme Court reinstated it, holding that the state Constitution's Equal Rights Amendment prohibited the denial of marriage licenses to same-sex couples unless the state could demonstrate a "compelling interest" in denying the licenses to same-sex couples. In a historic 1996 ruling following a trial on the merits,

Circuit Court Judge Kevin Chang held that the state had shown no compelling interest in denying marriage licenses to same-sex couples. The state appealed. While the appeal was pending, the legislature authorized a ballot initiative proposal that would amend the state Constitution to allow the legislature to deny recognition of same-sex marriages. That initiative passed with 70 percent of the vote in November 1998.

Right-wing activists and organizations heralded the state Supreme Court's 1999 decision holding the same-sex couples' lawsuit to be moot in light of the 1998 state constitutional amendment. Mike Gabbard, chair of the Alliance for Traditional Marriage, said, "Thank you to the Hawaii Supreme Court for affirming what we've known all along: that marriage, by God's definition, is between opposite-sex couples." Robert Knight of the Family Research Council (see p. 355) said, "Contrary to pro-homosexuality activists' rhetoric, marriage is not the construct of man that can be retooled and manipulated, but an institution established by God and protected through 6,000 years of human history." Jan LaRue, a legal analyst with the FRC, said, "Homosexual activists contended the state's support of traditional marriage amounted to gender discrimination... But the law applies equally to men and women as well as homosexuals and heterosexuals. Just as two heterosexual men cannot marry, so two homosexual men cannot marry." Jack Hoag with Save Traditional Marriage hoped the state Supreme Court's 1999 ruling would finally kill an issue he felt had divided communities across the state.

> "We had our rights stripped away from us yesterday. We're now no longer equal. We're second-class."
>
> — Sue Reardon, counselor to a Hawaii youth group, after a lawsuit by same-sex couples seeking marriage licenses died in the Hawaii Supreme Court.

Advocates of the legal recognition of same-sex marriage were disappointed. Joe Melillo, one of the plaintiffs in the lawsuit, said, "I felt a little let down. I just felt that the judiciary here is a bunch of wimps... that they just copped out." Sue Reardon, counselor to a youth group in Hawaii, said, "We had our rights stripped away from us yesterday. We're now no longer equal. We're second-class." Reardon was particularly upset with those who had organized the push for a constitutional amendment. "What I think is a very small group of hateful people put out a lot of misinformation, and created a scapegoat, and caused a lot of fear," she said.

People For the American Way Foundation, along with other groups, filed an *amicus curiae* brief in the state Supreme Court urging the Court to uphold Judge Chang's decision.

Honolulu: Alleged transgender discrimination

In August, the Hawaiian Canoe Racing Association reiterated its policy on assigning qualifying participants to teams competing in races the association sponsors according to their sex at birth after complaints from a transgendered athlete. The association had originally instituted the policy in December 1998. Before an August 1999 competition, the association told paddlers to bring their birth certificates or submit to DNA testing in order to establish the categories in which they would compete. It said it would disqualify trans-gendered athlete Li Anne Taft if she qualified for its championship race and tried to compete as a woman. Taft was born male, but has since become a male-to-female transsexual. Surfing club coach Tim McCandless said that several female paddlers felt it would be unfair to compete against Taft because of her build. Another coach, Joe Kim, disagreed, saying Taft has no advantage over other women and that he had seen female paddlers bigger than Taft.

Taft filed a complaint with the Hawaii Civil Rights Commission and city of Honolulu claiming the policy allows the canoe association to discriminate against her. Her attorneys contend that state laws prohibiting discrimination based on gender protect her from the type of discrimination Taft alleges to have suffered from the association. Taft initially said she would not use her birth certificate to establish her sex because it had not been accurate since she became a transsexual. She later agreed to sit out the competition rather than create difficulties for her teammates.

IDAHO

Statewide: Broadcast of "It's Elementary" denounced

Religious Right groups and politicians denounced Idaho Public Television's decision to air the award-winning documentary, "It's Elementary: Talking about Gay Issues in School." The film, intended for teachers and adults, features discussions of homosexuality in schools across the country. The Idaho Christian Coalition and several state and local politicians all called on IPT to drop the film. Nancy Bloomer, the Coalition's executive director, asked, "When are we going to see a halt to the misuse of taxpayer money to promote the radical left's pro-homosexual agenda?" She claimed that the fact that "It's Elementary" was being broadcast on a state-supported channel by government money was the most objectionable aspect of the controversy. Idaho Public Television receives about 30 percent of its operating budget from the state government. The state board of education holds the broadcasting license for the station.

Some critics also called on IPT to broadcast the American Family Assocation's (see p. 352) video "Suffer the Children," made in response to "It's Elementary." The state attorney general, however, cautioned the station not to broadcast the AFA video because of a copyright lawsuit against AFA charging that the AFA illegally used clips from "It's Elementary" in its video.

Idaho Public Television General Manager Peter Morrill defended the station's decision to air "It's Elementary." He said that out of 340 messages the station had received about the program, 290 wanted it to air. In June, the state Board of Education voted unanimously in favor of supporting the decision to air the program. State Board of Education member Tom Dillon said bowing to pressure not to air would be a "horrible mistake and a bad precedent." The board also recommended the station provide equal time to people who opposed the program, a recommendation the station adopted. Morrill offered the Idaho Family Forum and the Idaho Christian Coalition up to an hour of on-air time to explain their grievances about the program, but both groups turned that down, saying that to rebut the film would give it credibility.

Elected officials began discussing withholding funds from IPT because of its decision to air the documentary. State Sen. Atwell Parry, who sits on the committee charged with IPT's budget, wrote Morrill that "From my viewpoint, there is a real firestorm brewing over this. It might do public TV more harm than good if you go ahead with the showing." Sen. Stan Hawkins said, "I have to question Morrill's judgment at this point... this calendar year we've seen a giant step backward to the days when [former head of IPT Jerold] Graber was running documentaries about sex changes and homosexuality... I don't think taxpayer dollars should be used for this purpose."

Pressure not to air the program further escalated in August when businessman Frank VanderSloot announced he would put up billboards across the state denouncing IPT and "It's Elementary." They read, "Should public television be teaching your children about the homosexual lifestyle? Think about it." He said, "Why is public TV, paid for by our tax dollars, going to show this to our families, to our children?... I'm really concerned that if this isn't stopped, a lot of little kids will watch this program and create questions they've never had, raise curiosities that they shouldn't have at those ages." VanderSloot and state officials met with the station's management in August to discuss the program and state funding for IPT. Gay and lesbian youth reportedly began a boycott of VanderSloot's company, which makes vitamins, skin-care and pet-care products, and home cleaning supplies.

Opposition also came from the grass roots. Another group, Idahoans for Responsible Public Television, emerged in August. It called on the station to delay its broadcast until greater community input could be solicited. Elk River parent Shelley McLam said, "My feeling is it's a moral issue and it needs to be taught at home." Moscow Seventh-day Adventist pastor Ray Rother agreed, saying, "As an evangelical Christian pastor, I do not believe that the gay and lesbian agenda is an issue condoned or allowed by biblical standards." Sharon Crandall wrote to the South Idaho Press, "I am not interested in using our tax money to promote a bloodbath in this country or programs targeted to brainwash our children to accept homosexuality..." Helen Synder also wrote to that paper, saying, "Most gays are well educated and wealthy, and the mainstream media is able to feed off their wealth. They are not very apt to publish anything that might hinder that cash-flow, but they are quick to defend homosexuals by promoting the perceived bigotry and homophobia." By the middle of August, 59 percent of people contacting the station opposed showing the documentary. In September, opponents held a community meeting in Jerome and urged people to contact the governor and state legislators to register their opposition.

As part of a compromise, Gov. Dirk Kempthorne got the station to air the program at 11 p.m. instead of the original time of 10 p.m., to make it more likely that children would not be watching. In explaining that decision, Kempthorne said that while he appreciated parts of the film for its message of tolerance, the approach it showed to dealing with homosexuality was not appropriate for Idaho or his own child.

"It's Elementary" aired on the scheduled date, September 7. That day, the station received 25 supportive phone calls and e-mails and 17 in opposition.

Debra Chasnoff contributed an essay about the campaign against "It's Elementary" to the 1999 edition of Hostile Climate.

Statewide: Hate crimes bill killed

The Idaho House State Affairs Committee rejected a bill that would have expanded the existing hate crimes law to include sexual orientation. Idaho's original hate crimes law was adopted in 1983, making it one of the first states to enact such a law. Religious Right activists spearheaded the effort to kill the bill, which was proposed by the Idaho Human Rights Commission. Kelly Walton of the Idaho Christian Coalition (see p. 353) asked, "Why should some victims be more important than others?" Rev. Bryan Fischer questioned whether the state should have any hate crimes laws, invoking Thomas Jefferson. Dennis Mansfield, of the Idaho Family Forum, an affiliate of Focus on the Family (see p. 355), claimed that Christian conservatives since the 1960s have supported the rights of "legitimate minorities," but that the bill was a "back-door" way to gay and lesbian acceptance. His organization opposed the bill.

Supporters of the bill pointed to recent anti-gay hate crimes and to the perception of Idaho as a home for intolerance. Leslie Goddard, director of the state Human Rights Commission, said, "A hate crime touches every potential subject of the victim's group, not just the victim." Mark Bangeter, a Boise artist, spoke before the House State Affairs Committee in January, telling legislators about how he had been beaten in front of his house because his attacker mistakenly thought he was gay. He was blinded in one eye by the attack and told committee members that he still lives in fear. "If you think you're safe, you're mistaken," he said. The head of Idaho's American Civil Liberties Union said that after coming to the defense of a gay man who was being beaten, he was struck with a baseball bat. Hewlett Packard executive Bill McGwinn told the committee that not passing the bill would send a negative message to other companies. He said that because Idaho has a reputation as a home for intolerance, he and other companies face difficulties in recruiting qualified staff. "We get the stigma of Idaho thrown in our face," he said.

Conservative committee members were not persuaded by the supporters' testimony. Rep. Jeff Altus (R) said, "It's flawed to think that something like that [an anti-gay hate crime] should have an increased penalty." State Rep. John "Bert" Stevenson (R) said that anyone voting strictly on emotion would have had to vote for the bill but that there were "other things" to consider.

The committee rejected the bill by a 14-7 vote. Committee chair state Rep. John Tippetts (R) argued that a "no" vote should not be perceived as condoning anti-gay hate crimes. "My desire is that all Idahoans deserve equal protection from the law," he said. Tippetts also claimed that the 1983 bill would probably fail it if were proposed now. Rep. Bill Deal offered a mixed message, after voting for the bill: "Certainly, I don't condone the gay or lesbian lifestyle. But I don't think people in Idaho have to live in fear. We don't have to have a reputation for bigotry and hate."

Religious Right activists vowed to target the bill's three Republican supporters in their next elections. Supporters of the legislation, however, vowed to continue pressing its passage.

Boise: Attempt to ban book

In November, the Idaho Family Forum publicized a letter it had written to the library board at the Ada Community Library in Boise asking it to remove "Daddy's Rommate" from the collection or at least keep it away from children. John Elliot, the library's new executive director, said that effort was prompted by a parent who complained that she had found the book on the floor of the library. "The Ada Community Library should respect the right of parents to choose the time they believe is most appropriate to discuss with their children the issue of human sexuality generally, and homosexuality specifically," the letter read. "We are concerned that the subject matter of this book is not in line with the traditional family values that parents are trying to teach their kids throughout the state of Idaho." Parent Stephanie Howard requested that the book be moved to the adult section as well. Her husband, Brian, said, "This is not politically motivated." Library Director Dian Hoffpauir said the book is shelved in the youth services nonfiction section and not with youth picture books. The library's board voted 3-1 to keep the book in its current section.

Boise: Diversity conference condemned

Religious Right activists assailed a business conference designed to celebrate corporate diversity. A coalition of businesses and the Boise Area Chamber of Commerce sponsored the event to promote corporate diversity in February. The Idaho Family Forum spearheaded an opposition campaign, claiming the event was a covert effort to endorse homosexuality. Dennis Mansfield, then the group's executive director, said, "This is a gay and lesbian issue and they're masking it under minority status using a hero to do it." Colin Powell was the keynote speaker at the conference. Mansfield cited Hewlett Packard's support for a recent hate crimes bill applicable to anti-gay violence as evidence of the company's pro-gay agenda. Hewlett Packard was one of the main sponsors of the conference.

Mansfield warned that the Forum would launch a radio and television ad campaign against the conference and sponsored its own speaker. "Somebody had to speak up... We're a conservative, faith-based state, and homosexuality is a lifestyle that's not accepted here," Mansfield said. Alveda King, a niece of Martin Luther King Jr. known for her opposition to gay and lesbian rights, spoke on what she contends is the difference between anti-gay discrimination and race-based discrimination. King claimed that gay men and lesbians do not deserve legal protections against discrimination and violence directed at them. She told the crowd, "Gay members of society have never been told as a class and a group, 'Sit on the back of the bus, you can't vote, you cannot buy property.' "

Hewlett Packard, which employs thousands of people in Boise, denied Mansfield's allegations. "We're certainly not attempting to focus on the gay-lesbian issue or any other issue for that matter," a company spokesperson said. Other business leaders supported the conference, saying that Idaho's image as a refuge for hate groups hinders their ability to recruit top-quality employees.

Elk City: Community center opposed

Opponents sought to derail plans for a community center in part out of an asserted fear that it would attract gay men and lesbians and teenagers seeking abortions. Organizers proposed an $800,000 community education and performing arts center to be built with money from a variety of state and national grants and donations. But Rev. Robert Heitzman, pastor of the Church at Elk City, said that because the center would be built on public land, the town would not be able to restrict access to it. "Whenever there is something like this presented to the public, then it's open to every person in the U.S... Our government is pushing this, and I just feel it in my bones the homosexuals would be using it as a performing arts center to put on a show." In elaborating on why he opposed the center, Heitzman said he feared that gay men and lesbians would recruit local youth: "They [gay men and lesbians] will use that [the center], I'm sure, to go in there and put on some sort of a play that would encourage young people to take up their lifestyle." Heitzman also said that if the center were built on school proper-

> "They will use [the center] ... to go in there and put on some sort of a play that would encourage young people to take up their lifestyle."
>
> — Rev. Robert Heitzma, pastor of an Idaho church, expressing opposition to a community center because it would be open to gays.

ty "socially it will be worthless to the community" because people would not be allowed to drink, smoke, or have guns. Mike Edmondson, another opponent, and Heitzman claimed the project never had local support. Dolores Chandler, a local resident, drew up a petition signed by 132 people who also opposed the center for a variety of reasons.

Supporters of the center said the opponents continually changed the reasons behind their opposition, never allowing them to be fully addressed. "Since their reasons changed, it would be nice to know the real reason they're opposed to it," said Ian Barlow, a national forest ranger and center supporter. "We've tried really hard to work out some of those differences… " Susan Borowicz, principal of the Elk City School, said that students would benefit from the center's hands-on learning programs and be able to help plan a system of wilderness trails around the proposed center.

Nampa: Attempt to move or ban books

Conservative citizens and Religious Right activists called on a public library to remove children's books that dealt with homosexuality. The controversy started when two Nampa residents requested that their public library move "Daddy's Roommate" and "Heather Has Two Mommies" from the children's picture book section to the adult section in June. The books, geared for elementary and school children, portray examples of life in gay and lesbian households. Yvonne Buus, one of the residents who filed a formal complaint, said, "This is an adult subject placed in the children's section… If people want to check them out, I have no problem with that. But they don't belong in reach of my children." Gretchen Gardner, owner of a local bookstore, claimed that library officials responded to the objections by making access to the complaint forms difficult. "Several people had a great deal of trouble trying to [locate] the form. Then they were told they would have to make an appointment, or to not worry, others were filling out the form." Gardner collected almost 600 signatures on a petition asking the library to move the books. She also withdrew her store's support for a summer reading program at the library, saying "I can't understand why these are in the preschool section instead of under parenting, in the adult section." Other supporters of moving the books made phone calls and sent e-mail to the library staff. An ad hoc group, Nampa Citizens for Parental Rights, formed to organize support for the books' removal from the children's section.

Responding to the criticism, library officials moved both books to the juvenile nonfiction section. Katy Curl, the youth services librarian, said the library's Board of Trustees made the move "in the spirit of compromise." However, Buus felt that decision was inadequate. She wanted the books placed in the adult section. "I just don't think they're appropriate in the children's section at all. They both address adult material." Library Director Karen Ganske responded, "We are responsible to the taxpayers of this community… We're trying to determine what role is appropriate for someone who does not carry a card from this library or does not live in Nampa."

Although the first complaints focused on moving the books, opposition to the library's policy quickly shifted to calling for an outright ban on "Daddy's Roommate" and "Heather Has Two Mommies." Resident Dan Willey said that would be the only solution to the dispute. "It's inconsistent with ethics for a public institution to promote an illegal activity. While sodomy is illegal, why are we teaching our children to be acceptable of that lifestyle?"

Activists for the Religious Right also lined up to oppose the library's actions. Dennis Mansfield, then head of the Idaho Family Forum, a Focus on the Family (see p. 355) affiliate, said nearly 1,000 people had signed another petition to restrict the library's open access policy. The petition also requested the creation of an advisory committee on controversial books and an adult-only section where children would need parental permission to browse. "Our observation has been that the [library's] policy does not match the way Canyon County or Nampa have traditionally believed," Mansfield said. "Now, because of a culturally elite attitude, we're supposed to allow the library board to let first-, second-, and third-graders have access to this material." His group's executive administrator, Teresa Kidwell, claimed that any book discussing homosexuality was inappropriate for children. The Forum held a news conference with the citizens group to announce their joint effort at changing the library's policies.

The Idaho Christian Coalition (see p. 353), which Mansfield helped found, mailed a survey to 22,000 citizens in July seeking their input on the issue. Coalition officials said their members overwhelmingly opposed the library's actions. "I haven't seen anything like this," said Mansfield, who by October had declared his candidacy for the seat occupied by retiring U.S. Rep. Helen Chenoweth-Hage. The survey also questioned recipients' views restricting the library's Internet access.

A group of people opposed to the attacks on the library held a rally in July as a show of support. About 25 residents gathered at the Nampa Public Library in support of the staff. Barbara Watkins, a library supporter, said, "We all use the library. We support the library in its decision [not to remove the book] and object to censorship and someone else telling me and my children what we can and cannot read." Dan Willey, who wanted the books removed, interrupted a speaker at the rally, saying, "They [the books] cover a homosexual topic. The only one who could benefit is a pedophile."

> "They cover a homosexual topic. The only one who could benefit [from reading them] is a pedophile."
>
> — Nampa resident Dan Willey, arguing against having gay-themed books in the public library.

Elected officials quickly became involved in the controversy. In June, several City Council members said they supported the effort to move the books to the adult section. The next month, with only one dissenter, the council sent a letter to the library's board suggesting the books be moved from the children's section. In August, Mayor Maxine Horn appointed a City Council member to the library's board as a liaison and asked the library to hold a town meeting to address the issue and to form an ad hoc committee of citizens from both sides to make recommendations. The liaison position had previously been left vacant. But the trustee board turned down Horn's request to hold a town hall meeting, saying it would inflame rather than quell passions on both sides of the issue. The City Council later voted to withhold $50,000 in library funding until the library put Internet filters on its public computers, simplified the patron complaint procedures, and provided parents with more information about what their children check out of the library.

ILLINOIS

Statewide: Non-discrimination bill defeated

The Illinois Legislature rejected a bill that would have prohibited various types of discrimination based on sexual orientation. Sponsored by state Rep. Larry McKeon and supported by Gov. George Ryan and the Illinois Federation for Human Rights, a statewide gay and lesbian rights group, the bill would have prohibited discrimination based on sexual orientation in housing, employment and public accommodations with few exceptions. Supporters had secured initial bipartisan support for the bill. Although it prohibits hate crimes, Illinois does not protect gay men and lesbians from employment and housing discrimination.

> "Giving protected status to homosexuals grants protections that some other groups, smokers for instance, do not enjoy."
>
> — Karen Hayes, Illinois director for Concerned Women for America, opposing a bill in the state legislature that would have protected gay men and lesbians from discrimination.

Critics outside the legislature claimed the bill amounted to "special rights" legislation for gay men and lesbians. Karen Hayes, the state director of Concerned Women for America (see p. 354), claimed the bill lends government credibility to homosexual activity. She claimed that giving protected status to homosexuals confers on them rights that some other groups, smokers for instance, do not enjoy. She said, "We see this, certainly, as an attack on the family. The attempt to normalize homosexual behavior, in our view, undermines traditional families with a mom and dad."

Republican predictions of an uphill battle proved true. State Rep. Terry Parke (R) said, "I don't tolerate discrimination, but we have a constitution that is very clear… That ought to be enough." House Republican leader Lee Daniels echoed those statements. State Rep. Cal Skinner (R) told a reporter that passing the bill "would be enabling an addiction" that kills people by transmitting AIDS. The House defeated the measure by one vote, 57-59, with one abstention.

After the vote, the McHenry County Human Relations Council demanded that two state representatives from that county explain their votes against the measure. State Reps. Jack Franks and Cal Skinner both turned down the opportunity to respond. Members of the McHenry County Board, which created the Human Relations Council, said that body had overstepped its mandate in demanding an explanation from the legislators. Board member Donald Brewer said that if the council had consulted the board it would have praised the legislators' no votes. Board member John Jung said, "We do have to remind [the Human Relations Council] once in a while that they can't get carried away."

Champaign County: Hate crimes resolution

Despite significant opposition, the Champaign County Board of Supervisors adopted a resolution in November condemning hate crimes, including those based on sexual orientation. The resolution was proposed after a Fourth of July shooting spree by avowed racist and homophobe Benjamin Smith, whose rampage left two people dead and eight wounded. One of his victims, Steven Kuo, was shot in the leg in Urbana. In response, a "Stop the Hate" march from Urbana to Champaign was held in October, calling for an end to hate crimes, including those based on sexual orientation, and demanding the Board of Supervisors issue a resolution condemning them. At that time, the board considered but tabled the measure.

When the board took up the measure again in November, board member Joan Dykstra said that she would not vote for a resolution that made gay men and lesbians "a special class of victims." She said she believed the resolution would restrict the right to free speech for heterosexuals. Board member Scott Tapley agreed. "In Canada, believe it or not, it is a hate crime to say anything bad or negative against homosexuality." Tapley said, "It's destroying freedom of speech there." Supervisors Dave Johnson and Stu Trumbo voted in favor of the resolution reluctantly. Johnson expressed his discomfort with a resolution that mentions sexual orientation, and Trumbo said the resolution would accomplish nothing. However, Supervisor Teresa Miles said the opposition and reluctance to support the resolution was the product of homophobia. She received numerous letters filled with anti-gay sentiments. Referring to the letters, she said, "There's a word for this. This is hate."

The resolution passed by a 15-10 vote, making Champaign County the last area targeted during the July shooting spree to approve a measure condemning hate crimes.

Champaign: "Hell House" features AIDS patient

The Curtis Road Church of God organized a Hell House for Halloween, depicting images of Hell. One scene featured a young man in a casket, dying of AIDS. Another showed a woman after a botched abortion. The church used a nationally distributed package for conducting Hell Houses, which had included a same-sex wedding, having adapted some of the scenes. The original package features a gay couple whose honeymoon bed is replaced by a hospital bed because one of the spouses has died of an AIDS-related illness. Curtis Road modified that package by eliminating the same-sex wedding and removing explicit condemnation of the AIDS patient's homosexuality. The skit did express how the victim's friends and family abandoned him. In addition, an actor playing Satan guided guests through the scenes.

Human rights activists condemned the event. Sandy Sexton, who works at Outpost, a local gay and lesbian community center, said that the Hell House "has hate crime written all over it." Ruth Wyman of the National Organization for Women, said, "the idea that because you're gay or had an abortion means that you're going to hell is radical and uncaring, and not mainstream Christianity." The production ran for four days, ending on Halloween night.

Chicago: Anti-lesbian judge

In February and again in March, Cook County Circuit Court Judge Susan McDunn tried to invalidate a court's ruling that granted adoptions to two lesbian couples. In 1998, McDunn disrupted normal adoption procedures for two unnamed lesbian couples because she said no one questioned the suitability of lesbians' raising the children in question. During those proceedings, she tried to award the Family Research Council (see p. 355) second guardianship of one couple's child, disclosing the names of the parents to that group. Presiding Judge Francis Barth removed McDunn from the cases, admonishing her for her bias, and assigned her to traffic court in September 1998. That winter, Barth also invalidated McDunn's earlier rulings and granted the parents the adoptions. Although she had been removed from family court, McDunn sought to circumvent her superior's authority in February and March of 1999 and issued orders from the traffic court voiding her own removal from the case and declaring the adoptions invalid. At that time, McDunn also moved to bring in the Family Research Council, which until then had had no involvement with the case.

An appeals court finally settled the matter in June 1999, having issued a ruling from the bench. Not only did three Illinois appeals court judges invalidate McDunn's ruling by affirming the adoptions, Justice Martin Zwick apologized to the parents on behalf of himself and the two other justices. Zwick called McDunn's rulings "an inexcusable injustice," and said McDunn had exhibited "predetermined bias against lesbians" and brought discredit to the judiciary. The court admonished Judge McDunn in July when it issued its written opinion. At that time, the state Judicial Inquiry Board had begun investigating McDunn's activities related to her rulings in this matter. The Chief Judge of the Circuit Court of Cook County placed McDunn on inactive status, having already been barred from hearing cases in traffic court.

> ## "Punch 64, Don't Vote for the Whore."
>
> — A sign in a van opposing Chicago Alderman Helen Shiller, a lesbian who successfully ran for re-election.

Chicago: Campaign against Helen Shiller

Zealous supporters of Saundra Reed, a Democratic primary candidate for alderman in Chicago's north Lakefront district, engaged in several anti-gay campaign tactics on election day in February. Reed was running against incumbent Alderman Helen Shiller.

Witnesses spotted a van with Reed's campaign signs driving through the district filled with people yelling, "Fags Love Shiller" and "Windy City Times Loves Shiller" to people on the streets. The Windy City Times is one of Chicago's gay and lesbian newspapers. The van also had signs calling Shiller a "queen" and a "poverty pimp." Activist Larry Ligas, who claimed to work for the Reed campaign, had used those labels for Shiller during the campaign. Another van was also seen ferrying people from Uptown Baptist Church, well-known for its anti-gay activity and where Reed is a member, to the polls. Saundra Reed's campaign renounced any connection with these tactics and denied Ligas was part of its operation. Reed's gay supporters claim she is not homophobic. One supporter said that she backs same-sex marriages. Yet another van sported a sign that read, "Punch 64, Don't Vote for the Whore." That number referred to the position that another challenger, Cindi Anderson, had on the ballot.

Shiller defeated Reed in a primary runoff election in April to become the party nominee and eventually was re-elected.

Chicago: Campaign against Lorna Brett

Republican ward committeeman John Curry tried to stir up anti-gay sentiment with a homophobic mailing in February that attacked a candidate for city alderman. Although the race took place during a nonpartisan election in which candidates run without the official support of political parties, partisanship still factored into the contest. The letter Curry sent claimed challenger Lorna Brett supported "pro-radical gay rights" and "a radical feminist agenda." Curry sent the letter to 700 registered Republican households to encourage them to vote for Brett's opponent, incumbent Alderman Theodore Matlak. The district, Ward 32, is heavily Democratic, one of Chicago's most diverse, and encompasses several largely gay neighborhoods. Matlak had never cultivated ties to gay or lesbian groups. He had previously referred to local anti-discrimination laws that protected gay men and lesbians as "special protections."

Though Matlak said he had no knowledge of the mailing and did not agree with it, Curry told a local reporter that he and Matlak had financed the mailing and that Matlak was well aware of it. Brett accused Matlak of engaging in "the politics of hate," saying, "Mr. Matlak did not have the courage to stand by his political attack… He is running a divisive campaign."

Matlak won the election with 54 percent of the vote.

Chicago: Controversy over gay-themed documentary

Although a Dallas-based gay and lesbian church paid for a program to air on a Chicago cable television station, the management of WGN decided initially not to broadcast it. The Cathedral of Hope, the nation's largest predominantly gay and lesbian church, signed a contract with WGN to broadcast its documentary "Holy Homosexuals," which affirms the role of gay men and lesbians in Christianity and declares that God loves all people regardless of their sexual orientation. WGN pulled the program without explanation days before it was set to be broadcast. The Cathedral of Hope sued for breach of contract. WGN settled out of court and agreed to broadcast the program in April. Church officials agreed to change the program's name to "Cathedral of Hope." Although the Cathedral of Hope tried to broadcast the program on television stations across the country, WGN was the only television outlet that agreed to air the program.

Chicago: Controversy over training film

Efforts to have Chicago school officials show Debra Chasnoff's award-winning film "It's Elementary: Talking About Gay Issues in School" to school principals and teachers sparked a controversy in the weeks leading up the start of fall classes. According to press reports, Blondean Davis, chief of school operations, agreed to show the film at a training session for school principals on diversity and anti-harassment issues. Mary Morten, the mayor's liaison to the gay community, said officials also agreed to allow teachers at individual schools to see the documentary, which features discussions of homosexuality in elementary schools across the country, if they wanted to view it. Chicago public schools Chief Executive Officer Paul Vallas rescinded the plan and denied that he or Davis ever intended to show the film to principals or teachers. Vallas did note that the film had been shown to counselors and crisis intervention specialists within the school system and that it would be made available to principals who wanted to show the video to teachers in their school. Vallas said he objected to making it mandatory that school principals view the film, saying, "We have very few instances that warrant the use of this tape." He accused Morten, of "making this up as she goes along," referring to her claim that Vallas and others had agreed to show the video to all principals. Morten had previously conducted general training on protecting gay and lesbian students from harassment. Eva Nickolich, a regional education officer, said she may have made a mistake if she had agreed to show the film. "I may have said that and I didn't mean it... She caught me when I was tired," she said.

Although Chicago Mayor Richard Daley said that he saw nothing wrong with the film, Valles' operating plan remained in effect.

Debra Chasnoff contributed an essay about the campaign against "It's Elementary" to the 1999 edition of Hostile Climate.

Chicago: Epithets shouted from bus

After enduring months of being called "faggot" and other anti-gay epithets, an employee and a customer of the Brown Elephant secondhand store halted a school bus carrying several students who had been yelling the epithets. In April, Bill Salek, a store employee, said the students yelled, "Hey, you AIDS-infected four-eyed faggot behind the cash register," and he ran out to stop the school bus from the Louis Nettelhorst Grammar School. Salek and a customer, Tim Boisvert, got in front of the bus to prevent it from leaving the scene. Then Salek attempted to board the bus while Boisvert remained in front of it. Before Salek could board, the bus driver, who, according to Salek, appeared sympathetic to the students, lurched the vehicle forward, Salek claimed, to frighten him and Boisvert out of the way. Salek said he reported the students' harassment to the driver, who, according to Salek, was unreceptive to the complaints. The police officers arrived quickly and ordered the driver off the bus. Salek and Boisvert said the officer told the driver that that he was facilitating a hate crime.

Unsatisfied, Salek called school Principal Cynthia Dougal to complain. Although Salek said he had twice last year written letters to the principal complaining of the harassment, Dougal claimed to be unaware of the harassment. This time, she responded, meeting with local gay and lesbian activists and law enforcement officials later in April. Dougal said that the school would implement educational programs that encompassed sexual orientation discrimination and harassment.

Chicago:
Lesbian allegedly fired for commitment ceremony

Officials at the Cook County Jail fired a lesbian correctional officer in July 1999 following her participation in a same-sex commitment ceremony with an inmate. The officer, Lynn Harper, and female inmate Jacqueline Montanez reportedly exchanged wedding rings in July 1997, and Harper was suspended without pay the following December. Prison officials accused Harper of violating jail regulations that prohibit correctional officers from fraternizing with inmates. Harper denies those allegations, saying they come from a "snitch," who lied about her relationship with Montanez. Harper claims jail officials wanted to fire her because she is a lesbian and that they conspired with the inmate to have a basis for that firing. Harper has sued the jail, seeking to be reinstated to her job and to receive back pay and benefits. At press time, the Cook County Circuit Court had not ruled on her case.

Chicago: Lesbian mother denied visitation rights

A three-judge panel of a state appeals court denied a lesbian mother's right to visit the daughter she had raised with her former partner. The ruling held that the appeals court lacked the legal authority to establish visitation rights, thereby affirming the ruling of a lower state court, which held that "Amanda," as the non-biological mother was identified in court records, had no legal standing to make such a claim. For four years, Amanda and her former partner "Helen" had raised a child to whom Helen had given birth through artificial insemination. After their breakup, Helen married a man and eliminated all contact between Amanda and their daughter. Attorneys for Amanda claimed she was a "common law parent" with many of the primary responsibilities for raising her daughter. The court disagreed, even though in 1996 it had awarded visitation rights to a man who mistakenly thought he was the biological father of his unmarried female partner's daughter. In Amanda's case, the court held that the state legislature must determine the visitation rights of non-biological gay and lesbian parents. Heather Sawyer, an attorney for the Lambda Legal Defense and Education Fund who represented Amanda, said, "The court has abdicated its responsibility to look out for this child's best interest, abandoning its historic role of protecting relationships that fall outside statutory definitions."

Chicago: Restaurant accused of ignoring theft

A Chicago gay man who was assaulted at a Checkers restaurant in August said employees there ignored his pleas for help. Steven Schering, the victim, said the workers refused to contact the police or to intervene as three attackers tried to steal his wallet. Schering was hurt during the attack. In September, Chicago gay and lesbian activists led by the Chicago Anti-Bashing Network staged a series of protests. Checkers employees yelled anti-gay insults at the protesters. Recalling the attack, one worker said he wished he could "beat [Schering's] fag ass myself." The protesters also targeted a local police station whose officers they claim were unresponsive after arriving at the scene. In addition to the protest, they called for a boycott of the entire Checkers chain.

Cook County: Domestic partner benefits policy opposed

Over the objections of determined opponents, the Cook County Board of Commissioners extended family benefits to the domestic partners of county employees. Commissioner Mike Quigley, whose district encompasses several gay and lesbian neighborhoods in Chicago, introduced the proposal in January. At a hearing two months later, several citizens opposed the plan because they believed it endorsed homosexuality.

Much of the opposition came from within the commission. Board member Carl Hansen argued that the proposal would force taxpayers to subsidize a lifestyle that many people find abhorrent: "If someone has a particular lifestyle and that's the way they want to live, that's not a concern of the taxpayers," he said. Hansen claimed the proposal was also ripe for abuse because he assumed there was no way to verify a recipient's relationship to a county employee. He attempted to delay consideration of the proposal by proposing to hold public hearings. Commissioners, fearing the plan would create a "traveling circus," defeated it after a series of shouting matches between several of its members. During a March hearing, several citizens representing religious groups continued to express their opposition to the proposal. They referred to homosexuality as "immoral" and "ungodly." The proposal passed by a three-vote margin, with six of the board's 17 members voting it and two members voting "present."

Des Plaines: Families evicted from religious campground

A campground affiliated with the United Methodist Church tried to expel a family for its support of a gay couple who had been banned from the campground without explanation the previous year. The conflict started at the end of the summer of 1998 when officials at the United Methodist Historic Campground told a gay couple, Bob Carroll and Russell Elenz, that they would not be allowed to rent a cottage at the campground again. Carroll is the son of a Methodist minister and certified lay speaker for the church, and Elenz works for a Methodist agency. At the end of that summer, William and Nannette Graham, who had befriended the couple, wrote a letter to the campground's officials in which they criticized the campground's action against Carroll and Elenz. The Grahams also told officials that they would host the couple in their cottage. The Grahams' 16-year-old daughter posted signs in their cottage at the campground reading, "Gays and lesbians, bisexuals, and transgenders, welcome" and called their home a "reconciling" cottage, a reference to a group of Methodists who affirm the place of gay men and lesbians in the church.

In June 1999, the campground's management, the Chicago District Camp Ground Association, wrote the Grahams a letter telling them that because they violated the "privilege of ownership of a cottage," they would be evicted. The letter read, "The sign displayed in your cottage windows incites conflict and inhibits [the] harmonious environment of the campground." The campground, which operates much like a condominium or townhouse association, in which owners are subject to bylaws established by an owners group, ordered the Grahams out in less than a week. The campground also began proceedings to revoke the Graham's ownership rights and planned to change the locks to keep them out.

The Grahams' response caused an uproar within the camp. They chained the doors to their cottage, changed the locks, and posted notices that anyone entering their property would be trespassing. Nannette Graham said, "This is a bigger issue than gay or lesbian rights to us. We would have taken a stand for anyone's civil rights." Reportedly fearing media coverage unfavorable to the campground, the association chained shut the entrance gates to the campground and barred the media from entering the property, permitting only campers to enter. The pastor of the Grahams' church, Rev. B.J. Birkhan-Romelfanger, said, "I'm horrified that the campground would be treating anyone this way." The Northern Illinois Conference of the United Methodist Church stepped in to mediate the dispute, holding a hearing at which both sides presented their cases.

Campers barricaded the entrance gates once again in August when about 30 Methodist clergy and parishioners staged a protest against the campground's discriminatory practices. Protest organizers said they were shocked at the level of hostility they their protest faced. "The very fact that they would bar the gates to the Methodist clergy is very offensive," Rev. Judith Kelsy-Powell said. The protesters had hoped to attend a campground association meeting to register their disgust with the ordeal.

In August, both families filed complaints with the Cook County Commission on Human Rights. The Grahams' complaint sought an injunction against the campground's effort to revoke their ownership rights of their cabin at the campground. The complaint also sought an unspecified amount of damages. The complaint filed by Carroll and Elenz claims that the campground discriminated against them on the basis of sexual orientation on two occasions — when it canceled a church service because Carroll had been scheduled to speak and when it told them that they would not be allowed to rent a cottage at the campground again. Carroll and Elenz also claim that other families at the campground harassed them by walking around their cabin reciting passages from the Bible in an effort to convert them to heterosexuality. According to Carroll, one of the campground's trustees called him a pedophile. Their complaint sought $500 a day for each day the prohibition continued and damages for lost vacation time and emotional distress. Kenneth Dobbs, an attorney for Carroll and Elenz, said, "I just don't understand any longer, in this day and age, why somebody wants to punish someone because of their sexual orientation."

The campground denied all the charges of discrimination. In a written statement, officials said that the Chicago District Campground Association "does not discriminate against anyone. We welcome all, regardless of race, gender, national background or sexual or other practices." But they added, "Unfortunately, some persons have tried to use the campground for political purposes or to advance agendas other than spiritual." The campground's attorney, John Juergensmeyer, would not explain precisely why Carroll and Elenz have not been allowed back at the facility. He did say that the discrimination charges are pointless because of the religious exemption in Cook County's non-discrimination ordinance.

In September, the Commission on Human Rights found that the campground had discriminated against the Grahams, and, in accordance with Cook County law, referred their case to the Cook County Circuit Court. The commission also petitioned that court for a temporary injunction prohibiting the campground from evicting the Grahams while the suit is pending. The commission said it would wait for a decision on that petition before ruling on the complaint filed by Carroll and Elenz.

In November, an executive committee of the Northern Illinois Conference of the United Methodist Church concluded that the campground had violated the social principles of the Methodist Church and cultivated a "pervasive atmosphere of intolerance and inhospitality" in its actions against the Grahams and Carroll and Elenz. The Conference asked the campground to remove the church's name, insignia, and logo from its property. Juergensmeyer called the committee's findings "totally inaccurate" and claimed it was swayed by media. "This has become a media circus rather than a truth-seeking forum," he said.

In December, Cook County Judge Thomas P. Durkin dismissed the Grahams' petition for an injunction to stop the campground from revoking their ownership rights. Judge Durkin ruled that granting an injunction against the eviction would violate the campground's First Amendment rights. Ken Dobbs, an attorney for Carroll and Elenz, said that Judge Durkin wrongly reasoned that the Methodists' Book of Discipline condones discrimination against gay men and lesbians. Shortly after Judge Durkin issued the ruling, the Grahams were evicted from their cottage. The Human Rights Commission filed a motion with the Circuit Court to reconsider Judge Durkin's ruling. The court granted that motion thus prohibiting the campground from selling the Grahams' cottage and disposing of its contents. At press time, however, the Grahams remain evicted and the commission was still deliberating on the complaints brought by Carroll and Elenz against the campground.

Downers Grove: Methodist minister suspended

A United Methodist trial court convicted Rev. Gregory Dell of performing a same-sex commitment ceremony in 1998. Finding him guilty of "the offense of disobedience to the Order and Discipline" of the denomination in March 1999, the church originally sentenced him to an indefinite suspension. The church's sentence, scheduled to begin in July, prohibited him from practicing his ministry, ordered him out of his pastoral home, and revoked his $35,000 annual salary until he signed a pledge not to violate the church's ban on the blessing of same-sex commitment ceremonies. Dell was not, however, stripped of his ordination as a minister.

Dell vowed to continue his affirming ministries and filed an appeal in April 1999. "I will never sign such a pledge. That would be a violation of what I believe the spirit of God and all these people signify," he said. In June, the Northern Illinois Annual Conference of the United Methodist Church selected him as a local delegate to the denomination's national convention in 2000. However, in September, a Methodist appeals court upheld his original conviction but modified his sentence to a one-year suspension. The Broadway United Methodist Church allowed Dell and his wife to continue living in its parsonage and created a special position for him heading In All Things Charity, an organization committed to expanding the Methodists' ministry to gay men and lesbians.

Urbana: Attacks on "It's Elementary"

The Religious Right attacked a television station's broadcast of the award-winning documentary "It's Elementary: Talking About Gay Issues in School," by Debra Chasnoff. The film features discussions of homosexuality in elementary schools across the country. The Illinois Family Institute (see p. 355) targeted public television station WILL when it decided to broadcast the film. The institute's director of legislative research, Virginia Nurmi, called the film an "artful piece of propaganda" that appeals to emotions rather than facts. She also disputed statistics showing high levels of gay teen suicide. Nurmi maintains that homosexuality is a chosen orientation and, therefore, should not be tolerated in schools. "We don't do special videotapes or pride days on abusive families or on alcohol abuse in families. Because we don't talk about them or those types of families, does it make those children feel bad?" she asked. Nurmi claimed that gay and lesbian teachers featured in the film encourage heterosexual school children to change their orientation. She also claimed the film forces children who are not attracted to others of the opposite sex to question their sexuality. WILL station manager Ellis Broomberg noted several letters the station received condemning its decision to broadcast "It's Elementary."

The station drew further criticism when it elected not to also air "Suffer the Children," a video produced by the American Family Association (see p. 352) that claims "It's Elementary" is a recruiting tool for gay men and lesbians. "Suffer the Children" also claims that teaching tolerance for sexual diversity in schools is immoral and implies that gay teachers are often pedophiles and features extensive clips from "It's Elementary" that were never authorized. The station said the "Suffer the Children" was an ineffective rebuttal of "It's Elementary." Conservative groups around the state urged WILL to air "Suffer the Children."

In response to those requests, the station hosted a program featuring supporters and detractors of both films.

Debra Chasnoff contributed an essay about the campaign against "It's Elementary" to the 1999 edition of Hostile Climate.

Union: Transgendered employee asked to resign

The Board of Directors of the Illinois Railroad Museum asked a transgendered woman to resign in November. At a meeting that month, Julie Ann "Jim" Johnson officially came out as a transgendered woman to the museum's board of directors. She had always presented herself as a male while on the job as president of the museum and said she would continue to do so. Johnson said the board quickly asked her to resign. She contends that several board members had already known about her struggles with gender identity. Johnson was reportedly the largest donor to the museum as well as a longtime volunteer.

Johnson sent a scathing letter of resignation to the board. "That some of you are uncomfortable with me I cannot help. Nor can I help that you are not possessed with enough tolerance for individual differences or respect for me as a person to judge me on the merits of my performance rather than on my gender." She said, "The board has today given in to the basest kind of undiluted prejudice," and warned board members that society would not stand for their intolerance much longer.

Western Springs: Support withdrawn from "outed" nominee

Three days after the local president of the Western Springs chapter of the American Association of University Women nominated a respected retired professor, whose name has been withheld, to the position of co-president, the acting president rescinded her support when she discovered the candidate was a lesbian. The acting president said the candidate's sexual orientation was "too controversial," though the nominee said she was only "out" to one other AAUW official. The candidate complained to the state and national presidents of the AAUW that she had been discriminated against because she is a lesbian.

Those officials supported her claim and reaffirmed the organization's opposition to discrimination based on sexual orientation. Saying that she felt "isolated and suspected," the candidate withdrew her nomination. "If they treat me like this, how do they treat their gay and lesbian sons and daughters?" she asked.

Wheaton: Exodus Ministries conference

Exodus International, a federation of so-called "ex-gay" ministries, staged its most successful conference ever in July. The conference took place at Wheaton College, an evangelical Protestant school outside Chicago, and was attended by more than 1,000 people who profess to have left homosexuality behind. Presbyterian minister Bob Davies, the organization's director, hailed the conference as a success. He announced that "a whole new chapter has opened for Exodus" because of the group's visibility since its anti-gay "Truth in Love" campaign began in 1998. That campaign spread the group's message that gay men and lesbians can and should change their sexual orientation and become straight through religious devotion. Founded in 1976, Exodus maintains that "freedom from homosexuality is possible through repentance and faith in Jesus Christ."

Exodus' growth and visibility have skyrocketed since hitting a plateau in the early 1990s. Renewed outreach to religious media and newly-formed alliances with the Religious Right have reinvigorated Exodus' message. The organization began publishing numerous stories about how its members have renounced their homosexuality through religious devotion and began promoting its message through speaking engagements. In 1995, Exodus started sponsoring "National Coming Out of Homosexuality Day" along with other right-wing organizations. The "Truth In Love" campaign in 1998 ran in several major newspapers and on television stations across the country,

> "The board has today given in to the basest kind of undiluted prejudice."
>
> — Julie Ann "Jim" Johnson, in a letter to the Board of Directors of the Illinois Railroad Museum. The board fired her as museum president after she came out as a transgendered woman.

directing the attention of news outlets to its anti-gay message. Press reports of the 1999 conference followed up on that coverage.

Reporters from several national wire services and daily newspapers detailed the messages and instructions given at the conference, including a new project intended to prove scientifically that sexual orientation can be changed. Panelists reportedly trained attendees on changing their orientation through religion. Participants listened to testimonials from members who claimed to have changed their sexual orientation. At one panel, John Paulk, chairman of the Exodus board of directors and self-proclaimed "ex-gay," said that he feared using psychological conversion, a practice some speakers had advocated. He said counselors risked losing their certification and licenses to practice. "The gay lobby is so powerful, much more than we are, that it could happen," Paulk said. Amy Tracy, who works with Paulk at Focus on the Family (see p. 355) and another "ex-gay," agreed, saying, "The gay activist community is very threatened by Exodus." She went on to tout the importance of "ex-gay" ministries. "[The gay] civil rights campaign is based on the belief that homosexuality is immutable. Yet people have changed. We are here." Increased press coverage helped conference organizers almost double the number of participants at this conference over the previous one.

Members of the Metropolitan Community Church of Incarnation led a protest of about 50 people. One member, Cynthia Marquardt, denied that sexual conversion is possible. She said, "We're putting the Religious Right on notice we are not going to stand by silently and listen to rhetoric that has endangered the lives of innocent people... They are nice people, but their attitude and behavior are so dangerous to our community."

Statewide: Anti-gay adoption bill

The state legislature considered a bill that would have prohibited gay men and lesbians from serving as foster parents or adopting children who were in the state's custody. Conservative Republicans and Religious Right activists united in support of the measure. Similar bills were introduced in both houses of the legislature in January, but only the Senate version made it out of committee. Rep. Woody Burton (R), author of the House bill, said, "A person's lifestyle is their own business, it is not my job to judge that, but my concern is that it puts children who are already at risk at an even higher risk because of discrimination." He claimed that children adopted by gay men and lesbians face social chastisement because of the discrimination against their adoptive parents. Burton said he was motivated by a case in which the state awarded permanent custody of three children, who had been temporarily placed with a heterosexual couple, to a gay couple. Burton, the author of the 1997 bill that prohibited the state from recognizing same-sex marriages, claimed that married, heterosexual couples are the best role models for adopted children.

The Christian Coalition of Indiana (see p. 353), the Indiana Family Institute, an affiliate of James Dobson's Focus on Family (see p. 355), and Advance America all supported a legislative agenda that included the proposed adoption prohibition and defeat of a hate crimes bill that included sexual orientation. Eric Miller, head of Advance America, a coalition of 3,400 conservative churches in the state, said, "We believe it is in the best interest of children to be raised in a traditional family setting." Micah Clark, director of public policy for the Indiana Family Institute, wrote a guest column for the Indianapolis Star in which he cited statistics allegedly proving that children raised by gay parents were more likely to be gay or lesbian. Saying that "Homosexual couples do not provide a stable environment for children," he claimed that such unions last an average of three years and that gay men and lesbians die younger "in part due to disease, suicide, promiscuity, and drug usage."

Some state government officials opposed the adoption prohibition. The state's Family and Social Services Agencies said it was unnecessary. A spokesperson for Gov. Frank O'Bannon said, "[T]he law is geared so that the decisions are made locally and are geared to each specific case... The governor believes that is the way it should stay." Democrats in the legislature also voiced their disapproval. Rep. Earline Rogers said, "The focus should really be on the child and their needs... The sexual orientation of the parent should play no part in the decision." Saying the bill violated the state and U.S. Constitutions, Sen. Timothy Lanane predicted a legal challenge if the bill became law. Sen. Anita Bowser said, "The motivation behind this is discriminatory, and I find that offensive."

The Senate sponsor of the adoption proposal, Sen. John Waterman (R), withdrew the bill in February, saying that it would not pass because House Democrats opposed an outright prohibition. Instead, he introduced another bill that would have restricted adoptions by anyone "not living with that person's spouse in an intact marriage recognized under Indiana law." Rep. Burton supported that effort, saying "The ideal way to raise children is a mother and a father at home. That's why I believe it's detrimental to put children in the homes of homosexuals." The Senate Judiciary Committee approved Waterman's bill 5-4.

The bills outraged supporters of gay and lesbian civil rights. Wally Paynter, head of Justice Inc., a statewide gay rights organization, said, "This is just a piece of bad legislation that is really inappropriate... What we are really talking about is morality and a way to legislate morality." Women in the Arts member Mary Byrne said, "I don't want any special rights. I just want equal rights as a woman and equal rights as a lesbian." Sean Lemieux, an attorney with the Indiana Civil Liberties Union, asked, "What is wrong with an adoption standard that says judges and professionals should decide adoptions based on what is in the best interest of the child?"

Media scrutiny and high-profile opposition weakened support for Waterman's second attempt at prohibiting adoptions by gay men and lesbians. Using a parliamentary maneuver, senators quickly killed the bill in late February without any vocal objections from the Senate's Republican leadership. Waterman said, "It was obviously an organized effort."

Rep. Burton said he would continue his crusade to outlaw adoptions by gay men and lesbians and would reintroduce the measure in the 2000 legislative session. However, he never filed a bill to that effect. Meanwhile, the adoption case that Burton said had motivated him to introduce the proposal took a tragic turn in May 1999. The foster father, Earl "Butch" Kimmerling, was charged with four felony counts of molesting his foster daughter. His wife reportedly contacted police after the girl told her about the alleged abuse. Police said Kimmerling had admitted to sexual contact with the girl "many times since April or May, 1998."

Statewide: Hate crimes bill defeated

The state legislature killed a hate crimes bill that would have included sexual orientation. Co-sponsored by state Rep. William Crawford (D), the bill would have required police departments to maintain statistics on hate crimes and to conduct special training on how to deal with them. Judges would have been allowed to extend the sentences of those convicted for committing hate crimes. The bill also would have allowed victims to file civil suits against their attackers to recover damages. Though the legislature rejected similar measures in the past that included sexual orientation, early action on the 1999 bill suggested it might be passed. The House Court and Criminal Code Committee voted 8-3 to pass the measure on to the full House. Rep. Jesse Villalpando (D), a supporter, said, "Violence against certain people is more prevalent because of who they are."

Opponents of the bill, however, argued that it singled out specific groups for special protections. Rep. Brent Steele (R) said, "All crime against another human being is about hate. If you cross that line, it doesn't matter what your motivation was." Rep. Woody Burton (R) asked, "I'm a heavy-set person. If someone beats me up because I'm fat, does that mean they should face a tougher penalty?" Micah Clark, public policy director with the Indiana Family Institute, an affiliate of the Focus on the Family (see p. 355), told a House committee, "I don't see why pushing a homosexual out of a window and pushing an old lady out of a window should be treated differently under the law." Eric Miller of Advance America said the bill would punish thought.

Other opponents feared the bill would compromise free speech. Brett Shankman, with the Jewish Community Relations Council, said, "This gets uncomfortably close to [restricting] free speech and we ought to be careful there." Although Shankman said he opposed the bill as written, he said he supported its intent. Chris Gibson with the Indiana Civil Liberties Union said his organization shared the same concerns and did not support the proposal.

Those who specifically opposed the inclusion of sexual orientation in the bill led the effort to defeat it. Along with two other representatives, Rep. Burton made a failed attempt to file an amendment that would strike sexual orientation from the bill. Rep. Jerry Denbo said, "The main problem with me, and I think with most conservative-minded Democrats, is that it gets into civil rights by making homosexuals a minority... I think it's terrible having things like this, but I hate seeing them [homosexuals] as a minority." Rep. Peggy Welch and House Speaker John Gregg both said they opposed the bill because it included sexual orientation. Without debate, by a 49-44 vote, the House defeated the bill.

Supporters were angered by that defeat. Rep. Crawford said, "I see that as a lack of courage to do the right thing." Marla Stevens of LGBT Fairness Indiana said, "My sense is many of the representatives cannot understand the difference between a childhood prank and someone scrawling threats on their house."

Carroll County:
Lesbian officer sues over alleged discrimination

In September, the Indiana Civil Liberties Union brought suit on behalf of an openly lesbian probation officer against two Carroll County judges in federal court for allegedly failing to promote the plaintiff because of her sexual orientation. Sheri Moore claimed that Circuit Court Judge Joseph Cary and Superior Court Judge Jeffrey Smith together decided against promoting her to chief probation officer. Moore said she requested the job two days after the employee formerly holding the position had resigned, and that Judge Smith told her that he and Carey would not promote her because she was a lesbian. In her lawsuit, Moore asserts that, "[Judges Cary and Smith] acted out of personal bias and their actions constitute a conspiracy to deprive [me] of equal protection." Moore also claims that Judge Smith told her that she was embarrassing the court by dating a woman, and that he had asked other court employees about her sexual orientation and personal life. According to Moore, a man with no prior probation experience was promoted to the position. The judges denied violating Moore's rights, saying they hired the other officer "after careful consideration." Judge Smith added, "We did what was in the best interest of the county and the court system." Moore is seeking monetary compensation and damages. The case was still pending as of press time.

> "If gay and lesbian people wish to introduce their lifestyle to children, let them do so with their own children. If that's possible."
>
> — Kristine Momper, in a letter to the Fort Wayne Journal-Sentinel thanking PBS station WFWA for not airing the documentary "After Stonewall."

Fort Wayne: Station declines to air "After Stonewall"

Fort Wayne's PBS station decided not to broadcast the documentary "After Stonewall," drawing criticism from the gay and lesbian community and support from right-wing Christians. The documentary, which chronicles the history of gay and lesbian activism from the Stonewall Riots of 1969 to the present, was broadcast on PBS stations across the country. However, station executives at WFWA Channel 39 chose not to broadcast the documentary in June, claiming that its brief depiction of nudity forced them to pre-empt the program. Gay and lesbian residents held a community forum to discuss that decision and resolved to seek a meeting with station officials. Cat Voors, one of the organizers of the meeting, said, "Basically, we want to approach the general manager and programming manager and get their thoughts." She said they also wanted the station to air "It's Elementary," a documentary featuring discussions of homosexuality in elementary schools across the country.

WFWA station officials said the decision not to air "After Stonewall" was a difficult one. Bob Petts, the station's program manager, said they learned the documentary had brief scenes of nudity only a week before it was schedule to air. Petts and station President Roger Rhodes decided to pre-empt the program at the last minute because they did not have enough time to discuss their handling of the nude scenes. Rhodes, however, said the station has not ruled out airing "After Stonewall" in the future.

Letters to the editor and an editorial in the Fort Wayne Journal-Sentinel suggested broad support for the program's cancellation from many of the station's viewers. One letter writer, Mike Hein, told readers that not only does "the Bible condemn homosexuality" but it also "strongly condemns those who cause others to sin." He said that Christians "are not instructed to teach children to accept their 'differences' produced by sin." He also wrote, "… there is no obligation on the part of society to publicize or popularize their [gay men's and lesbians'] views or motives." Kristine Momper, who also wrote to the newspaper, thanked the station for not airing the program, calling that decision "tasteful." She wrote, "If gay and lesbian people wish to introduce their lifestyle to children, let them do so with their own children. If that's possible." An op-ed by resident Fred Hannan linked objections from gay men and lesbians to a "gay agenda" that included the legal recognition of same-sex marriage. He feared the push for equal rights, safer schools, and domestic partner benefits for gay and lesbian employees "must be understood in this context." Saying that he was "very disturbed" about an article on the gay community's response to the controversy, Hannan called their response "another ploy by the homosexual community to have us accept their lifestyle as normal." He said his religious beliefs prevented him from supporting equal rights for gay men and lesbians.

A gay and lesbian group reportedly urged viewers to withhold contributions from the station to protest the pre-empting of "After Stonewall." In response, Momper wrote, "I am not waiting for Channel 39's fund drive to send money. My check is in the mail."

South Bend:
Notre Dame rejects anti-discrimination proposal

A controversy erupting from the University of Notre Dame's decision not to include sexual orientation in its official non-discrimination policy lasted through most of 1999. In November 1998, the Academic Council, the highest representative governing body at the Catholic-affiliated school, proposed that the university add sexual orientation to all of its non-discrimination policies, including those covering hiring, promotions, access to activities and facilities, and admissions.

The Progressive Student Alliance (PSA), a two-year-old student group working for social justice, coordinated much of the campaign to have the proposal adopted. About 80 students held a hunger strike during a February meeting of the Board of Trustees, hoping to influence the vote. Former talk show host and Notre Dame alumnus Phil Donahue visited the campus before the board meeting to speak in favor of the proposal. "What more noble purpose can we assign to ourselves than a fight for freedom?" he asked. "We're not even asking the university to break any new ground." The student activists had expected the support of Notre Dame's president, Rev. Edward Malloy, and were disappointed by his inaction on the matter. David Hartwig, a member of the PSA, said, "It's very frustrating. All this work, and finally it comes down to a showdown between this small, unresponsive cabal of administrators versus a large majority of the faculty and students."

During its February meeting, the board voted against the proposal. A university spokesperson said that homosexual sex is a sin and that the school, which is affiliated with the Catholic Church, could not submit to all secular norms. Student activists were disappointed. "They're leaving open the possibility of unjust discrimination to exist for students, staff and faculty at this university," said Mark Massoud, a member of the gay and lesbian student group OUTreach ND.

Openly gay professor Mark Jordan resigned in March over the vote. Jordan, a tenured professor of medieval studies, said President Malloy's opposition to the proposal was a "moral failure." He told the South Bend Tribune, "Now they are forfeiting [their credibility] because they are stubbornly standing by this policy that no one else can see makes sense." Saying Notre Dame is "no longer a place that I think I can be a Catholic scholar," Jordan took a job at Emory University as the Aquinas Chair in Catholic Studies. Emory offers domestic partner benefits to its employees and includes sexual orientation in its official non-discrimination policy. Jordan was the second professor in as many years to leave Notre Dame because of its policies toward gay men and lesbians.

Controversy surrounding gay and lesbian issues carried over into the fall semester when, in November, the university's student newspaper, The Observer, ran an advertisement from the Gay and Lesbian Alumni Association (GALA). President Malloy had written the newspaper a letter in August, saying the newspaper could not publish GALA advertisements or ads from other groups "that, directly or indirectly, espouse positions contrary to the moral teaching of the Catholic Church." Editor-in-chief Michelle Krupa said Malloy never responded to her requests for evidence that GALA contradicts Catholic doctrine. The paper maintained that it was an independent institution, but Malloy said, "The administration is legally and symbolically the publisher." In December, the Faculty Senate voted 31-1 in favor of a resolution supporting the paper's action.

Terre Haute: Textbooks opposed

A Vigo County School Board member objected to a host of textbooks, one of which dealt with homosexuality. Mark May questioned the way the school system's new textbooks dealt with evolution, global warming, ozone depletion, overpopulation and homosexuality. "We are on the cutting edge of political correctness," he said. "They promote a system of beliefs... as though they are facts. They are not facts, they are beliefs." He specifically targeted a health book's discussion of homosexuality. The book reportedly included a picture of a gay pride parade with the caption, "Everyone needs to be accepted by a community." May said, "It's quite disgusting... It paints them in such a nice light." He said he felt the school system could do a better job of selecting textbooks. A textbook advisory committee composed of teachers, parents and students had reviewed the books for the district's schools. At a school board meeting, several educators voiced their support for the books, but two Terre Haute South Vigo High School students praised May for his criticism. The school board approved all the books by a 6-1 vote.

Statewide: Executive order prompts backlash

When Democratic Gov. Tom Vilsack issued an executive order prohibiting discrimination based on sexual orientation and gender identity in state employment, conservative lawmakers and right-wing activists began a campaign to have the order rescinded. In September, Gov. Vilsack signed the order, which was drafted in consultation with the Gay and Lesbian Caucus of the state's Democratic Party and the Iowa Coalition for Human Rights. The order also included such other protected categories as race, age, marital status and mental disability. The National Gay and Lesbian Task Force praised the governor for making Iowa the first state where transgendered state workers were protected from employment discrimination by an executive order. By mid-October, however, the backlash that the governor faced from the right wing seemed to overshadow that earlier praise.

Bill Horn, head of Straight From the Heart Ministries, an evangelical group that seeks to change the sexual orientation of gay men and lesbians through religious devotion, criticized the governor in statements laced with anti-gay rhetoric. Horn called the order "an extreme position" adopted "in secrecy" and claimed the governor's action would allow transvestites to use female bathrooms in government buildings. He also claimed the order would establish "affirmative action programs that require the state to recruit cross-dressers, transgenders and she-males" for state jobs. Horn added that protection for gender identity "is something he could not get through the legislature. It is not the will of the people. It's his payback to a bunch of homosexual activists." Labeling the order part of the "homosexual agenda," Horn personally attacked Vilsack: "If the governor wants to wear a dress at home, that's fine. But when he goes out and represents the state of Iowa... I would appreciate it if he would dress appropriately."

Republican state legislators also criticized the governor, most of them objecting strongly to the inclusion of gender identity. Senate Majority Leader Stewart Iverson (R) said, "Iowa should be on the cutting edge of educating our children, not the cutting edge of extending civil rights to transsexuals." He dismissed the need for employment protections, saying, "I have friends who are homosexual, but they do their job and that isn't the issue. When you talk about gender identity and transsexuals, that is unbelievable... how far do you go in setting up special classes of people?" Iverson later called on the governor to rescind the order. House Speaker Brent Siegrist (R) said the order went against the will of most legislators, noting that the legislature had rejected several bills to add sexual orientation to the state's non-discrimination law. Saying Vilsack had pushed the limits of executive authority, Siegrist added that the order might face a challenge in the courts or the legislature. State Sen. Steve King (R) issued a press release saying, "For white, heterosexual, Christian males, the circle of special rights has finally closed entirely around you. You are now the only unprotected class." In a letter to the editor of the Des Moines Register he wrote, "This executive order's only purpose is to establish a quota system for homosexuals and transsexuals." Legislative opponents of the order were surprised to discover that the Assembly's own employment guidelines bar discrimination based on sexual orientation. Iverson said they would consider eliminating those guidelines.

> "If the governor wants to wear a dress at home, that's fine. But when he goes out and represents the state of Iowa... I would appreciate it if he would dress appropriately."
>
> — Bill Horn of Straight From the Heart Ministries, criticizing Gov. Tom Vilsack for issuing an executive order protecting gay and transgendered state employees from discrimination.

Vilsack argued that his order was morally right and a necessary tool in recruiting qualified state employees. "We are essentially competing with people for qualified help. As far as I'm concerned, what you do in the privacy of your own home shouldn't impact or affect your ability to do that job you are being hired to do." He also said the legislature lacked the authority to overturn his order.

Campaigning in Iowa, then-presidential candidate Gary Bauer, former head of the Family Research Council (see p. 355), joined the fray. He said, "Governor Vilsack has joined the ranks of his friend Bill Clinton by working to impose a set of values without allowing the people or their representatives to decide." Bauer called the gay and lesbian groups with whom the governor worked "anti-family." John Norris, Vilsack's chief of staff, responded, "This is exactly what I would expect from a far-right conservative, and why I'm confident we did the right thing." Iowans from across the state echoed those sentiments in state newspapers.

Horn helped orchestrate a media relations campaign attacking the governor's order and, in late October, vowed to spend "several thousand dollars" on ads for two radio stations. Horn said in his ad, "By issuing a secret executive order, [Vilsack] is now welcoming crossdressers and transvestites to come work in our state government. He says in the newspaper it's civil rights, but we say it's insanity. This is a big political payback to his transvestite and cross-dresser supporters." Horn organized an anti-Vilsack rally featuring Bauer and former pro football player Reggie White. Introducing White to the crowd, Horn said, "Reggie doesn't hate homosexuals; he loves them so much he is going to be honest with them and tell them that what they are doing is destructive." White told the crowd, "Every black person in America should be offended that a group of people should want the same civil rights because of their sexual orientation." Bauer called on Vilsack to admit his order was a mistake.

Ames: Methodists' conversion proposal

A group of right-wing United Methodists at a state conference introduced a proposal to support ministries seeking to change the sexual orientation of gay men and lesbians. United Methodists Organized for Renewal and Evangelism offered the proposal at the Iowa Annual Conference in June. David Stanley of Muscatine, who said the church was too sympathetic to homosexuality, offered a proposal that would have encouraged the church to study the work done by Transforming Congregations (see p. 357). Stanley said, "We've got to offer God's grace for the healing and overcoming of homosexual practice." Rev. William Cotton of Des Moines disagreed, saying the conversion movement "creates havoc for those of us who minister to gay and lesbian people in our churches... I wish we could just lower our voices, and let's keep the word 'sin' out of this." Stanley's proposal was defeated 789-447. Charles Wesley Jordan, the state bishop, stopped another resolution to affirm the church's ban on same-sex marriage ceremonies, calling it out of order.

Cedar Rapids: Gay rights ordinance

Opponents tried to derail a proposal to add sexual orientation to the city's human rights code, which prohibits discrimination in employment, housing, public accommodations, credit and education. The city's Civil Rights Commission voted 6-1 in November 1998 to recommend that the City Council adopt the measure. Opponents criticized the proposal at several City Council meetings between December 1998 and January 1999. At a December meeting, one resident said, "The Bible says if you live a gay lifestyle, you will not go to heaven. It's as clear as day." Another said others at the meeting feared the impact the proposal would have on those who object to homosexuality on religious grounds. Anti-gay activist Marvin Beer submitted a list of signatures of people supporting a referendum on the issue. For the proposal to pass, it needed to be approved during three hearings by the council.

The proposal was approved during the first two hearings, both held in December, but not without opposition. Members of the Alliance for Families and Businesses, one of the leading opponents, said its members objected to the proposed ordinance on moral and economic grounds. Mike Cambridge claimed the proposal would grant gay men and lesbians "super-rights which will change dress and behavior codes for a privileged few." Bill Nissen, pastor at River of Life Ministries, said, "Homosexuality is a perversion," while Bernard Hayes, a black minister, objected to comparisons between the civil rights of gay men and lesbians and those of people of color. "To say we're facing the same discrimination hurdles that these folks have, it's not true," he said.

By the third hearing, in January, opponents enlisted the aid of high-profile anti-gay activists. Attending a rally sponsored by the Alliance for Families and Businesses, former head of the Family Research Council (see p. 355) Gary Bauer, then a possible GOP presidential candidate, spoke out against the measure the night before the council's final vote. He said that lawmakers' attention was more devoted to a "gay rights" law than to the problem of drug use and the farm economy. Bauer told the crowd of over 600 that gay men and lesbians would demand inclusion in the school curricula and legal recognition of same-sex marriage. Alveda King, niece of Martin Luther King Jr., also spoke against the proposal. Supporters of the proposal also organized their own rally that same day.

So many people turned out for the final hearing on the proposal that the council held the session at a neighborhood recreation center and brought in police for added security. The council voted 3-2 in favor of the proposal, making Cedar Rapids the third city in the state with a civil rights law protecting gay men and lesbians. Rev. Larry Johnson, one of the opposition leaders, said he would rally support for a new slate of council members: "The mayor said to us that our alternative is to remove her from office. I think we'd take her pretty seriously along those lines." He said the Alliance for Families and Business planned to become politically active and more involved in "morality issues" in local government.

Des Moines:
Presidential candidates sign anti-gay pledge

An anti-gay coalition ran a full-page ad in the Des Moines Register in August calling on presidential candidates to sign a pledge opposing gay and lesbian rights. Its signers pledged to oppose domestic partner benefits, legal recognition of same-sex marriage, adoptions and foster care by gay men and lesbians, discussion of homosexuality in public schools, and civil rights for gay men and lesbians. Right-wing activists Bill Horn and Reggie White helped coordinate the effort, which involved the American Family Association, Americans for Truth About Homosexuality, the Center for Reclaiming America, the Christian Family Network, Citizens for Community Values, Concerned Women for America, Coral Ridge Ministries, Family First, Kerusso Ministries, Liberty Counsel, Mission America, National Legal Foundation, Stop Promoting Homosexuality, Straight from the Heart, and Toward Tradition (see p. 352-357). Rich Tafel, executive director of the Log Cabin Republicans, said, "It may be the most gratuitously intolerant pledge to surface in any presidential campaign." Horn and the Register's staff said that six candidates, all Republicans, had signed on — Gary Bauer, Pat Buchanan, Malcolm W. "Steve" Forbes Jr, Alan Keyes, Orrin Hatch and Dan Quayle. Neither of the Democratic candidates signed the pledge, nor did Republican candidates George W. Bush, Elizabeth Dole or John McCain. Peter LaBarbera, head of Americans for Truth About Homosexuality, publicly criticized Dole for not signing the pledge and for not speaking out against a New Jersey Supreme Court decision that the Boy Scouts' prohibition on gay members violated state law.

Des Moines: Pro-gay Catholics criticized

Two Catholic scholars who teach that sexuality is a gift from God came under fire in October for a series of speeches they gave in the Des Moines area. James and Evelyn Whitehead, faculty members at the Institute for Pastoral Studies at Loyola University in Chicago, were to discuss a variety of theological issues, including sexuality. According to the Des Moines Register, an anonymous flier appeared on cars at several area parishes sarcastically inviting "queer" Catholics to hear "Catholic dissenters" James and Evelyn Whitehead "affirm your homosexuality and give you a new theology to replace Catholic beliefs." The flier said that Catholic teachings made homosexuality a sin and included a picture of two men kissing, with a caption reading, "[Iowa Catholic] Bishop Charron's sexual dissent night with speakers affirming sodomy, self-sex, birth control." It also linked the Whiteheads with Call to Action, a group advocating change on social issues within the Catholic Church. James Whitehead and a spokesperson for the Diocese of Des Moines both said the discussion did not address homosexuality. Whitehead denounced the flier, saying, "It's beyond uncharitable... it's bitter and sinful. I don't think it demands a response."

Later that week, an Imogene minister, John Clarke, published an ad in the Register claiming that the Whiteheads promoted homosexuality and called for a demonstration at one of their speeches. Clarke's ad said the two were "heretics" and "avid advocates of contraception, masturbation, homosexuality, and divorce."

Dubuque: Rights ordinance rejected

In August, Dubuque's City Council rejected a proposal to prohibit discrimination in housing, employment, credit, and public accommodations based on sexual orientation. The month before, the city's Human Rights Commission had unanimously recommended that the City Council adopt the proposed ordinance. But despite support from the council's chairman, Thom Determann, members rejected it 5-2. One of those who voted against the recommendation said he believed sexual orientation was not a category of discrimination that warranted legal protections. Councilman John Markham said, "I'm not in favor of naming specific classes in an ordinance." The council allowed no public comment during the meeting, so supporters showed their concerns through buttons and stickers.

The vote had the support of many in the community. Steve Seng, a local seminary student, said the ordinance conflicted with his religious beliefs. Sheila Everts, a resident who previously spoke before the Human Rights Commission, said, "My religious view, that homosexual acts are immoral, places homosexuality in a different category than race, gender, or religion... I feel that homosexuality is a weakness, like other sinful weaknesses." Local resident Marvin Schlitzer wrote a letter to the editor of the Dubuque Telegraph-Herald in

October commending the council for its vote. He personally thanked Seng for his comments in the paper and said the council's vote reflected the will of the community. "[T]his issue is not as much of a rights issue, but one of promoting a lifestyle," he wrote.

The ordinance's supporters, who were angered by the vote, formed an ad-hoc group, Dubuquers Against Discrimination, and staged a rally at the September City Council meeting. They carried signs reading, "We are people, too," "We are the people you choose to ignore," and "Were you afraid of discussion?" They also protested in front of the Carnegie-Stout Public Library, where the City Council meets. They hoped to convince the City Council to reconsider its vote but failed. They objected both to the vote and being denied a chance to speak. Kevin Menning, said, "If they [council members] are unwilling to hear the public in chambers, then they will hear and see us on the streets." Parents, Families and Friends of Gays and Lesbians (PFLAG) organized another protest in October.

Fairfield: Attempt to ban book

The parent of a Fairfield Middle School student tried to have a book dealing with adolescence and homosexuality removed from two school libraries. In April, Nancy Hesseltine requested that the town's entire school board review of "Am I Blue? Coming Out from the Silence," which includes accounts of initial homosexual experiences. The school board's book review committee met with her in May and unanimously decided to keep the book in the libraries of the middle and high schools. Hesseltine asked to appeal that decision to the school board, claiming that she did not understand the proper book review school procedures. A meeting was held in January 2000, and 20 people from a crowd of about 150 addressed the board on the book. Most of the speakers favored removing the book. Hesseltine described the book as sexually explicit and questioned whether it was age-appropriate, especially for middle school students. Some board members said they learned more about alternative lifestyles from reading the book, while others said nothing in it surprised them. Most board members, however, said the subject matter made them uncomfortable. Board member Douglas Flournoy, who opposed keeping the book, said that he had to follow his own value system. Nevertheless, the board voted 5-2 to keep the book in both school libraries. Hesseltine said, "I would like to have it removed from everywhere, but removing it from the middle school would have been the second best thing."

KANSAS

Topeka: White-Phelps meeting

A meeting between Rev. Mel White, head of Soulforce, an organization advocating spiritual equality and civil justice for gay men and lesbians, and Rev. Fred Phelps (see p. 356) fell short of meeting White's goal of getting Phelps to tone down his rhetoric and anti-gay activities. Phelps, his family, and members of his church picket gay pride parades, funerals of well-publicized gay men and lesbians, and churches he believes are insufficiently harsh toward homosexuality. Phelps and White met in December at Westboro Baptist Church, where Phelps is pastor. Phelps originally wanted to have a public debate with White entitled "Is Homosexuality an Abominable Sin or an Innocent Alternate Lifestyle?" but White turned that request down. Both described the meeting as amicable, but disagreed over the impact of Phelps' picketing. White said they agreed not to publicly discuss the details of their meeting, but Phelps talked to a local reporter the day after their meeting. He said, "[White] calls Bible meetings we have on the street a 'public hate demonstration.' Well, I'm not willing for them to take over the lexicon. It is a gospel meeting we have on the streets, not a public hate demonstration." White said that Phelps' protests are acts of "spiritual violence." White led a demonstration at Westboro Baptist Church and at the Phelps home a day after their meeting. Their placards read, "God even loves Fred." White said, "It was done to say, 'Fred, I love you. God loves you. But I am protesting that you say God doesn't love gays, and that breaks the heart of God.' " White later told a crowd at Washburn University, "We have to believe that Fred Phelps also can change."

KENTUCKY

Statewide: "It's Elementary" not broadcast

Kentucky Educational Television (KET), the state's PBS affiliate, decided not to broadcast the award-winning documentary "It's Elementary: Talking About Gay Issues in School" by Debra Chasnoff. The documentary features discussions about homosexuality in elementary schools across the nation. Answering complaints from University of Kentucky professor Joan Callahan, a KET spokesperson said the documentary "simply does not, in our opinion, rise to the standards necessary for inclusion in a KET broadcast." On an e-mail bulletin board, Callahan responded, "My goodness, can you say precisely what these standards are? Does KET realize that every day children are harassed in Kentucky schools because of their real or perceived sexual orientation?... Are there standards that are higher than protecting the very lives, welfare, and educational equality of our children? If so, I have no idea what they might be." KET was one of several PBS outlets across the nation that either chose not to broadcast the program or came under fire for doing so.

Debra Chasnoff contributed an essay about the campaign against "It's Elementary" to the 1999 edition of Hostile Climate.

Bowling Green: Civil rights ordinance opposed

A proposed civil rights measure to prohibit discrimination based on sexual orientation in employment, housing, and public accommodations came under fire from right-wing citizens. Residents opposed to the "Fairness Ordinance" voiced their concerns in letters and calls to the Bowling Green Human Rights Commission, letters to the editor of local newspapers, and at public hearings on the matter.

By the end of October, the commission reported that over 150 people had contacted it in opposition to the proposal, but only 25 had registered their support. Resident Jane Howell wrote, "I am appalled that your organization is even considering 'special rights' for members of the homosexual movement... Why should we give any one group more protection or significance than another?" An unidentified resident wrote, "The words 'fairness ordinance' sound harmless, but are they are the first step in using the force of the law and power of government to legislate a new morality?... What then? Put their agenda into our school, teaching our children that their lives, their alternative lifestyle is acceptable. I think not!"

Churches also organized against the proposal. Greenwood Baptist Church sent a petition to the commission signed by more than 100 members in opposition to the proposed ordinance, saying the law would open up a "floodgate of demands upon our public schools, such as teaching to our children the acceptability of the gay or homosexual lifestyle in violation of both the teachers' and parents' beliefs." Hillvue Heights Church also sent a letter to the commission saying it was opposed to "special rights" for any group based on behavior.

In November, the commission held a public hearing during which supporters and opponents of the proposal squared off. Bruce Wilkerson, a retired police officer, said that in his 20 years on the force, he never heard of any anti-gay hate crimes. He said the police department told him that there were only three in the last three years. "Such an ordinance would provide special legislation protection for homosexual conduct... This commission is being asked to take a very strong medicine for an illness that does not exist," Wilkerson said. Kathy Bussey told supporters, "If your mothers and fathers had fought for what you want, some of you wouldn't be here tonight." Supporters, on the other hand, wore buttons reading, "Fairness, No More, No Less." Several spoke about discrimination and harassment they or people they knew had faced because of their sexual orientation.

The Human Rights Commission voted to recommend that the City Commission draft and adopt the fairness ordinance. Members of the commission took several votes on component issues, all 14 having voted in favor of the concept of a civil rights ordinance. They voted 11-2 for protections in employment, 8-5 for protections in housing, and 9-3 for protections in public accommodations, with some members abstaining on each vote. They also voted to recommend that the state legislature adopt civil rights protections in the same areas for gay men and lesbians. Prior to those votes by members of the Human Rights Commission, all of the City Commissioners had announced that they would not sponsor or vote for the proposed ordinance. Commissioner Jim Bullington Jr. said, "It's not civil rights legislation; it's not a civil rights issue; it's something you could really place the same rationale for about any group."

Fort Campbell: Military base's continued hostility

Weeks after Army Pfc. Barry Winchell was murdered in July, homophobic chants continued at the Fort Campbell military base. Pvt. Calvin Glover murdered Winchell, who was being harassed by fellow soldiers who believed him to be gay, with a baseball bat in his barracks while Winchell was sleeping. Days before the murder, Winchell and Glover had reportedly fought each other, and Glover reportedly lost. On the CBS television program "60 Minutes," Pvt. Javier Torres reported that weeks after Winchell's murder, a sergeant had led a platoon cheer, "Faggot, faggot, down the street. Shoot him, shoot him, till he retreats." Torres told Ed Bradley, one of the show's correspondents, "It's supposed to be our motivation to run... I sang it. I had to... I couldn't be the only one." He reiterated those points during sworn testimony for the Servicemembers Legal Defense Network. Torres said that complaining about the cheer would have raised suspicions about his sexual orientation, triggering a dismissal investigation under the "don't ask, don't tell" policy on gays in the military. Torres said he later came forward and acknowledged being gay because he was scared to death, having known about what had happened to Winchell. He was later dishonorably discharged for being gay. Military officials reportedly declined to appear on "60 Minutes," but said that the military has a "zero tolerance" policy on the harassment of gay men and lesbians. In discussing the murder of Private Winchell, Torres said, "There was some [who said]... 'It's just one less fag to deal with... They don't really belong here.' "

> "Faggot, faggot, down the street. Shoot him, shoot him, till he retreats."
>
> — Pvt. Javier Torres told "60 Minutes" that his Fort Campbell platoon was made to chant this a few weeks after the murder of Pfc. Barry Winchell.

A personal essay by Winchell's parents, Pat and Wally Kutteles, appears on p. 22.

Henderson: Civil rights ordinance opposed

An effort to pass a civil rights ordinance prohibiting discrimination based on sexual orientation in housing, employment, and public accommodations came under attack from anti-gay citizens and the Religious Right. Many of the proposal's supporters were members of Zion United Church of Christ, which for several years has been an "open and affirming congregation," welcoming gay and lesbian members. The proposed ordinance would authorize the Henderson-Henderson County Human Relations Commission to hear cases in which discrimination was alleged. The original proposal would have provided civil liability for violators and fines ranging from $1,000 to $10,000.

After a coalition of local residents began their push for the ordinance in May, the Green Valley Baptist Association, which represents 30 local Southern Baptist churches, adopted a resolution condemning the effort. Rev. Steve Thompson, the group's executive director, said, "We feel like they're trying to use the law to coerce Bible-believing Christians to go against their principles and give up their rights... And, therefore, [those Christians are] being treated unfairly and being forced to make decisions in terms of housing, employment, and public accommodation that they don't want to make." The resolution listed the group's reasons for opposing the proposal, among them- the contention that homosexual behavior "greatly exaggerates" the spread of AIDS and other sexually transmitted diseases, and that protecting homosexual behavior "degrades the beauty of God's good gift of sexuality between a husband and a wife by making sexuality solely an issue of desire."

Some elected officials also opposed the proposed ordinance. City Commissioner Robby Mills asked, "Why should a little town like Henderson be looking at this issue that even our state and federal officeholders cannot decide on?" He claimed the proposal was supported by a "very narrow, special-interest group that has the ears of some elected officials." He also claimed the proposal would harm small businesses.

In an effort to better organize, opponents, in June, formed a local chapter of the American Family Association (see p. 352), calling it the Family Foundation of Kentucky. Mills noted that the AFA had helped organize opposition to a similar ordinance adopted earlier in the year in Louisville. At an organizational meeting, Mills told opponents to attend a July meeting of the Human Relations Committee, the group that would hear cases under the proposed law. Kevin Stone, youth pastor at a local church and another organizer of the local AFA, claimed that the proposed ordinance would limit his religious freedom and legitimize "behavior I consider from a biblical standpoint to be sin." He agreed with Mills that the law would hurt small businesses.

At a June meeting of the City Commission, opponents voiced their concerns. Resident Blaine Holder said he feared "they're going to slip it [the ordinance] under the rug when we're not looking." He added, "People have the right to live the way they want to, but they don't have the right to force their values on others. We don't need this in our town." He urged the commission to uphold Christian values, saying, "If this commission doesn't believe in God, any one of you, then you need to step down." Rev. Jake Carter, a local pastor, said, "God does not bring justice to sin." Another opponent said, "I encourage you to legislate right living," while yet another said he feared the city would be punished with tornadoes and earthquakes if the commission passed the law. Residents also spoke out against the proposal with letters to the editor of The Gleaner, a local newspaper. The tone of the letters became so harsh that the editor placed a moratorium on publishing them.

Although the final version of the ordinance did not include the civil liabilities clause and lowered the cap on fines to $250, opponents were still not satisfied. Commissioner Russell Sights said, "I really believe that we have uncovered more problems than believed with this ordinance. We are creating a monster that does not need to exist in our town. The need has not been justified." An August edition of The Gleaner included an insert from the Family Foundation. The insert, a newsletter called "The Kentucky Citizen," contended that the proposed ordinance was funded by the National Gay and Lesbian Task Force. Kent Ostrander, head of the Family Foundation, said, "We see this so-called fairness ordinance actually as a grasp for power by one small segment of our society. We are for equal rights, not special rights granted to this group or that group." Rev. Ben Guess, co-chair of the Henderson Fairness Campaign, denounced the insert and said the campaign had not received any money from NGLTF.

During the September meeting of the City Commission, at which the first reading on the proposed ordinance was held, opponents continued their campaign. About 575 people attended, and over 90 people signed up to comment on the proposal, turning the commission's meeting into a seven-hour marathon. The meeting ended with a 3-2 vote in favor of the proposal.

At the second and final reading of the ordinance in September, the commission again voted 3-2 in favor. Crowd estimates at the five-hour meeting ranged from 300-400. The final version included even more changes. One amendment stipulated that the ordinance would only apply to the City of Henderson and not to the rest of the county, but opponents remain unsatisfied. James Hickerson said, "Look at what happened to Sodom and Gomorrah and the surrounding cities, and include Henderson." Opponents vowed to overturn the measure, though Kentucky law does not provide for repeal referendums.

In November, Pat Robertson's American Center for Law and Justice (see p. 352) filed suit in Henderson Circuit Court on behalf of Rick and Connie Hile, challenging the ordinance. The Hiles contend that the ordinance requires them to violate their religious beliefs by not allowing them to deny housing because of a renter's sexual orientation. "This ordinance tramples on a landlord's constitutional right to the free exercise of religion," said Francis Manion, an official at the ACLJ-Midwest. "This is a clear example of government attempting to legislate its own view of morality at the expense of the fundamental rights of its citizens." The suit also contends that the law requires the Hiles "to abandon and act contrary to beliefs which are central to their Christian faith." In August 2000, the lawsuit was dismissed, the judge having ruled that the ordinance did not apply to the Hiles.

Jefferson County: Civil rights law challenged

Right-wing organizations challenged a civil rights law that included sexual orientation in Jefferson County. The controversy began when Jefferson County commissioners considered a proposal to prohibit discrimination on the basis of sexual orientation and gender identity in housing, employment and public accommodations. After three county commissioners announced their support for the proposal in August, the lone opponent, Judge-Executive Rebecca Jackson, used a parliamentary maneuver to delay a final vote. Jackson said she was not convinced the measure was necessary and was generally opposed gay rights laws. She serves on the Jefferson County Fiscal Court, which is the legislative body for the county and is composed of four elected officials — three county commissioners and one judge-executive. The court voted 3-1 in favor of the ordinance in October. The final version exempted churches, religious-based agencies and private clubs. A group primarily composed of religious activists staged a demonstration against the court outside of the courthouse just before that vote.

In November, Pat Robertson's American Center for Law and Justice (see p. 352) followed through on its threat to challenge the county's new civil rights law. The ACLJ filed a lawsuit in federal court on behalf of Dr. J. Barrett Hyman, who claimed that the law forces him to violate his religious beliefs. "We believe the ordinance is not only unlawful but unconstitutional as well," Francis Manion, counsel for the ACLJ, said. Jackson said she was not surprised, having voiced concerns before the ordinance was passed that this would happen.

Opponents later mounted a campaign to unseat Commissioner Joe Corradino, who was the last member to announce his support for the measure and the key swing vote. The Organization of Christian Democrats led the anti-Corradino campaign. It mailed 10,000 leaflets to voters denouncing Corradino's support for "special rights" for gay men and lesbians. It urged voters to defeat Corradino "and the radical, anti-God element that is trying to take over our Democratic Party." Jerry Stephenson and other anti-gay black ministers signed the leaflet along with Frank Simon, head of the Kentucky affiliate of the American Family Association (see p. 352). Rev. Charles Elliott specifically told his congregation to vote Corradino out of office: "When you vote a law in that will... go along with wrong and condemn Jesus, I'm not going to bow to it... I'm going to pull a campaign to vote everyone out that voted for that cause. Will y'all help me?" Corradino was defeated in the November general election.

At press time, the ACLJ's lawsuit was pending.

Lexington: Non-discrimination ordinance opposed

Right-wing citizens sought to derail an attempt by the Urban County Council to pass a proposed ordinance prohibiting discrimination on the basis of gender identity and sexual orientation in housing, employment and public accommodations. Private organizations and churches would largely be exempt. The council held a public hearing in July during which supporters and opponents were given a chance to be heard. Rev. Wally Rendel, pastor of a local church, said, "God has spoken clearly about human sexuality. The sin that invited that judgment was the sin of homosexuality." Attorney Patrick Moores warned the council of the legal problems the county would face if the ordinance were passed, saying, "You have no idea of the potential liability and risk exposure you're putting on employers." Mike Alsmen, who said he represented a group of insurance agents, told the crowd, "You ministers who are for the fairness ordinance need to read your Bible... What are you going to do when you're dying of AIDS? What are you going to do when you're dying because of your immoral lifestyle?" Other opponents in the audience reportedly feared the proposed ordinance would clear the way for the legal recognition of same-sex marriage or impose hiring quotas for gay men and lesbians. The Kentucky Family Foundation, an affiliate of Focus on the Family (see p. 355), also opposed the proposed ordinance. Its president, Kent Ostrander, objected to how quickly the council put the proposal to a vote. "This fast-track process here in Lexington is unfortunate and I believe detrimental to the city," he said. "I believe that the ordinance is so aggressive that its language makes it vulnerable to some kind of lawsuit."

Several of the original opponents on the council apparently struggled with the proposal before the final vote. Council member Sandy Shafer said, "there is an issue that I have not been able to get beyond, and that is how a government can regulate a lifestyle." Council member Bill Farmer said that he objected to the inclusion of gender identity. He proposed deleting that section, but the council voted 10-4 to keep it in.

The council voted 12-3 to adopt the proposal. Supporters did not expect such a large margin of victory, but several amendments adopted prior to the final vote brought a few previous opponents on board. Those amendments exempted religious organizations and landlords renting a unit of a building where they or their relatives live. The amendments also allowed businesses to establish dress codes that would prevent cross-dressing and to designate gender-specific bathroom and shower facilities. The ordinance charged the Human Rights Commission with the power to investigate complaints of discrimination. Council members Shafer and Farmer both voted for the proposal in the end.

Louisville: Civil rights ordinance opposed

Opposition to proposed gay rights ordinances from conservative citizens and Religious Right organizations lasted through much of the year. Supporters had hoped the proposed ordinances would have a better chance of being passed this year because of plans to vote separately on each of the proposal's component parts. Proponents of the proposals also hoped that the well-publicized firing of an openly lesbian therapist from the Kentucky Baptist Homes for Children would increase the amount of support they would receive. The three proposed ordinances would have prohibited discrimination based on sexual orientation and gender identity in employment, in housing, and in public accommodations, respectively.

Two local anti-gay activists led much of the conservative religious community's opposition to the proposals. At an early January City Council meeting at which the proposals were first introduced, Frank Simon, director of the Kentucky affiliate of the American Family Association (see p. 352), said, "This is basically an anti-Christian bill... It's like spitting in God's face." The Board of Aldermen decided not to hold public hearings on the proposals, noting that they had considered similar measures since 1991. Rev. Jerry Stephenson, head of Metro African-Americans for Morality and Justice, later objected: "If a public hearing was held, and a couple of [aldermen] truly understood where people are in this community, I believe they would reconsider their vote."

Simon and Stephenson tried have local television station WDRB broadcast a television commercial opposing the proposed ordinances and the aldermen who supported them.

The ad linked gay men with pedophiles using an article from the Journal of the American Medical Association. The article's author said that Simon and Stephenson had misinterpreted his information. The commercial featured the voice of a man stating that as a child, he had been molested by a gay man, and then he cited the article. During another part of the commercial, Gayle Slaughter, an attorney, said, "… I have seen how the homosexual agenda poses a real threat to black children, including their demand to eliminate the age of consent laws." She then urged residents to call the Board of Aldermen to state their opposition. The station declined to broadcast the commercial, prompting criticism from Simon and Stephenson.

During the last week in January, the council adopted an amended version of the non-discrimination proposal concerning employment by a 7-5 vote, making Louisville the first city in the state with a gay and lesbian rights law. Among the vote's detractors was Rev. John Cummings, a local minister, who said, "It's against God, against His laws," as he left after the vote. Alderman Barbara Gregg objected to the process by which the proposal had been adopted, saying, "I'm totally disgusted with the manner in which it proceeded… This is an insult to the legislative process." Stephenson continued to denounce the ordinance, ignoring a poll showing

"You ministers who are for the fairness ordinance need to read your Bible… What are you going to do when you're dying of AIDS?"

— Mike Alsmen of Lexington, at an Urban County Council hearing on a proposed ordinance prohibiting discrimination on the basis of sexual orientation.

that 65 percent of Louisville residents supported it. "I think their constituents are disappointed, and my plea to the aldermen is for them to listen to their constituents," he said. The board tabled the other two non-discrimination measures.

In September, Pat Robertson's American Center for Law and Justice (see p. 352) sued the city, the mayor and other officials in federal court on behalf of a local doctor, J. Barrett Hyman, claiming that the law forced him to violate his religious beliefs. "By forcing employers who object to homosexuality and transgenderism to hire people who practice those lifestyles, the city of Louisville is attempting to legislate its own view of morality at the expense of the fundamental rights of its citizens," said Francis Manion, legal counsel for the ACLJ. "It forces an employer to choose between following the dictates of his conscience and going out of business." At press time, the lawsuit was pending.

Louisville: "Corpus Christi" protested

In July, members of Louisville's religious community protested a local production of award-winning playwright Terrence McNally's play, "Corpus Christi." The play depicts a Christ-like character as a gay man with 12 gay disciples. Louisville's production was one of the first after the original New York run. Jerry Stephenson, chairman of the

Metro Afro-Americans for Morality and Justice, led many of the protests. Before the production began, Stephenson led protesters in prayer outside the theater, saying that he was praying for the cast. He later told the protesters, "This is a slap in the face to the... Christian values that people in this community hold true." Although Stephenson admitted that he had never seen the play, he did say, "We used to call this thing blasphemy... Now we call it art."

Other right-wing activists joined Stephenson in the protests. Frank Simon, head of the Kentucky chapter of the American Family Association (see p. 352), also protested outside the theater during the week leading up to the opening show. Simon said that 15 other area churches had joined him in the protests. On opening night, the protesters numbered about 50. They sang hymns and prayed again outside the theater. "We're here to let them know we're defending our Lord," said Bertha Lloyd. "I've come to criticize this. It's blasphemy." Older women with statues of the Virgin Mary, young Protestant churchgoers, and members of the Ku Klux Klan joined the protests at various times.

Despite allegedly overt threats, the production continued. Artswatch, the group locally producing the play, said that it had received several anonymous threatening phone calls and letters. Cast members were reportedly threatened as well. Artswatch Director Joe Conroy said, "We won't be intimidated by the KKK or Frank Simon or his McCarthyist tactics." Robert Coulter attended opening night to support a friend who was in the play. "It [the protest] doesn't bother me. It would worry me if there weren't any protesters," he said. The play's director, Don Cox, felt differently. "I guess I thought that in 1999 the world had changed enough that it would allow people to speak and it would not create a furor," he said. He added that the production was an example of artistic freedom, not theology. "This is not Christianity. This is a play," he said. Supporters, many members of the Fairness Campaign and Anti-Racist Action, staged a counterprotest during one of the nights the play ran.

LOUISIANA

Baton Rouge: Council members walk out

City Council members Mike Tassin and Jim Benham walked out of a March council meeting during which a gay and lesbian group gave a presentation on discrimination. Lambda Group Inc. gave the council postcards from 300 people supporting a state law to prohibit anti-gay discrimination in employment. Tassin tried to block the presentation but was overruled by his fellow council members. Tassin said he objected to having the group's literature placed at this desk, calling the pamphlets "crap." He left saying he disagreed with the group's message. Carrie Evans, a member of the group, noted that more constituents from Benham's district had signed the cards than from anywhere else.

New Orleans: Gay billboards blocked

An advertising company rescinded an agreement to lease a billboard space to a gay and lesbian rights group. The Louisiana Electorate of Gays and Lesbians (LEGAL) paid Outdoor Systems Inc. to put up billboards reading, "Louisiana Says It's Okay to Fire People Because They Are Gay — Is That Fair?" The billboards were part of a campaign to get the state legislature to pass a non-discrimination bill protecting gay men and lesbians. LEGAL put the same message up in other cities around the state. Outdoor Systems' general manager said, "We are concerned about the content of that ad, not the issue." The company claimed the message was not entirely accurate because the city of New Orleans does have a non-discrimination ordinance that covers gay men and lesbians. Martha Kegel, LEGAL's spokesperson, said, "This illustrates precisely the point of our campaign. This is just the type of irrational discrimination against gay people that exists everywhere." A representative from one of Outdoor System's competitors, Lamar Advertising, said, "They [LEGAL] have the right to engage in political speech, as long as they put a disclaimer on it saying who is buying this advertisement. You don't have to necessarily be 100 percent right when it comes to people's First Amendment rights." Christopher Daigle, a member of LEGAL's board of directors, said, "[W]e are yet another example of gay and lesbian people being discriminated against."

MAINE

Statewide: "It's Elementary" opposed

Anti-gay religious activists opposed the local broadcast of Debra Chasnoff's award-winning documentary "It's Elementary: Talking About Gay Issues in School." In July, the Christian Civic League of Maine staged a protest at the Lewiston offices of Maine Public Television. The group's executive director, Michael Heath, called the film "morally repugnant" and claimed it promotes homosexuality. The League urged its 200 member churches to contact Maine Public Television and tell it not to broadcast the program. He added, "There's no doubt that this program is a tool for persuading everyone to accept a view of homosexuality that's highly controversial... " The American Family Association (see p. 352) said "It's Elementary" is an attempt by gay men and lesbians to "capture the hearts and minds of the next generation."

Rhonda Morin, a spokesperson for the station, said the station had received a large number of calls, many of them requesting it to air "Suffer the Children," a video produced by the AFA purporting to refute "It's Elementary." Morin denied that the station had a bias, saying, "We don't advocate any point of view. We strive to offer our viewers programs with diverse perspectives. Our hope is these will inform viewers, then create a forum of free speech."

Debra Chasnoff contributed an essay about the campaign against "It's Elementary" to the 1999 edition of Hostile Climate.

Bar Harbor: Domestic partner benefits opposed

In November, political opposition stalled a measure to provide domestic partner benefits for city employees. In October, the Maine Municipal Employees Health Trust had begun offering domestic partner benefits to government employees, if individual towns requested the coverage. The Bar Harbor Town Council deadlocked 3-3 in November on whether to add the coverage. Councilor Tom Burton, one of the more vocal opponents, said, "I don't have a problem with the sexual orientation part of it. I have a problem with people just living together not making a lifetime commitment. Getting on a health plan is traditionally one of the reasons why people get married." Councilor Matt Horton added, "… those of the opposite feelings should be able to say we think people should be married." Councilor Ken Smith also voted against the proposal. The one councilor who was absent can bring the measure back up for a vote. At press time, no further action had been taken.

Falmouth: Attempt to repeal non-discrimination law

Right-wing citizens fought to overturn an anti-discrimination ordinance that included sexual orientation, which the Town Council had unanimously passed in April. The ordinance, which prohibits sexual orientation discrimination in employment, housing, credit, education, and public accommodations, was widely viewed as a response to the 1998 referendum that nullified a similar statewide anti-discrimination law.

> "I was walking through the hallways and wondering, 'Is this the person who wants me dead because I'm gay?'"
>
> — Chris O'Connor, assistant director of student life at the University of Southern Maine, after anti-gay graffiti with threats of violence was written outside his dorm room.

By the time the council adopted the measure, conservative activist Mark Finks had already collected two-thirds of the signatures necessary to place a referendum on the ballot in the fall that would have effectively repealed it. The proposed referendum would have amended the town charter to prohibit the town from making any "ordinance, policy, or regulation regarding sexual orientation," and would have been applied retroactively. Over the summer, Finks helped form the Falmouth Concerned Citizens Ad Hoc Committee on Sexual Orientation to organize support for the proposal. Finks said members "are not trying to legalize discrimination. They are trying to exercise their rights of freedom of conscience under the law." The committee reportedly was helped by Maine's chapter of the Christian Coalition (see p. 353). By August, the committee helped collect enough signatures to place the proposed repeal measure on the November ballot.

Finks claimed to speak for other supporters at a September town council meeting, but was the only one to push for the referendum. He claimed that "some families of faith" had been discriminated against at a local school program on diversity by being excluded, and added that council members should not make policy based on their consciences. He maintained that there was widespread support for the charter change despite the relative silence of his backers. When reminded that he had distributed the virulently anti-gay publication "The Gay Agenda" in a failed bid to defeat the 1998 anti-discrimination proposal that included sexual orientation, Finks reiterated his support for that report. "I stand by every comma, dot, and question mark," he said. "The Gay Agenda" claimed that gay men and lesbians want to infiltrate public schools and "convert" schoolchildren and that gay men eat fecal matter.

In October, the Ad Hoc Committee announced that it would be distributing copies of "The Gay Agenda" again. Instead, it placed a newsletter, "Sexual Disorientation: Faulty Research in the Homosexual Debate," produced by the Family Research Council (see p. 355) in The Portland Press Herald and Maine Sunday Telegram home delivery tubes. The newsletter claimed that gay men and lesbians make up less than 10 percent of the population and that many gay men are child molesters. The newspapers denied having anything to do with the distribution. Finks did say that his group had distributed about 4,000 copies of the newsletter to homes around the town. One other pamphlet said, "Stop special rights. Vote 'yes' on 1."

Falmouth voters defeated the proposed anti-gay charter amendment, 59 percent to 41 percent.

Portland: Anti-gay vandalism in dormitory

Residents of the University of Southern Maine's Portland Hall dormitory twice found anti-gay graffiti written on the walls in September. The first incident was aimed at gay men and lesbians in general. The second included threats of violence against the openly gay assistant director of student life, Chris O'Connor, on the wall outside of his room. O'Connor said, "It really hit me hard... It hit me in my home, where I live and work... I was walking through the hallways and wondering, 'Is this the person who wants me dead because I'm gay?' " In response, the university held a Community Forum to End Hate and Intolerance at the dormitory. Stephen Wessler, head of the university's Center for the Studies and Prevention of Hate Violence, advised students that silence following such incidents can be disconcerting and that they need to confront other students who use degrading language.

Portland: Domestic partner policy opposed

A right-wing religious activist opposed a plan for city employees to receive domestic partner benefits. George Thebarge, an adviser with the Christian Civic League of Maine, spoke out against a proposal to provide health, family leave and death benefits for the domestic partners of city employees. He claimed that the proposal would recognize same-sex unions and that doing so would diminish the value of heterosexual families. Thebarge claimed the package would be ripe for abuse, especially fraudulent insurance claims. Under the proposal, qualifying employees would be required to present evidence of their relationship and sign an affidavit attesting to it.

Supporters disagreed with Thebarge's charges. Karen A. Geraghty, a former president of the Maine Lesbian and Gay Alliance, said the proposal would "level the playing field" for all city employees. "In the same way that we don't pay people differently for doing the same work, we shouldn't provide different levels of health coverage," she said. Mayor Thomas Kane also supported the measure. "Maybe some people will object on moral grounds. But I'm a firm believer that the city needs to be a leader on these kinds of work-place issues," he said. The City Council adopted the program in April, making it the first municipality in Maine to do so.

Statewide: Anti-discrimination bill defeated

A bill that would have prohibited discrimination against gay men and lesbians in employment, housing and public accommodations was proposed in January by Gov. Parris Glendening, who called it a legislative priority and testified personally before a legislative committee. Political opposition from conservative state senators and the conservative religious community doomed the bill, however. Jim Rogers, a resident who lobbied the state on a range of other conservative issues, called the bill "wrong," and said, "we'll stand against it as long as we have life and breath." Sen. Alex Mooney asked, "Do we really think a tan or black skin color is the same as homosexuality?... To give skin color and a lifestyle choice equal protection in law is wrong." Sen. Philip Jimeno voiced other concerns, saying, "I think it needs so much work, that to put this into law would, at this point, be a major leap... How will an employer know if he's acting legally against inappropriate behavior or violating the worker's rights?" Rev. Emmett Burns, a state legislator and minister, said, "I don't want to improve the chances for someone who is of gay persuasion to ply their behavior."

Many legislators objected to the bill's inclusion of transgendered people as originally introduced. As a compromise to get the bill out of the House Judiciary Committee, legislators dropped that provision from the bill. "How much do you think your child would learn if he or she were being taught by a man dressed as a woman?" Mooney asked. "This is obviously an attempt from militant homosexual and transgendered rights people to force the acceptance of their lifestyle on the people of Maryland." Some committee members insisted that transgendered people would still be protected.

Gov. Glendening gave unprecedented testimony before a legislative committee in support of the bill. He said his efforts were motivated by his brother, who was gay and died of

AIDS-related illnesses after years of serving in the Air Force. Telling the legislature, "It's the right thing to do," the governor said passing the bill would make Maryland a more fair society. He told The Baltimore Sun, "No one should be in fear [for] their job, no matter what their occupation, because of their sexual orientation."

The bill passed the House but stalled in a Senate committee, killing its chance at passage, making 1999 the seventh year in a row such a bill had failed. Gov. Glendening announced in October that the bill's passage would not be a legislative priority in the next session unless the Senate's conservative Judicial Proceedings Committee changed membership or the bill was moved to another committee.

Statewide: Harassment policy opposed

The state Board of Education turned down a proposal to explicitly prohibit anti-gay harassment in public schools. The Board first considered a proposal from the state Department of Education that included anti-gay harassment among other types of harassment that the state should prohibit. As complaints from right-wing parents, educators, and residents grew, state Superintendent Nancy Grasmick withdrew that proposal and offered a blanket anti-harassment policy. Doug Steigler, head of a Religious Right group called the Family Protection Lobby, claimed that the original policy would have encouraged gay and lesbian students to sue school districts, force educators to teach gay and lesbian issues, and force schools to fund gay and lesbian student groups. Deputy state Superintendent Richard Steinke said his department had received about 20 letters and several phone calls, most of which objected to listing specific groups protected under the proposed guidelines.

The policy the board adopted by a 10-2 vote states that "all students in Maryland's public schools, without exception, have the right to educational environments that are safe, optimal for academic achievement and free from any form of harassment." Maryland's Christian Coalition (see p. 353), Citizens for Parents Rights, and other right-wing organizations reportedly took credit for the change. Tres Kerns, of Citizens for Parents Rights, said, "[W]e sent a very clear message that they [sic] don't want to see homosexuality promoted or taught in the public schools." Bunny Galladora, spokesperson for the Women's Christian Temperance Union of Montgomery County, said, "This is an action to expand on a state level the indoctrination of my children... The home, church, and school should be safe places for our children, not battlegrounds for their bodies and minds."

Baltimore: Gay ministry silenced

The Vatican issued a directive in July to a nun and priest to stop their ministry to gay men and lesbians. Father Robert Nugent and Sister Jeannine Gramick of the New Ways Ministry were ordered to stop their outreach to the gay community. The order, issued with the Pope's approval, said the two were "permanently prohibited from any pastoral work involving homosexual persons." The Congregation for the Doctrine of the Faith, an organ of the Catholic Church, asked Nugent and Gramick to respond to a questionnaire on the church's doctrine. Gramick's non-response and Nugent's response were deemed unsatisfactory. Francis DeBernardo, the Congregation's executive director, issued a statement calling the order "clearly misguided and patently unjust." Gramick and Nugent say that they do not disagree with the church's dogma, but they emphasize the needs of gay and lesbian Catholics instead. DeBernardo's statement also said, "Silencing Sister Gramick and Father Nugent will not succeed in ending the discussion of how to reach out pastorally to gay/lesbian people."

Both Gramick and Nugent agreed that they would comply with the order. Nugent said that he would no longer give messages on homosexuality as a matter of pastoral teaching. "As far as I'm concerned, I'm not prohibited from speaking, as long as it's not associated with a pastoral setting," he said. Gramick said she would abide by the order and called on fellow Roman Catholics to "help me find creative, collaborative ways to lift the burden of this directive from [my] shoulders." A statement signed by 4,500 U.S. Roman Catholics protesting the order appeared in a November edition of The National Catholic Reporter and called on the church's bishops to "exercise their collegial right and ask the Vatican to reconsider this decision." It was presented at a meeting of U.S. bishops in Washington, D.C.

Frederick: Non-discrimination ordinance defeated

A proposed ordinance that would have prohibited sexual orientation discrimination in housing, employment and public accommodations faced numerous hurdles and ultimate defeat after it was introduced to the county's Board of Commissioners in September. Lobbying by the Frederick Human Relations Commission prompted the proposal. Passage seemed uncertain early on when the Human Relations Chairman, Edward Jenkins, and County Commissioner John Thompson announced their opposition. Referring to a separate proposal that the County Commission request that the state add such protections for gay men and lesbians to state law, Thompson claimed the Maryland sodomy law prevented it: "I don't need to make a moral judgment because the legislature says it is inappropriate." The Frederick proposal, Thompson claimed, would violate the state's sodomy laws.

Residents also organized opposition to the proposal. Bill Devens, head of the Maryland Family Values Alliance and the Montgomery County chapter of the Christian Coalition (see p. 353), said the measure would open a "Pandora's box of perversion," including county-sanctioned pedophilia and bestiality. He told county commissioners, "Homosexuals have proven themselves to be irresponsible disease carriers, detrimental to the health of society." Another opponent described homosexual sex acts as "abominations" practiced by "sodomites." Rev. Richard Glass said, "We're not preaching hate. We preach against sin."

The night before the final vote, supporters held a candlelight vigil at the commissioners' building. The Board of County Commissioners voted unanimously in October not to adopt the ordinance and to refer the measure back to the Human Relations Commission for further study.

Montgomery County:
Domestic partner benefits challenged

A proposal to extend family benefits to the domestic partners of gay and lesbian county employees came under fire from right-wing activists and politicians. Council member Derick Berlage first proposed the measure, which would cover health care, survivor and family leave benefits, in June. The county's Republican Party denounced the proposal in October, when it adopted a resolution opposing it. Proponents of that resolution said the benefits sent a "message that homosexual behavior is a valid 'alternative lifestyle.' " A party official called the resolution a "defense of marriage" and not an attack on gay men and lesbians.

At several hearings on the matter, local residents voiced their opposition. At an October meeting of the County Council, Bunny Galladora of the Women's Christian Temperence Union (WCTU) said, "We believe that homosexuality is illegal, immoral, unnatural and unhealthy. An abomination to God." She equated the benefits proposal with supporting illegal and sinful activity. Rev. J. Grace Harley, a local pastor and self-proclaimed "ex-gay," said the proposal promoted "a dangerous lifestyle." She added, "any time you grant any special rights or hate-crime bills you are really treading on dangerous territory because you are saying to those who are not yet in the lifestyle... that the lifestyle is OK, and that scares me." The Catholic Archdiocese also came out against the proposal. Bill Devans of the county's Christian Coalition (see p. 353) joined that opposition, saying, "Homosexuals even attend AIDS parties" so they can contract HIV and warned "whatever the vote... the further you push Christians, the further they push back."

> "Homosexuals have proven themselves to be irresponsible disease carriers, detrimental to the health of society."
>
> — Bill Devens of the Maryland Family Values Alliance , opposing a proposed anti-discrimination ordinance in Frederick County.

In November, the council adopted the measure 6-3. During the vote, members of the WCTU held signs saying, "Say No to Sodomy Subsidies." Galladora claimed that sodomy was illegal in the state although a court decision earlier in the year had ruled that law unenforceable. She said, "This bill when made law will benefit those who are engaging in the unnatural, immoral, and illegal act of sodomy... We think this bill should more appropriately be named the Sodomy Subsidy Bill for the Gay '90s." Rev. Harley said, "We don't need to be stimulating more immorality and sinfulness... Sodomy is still a crime."

Opponents had already begun gathering signatures for a referendum on the benefits program in October anticipating that the council would adopt the proposal. Lawrence Lauer, a member of Montgomery County Watch, said his group had 100 members and had already began collecting signatures for the referendum. "I believe in democracy," he said.

"If the people of Montgomery County want it, let them decide." The group contends that the benefits amount to special rights for gay and lesbian employees. Lauer also said that he had contacted the American Center for Law and Justice (see p. 352) to possibly mount a legal challenge to the proposal. The WCTU, Maryland Family Values Alliance, and Montgomery County Watch together formed the Montgomery County Coalition for Family and Marriage to better organize their efforts, but failed to collect enough signatures by the March 2000 deadline.

Montgomery County: Private school workshop criticized

Anti-gay activists criticized a workshop focusing on making sexual orientation part of diversity initiatives during a Montgomery County private school conference. At the workshop, Green Acres School teacher Anita Marcus discussed her use of "Heather Has Two Mommies" in a kindergarten class. Peter LaBarbera of Americans for Truth About Homosexuality (see p. 352), who taped the conference, criticized her for the lesson and for having a larger discussion with the students about gay men and lesbians. Marcus later noted that the discussion in question was sparked when her students mentioned that they knew of families with two mothers or two fathers. Molly Burke, a parent and president of the PTA at Diamond Elementary, a public school, said, "I would be very concerned if someone came to me and said my son was being taught homosexual issues or any human sexuality… I would definitely need to be notified prior to that instruction."

> "We think this bill should more appropriately be named the Sodomy Subsidy Bill for the Gay '90s."
>
> — Bunny Galladora of the Women's Christian Temperance Union, describing a proposal to offer domestic partner benefits for Montgomery County government employees.

A story on the conference ran in The Montgomery Journal, which followed up with another story on how experts view discussing gay and lesbian issues in elementary schools. Dr. Olga Fairfax, a lobbyist for the conservative Family Protection Lobby (see p. 355), said, "If the innocence during that time is violated in any way, it leads to precociousness or promiscuity later in life," she said. Anthony Falzarano, head of Parents and Friends of Ex-Gays (see p. 357), expressed similar concerns. "If they are pre-homosexual and have tendencies toward acting out [of] homosexuality," such information "could incite them to act upon these desires prematurely," he said. Fairfax challenged the argument that homosexuality is innate and not something that can be acquired, saying, "When you have two lesbians or two homosexual males, that is not a family… The only way lesbians or homosexuals can reproduce is by recruiting. That is their agenda, by going into the schools, recruiting and just presenting that style or relationship as normal, which it is not, and which in the children's eyes looks acceptable."

Washington/Frederick Counties:
Anti-gay campaign letter

A Republican state senator came under attack for proposing to use taxpayer money to fund an anti-gay public relations campaign and for distributing an anti-gay campaign letter on what looked like official letterhead. Sen. Alex Mooney wanted to use his office funds to hire a public relations firm to help defeat a bill to add sexual orientation to the state's civil rights laws.

In March, Mooney tried to hire a consulting firm to work on getting an op-ed he wrote published in newspapers serving the districts of legislators still undecided about the bill. "This bill has important ramifications and it's misunderstood. It has lacked someone exposing it," he said. In the piece, Mooney claimed the bill would protect cross-dressers and transsexuals from employment discrimination. The firm he chose was one that had contributed to his campaign. The watchdog group Common Cause of Maryland and the legislature's Joint Ethics Committee called his actions into question. Common Cause/MD Executive Director Kathleen Skullney said, "There's a clear line on certain kinds of communication that can be paid for by legislative office funds, and this falls on the wrong side of the line."

In August, after the bill had been defeated, Mooney again created ethical concerns among legislators with an anti-gay fundraising letter he sent on what appeared to be official Senate letterhead to his Frederick and Washington County supporters. He said the "militant homosexual lobby is targeting me for defeat." He added, "I need your help to protect our beloved state from the left-wing agenda of [Democratic Maryland Gov.] Parris Glendening and the crazy, anti-business crusade of the militant homosexuals." The Associated Press said Mooney used the term "militant homosexual" six times in the letter. Once again claiming the bill would have granted job protection to cross-dressers and transsexuals, Mooney took credit for its defeat and asked for a donation of $500 or more. His letter used the Maryland state seal and resembled Senate letterhead, although a disclaimer said it was not printed at government expense.

The bill's supporters heavily criticized Mooney's activities. "He's using trans people as scare tactics," said Jessica Xavier, a transgendered activist. Cathy Brennan, a member of the gay rights group Free State Justice Campaign, said, "Mooney is exploiting the gay community to raise money for his PAC." Even Mooney's Republican colleague Sen. Martin Madden criticized him, saying, "I would have encouraged him to write a less inflammatory letter."

MASSACHUSETTS

Statewide: Same-sex marriage bill

A bill to prohibit the state from recognizing same-sex marriages drew support from the state's conservative activists and some religious leaders. State Rep. John Rogers introduced the measure in December, and opponents of gay and lesbian rights quickly announced their support. The original bill read, "A purported marriage contracted between persons of the same sex shall be neither valid nor recognized in the Commonwealth." It was later changed to say that the state only recognizes marriages between men and women. Rogers' spokesperson said that the original language was a mistake and not intended to be offensive.

The state's conservative religious leaders organized support for the bill. The Catholic Archdiocese announced its support early on. John Walsh, its spokesperson, said, "Our view on marriage is always of a man and a woman in an exclusive and monogamous relationship... That's according to natural law and to the whole of sacred Scripture." Rev. Ray Hammond, pastor of a Boston church, also spoke out in favor of the ban. Alveda King, niece of Rev. Martin Luther King Jr. and an anti-gay activist, echoed these pronouncements.

"Pro-family" groups, led by the Massachusetts Family Institute, an affiliate of Focus on the Family (see p. 355), also spoke out in support of the bill, citing religious justifications. Its president, Matt Daniels, said, "We will be religious groups all standing up and saying the same thing — that the Commonwealth should hold the definition of marriage as a union of a man and woman." In advance of the hearing, the Institute also held a press conference featuring King and other anti-gay speakers.

However, the state's religious community was divided on the issue. A coalition of 150 progressive religious leaders, among them Jews, Protestants, Catholics and Unitarians, signed a declaration of support for same-sex marriage in February. The declaration began, "The most fundamental human right, after the necessities of food, clothing and shelter, is the right to affection and the supportive love of another person." The coalition said they would fight to make sure that if same-sex marriages were legally recognized elsewhere, they would not be recognized by Massachusetts.

Elected officials also supported the bill. Gov. Paul Cellucci told reporters, "I am not for gay marriages." He added, "I think we need to encourage that basic family unit, and I think permitting gay marriages would detract from that." The coalition of religious leaders who supported same-sex marriage were holding a rally outside the state Capitol while Cellucci made the statements. His position upset many gay and lesbian activists. Jennifer Levi said, "It certainly is disappointing that the governor would not recognize the importance of strengthening gay families."

During May hearings on the bill, religious leaders from both sides testified before a legislative committee. Catholic Bishop Sean O'Malley claimed that families with opposite sex couples were best for raising children. He contended that same-sex marriage would "open the door to polygamy and incest." The state Catholic Conference issued a statement saying that possible pro-gay legal developments on same-sex marriage in other states made the bill necessary for Massachusetts to establish its own definition of marriage. Rev. Gilbert Thompson, pastor of New England's largest black church, said, "We came to proactively support the way marriage has been viewed for centuries... This issue goes further to tear down the family." Opponents of the bill argued that it violated the separation of church and state because its motivation was religious in nature. When Cambridge City Council member Katherine Triantafillou said the Bible did not define homosexuality as sin, many in the chambers jeered her. The bill stalled in committee in July, but was carried over into the 2000 legislative session.

A personal essay by Katherine Triantafillou appears on p. 49.

Amherst: Gay-straight alliance posters torn down

A vandal tore leaflets advertising a gay student group from a high school bulletin board in September. The board was used by Students United with Diverse Sexuality (SUDS), a gay-straight alliance at Amherst Regional High School. Posters for a girls' flag football game were also defaced. Led by Lyndsy Belliveau-Byam, members of SUDS drew up a petition signed by 200 students demanding action from school officials. After speaking with the group, Principal Scott Goldman made a schoolwide address. The student, who admitted to tearing down the SUDS posters, later apologized to the group's members. SUDS adviser Michael Bardsley said the apology was not part of the punishment. Goldman did not say what punishment the student faced. Belliveau-Byam left with a good impression: "I feel I have learned a lot from this experience and hopefully people who have discussed it in class have learned a lot, too."

Boston: Refusal to aid gay theater group

A gay theater group filed a discrimination complaint against Boston University, claiming that a BU program had refused to help the troupe design a brochure and logo because it is a gay organization and might spark controversy. Theater Offensive, a gay and lesbian theater company at the Boston Center for the Arts, solicited help from Boston University's AdLab, a student-run course in the College of Communications that provides production and advertising assistance for nonprofit groups, to promote an upcoming production in October. However, AdLab's faculty advisor, Sue Parenio, admittedly refused to provide assistance. Renee Farster, Theater Offensive's managing director, said Parenio told her that "... the majority of the students are 18. There are kids from Third World countries, and [I don't] want some angry parents complaining." When asked if the group had been rejected because it is predominantly gay and lesbian, Parenio allegedly said, "I hate to say this, but yes. I'm sorry, but I have to be honest." Parenio did offer her own services free of charge, but Farster turned them down, saying that AdLab would have provided a more complete campaign. Farster later filed a complaint with the Massachusetts Commission Against Discrimination.

The Boston Globe asked Parenio to describe the criteria for accepting new clients. She responded, "If it's not outright offensive, we probably will do so. But [not] if it is, if I have to spend time explaining to parents and to the people in the college here. I guess it's a judgment call." To illustrate what she felt was offensive, she cited "Greetings from a Queer Senorita," a play in Theater Offensive's annual Out on the Edge Festival.

Parenio had the support of university officials. Brent Baker, dean of the College of Communication, said, "If her judgment is that that's not an appropriate project, for whatever reason, that's within her bailiwick, as far as I'm concerned."

Theater Offensive Artistic Director Abe Rybeck said, "We work with high school-age kids every week... so it's strange that someone should think college-age kids would not be able to handle what our work is about... [I]'m also appalled by the lack of courage in standing up to that."

At press time, the case was still pending before the commission and Theater Offensive and officials at Boston University were in negotiations attempting to achieve a settlement.

Cambridge: Vandalism at Harvard University

Vandals struck a Harvard University dormitory twice during the fall semester. In October, anti-gay messages were left on a board in Mather House twice in one week. One of those targeted was resident tutor and adviser to the Bisexual, Gay, Lesbian, Transgendered, and Supporters' Alliance (BGLTSA), K. Kyriell Muhammad, who found homophobic graffiti posted on a message pad outside his door. He said that in the previous week, someone had torn down a picture of him wearing a dress, with the caption, "BGLTS Safe Zone." Posters advertising a gay and lesbian film festival were defaced.

Vandals targeted Muhammad's dormitory door once again in December. A BGLTSA poster outside his door was defaced. Days after this event, Muhammad announced that he would resign at the end of the semester, saying, "The disruption in my personal life has been profound, and I no longer feel capable of continuing in my capacity as a resident tutor... This is not a decision that I have made lightly." University officials condemned the incident and expressed their sorrow at Muhammad's departure.

Holyoke: Bank discrimination alleged

A woman claimed that a Holyoke bank had refused to give her a loan application because she was transgendered. The woman, Lucas Rosas, filed a sex-discrimination suit in federal court in April against the Park West Bank and Trust Company seeking an unspecified amount of damages because the bank allegedly violated federal and state laws in denying her an application. Rosas said that when she was asked to produce three forms of identification, one showed her in male attire, one in female attire, and another in which her gender was "indeterminate," according to her attorney, Jennifer Levi, of the legal group Gay and Lesbian Advocates and Defenders. Rosas said that after examining the identification, the bank officer refused to give her an application. Rosas said the experience was humiliating. "The loan officer had three photographs sitting in front of her to confirm who I was," Rosas said. "What I wear should not affect whether or not I get to apply for a loan." Levi described Rosas as "traumatized," and that the loan officer refused to give her the application and told Lucas to "go home and come back when you're dressed like a male." Levi added, "Refusing to extend credit to a person who was born male but dresses in female clothing and often passes for a woman is impermissible sex-stereotyping. Both state and federal law forbid such practices."

Bank officials would not comment on the case. U.S. District Judge Frank Freedman dismissed the case in November. Levi and her client appealed. Oral arguments were held in the court of appeals in May 2000, and in June, a three-judge panel of the appeals court reinstated the case, ruling that sex discrimination may have been involved in the incident.

Newton: Anti-gay school board campaign

Conservative activists distributed anti-gay campaign leaflets urging voters to support school board candidates who opposed having gay and lesbian issues discussed in schools. Stand Up Newton (SUN) developed a four-page pamphlet it distributed around town that endorsed a slate of school committee candidates and denounced gay-positive programs in the town's schools. It said, "The school committee allows a wide array of radical sexual and homosexual activists to come into the schools and present programs, give speeches, form clubs... Nearly all the 'information' given is little more than propaganda and scientific quackery... " In a section entitled "Bring back parental control over radical sexuality pushed at kids," the flier derided gay-affirming programs in the schools. The pamphlet also said the high schools supported "being gay" days and "celebrate the homosexual lifestyle." SUN also claimed that "students and adults talk about becoming homosexual and encourage kids who might feel so inclined, or confused, to do so." Another section listed the candidates — all eight challengers to the incumbents — endorsed by SUN for the school committee. The gay and lesbian Boston newspaper Bay Windows reported that one of those endorsed, Brenda Loew, published an adult, sexual magazine called, "Everyone is Doing Outrageous Sex" and affirmed her support for gay/straight alliances in the schools and sex education to another Boston gay newspaper. Although Loew said she welcomed the endorsement, she also said that the endorsement would not make her change any of her positions. Loew said she thought SUN would distribute about 15,000 of the pamphlets around Newton. Three of the candidates SUN endorsed, including Loew, lost their bids in November.

Sherborn: Anti-gay mailings

An anti-gay activist made two anti-gay mass mailings to most of Sherborn's residents in January and February. In January, J. Edward Pawlick mailed 15,000 copies of a booklet he described as an "in-depth feature story" entitled, "An Intelligent Discussion About Homosexuality... Will Massachusetts Listen?" In it, Pawlick discussed the discredited work of sociologist Paul Cameron, who claimed that "30 percent of homosexual men will be dead before age 30 or they will be HIV positive." He also quoted studies claiming that

> "We should not allow the most vulnerable of our young men to be indoctrinated by homosexual activists."
>
> — Activist J. Edward Pawlick, in an anti-gay pamphlet mailed to 13,000 Massachusetts schools and church groups.

gay people can change their sexual orientation and said that gay activists are spreading hate and teaching their "lifestyle" to children. In the latter story, Pawlick referred to the state's gay/straight alliances in public schools funded in part through state money. The 28-page booklet also included a copy of an ad run in the New York Times as part of the "Truth In Love Campaign" by so-called "ex-gay" ministries. Pawlick publishes a conservative online newspaper, The Massachusetts News, and has engaged in political campaigns around the state.

Gay and lesbian activists and residents were alarmed, fearing the mailing was part of the growing influence of the Religious Right in their town. Mark O'Brien said, "I am concerned because some people may read it and say, 'Oh, gee, this is what gay people are really like.' " Others feared the damage it might inflict on youth who were questioning their sexuality. Sue Hyde, a regional organizer for the National Gay and Lesbian Task Force, said, "This kind of written material about gay people comes from the right wing and is very anti-gay and defamatory and depicts gay people in the worse possible terms and light." Surina Khan, an analyst for Political Research Associates, which monitors the Right, said, "This is something we started to see in Massachusetts a few years ago, but I think it's an ongoing effort that I expect we will continue to see." Many said Pawlick's efforts might be a first step in targeting seats in the elections for the state legislature.

Pawlick sat down to elaborate on his activities with Bay Windows, a gay newspaper in Boston. He said he mailed the booklet to "test people's reactions" and spark a discussion about homosexuality. Pawlick claimed that reports about scientists who argue that sexual orientation is not genetic seldom garner attention, and that he was adding balance to the debate. When asked why he did not present arguments that homosexuality is genetic in his booklet, he said, "I am just one guy and that was a lot of work and there is just so much I can do." Pawlick also denied that he was part of the Religious Right despite his membership in several national organizations like the Family Research Council (see p. 355) and the Christian Coalition (see p. 353). On discussing homosexuality with children, he said, "As long as there is any doubt in anybody's minds, whether [gay people] are made or born, I don't think we should be telling [children] that... they are homosexual and that they cannot change." The Unitarian Universalist Area Church held a public forum to discuss the mailing and issued a public letter condemning Pawlick's activities.

Weeks after the Bay Windows interview and the church's organizing against intolerance, Pawlick mailed out copies of another pamphlet to town residents. It also went to 13,000 schools and church groups statewide. "We should not allow the most vulnerable of our young men to be indoctrinated by homosexual activists," it said. Pawlick said he was disappointed with the response the first mailing had received and was disturbed by the "personal attacks" against him. He wrote, "I think these adults [gay men and lesbians] are foolish to be homosexual, but that is their decision... It is our children about whom we should be concerned." The letter echoed many of the same themes in the first mailing, especially the claim that "homosexuals" were being recruited in public schools. Pawlick called Rev. Rosemarie Smurzynski of the Unitarian Universalist Area Church "intolerant."

The church again held a public forum, attended by Pawlick, to discuss the second mailing. Though many in the crowd said they left feeling somewhat enlightened, Pawlick said he felt quite the opposite. "I don't know what I've learned. I didn't really learn much, I don't think. I was obviously disappointed that it was a one-sided meeting. There is no group in the world that is totally happy, and they made it seem everything is wonderful." He also claimed that most residents were probably too scared to speak in support of him for fear of suffering "personal attacks."

MICHIGAN

Statewide: Bill to define marital status

Republican state Rep. Clark Bisbee introduced a bill in March that would have amended the state's civil rights law to define "marital status" as being lawfully married to someone of the opposite sex or as unmarried and not cohabiting. Bisbee introduced the bill in response to a 1998 Michigan Supreme Court ruling upholding civil rights protections in housing for unmarried couples. In that ruling, the court held that a landlord could not refuse to rent to an unmarried couple because doing so would discriminate against the prospective tenants based on their marital status. Bisbee argued that the government must protect the religious beliefs of what he called that "small minority of landlords." Gay and lesbian rights activists had heralded the ruling as a victory for same-sex couples.

Civil rights activists and housing experts quickly attacked Bisbee's bill. Jeffrey Montgomery, head of the Detroit gay rights group the Triangle Foundation, said that the bill unfairly targeted gay men and lesbians, whose relationships the state refuses to recognize as marriages. Thomas Coleman, executive director of the American Association for

Single People, called the bill "a rush job to strip three million unmarried Michigan adults of their civil rights... This is a meat cleaver approach to delicate legislative surgery." He called it "the worst assault on the rights of single people I have seen in the entire United States." Clifford Shrupp, executive director of the Fair Housing Center of Metropolitan Detroit, said, "[This bill] makes a mockery out of Michigan's Elliot-Larsen law, that prohibits discrimination based on religion, by attempting to change that law to allow people to legally impose their religious biases on the housing choices of other persons."

The bill died in the House Constitutional Law and Ethics Committee.

Statewide: Hate crimes bill stalls

A campaign by anti-gay groups and right-wing state legislators blocked passage of bill to amend the state's existing hate crimes law to include sexual orientation. The bill would also have made the current two-year penalty for commission of a hate crime consecutive with the commission of any other related felony.

Opponents claimed that hate crimes legislation threatens free speech. Steven Schwalm, an analyst with the Family Research Council (see p. 355), said, "When the law acts on attitudes and beliefs, it becomes dangerous." He added, "If hate crimes cannot be prevented in a state with the death penalty, how do you expect to reduce them in a state where the punishment is less?" During a public debate on hate crimes at the International Institute, Gregory Quinlan, president of the Pro-Family Network (see p. 357) and self-proclaimed "ex-gay," said, "Hate crime laws represent a desire to bring special rights to a group that was not born to do what they do."

> "Hate crime laws represent a desire to bring special rights to a group that was not born to do what they do."
>
> — Gregory Quinlan of the Pro-Family Network, opposing a bill to amend Michigan's hate crimes law to include sexual orientation.

Gay and lesbian rights advocates disagreed. Sean Kosofsky of the Triangle Foundation said, "by not supporting a bill that will save lives, you are encouraging violence." State Rep. Lynne Martinez disputed Quinlan's testimony saying, "What this bill does not do is create a protected category. This does not prohibit free speech. It does not prohibit the pastor saying from his pulpit that homosexuality is a sin."

The bill died in committee, but is scheduled for reconsideration in 2000. A similar bill had failed 1998.

Detroit: Anti-gay Radio Show

The hosts of the "Deminski and Doyle" radio show on WKRK-FM made anti-gay epithets part of its format. In September, Jeff Deminski and Bill Doyle began a segment of their show featuring what they called "faggy songs." They encouraged listeners to suggest songs that men "shouldn't be caught dead singing," especially those that made men feel less masculine. Callers responded, saying things like "I have a faggy song for you guys" and "I know a fag song." The hosts have used other derogatory terms on the show to refer to gay men.

Members of the Triangle Foundation, a statewide gay and lesbian advocacy group, called the program several times to challenge their stereotypes of gay men and to call for the show's termination. Sean Kosofsky, Triangle's director of policy and victim services, said, "This is an example of outrageous bigotry and overt homophobia." He continued, "If these radio personalities would have made disparaging epithets toward racial, religious, or ethnic minorities, they would have been forced by the station to apologize and would probably lose their job."

Triangle met with WKRK officials, seeking to stop the bigoted remarks. The station manager, Steve Sinicropi, refused to silence the radio personalities. He threatened to sue the Triangle Foundation for defamation because the organization had publicly labeled the show homophobic. The station's parent company, Infinity Broadcasting, finally stepped in and ordered an end to homophobic remarks on the show. It also offered Triangle an apology on behalf of the radio station. Although Deminiski and Doyle are still on the air, they have since refrained from making homophobic remarks part of their format.

Ferndale: Human rights ordinance repealed

A human rights ordinance that prohibited discrimination against gay men and lesbians and other minority groups was short-lived. The Ferndale City Council had considered writing the anti-discrimination provisions into a revised city charter but later decided to call for a separate ordinance to prohibit anti-gay discrimination in employment, housing, public services, and public accommodations. The Council adopted the anti-discrimination ordinance in September. Months later, anti-gay activists led a successful effort to repeal the measure by placing the measure on a ballot referendum.

The citizens committee charged with developing the language for the anti-discrimination proposal deliberated through much of the year, hearing from both opponents and supporters. Council member and former mayor Robert Paczkowski led the political opposition. Within a month of the formation of the citizens committee in December 1998, Paczkowski began speaking out against the proposal, saying that a "gay rights ordinance," as he termed it, would recognize the "unnatural union" of homosexuality. He called the ordinance "a smokescreen to promote homosexual lifestyles" and claimed it would become a financial burden to the city because of the number of lawsuits it would encourage. Although Paczkowski said his opposition was based in his Catholic faith, the Detroit Archdiocese offered no official objection to the ordinance. Committee member Kay Watson also cited her religious convictions as the basis of her opposition to the proposal. "I'm a Christian. I think homosexuality's a sin. I didn't say it. God said it."

A majority of the citizens committee, whose membership was diverse, ignored those arguments and recommended to the City Council that it adopt the proposed ordinance. The council adopted the measure in September, with Paczkowski providing the sole opposing vote.

Opponents of new ordinance quickly organized to have it repealed. In October, Paczkowski submitted enough signatures to secure a place for measure on the ballot as a referendum, hoping that voters would rescind the ordinance. A month later, the city suspended enforcement of the new ordinance pending the vote. The issue was placed on the February 2000 ballot, the same day as the state's Republican presidential primary.

A majority of voters chose to rescind the ordinance. Their margin of victory was small, however. Of his victory, Paczkowski said, "We have no duel with the gay community. We don't want them to push their lifestyle."

Holland: College hosts "ex-gay"

J. Ben Patterson, Dean of the Chapel at Hope College, invited self-proclaimed "ex-gay" speaker Mario Bergner to address the college in March. Patterson, who believes homosexuality is a sin, invited Bergner as part of a series focusing on "Sexual Brokenness." Affiliated with Pastoral Care Ministries, Rev. Bergner has written several books arguing that gays and lesbians can and should change their sexual orientation through religious devotion. His books discuss how he claims he renounced his homosexuality and joined a Christian ministry.

Patterson is well-known on campus for his views opposing homosexuality. He has said, "Homosexuality, along with all other sins, is sin" and that all sin turns "into human perversion." His homophobic messages have resonated with some students. "When I think of homosexuality, I think of it as another demonstration of Satan," student Todd Haulenbeek said. "It's a sin to commit acts of homosexuality in the same way people are tempted with stealing."

In response to Bergner's address, the college's Women's Issues Organization wanted to sponsor a "clothesline of intolerance" behind the campus chapel. The group was forced to place the display indoors after college officials denied its request, saying similar demonstrations had been held indoors in the past. Jill Pierson, president of the student group, felt otherwise: "To me, it seems like they're closeting the issue."

At the invitation of several student groups, including the Women's Issues Organization, Rev. Mel White spoke at campus Chapel the week following Bergner's address. One of those groups, the Student Congress rescinded its own invitation to White when some of its leaders claimed the issue became controversial. Other groups stood by their invitations. A nationally known gay minister, White had worked with several Religious Right leaders for decades before coming out of the closet. "Gays and lesbians are already at the heart of the church. We are important to the faith community. This should be a non-issue," he told the audience. He later addressed a local church whose denominational affiliation had been revoked because of the church's inclusion of gay men and lesbians.

Jackson: Proposed gay rights measure targeted

Right-wing politicians and religious leaders attacked a proposed addition to Jackson's existing human rights ordinance that would have protected gay men and lesbians from discrimination. In February, Jackson's Human Relations Commission (HRC) presented a proposal to the City Council that would add sexual orientation to the city's anti-discrimination ordinance to prohibit discrimination against gay men and lesbians in housing and employment. Frank Hampton Jr., of the Church of God in Jackson, assailed the proposal, arguing that people should be allowed to discriminate against gay men and lesbians if their religion instructs them to do so. "People should not have to violate their moral beliefs as landlords or employers. I feel homosexuals are a threat to the morality of our society," he said.

Criticism continued through the summer. Commissioners had expected to formally present the proposal at a July City Council meeting, but it was inadvertently left off the agenda. The City Council still provided time for opponents and supporters to voice their opinions. Although the majority of those who testified supported the proposal, City Council candidate Craig Radala called the measure unnecessary, unconstitutional, and a threat to the religious rights of landlords. The Jackson Citizen Patriot, a local newspaper, published an editorial claiming that there was no need to protect gay men and lesbians from discrimination.

Despite promises from the mayor that the proposal would be brought up for a vote, the council has not yet acted on the commission's recommendation as of press time.

Plymouth: Gay-themed displays censored in schools

District school officials forced a middle school teacher and a high school teacher to remove displays depicting gay and lesbian life. In October, Plymouth-Canton Schools Interim Superintendent Ken Walcott ordered Mike Chiumento of West Middle School and Tom Salbenblatt of Plymouth Salem High School to remove displays they had set up commemorating Gay and Lesbian History Month. Chiumento, an openly gay music teacher at West Middle School, had created a display featuring books, a newspaper article on Billy Bean, a professional baseball player who had recently revealed his homosexuality, and several small pieces of gay iconography. Salbenblatt had put up a bulletin board featuring statistics on the nation's gay population, gay historical figures, and a statement by Coretta Scott King assailing homophobia. He said his bulletin board was consistent with the high school's motto: "Dignity and Respect for All."

Maureen Murphy, West Middle School's assistant principal, altered Chiumento's display. She removed one of the gay-themed books and replaced it with books on blacks and Native Americans. Explaining her actions, Murphy said, "I was just told by Mr. Chiumento he wanted to do a display on diversity, so I let him... I didn't know it was going to be a one-issue display, and I told him we needed to make it more diverse." Chiumento said that a similar display put up by a heterosexual teacher had been shown in previous years without interference from school officials. Chiumento replaced the display with a sign reading, "Censored." He believes the directives came because he and Salbenblatt are openly gay. "I'm a gay man, so they say I'm promoting my lifestyle," he said. "They think I'm recruiting."

> "This is the last straw. If the police are more interested in covering up for their own than in protecting me, then I'm not going to stick around."
>
> — William Krout, who decided to close his Royal Oak shop after learning that the father of a boy who allegedly vandalized his store was a police officer. Another officer responding to Krout's complaint declined to file a report.

Having also been told to dismantle his display, Salbenblatt replaced it with a quote from Goethe: "There is nothing more frightening than active ignorance." Salbenblatt said that several of his students questioned him about why the display came down so suddenly. "I told them it was censorship. It's telling students it's not OK to be different," he said.

Walcott said he ordered the displays taken down because they were not curriculum-related and parents objected to them. "Last week, I received calls from [over 200] parents who thought the displays were inappropriate... It isn't part of our curriculum. If these bulletin boards were recruiting people to Catholicism, we wouldn't allow that either." He said that freedom of speech was not the central issue.

Walcott's decision had the support of several school board members and parents. School trustee Darwin Watts said, "Gay material and sexual preference are not a function of educating our kids." Trustee Judy Mardigian said, "I wonder why we would post information about gay lifestyle in a middle school hallway. And what does it have to do with a high school math class?... Parents need to be notified of this kind of exposure." School board president Sue Davis said, "If you want to talk about lifestyle, then why don't you talk about S&M? That's a lifestyle." Canton parent Sandy LaMassee said, "I think it's kind of inappropriate, especially at the middle school... These aren't issues for school." Another parent said, "This debatable subject matter doesn't need to be in the schools." She continued, "I didn't sign any paper to have my child taught this type of sex education."

Criticism of the displays continued in local newspapers. Harold Monet wrote a letter to the editor in The Crier calling Gay and Lesbian History Month "homosexual perversion history month." He challenged statistics that point to the high number of gay and lesbian teens who commit suicide. "I would suggest the suicides occur because of some physical or mental instability," he wrote. "I do not believe they have a civil right to promote and inform children of their persuasion through displays in Plymouth-Canton schools."

Chiumento, Salbenblatt, and their union filed a grievance against the school district for violating the academic freedom clause in their employment contracts. They sought an end to the censorship and a reinstatement of the gay-themed displays. The American Family Association's Center for Law and Policy (see p. 352) offered free legal services to the school board and applauded Walcott for ordering the displays taken down. The AFA of Michigan's president Gary Glenn said, "We join parents in applauding Superintendent Walcott for acting in the best interests of children rather than submitting to homosexual activists' political agenda... It is wrong to use our public school classrooms, and the tax dollars to fund them, to promote homosexuality or any other behavior that puts our children at risk." At a subsequent school board meeting, advocates of free speech and gay and lesbian rights criticized the district's actions and supported the displays.

An assistant superintendent, who was designated as an administrator for the proceeding, heard the grievance in November. Because the district took no action on the grievance, Chiumento and Salbenblatt brought the matter before an arbitrator. At press time, the arbitration was pending. The American Civil Liberties Union said it would sue the school district if the teachers lost their grievance.

In the wake of the controversy, district high school students voted to establish a Gay-Straight Alliance. The new group held its first meeting in December.

Royal Oak: Complaints allege police unresponsiveness

Allegations that Royal Oak police failed to address complaints from gay and lesbian residents and other minority groups led the City Commission to form a citizens review board for the police department in June. Jeffrey Montgomery, head of Detroit's Triangle Foundation, a gay and lesbian rights organization, said that police had repeatedly mishandled cases involving gay men and lesbians. In April, about 10 people told the City Commission about problems they have had with the police department's response to harassment and personal assaults they suffered. In a survey of 156 citizens' complaints from across the community, reporters from The Detroit News found that police were 10 times as likely to dismiss complaints as they were to find that they had merit. Only 8 percent of complaints were substantiated by the department. Two widely publicized incidents affecting gay men prompted gay and lesbian demands for the review board.

In one incident in March, the son of a police officer reportedly dropped a glass vial containing a foul-smelling substance in a store owned by a gay man. William Krout, co-owner of the shop, said he smelled the odor, which had come from a stink bomb the 7-year-old boy had dropped. Krout reported that he followed the boy and his parents out of the store and confronted them. According to Krout, the boy's father, a police detective who was off-duty at the time, denied his son dropped the stink bomb and began to verbally harass Krout. The father allegedly threatened Krout with anti-gay epithets and told him to commit a sex act and "go die of AIDS." Krout then summoned the police to his shop. Krout said the responding officer first discouraged him from filing a report, then refused to write one up. Krout said that four days later, he discovered that the boy's father was a police detective. He has since decided to close his shop and move elsewhere, saying "This is the last straw. If the police are more interested in covering up for their own than in protecting me, then I'm not going to stick around." State Police said they had been conducting their own investigation. Sean Kosofsky, of the Triangle Foundation, said, "This is one of several incidents involving gays which show Royal Oak police neglect duties and sometimes are the actual problem."

> "His schoolwork suffered, and he experienced great shame, terror, embarrassment, and humiliation in and while going to school."
> — From a complaint filed by Jesse Montgomery, who claimed he suffered anti-gay harassment in Duluth's public schools.

In another well-publicized incident, Michael Sharp, a local hairdresser, complained that several teens had taunted him about being gay and having a rainbow gay pride sticker on his car before both parties were involved in a car collision. Sharp alleged that the teens kicked in his car's windows and spat on him. Sharp, who received a citation for careless driving, was the only one initially charged in the incident. He vowed to show that the teens had caused the accident and filed a lawsuit in local court seeking damages from the teens. One of his attorneys said, "Both cases [Krout's and Sharp's] exemplify the Royal Oak Police Department's callous indifference to harassment against gays in Royal Oak." The first judge assigned to the case recused himself because his son knew the teens involved. One of the teens involved in the incident was later charged with assault and sentenced in October to probation. At press time, no final trial date has been set in the civil suit against the teens, but a pretrial hearing took place in June 2000.

Royal Oak: Gay rights proposal opposed

Religious Right activists joined right-wing Royal Oak residents and elected officials in attacking a proposed human rights ordinance that would have included sexual orientation. Resident Leslie Thompson called for the measure in September after working with local gay and lesbian activists to end police indifference toward complaints of harassment by gay and lesbian residents. Commissioner Laura Harrison became the lead sponsor, modeling the proposal after a human rights ordinance passed in neighboring Ferndale.

The topic became an issue in the city's fall campaign for mayor. Incumbent Mayor Dennis Cowan said he would consider the measure when it reached the City Commission. His opponent, Mike Andrzejak, favored forming a citizen's committee to study whether the measure was needed. Current Ferndale Councilman and former mayor Robert Paczkowski, who helped organize a petition drive against Ferndale's human rights ordinance, claimed to have received several calls from Royal Oak and Ferndale resident opposed to the proposed ordinance.

Religious Right groups also organized opposition to the proposal. The Michigan affiliate of the American Family Association (see p. 352) sent a letter to Royal Oak's city commissioners urging them to oppose the measure. "If Royal Oak's leaders adopt special minority-status rights on the basis of sexual orientation, we will assist the citizens of Royal Oak in amending their charter to strike this," threatened its leader, Gary Glenn. Auburn Hills Mayor Tom McMillin, also active in the campaign to repeal Ferndale's gay-friendly anti-discrimination ordinance, began gathering support to defeat the proposal in Royal Oak. He reportedly vowed to target similar non-discrimination proposals in other suburban Detroit communities.

Defeat of the Ferndale human rights ordinance in February 2000 reportedly made Royal Oak's City Commission cautious. The commission has refrained from moving forward on its plans to adopt its own ordinance, reportedly fearing that opponents would quickly repeal it through a ballot initiative.

MINNESOTA

Duluth: Schools sued over alleged harassment

In March, a former Duluth public schools student sued the Duluth School District in state court, asserting that he had endured anti-gay harassment and that teachers and school officials had failed to address that harassment. Jesse Montgomery claimed that he had been verbally and physically harassed while attending the district's elementary, junior and senior high schools. He said that he and his parents had reported the harassment, which allegedly included being called "faggot," "queer," and "Jessica," to the superintendent and the school board. Montgomery's parents said officials' failure to adequately address the harassment forced them to remove him from public schools and enroll him in a private high school. "His schoolwork suffered, and he experienced great shame, terror, embarrassment, and humiliation in and while going to school, knowing he would not receive protection from the school," the complaint read.

> "The chancellor and the majority believe a minor is best served by living in an explosive environment in which the unemployed stepfather is a convicted felon, drinker, drug-taker, adulterer, wife-beater, and child-threatener."
>
> — Mississippi Supreme Court Justice Charles McRae, dissenting from a ruling that placed David Weigand's son in an abusive home rather than in Weigand's custody, on the basis of his "moral fitness" as a gay man.

The school district, however, denied all of the charges in a five-page response to the suit. The district contended that it had exercised reasonable care in preventing the alleged harassment and did not have a duty to protect Montgomery from harm inflicted by other students. The district also said that Montgomery had unreasonably failed to take advantage of preventative opportunities provided by the district to avoid the alleged harassment.

Jesse Montgomery said, "This case isn't based on my sexuality. It's based on how I was treated in high school and the harassment I took because people thought I was gay." The suit seeks compensatory and punitive damages and asks the district to institute a school policy prohibiting harassment based on actual or perceived sexual orientation. Montgomery's attorney, Kyle Torvinen, said the state Department of Human Rights had investigated the case in 1996 and found that probable cause existed to substantiate a discrimination claim. The department also certified the case for a hearing. Torvinen said Montgomery chose to bring a lawsuit instead. The lawsuit was pending as of press time.

MISSISSIPPI

Statewide: Court upholds denial of custody

The Mississippi Supreme Court upheld a lower court's ruling that left a 15-year-old boy in an abusive home rather than in the full custody of his openly gay father. The state Supreme Court ruled 5-3 that David Weigand's "moral fitness" was inadequate for him to be awarded full custody of his son. The court did, however, overturn a lower court's order denying Weigand visitation rights while his partner of eight years was at their home.

Weigand filed for sole custody in 1997 after his son called 911 because of domestic abuse occurring at his ex-wife's house. Weigand's ex-wife, Machelle Houghton, had been in an abusive relationship with her third husband. Court records showed that boy's stepfather twice had been charged with beating Houghton and had once threatened her and the boy while drinking. The stepfather was convicted of simple assault in one of these incidents, but Houghton claimed that her marriage had stabilized. Houghton worked two jobs and admittedly spent little time with her son. The boy, however, told a Mississippi judge that he was indifferent about which parent he lived with.

Weigand said, "My son, my partner, and I have built a wonderful family together. It makes me sad and deeply worried for my son to know that the Court cares more about the gender of my life partner than about giving my son a good home." Weigand and his partner live in California. Five University of Mississippi psychology professors and the American Civil Liberties Union filed *amicus curiae* briefs with the state Supreme Court, arguing that gay men do not lack parenting skills and instincts. The state Supreme Court acknowledged that Weigand had the stronger claim to providing a stable home, but still awarded custody to Houghton.

In a dissenting opinion, Justice Charles McRae said that the court had been "blinded" by the issue of homosexuality. "The chancellor and the majority believe a minor is best served by living in an explosive environment in which the unemployed stepfather is a convicted felon, drinker, drug-take, adulterer, wife-beater, and child-threatener, and in which the mother has been transitory, works two jobs and has limited time with the child," he wrote. "The chancellor makes such a decision despite the fact that [the minor's] father has a good job, stable home, and does all within his power to care for his son."

MISSOURI

Statewide: Anti-gay clarification sought on sodomy ruling

Missouri Attorney General Jay Nixon sought clarification of a state appeals court's ruling striking down the sodomy statutes so that sex between consenting gay and lesbian adults would continue to be prohibited. In July, a state appeals court overturned a Kansas City man's conviction on a sexual misconduct charge because the person with whom he had had sex consented to the acts. The man, William Cogshell, continues to serve a sentence for his convictions on two counts of statutory sodomy with the same person, who was 13 and 14 during the incident in question. In August, Nixon requested from the court a clarification of its ruling. The sexual misconduct statute prohibits "sodomy," "sexual contact," and "sexual contact through clothing" "without that person's consent." Nixon asked the court to clarify whether or not the "consent" portion applied to all three areas covered by the law. He wanted the court to rule that the "consent" provision did not apply to those engaged in a homosexual sex act.

Gay and lesbian activists criticized Nixon's reading of the law. Tara Jensen, an attorney representing Cogshell, said, "The legislature obviously did not mean to criminalize all sexual acts in the state of Missouri." Pat Logue of the Lambda Legal Defense and Education Fund called the attempt to criminalize gay sex exclusively "a strange argument." She added, "The court itself knows what it was trying to say in its opinion." The court issued no ruling in response to Nixon's request. Attorneys at Lambda Legal maintain that the court's refusal to respond to Nixon's request means that state laws no longer prohibit consensual sex between consenting adults, in accordance with the court's July ruling.

Statewide: Hate crimes bill criticized

A bill to add actual or perceived sexual orientation to the state's existing hate crimes laws faced criticism in and outside of the state legislature's chambers. The bill, the Criminal Intimidation Act, would replace the Ethnic Intimidation Act with new provisions that would allow prosecutors to classify hate-motivated crimes as felonies if they can prove that bias motivated by the victim's sexual orientation, sex, or disability played a role in the crime. State Rep. John Loudon (R) ridiculed the idea of listing specific minority groups that would be protected under the bill. "Where's the protection for fat people or bald people or rich people? People are attacked every day for certain characteristics," he said. State Rep. Michael Gibbons (R) tried to have the existing hate crimes law repealed. After saying, "We are carving ourselves into such small sections... It's time we look at the broader picture," he sparked an emotional backlash from a few black legislators. State Rep. John Hickey responded, "I find it sad in this body that some of the same people who want to put you in jail for burning the flag want to make it legal for you to burn a cross." Gibbons withdrew his proposal. The Senate version of the Criminal Intimidation Act was passed in April by a 20-14 vote. In May, the state House of Representatives passed the bill after what one newspaper characterized as a "raucous debate." Gov. Mel Carnahan signed it in July.

Statewide: Non-discrimination proposal rejected

In January, the Missouri Board of Curators, the state board governing the University of Missouri system, ignored requests to restore sexual orientation to the university system's non-discrimination policy. The board had removed sexual orientation from its discrimination policy in 1995. In December 1998, several professors personally asked the board to make the changes. For several months in spring 1999 semester, students and faculty throughout the university system had been petitioning the board to restore the non-discrimination provision. In January 1999, University of Missouri System President Manuel Pacheco recommended that the board adopt a strengthened version of his existing executive order, which prohibits discrimination without delineating which groups are protected. His proposed policy would simply urge campuses to provide a "positive working environment," to design programs that "help develop healthy attitudes toward different kinds of people," and to develop training programs that include sensitivity to gay and lesbian issues. The board voted 7-2 in favor of that proposal. Board member John Matthes denied any implication that the board's vote constituted an endorsement of anti-gay discrimination.

Student and faculty activists at the University of Missouri at Columbia, however, led several protests against the board's vote. At the meeting at which the president's proposal was adopted, several students shouted, "Inclusion Now!" and "Full Inclusion!" Student volunteer Dean Anderson said, "Executive Order No. 3 is nothing more than bureaucratic double-speak." Missouri politicians joined them in frustration. Democratic state Rep. Vicky Riback Wilson said, "I am very disappointed that the university has not included sexual orientation in the list of other protected classes." Fellow legislator Tim Harlan agreed, saying, "I'm disappointed that President Pacheco and the Board [of Curators] didn't go ahead with the full inclusion... "

Despite the Board of Curators' action, three schools within the University of Missouri at Columbia in April elected to add protections for gay men and lesbians. The new policies were prompted by a request from the Missouri Students Association. Dean of Arts and Science Ted Tarkow said, "The majority of our faculty believes there are ethical obligations. Prejudicial actions are not tolerated."

In June, two openly gay professors at the Columbia campus resigned in protest at the board's failure to restore the non-discrimination provision covering sexual orientation. Horace Griffin said the board should have included the

> "I can truthfully say I would not have been looking for another job had the board decided to include sexual orientation."
>
> — Former University of Missouri-Columbia professor Denny Schrock, who resigned from the faculty when the Missouri Board of Curators ignored requests to restore sexual orientation to the university system's non-discrimination policy.

protection if only as a symbolic measure "to recognize and affirm lesbians and gays as equal within the institution." Denny Schrock resigned to take a position at the University of Illinois at Champaign-Urbana, where the administration specifically protects gay men and lesbians from discrimination. He said, "I can truthfully say I would not have been looking for another job had the board decided to include sexual orientation."

Columbia: Non-discrimination for schools criticized

A decision to prohibit discrimination based on sexual orientation within Columbia's public schools drew the ire of many parents and residents. Students had petitioned the school board for several months to adopt such a policy and were ejected from a May board meeting when they tried to speak on the matter. The board entertained their proposal a month later. Lynnanne Baumgardner, a sympathetic school board member, said, "Our responsibility as board members is to determine what the climate, the environment — what our culture will be within school buildings."

Opponents fought the measure on religious and moral grounds. Resident Don Schoengarth said, "If we pass this, Christian teachers can't talk about their life with Christ, Muslim teachers can't talk about Allah. But gay teachers can talk about the joys" of sexual activity between people of the same sex. Schoengarth went on to urge the board to ban discussion of homosexuality in schools. He worried that none of the supporters of the new policy had discussed the impact of AIDS on gay teens' lives: "It's very important to discourage any type of gay sex until children are older, or until they understand they are mortal." Attorney and school board member Elton Fay joined Schoengarth in denouncing the new policy. "They do not want tolerance." Fay said. "They want affirmation of their lifestyle." He said he feared the proposed policy would prohibit teachers from being able to speak out against homosexuality and drive parents away from public schools: "It's another indication of a society not willing to have a moral code."

In June, the school board voted 4-3 to adopt the proposal.

Kansas City: Jury decision in lesbian foster care dispute

A federal jury found that the Missouri Department of Social Services had discriminated against Larry Phillips when officials there reprimanded him for refusing to approve a lesbian as a foster parent in 1995. Phillips had said his religious beliefs did not allow him to grant the woman a license. Phillips had later claimed he received low performance evaluations and was ultimately terminated in 1996. Phillips, represented by Pat Robertson's American Center for Law and Justice (see p. 352) in his discrimination lawsuit against the Department, maintained that his supervisors had told him he "was being intolerant and his religious beliefs were affecting his ability to perform his job effectively" when he raised questions about the foster parent case in question. Phillips characterized the prospective parent as "sexually confused" to his superiors. The jury assessed $26,000 in actual and punitive damages in Phillips' favor.

The ACLJ heralded the jury's verdict. Francis Manion, regional director of the ACLJ's Midwest office, said, "This verdict sends a strong message to employers that Christian employees who hold religious beliefs do have rights." He added, "Employers are not free to treat Christian employees as second-class citizens just because their religious beliefs might not be politically correct." In an earlier press release, Manion had stated, "By attacking and terminating this employee, the state of Missouri has given its tacit approval to the militant homosexual lobby that is attempting to radically change the life-style and values of a society based on Judeo-Christian principles."

Pleasant Hill:
School district sued over alleged harassment

In June, a student who claims that he was harassed for four years by classmates whom, he says, believed he was gay sued the Pleasant Hill School District in federal court. The lawsuit alleges that school officials did nothing to halt the student's harassment even after he reported the abuse. The student says he was called names in the school cafeteria and hallways, physically assaulted, and nearly run over by one student's car. Although a school official spoke with a few of the students who allegedly harassed the boy, "the harassment of plaintiff only intensified," the lawsuit maintains. The student says he sought professional counseling and eventually dropped out of school.

His lawsuit was filed less than two weeks after the U.S. Supreme Court ruled that school districts receiving federal money may be liable for sexual harassment directed against their students. Katherine Argent, the student's attorney, said, "[The Supreme Court ruling] clearly tells the school they can't turn their backs anymore and talk about budget constraints." She added, "If schools can feel it in their pocketbooks, we can expect to see these kinds of problem behaviors really clamped down on."

In July 2000, the U.S. Attorney General Janet Reno filed a motion in the case asking U.S. District Judge Fernando Gaitan Jr. to order the school district to implement anti-harassment policy. An attorney for Lambda Legal Defense and Education Fund said that this was the first time the federal government weighed in on a case involving alleged anti-gay harassment in a school. The district settled the case later that month, paying the student $72,000 and agreeing to establish a two-year program to "prevent, identify and remediate harassment and discrimination" on the basis of sex or sexual orientation.

St. Louis: Anti-gay cab driver

In December, a cab driver refused to transport a customer to a gay bar. When Mike Gentle told his Yellow Cab Company cab driver the address of the club he would be visiting, the driver asked if that was a "fag" bar. Gentle corrected him, saying that it was a gay bar. The driver tried to eject Gentle about two blocks from his home, but Gentle refused to leave the car. Instead, Gentle grabbed the cab's microphone and tried to alert the dispatcher about the situation. "I just couldn't believe it. All I wanted to do was get a ride to a bar," he said. "I just wanted to be treated like a human being." Another driver arrived and took Gentle to his destination. Gentle was unable to get the first driver's name. The cab company's owner, Jack Seibert, said he did identify the first driver, but refused to reveal his name. Seibert offered a public apology to Gentle. The driver maintained that his religious beliefs prevented him from taking a passenger to a gay bar. Although Seibert said the driver would be reprimanded, he was unsure whether further actions could be taken because the driver claimed that he based his actions on his religious beliefs.

St. Louis: Pride week marred by vandalism

Vandals tore down a banner outside a gay and lesbian student center, and a lesbian student said she was verbally harassed during Gay, Lesbian and Bisexual Awareness Week at Washington University. A banner valued at $300 was stolen from in front of the offices of the Spectrum Alliance, a gay and lesbian student group. The incident was reported to university police. Because they had no witnesses, police were not optimistic they could find the thief. Washington University police Sgt. Mark Werner said that fraternities typically stage such incidents. He also expressed doubt about whether the theft was motivated by homophobia. Spectrum Alliance vice president Rebecca Bishaf said the position of the banner required someone to use a ladder to remove it. She added that the timing of the theft, during Gay, Lesbian, and Bisexual Awareness Week, should leave little doubt that this was an anti-gay theft. Later that week, Bishaf reported to university police that two men whom she could not identify had verbally assaulted her in a campus parking garage. She said that their comments targeted her sexuality. Police, again, said they could not identify any suspects because the victim could not identify them.

St. Louis: Right wing attacks beer company

Two right-wing groups sponsored a press conference in November to launch a nationwide boycott of Anheuser-Busch beer products because the company regularly sponsors gay and lesbian pride events. Peter LaBarbera and Jim Hanes of Americans for Truth About Homosexuality (see p. 352) and Joe Glover of the Family Policy Network (see p. 354) both addressed the media. Video clips of a few small gay and lesbian groups at the Folsom Street Fair in San Francisco were the focal point of the presentation; Americans for Truth claimed the footage showed sadism, cruelty, "simulated sex acts," and "human degradation." Bud Light, an Anheuser-Busch product, was a main sponsor of the fair.

> "All I wanted to do was get a ride to a bar. I just wanted to be treated like a human being."
>
> — Mike Gentle, after a taxi driver refused to take him to a gay bar in St. Louis.

Although LaBarbera and Glover acknowledged to reporters that the clips did not represent all gay people, they used them as a basis for denouncing the company's sponsorship of lesbian and gay pride events across the nation and its policy of extending family benefits to the domestic partners of its employees. LaBarbera and Glover called the company's sponsorship of pride events "unconscionable." The two said Anheuser-Busch has a marketing strategy of courting gay men because they have above-average incomes, though many studies do not support this assertion. "August A. Busch III needs to take responsibility for the perversions his company is promoting and put an end to this nonsense," LaBarbera said. He called on St. Louis residents to force the company to drop its pro-gay policies and marketing, saying, "It's time for the people of St. Louis and the rest of America to see the activities that Anheuser-Busch is helping to make possible." He added, "Anheuser-Busch executives are hypocrites for putting forth an all-American image through their TV ad campaigns while ignoring calls by pro-family groups to stop promoting homosexuality... "

Anheuser-Busch stood by its employment policies and its sponsorship of gay and lesbian festivals, saying it supported fair because of the "benefits the event brings to the San Francisco community."

MONTANA

Statewide: Failure to repeal sodomy statute

The state legislature refused to take Montana's sodomy law off the books even though the state supreme court had ruled it unconstitutional. Opponents of Rep. Joan Hurdle's bill to remove the sodomy statute said they feared doing so would encourage more gay men and lesbians to move to the state. Rep. Bob Clark said, "The Supreme Court didn't say we had to take this law off the books." Rep. Dan McGee, said, "The court has granted to the homosexual community the right to exercise that homosexuality in private, and that is all." Rep. Verdell Jackson quoted the Bible as he explained his opposition. Others said they feared that homosexuality was being viewed as "different but normal," rather than a deviant behavior. The bill failed with a 50-50 tie vote in the state House.

Led by Hurdle, several Democratic members made emotional speeches in favor of reconsidering the bill, and the House voted 50-46 to do just that. Rep. Mary Ann Guggenheim, the only openly gay legislator, said, "Who are we? We're your children, we're your siblings, we're your constituents." Minority leader Emily Swanson said, "Let's do what's right by people like my sister [who is a lesbian]." Before the bill came up for a second vote, state Rep. Jim Schockley, an opponent to the bill in its original form, sponsored an amendment that would have prohibited same-sex sexual activity that was non-consensual, conducted in public or conducted commercially. Adding that amendment caused many of the original bill's supporters, including Hurdle, to vote against the amended bill. On the second vote, the amended bill was soundly defeated 37-63. Rep. Carol said that Williams said that the amendment "eviscerated" the original bill and that "the power of the radical right" was thriving in the state legislature.

Statewide: Gay rights bill opposed

Conservatives opposed a bill that would have added sexual orientation to the state's existing civil rights laws. State Sen. Jon Ellingson's bill would have prohibited discrimination against gay men and lesbians in housing, employment, public accommodations, education, and credit. Most of the bill's opponents claimed that homosexuality was a choice, and therefore, not worthy of inclusion in the state's anti-discrimination laws. Laurie Koutnik, head of the Montana Christian Coalition (see p. 353), was one of the most vocal opponents. She claimed that because gay men and lesbians are not disadvantaged members of society and that the courts would not look favorably on claims that they need legal protections from discrimination. She argued that gay men and lesbians routinely made more money and were better educated than straight people, and referred to gays' "lifestyle or deathstyle; call it what you choose." Koutnik also asserted that landlords should be able to deny housing to gay renters if the landlords' religious beliefs justified it. The Eagle Forum (see p. 354) also opposed the bill.

The Senate Judiciary Committee took no action on the bill.

Statewide: Hate crimes bill dies

A committee of the Montana legislature killed a proposal to add sexual orientation to the state's existing hate crimes law. State attorney general Joe Mazurek developed language for the measure, and passage seemed possible early in the session, although conservative legislators and right-wing organizations later challenged it. Publicity over the murder of gay University of Wyoming student Matthew Shepard increased pressure for a gay-inclusive hate crimes law. Gov. Marc Racicot had said early on that he would support such a bill. Arlette Randash, with the Eagle Forum (see p. 354), discounted the need for such a bill, saying, "If you reflect back on what happened in Wyoming, the people who perpetuated that crime were able to be brought to justice under existing laws." She added, "I believe that hate crime legislation, in large part, is being used as a front to move the homosexual agenda forward so it is accepted by people as an accepted standard in our community." She claimed the bill would make sexual orientation equal to "the immutable characteristics such as race, creed, religion, color." Randash said that she was the victim of harassment from the state's gay newspaper: "I felt very intimidated."

> "I believe that hate crime legislation, in large part, is being used as a front to move the homosexual agenda."
>
> — The Eagle Forum's Arlette Randash, explaining her opposition to a bill adding sexual orientation to the state's hate crimes law.

In opposition to the bill, state Sen. Lorents Grosfield introduced his own measure to repeal all laws that designate as felonies specific types of bias-motivated crimes and laws that require judges to increase sentences for people convicted of such bias-motivated crimes. Claiming that the state had too many laws on the books, Grosfield said his bill would simplify enforcement by making the law more fair. He said that bills should not be passed because of "popular sentiment of public opinion at a specific time." Gay rights advocates feared Grosfield's bill was too broad to be enforceable. Gov. Racicot said that he would veto Grosfield's bill if it were sent to him.

Both bills died in committee in February. After consulting with the attorney general, Senate Majority Leader Hank Coe said Mazurek's bill was unnecessary because the number of anti-gay bias crimes was so low.

Statewide: Methodists reject marriage policy

In June, the Nebraska Conference of the United Methodist Church rejected proposals to liberalize the church's policies toward homosexuality. A proposal introduced by Rev. Lauren Ekdahl of Lincoln would have removed from the Book of Discipline the section prohibiting ministers from blessing same-sex marriages. The Book of Discipline contains the guidelines and rules that constitute church policy. Ekdahl's proposal would have replaced the section on the blessing of same-sex marriages with the phrase: "We urge our ministers not to perform ceremonies that celebrate homosexual unions or to conduct such ceremonies in our churches." Ekdahl, who prosecuted Rev. Jimmy Creech in 1998 for performing a gay marriage ceremony, said the wording was a good compromise between same-sex marriage supporters and opponents. Her petition was the only proposal that drew comments from more than one speaker. Another defeated proposal would have petitioned the church to delete language condemning homosexual acts and prohibitions on the ordination of gay men and lesbians from the Book of Discipline.

The conference also selected delegates to the General Conference to be held in 2000. In a victory for conservatives, three of the five lay members selected as delegates were backed by the Association of United Methodist Evangelicals in Nebraska, the group that led a demonstration at Creech's second trial in 1999 for performing a same-sex marriage ceremony in North Carolina in April.

Statewide: Same-sex marriage bill

Right-wing members of the state legislature sponsored a bill that would have prohibited the state from recognizing same-sex marriages regardless of where they were performed. Although the state attorney general noted that Nebraska has never recognized same-sex marriage, state Sen. Jim Jones (R) still introduced the bill. At a Judiciary Committee hearing in February, several of the state's right-wing activists registered their support for the bill. Jeff Johnson, a professor at the University of Nebraska and a representative of Pilots for Christ International, asked, "If we cannot draw the line in what is morally acceptable, where can we draw the line anywhere?" Claiming that homosexuality is a choice, Johnson maintained that the state would be "doing what is right" by passing the bill. Gordon Opp, a self-proclaimed "ex-gay," also testified in favor of the bill, saying, "If the state of Nebraska put a stamp of approval on anything other than marriage between a man and a woman, I might have been tempted [to be in a homosexual relationship]."

Opponents of the bill said that it amounted to anti-gay discrimination. Steven Charest, an attorney for the Lincoln chapter of Parents, Families and Friends of Lesbians and Gays, said, "I believe a family is two people who decide to take on life together as a team… This bill says you must take on life as a handicap. No laws are going to stop people from falling in love." Abby Swatsworth, a Lincoln resident, said that the legislation could add to the "culture of hate" against gay men and lesbians.

Jones' bill died in committee, just as a similar bill did in the previous session.

Grand Island: Methodist minister defrocked

Rev. Jimmy Creech, a Methodist minister from Omaha, was stripped of his ministerial credentials by a church jury for performing a same-sex "holy union" ceremony in North Carolina in April. Creech had blessed the union of Jim Raymer and Larry Ellis at Binkley Memorial Baptist Church in the couple's hometown of Chapel Hill. Since 1997, the Methodists' Book of Discipline has forbidden ministers from performing same-sex marriage ceremonies, and church officials continue to charge ministers who perform "holy unions" with violating church doctrine. Creech had narrowly avoided conviction in 1998 for previously performing a similar ceremony. In the wake of that outcome, Nebraska Bishop Joel Martinez chose not to reappoint Creech to First United Methodist Church, where Creech was pastor. Creech then moved back to his native North Carolina to begin work on a book about the trial and how the Methodists have dealt with homosexuality, although he had remained on the Nebraska roster of clergy.

Martinez, who had advised Creech not to perform the April 1999 ceremony, brought charges against Creech in May on behalf of the church's Nebraska Conference, after two Nebraska ministers complained about the ceremony. "It's a sad statement on where the church is to devote time and money to uphold the persecution of gays and lesbians," Creech said. The United Methodist trial was held at a church in Grand Island and lasted 90 minutes. All 13 jurors were Methodist clergy from Nebraska, and Bishop William Grove presided over the trial.

Outside the church, protesters gathered to criticize Creech. Fred Phelps (see p. 356) led a delegation from his Westboro Baptist Church in Kansas. He said that Creech's work is "damnable" and that he was "going straight to hell." He added, "We're following brother Creech around like an ugly dog." Phelps and his church members brought many of their trademark placards. They had also protested the Chapel Hill church where Creech conducted the "holy union" ceremony for which he was being tried. Members of the Association of United Methodist Evangelicals in Nebraska, hoping to marshal 200 protesters, was only able to gather about 30 demonstrators. They walked around the trial site reading Scriptures from the Christian Bible and praying. They had planned to read the entire Christian Bible before the trial ended. "We believe if we read the Bible and pray, it will help participants in the trial discern God's will," said Rev. Mike Moyer.

Supporters of Creech also demonstrated. Rev. Mel White, who heads Soulforce, an interfaith group that uses non-violent techniques to oppose discrimination against gay men and lesbians, led a delegation of 100 in a 24-hour vigil around the church where the trial was held. More than 70 were arrested for blocking the church entrance — two of them children from Creech's Omaha church who sang "We Shall Overcome" in the lobby of a makeshift police headquarters while the adults were being booked. The night before the trial, Creech performed a "renewal of vows" for the same couple whose April ceremony was the subject of the charges against him. They had to hold that ceremony in a local hotel because none of the local churches would allow them to use their facilities.

At the trial, Creech acted as his own attorney, saying he would not cooperate with an unjust trial. "If you vote guilty, you will be honoring that law [prohibiting ministers from officiating at same-sex ceremonies]," Creech told the jurors. The jury unanimously rendered a guilty verdict. An undisclosed majority of the jurors voted to strip Creech of his ministerial privileges by defrocking him. Those decisions disheartened Creech, who said, "I'm not surprised, but I'm really quite disappointed... I'm mostly disappointed that it was a unanimous decision... This is a loss of something I love dearly." He added, "This is the pettiness of the church and not the spirit of God that has acted here today." Creech planned to remain with the church, but will no longer minister. He does, however, plan to continue performing same-sex ceremonies as a layperson.

A personal essay by Rev. Jimmy Creech appears on p. 33.

Lincoln: Coach's anti-gay remark

University of Nebraska football coach Ron Brown ignited a controversy when he called homosexuality sinful on a sports radio broadcast in September. On that episode of his show, "Huskers Sports Report with Ron Brown," the university's head football coach discussed his view that Christians should minister to gay men and lesbians so they would learn that homosexuality is a sin and turn to Christ. "No question, homosexuality is clearly wrong according to God's word... We've left the homosexual on the side of the road, beaten and hurt, to a politically correct world that honors this lifestyle... who exhorts them with its liberal religious clergy and provides mercy to them from its government in the form of dollars, media time and accepted entry into school curriculums." Brown added, "The homosexual is both lost and beaten up, despite his strong appearance... The boy sissies of yesteryear that I physically abused have grown up to be overt homosexuals, as have the young college gays, no men, some with AIDS, all lost without Christ." Brown has frequently aired religious views during his sports update program.

Although Brown enjoyed support from across the state, many of his critics complained that his prominent position as the coach of a major college football team blurred the lines between his roles as a state employee and an advocate for anti-gay Christian beliefs. Some of his defenders, however, supported his right to speak out on the grounds that he did so as a private citizen and not as a representative of the university. Others supported his views on the sinfulness of homosexuality, saying his status as a state employee did not override his right to speak out about his Christian beliefs.

Gay and lesbian advocates and community groups criticized Brown for his remarks. Led by Citizens for Equal Protection, state chapters of Parents, Families and Friends of Lesbians and Gays, and a host of clergy, critics called on Brown and the University to apologize for the remarks. Rev. Sky St. John, an Omaha minister, said, "People who are righteously indignant about homosexuality have found a way to stone others and still call themselves 'Christian.' I wish that Ron would close the Bible and open his heart." Rabbi Aryeh Azriel said, "Nebraska is not a Christian state. The University of Nebraska is not a Christian university." Nancy O'Brien, chair of the Board of Regents, said, "I just can't support taking advantage of one's position at the university to preach their own ideas, regardless of what those ideas might be." She also said that the line between Brown's personal and professional activities "seems to be pretty thin and pretty unclear."

> "The boy sissies of yesteryear that I physically abused have grown up to be overt homosexuals ... some with AIDS, all lost without Christ."
>
> — University of Nebraska football Coach Ron Brown, on his radio show.

Brown's critics and supporters squared off in the Omaha World-Herald and Lincoln Journal-Star. The World Herald's editorial staff characterized Brown as courageous. Even though Brown had changed the name of his show to "The Ron Brown Show," the editorial staff at that paper wrote, "people who would subject him to further sanctions, up to and including being fired, ought to back off." Lynn Hamill wrote a letter to the editor of the World-Herald saying, "There is an atmosphere of nearly total intolerance by the homosexual community and its supporters of any disagreement with them about homosexuality. They are in effect forcing the entire nation to accept, condone, and celebrate a behavior that many, if not most, people in this country still believe to be of a deviant sexual nature." Ken Kohl, a season ticket holder for University football games, told a reporter for the Lincoln Journal-Star, "I don't mind him spreading the religion, but when he's spreading the religion against homosexuals, that's wrong."

Brown defended his views and his right to air them publicly. Talking to the World-Herald, he said that he broadcasts his religious views as a private citizen. He added that he does not wear University apparel when giving religious speeches. Brown had the support of many University officials. Chancellor James Moeser said Brown did not violate the University's non-discrimination policy, which includes sexual orientation, and that he did not speak for the University. "I personally disagree with Coach Brown," Moeser said, but "he has the right to state his opinion."

Lincoln: Women's studies program criticized

The Women's Studies program at the University of Nebraska-Lincoln came under heavy criticism for its lesbian content. The controversy started with a critical column in a January edition of the student newspaper by self-described "Christian conservative" undergraduate Jessica Flanagain. "I am asking if a well-developed program is one that devotes the most study to a faction of society that makes up only 10 percent of the population," Flanagain wrote. She suggested the program was a "political campaign," and claimed that if it were, the university would need to be investigated for violating federal campaign laws. She claimed that 70 percent of the required reading for a course on 20th century women writers was lesbian literature. "The current focus of the course material does not present an accurate cross-section of the experiences and contributions of women," she wrote. "It is heavily weighted toward advocating lesbianism."

Flanagain was soundly criticized for her remarks by faculty and fellow students. Joy Ritchtie, professor of a class whose content Flanagain questioned, disputed Flanagain's course content calculations, saying that only eight out of 40 women authors whose works were read during the class in question were lesbians. Another professor wrote, "If we deem subjects worthy of study based only upon the proportion of the population they refer to directly, then entire courses in, say, Western Civilization, Art, History... would have to be scrapped because men represent only 50 percent of the population." One student wrote, "I see Ms. Flanagain is again attacking women, and this time she decided to pick on the lesbians. What's her 'political agenda'? Do we accuse English classes outside of the realm of women's literature as 'overly promoting' a heterosexual curriculum?"

Only one letter to the editor supported Flanagain's concerns. Daphne Patai, a professor at the University of Massachusetts, wrote, "Flanagain is brave to voice a criticism that she knows will bring a predictable response. But she is right; there is indeed a difference between balancing a curriculum and proselytizing for a particular political agenda."

The controversy carried over into the fall semester when Flanagain wrote another column criticizing the Women's Studies program. "So, the women's studies department at the University of Nebraska-Lincoln not only seeks to advance a lesbian agenda, it's intolerant of any opinions that don't mesh with the liberal rhetoric of the academe" and "rejects 'alternative' points of view, like... a biblical one," Flanagain wrote. She then told students not to take any classes in the department "under any circumstances" since the department became "hysterical" in the wake of her January column. She was again roundly criticized in the student newspaper. One student, who said she had attended a Women's Studies class with Flanagain, said, "Jessica hardly ever attends class."

Omaha: Station cancels interview

An ABC television network affiliate canceled a scheduled interview on National Coming Out Day because station officials deemed the subject "too controversial." National Coming Out Day is designated every October to encourage gay men, lesbians and bisexuals to openly acknowledge their sexual orientation and educate the public on a range of issues affecting them. To acknowledge the event, KETV reporter Carol Kloss had scheduled an interview with the local organizer of the event to discuss local activities and to help people better understand the meaning of National Coming Out Day.

After meeting with the station's general manager, however, the news director, RoseAnn Shannon, canceled the interview, saying, "We have a policy on the types of interviews we allow on our newscasts. All interviews promoting a certain event must be non-controversial." Kloss was out of town when Shannon made the decision. After being asked why National Coming Out Day was deemed controversial, Shannon replied, "I'm not even going to go down that road." She said that she could not remember any other time when a planned interview was canceled because the station felt it was too controversial.

Viewers eager to see the interview called the station to complain. Deanna Zaffke, a member of the University of Nebraska's Gay, Lesbian, Bisexual, and Transgender graduate group, said, "Homophobic people are everywhere, and sometimes those people are gatekeepers. RoseAnn Shannon is one of those gatekeepers… This is a terrible situation for anyone who is gay or cares about gay rights."

NEVADA

Statewide: Non-discrimination bill opposed

Right-wing organizations tried to derail a bill to prohibit employment discrimination based on sexual orientation. Introduced by state Rep. David Parks, the state Assembly's only openly gay representative, the bill was attacked by one of the state's leading Religious Right organizations, the Eagle Forum (see p. 354). "This law ensures that employers can no longer take into consideration their most deeply held beliefs when making hiring and firing decisions," said Janine Hansen, the group's president. "It deals with sexual practices, and none of us should be asking each other what our sexual practices are, nor do we need special rights to protect them." She also claimed that the bill was part of the "world expansion of homosexual influence" and that it would require political parties to hire gay men and lesbians even if it were against the parties' will. Opposition to the bill became a family effort when Zachary Triggs, Hansen's son and a Boy Scout leader, testified before a legislative committee that "[The bill would] allow these sexual predators into our midst 24 hours a day." Daniel Hansen, Janine's brother, said, "In America, everyone should have the right to be a bigot."

The Religious Right launched a statewide lobbying campaign to defeat the bill. The Christian Coalition of Nevada (see p. 353) claimed that the bill would deny Christians the ability to make "theological statements about the immorality." Sheila Ward, a regional coordinator for the Christian Coalition, said, "We're against conferring rights based on behaviors that don't have anything to do with the immutable characteristics of what a civil rights characteristic is." Many members of the legislature who opposed the bill were members of the conservative Independent American Party. Former state Sen. Lori Lipman Brown, now with the American Civil Liberties Union's Gay and Lesbian Task Force, said that right-wing opponents had organized a call-in campaign to legislators' offices. She said that calls had been running nearly 4-1 against the bill.

> "In America, everyone should have the right to be a bigot."
>
> — Daniel Hansen, brother of Nevada Eagle Forum President Janine Hansen, testifying against a bill to prohibit employment discrimination against gay men and lesbians.

In April, the state Assembly passed the bill 30-11. The Senate later approved it after adding an amendment to exempt certain organizations, including the Boy Scouts. Gov. Kenny Guinn signed the bill, making Nevada the eleventh state to provide employment protections based on sexual orientation.

Las Vegas: Alleged job discrimination

A gay man and his heterosexual business partner alleged that their former employer had discriminated against them because of the gay partner's sexual orientation. Geoffrey Vanderpal and Michael Gordon sued Wells Fargo Bank in federal court in December for defamation and claimed that the bank had sabotaged their training and employment options by failing to provide working conditions as stipulated in their employment agreement. Vanderpal contends that he was targeted for discrimination because he is gay; Gordon contends that he was targeted because his former supervisors believed that he was also gay and in a relationship with Gordon. The two plaintiffs accused Ralph Pierro, their former supervisor at Norwest Corp., of referring to gay men as "queers" and of making derisive remarks about homosexual sex acts. Vanderpal and Gordon formerly worked for Norwest Corp., which later merged with Wells Fargo. Norwest's Employment Policies Handbook states that the bank is committed to equal employment opportunity and depends on people without respect to sexual orientation. The handbook gave examples of acts that constitute sexual harassment: "derogatory comments, slurs, jokes, or epithets of a sexual nature... and sexually degrading words used to describe an individual." Vanderpal also claimed that Pierro had failed to support his and Gordon's careers after Vanderpal told his supervisor that he, himself, had a romantic relationship with another man. Wells Fargo declined to comment on the allegations. The Gay Financial Network has ranked Wells Fargo on its top 50 list of gay-friendly publicly-traded companies. At press time, the case was pending.

NEW HAMPSHIRE

Statewide: Opposition to repeal of adoption prohibition

Right-wing activists tried to derail passage of a bill to repeal the state's prohibition on adoptions and foster parenting by gay men and lesbians despite broad support for the change. State Rep. Gay Torressen (R) claimed the bill would give special status to gay men and lesbians seeking adoptions and foster children: "I do believe we must be very careful about suggesting that any group or individuals should have the right to adopt... There is no right to adopt and to create one would be contrary to the best interests of children."

> "I do believe we must be very careful about suggesting that any group or individuals should have the right to adopt."
>
> — State Rep. Gay Torressen, arguing that gay men and lesbians should to prohibited from adopting children.

The Catholic Diocese of Manchester also opposed the repeal bill. The director of its office of public policy, Sister Margaret Crosby, testified against the bill in January, saying that gay "lifestyles" were not comparable to heterosexual ones and that children would be subjected to undue peer pressure if placed in the homes of gay men and lesbians. Richard Lessner wrote an op-ed piece published in the Manchester Union-Leader entitled, "Kids Aren't Guinea Pigs." He wrote, "Passing them [adoptees and foster children] out to homosexuals and lesbians living together in temporary domestic arrangements that merely mimic marriage? How can this be said to be 'pro-children'?" He added, "We do not believe that the state ever should place children in a home in which the adults are not bound to each other by the commitment and legal contract of matrimony."

The bill was overwhelmingly approved by both houses in April and later signed by Gov. Jeanne Shaheen. However, in November, Rep. Mary Lou Nowe (R) started fielding support for a bill that would overturn the new law and reinstitute the prohibition. State Rep. Ray Buckey (D), sponsor of the bill that repealed the prohibition on adoptions by gay men and lesbians, began his own campaign to block Nowe's measure.

Durham: Dispute over university's benefits proposal

In October, a committee of the Board of Trustees of the University of New Hampshire tried to derail attempts to adopt a domestic partner benefits policy for the unmarried partners of university employees. The Board of Trustees' Personnel Committee voted in June to offer dental, medical and tuition benefits to same-sex partners, but the board's financial affairs committee rejected that proposal in October by a 3-3 vote. A majority vote was needed for approval. Some of the trustees who voted against the measure claimed they did so for financial and not ideological reasons, saying the university could not afford the estimated $25,000 cost of the benefits package. "Offering a benefit to a group of people who have never had it before is inappropriate," said trustee Jane Hager, chair of the finance committee. However, in December, trustees of the University System of New Hampshire, which governs UNH, voted 21-1 to develop a benefits policy that includes same-sex partners of system employees. That body governs all state colleges and the College of Lifelong Learning.

Manchester: Bauer criticizes teen's question

Gary Bauer, former head of the Family Research Council (see p. 355) and then a Republican presidential candidate, criticized a teenage girl who questioned him about same-sex marriage while at Odyssey House, a home for troubled youth. One 18-year-old resident asked, "Don't you believe at the end of this century that gay couples... it's looking on two people who are emotionally attached in their minds and not their bodies, that they're together for one reason, and that's falling in love?" Bauer replied that no civilization had ever recognized same-sex marriage. "[I]t should be the intact family that brings a man and a woman together in marriage," he said. Other residents also questioned Bauer on same-sex marriage, prompting him to express amazement that "as young people who are wrestling with economic issues, and have experienced family breakdowns yourselves, that what you would be primed for today in talking to me is to promote the demands of the gay rights movement." He urged them to spend more time on "something other than promoting the political demands of a movement that 80 percent of the American people disagree with."

Manchester:
Students sue to permit gay/straight alliance

In April, school officials attempted to ban a Gay/Straight Alliance Club from West High School. In March, the school's principal told the students who wanted to form the club to submit a formal application. When the principal discovered that the club would deal with gay and lesbian issues, he allegedly rejected the application, telling the students to ask the city school board for approval. No other student group at West High has been required to obtain approval from the school board to start a club. In July, before the board rendered a final decision on the application, two of the current students and one former student filed a lawsuit in federal court, in which they were represented by the nonprofit Boston-based Gay and Lesbian Advocates and Defenders. The lawsuit contended that the principal's rejection of the application was a violation of the students' rights under the federal Equal Access Act, which prohibits secondary public schools that receive federal funds and that have non-curricular student clubs from discriminating against any of the student clubs based on the content of speech at club meetings. Members of the Gay/Straight

Alliance Club also contended that their rights had been violated when they were forced to bring their club application before the school board. One of the plaintiffs said, "I guess I knew deep down they'd oppose it, but I didn't think they'd be so adamant. I didn't want to believe it."

School board deliberations brought further delays. Some board members said they feared that by allowing such a group at a high school, they would have to allow it in the middle schools. Board member Lou D'Allesandro disagreed, saying, "We are taking a giant step backwards if we don't recognize people's individual differences." A former student and club organizer, Nick Panagopoulos, asked the board, "Look at me. Can you deny me access? Can you deny me my rights… ? Can you deny me the support I needed?" A board subcommittee voted 4-1 to recommend that the full board deny the group formal status as a non-curricular club. The subcommittee claimed that the group would be "detrimental to the maintenance of order, discipline, and the well-being of the students."

After consulting with its own legal staff and attorneys for the plaintiffs, the full board voted 7-6 to approve the club at West High School. Having obtained school recognition of their club, the students have dropped their lawsuit.

NEW JERSEY

Pomona: Alleged harassment at National Guard

A heterosexual pilot filed a lawsuit in a county court alleging that he had been the victim of anti-gay harassment by staff at the New Jersey Air National Guard and that his complaints about that had been ignored. Maj. Robert Scott sued four officers in the 177th Fighter Wing in March, saying he had been harassed by his peers who assumed he was gay because he was not married, did not have a girlfriend, and lived with female flight attendants. Scott claimed that fellow enlistees suggested he had a boyfriend and that Maj. Gen. James McIntosh, one of the defendants named in the lawsuit, had retaliated against Scott for complaining by issuing a written reprimand about his relationship with an unmarried woman. Scott also alleged that Capt. James Gordon, the unit's only black member, was taunted with racist epithets and jokes by his peers. According to Scott, after Gordon complained about the harassment, he was grounded from flying for 10 weeks. Retired Maj. John Barton corroborated the pilots' allegations in the lawsuit and said that he, too, had been ostracized for taking sides with the pilots. He said, "Maj. Scott and Capt. Gordon are extremely scared of what the military will do to them… There's no reason why they shouldn't be scared." A spokesperson said that the Air National Guard had completed its own investigation into the allegations in the spring but had not made public its findings. At press time, the case was pending.

NEW MEXICO

Statewide: Anti-discrimination bill defeated

The state House of Representatives defeated a bill that would have expanded the state's Human Rights Act to include sexual orientation. The bill would have prohibited anti-gay discrimination in housing, employment, public accommodations, credit and union membership, but would have exempted religious organizations. State Rep. Gail Beam, the bill's sponsor, said, "None of us is free from discrimination until all of us are free from discrimination." A majority of representatives, however, voted with state Rep. Daniel Foley, who voted against the bill, he said, because gay men and lesbians choose their lifestyle, and because their choice is "wrong." Foley said, "It's going to be challenged right away, and it's going to be found unconstitutional." Foley also claimed that gay men and lesbians are among the wealthiest citizens and do not need civil rights protections in the workplace. State Rep. Timothy Mack, said, "On the basis of morality, I urge the members of this House to vote no." The House defeated the bill by a 35-27 vote.

Supporters, however, were pleased that the bill got as far as it did. Linda Siegle with the Coalition for Equality, said, "We've never had a floor vote [before]… It helps us see who our allies are."

Statewide: Hate crimes bill vetoed

Gov. Gary Johnson vetoed a hate crimes bill in March that included sexual orientation. His action capped broad efforts by Republican legislators to defeat the bill before it left the Assembly. The bill would have authorized judges to impose longer sentences on people convicted of bias-motivated crimes. Even before state Sen. Pauline Eisenstadt formally introduced the bill, Johnson had promised to veto it as he had a similar bill in 1995. Opponents often focused on the inclusion of sexual orientation in the bill as a basis for their opposition. State Sen. Leonard Lee Rawson said he opposed protecting gay men and lesbians because, in his view, their sexual orientation is voluntary. He added that he might have supported a bill that did not include sexual orientation as a protected category. "Once you start making those judgments, they never quit… it makes a real problem in the judicial system, which is supposed to treat everybody the same, no matter who they are," he said.

The Senate passed the bill 26-12 in February largely along party lines. Republican state Sen. William Davis claimed the bill punished thought and opinions and that the state already had laws against violent acts. The bill would contribute to "the continuing fracturing of our society," he said. The state Republican Party's chair, John Dendahl, agreed, saying, "I'm just against this continuous Balkanization of our country, which seeks to separate out groups for special treatment." Praising those Republicans who voted for the bill, Linda Siegle, co-chair of the New Mexico Human Rights Coalition, said, "I'm happy to see that three Republicans could do the right thing today and support this legislation."

After the Senate vote, the governor reiterated his intention to veto the bill. The House gave him that opportunity by passing the bill with a 39-28 vote. Republican state Rep. Thomas Taylor, who voted against the bill, said, "There's no way to make a hate crime a greater offense without making the original crime a lesser offense." Fellow Republican Daniel Foley said the bill would force jurors to make judgments based on their feelings. Gov. Johnson quickly followed through on his promise and vetoed the bill, saying it was "a fundamental error to attempt in statute to qualify 'hate.' " Though both chambers of the legislature were controlled by Democrats, supporters did not have the two-thirds majority necessary to override Johnson's veto.

> Whether I wish to witness and bless the union of two willing adults is the business of my church. It is not the business of the state."
>
> — Rev. Holly Beaumont, head of the Christian Church of Santa Fe, responding to a bill in the state legislature that would have fined ministers for conducting a same-sex marriage ceremony.

Two weeks later, Senate Democrats tacked on an amendment to a bill on gang-related crimes that would have accomplished most of what the original hate crimes bill would have done. The Republican Minority objected to that tactic, saying "the hate crimes legislation is a separate issue." The Senate passed the bill, but it died in the House.

Statewide: Same-sex marriage bill

Right-wing members of the state legislature supported a bill that would have prohibited the state from recognizing same-sex marriages. Under the bill, those who perform gay or lesbian marriage ceremonies could have faced a fine of up to $50. That provision concerned Rev. Holly Beaumont, head of the Christian Church of Santa Fe. "I was stunned to read a bill that restricts my rights. Whether I wish to witness and bless the union of two willing adults is the business of my church. It is not the business of the state," she said. Beaumont added that the bill suffered from "clear problems of constitutionality." Sen. Leonard Lee Rawson, the bill's sponsor, told a crowd gathered at the state Capitol, "This is a spiritual battle, and I would just simply remind you that our God will not be mocked." He said this was not an issue of supporters trying to impose their morality on the bill's opponents. Rep. E.G. "Smokey" Blanton, another supporter, said the bill reflected what he maintained were America's Christian values. He said the story of creation is about "Adam and Eve, not Adam and Steve." Rep. Daniel Foley added, "We are at a crossroads in this country, a moral crossroads... This is the opportunity to take the right path." New Mexico's Roman Catholic bishops also supported the bill.

The first of two Senate committees to review the bill approved it in February, by a 5-3 vote. Rep. Rawson said, "This bill was not born out of fear and ignorance... This bill simply defines what a marriage is." The House and Senate Judiciary Committees tabled the measure in March, killing its chances for passage in the 1999 session.

Albuquerque: Gay rights initiative defeated

Voters in Albuquerque defeated a ballot initiative that would have added sexual orientation and mental disability to the city charter's human rights code. The code prohibited discrimination based on race, religion, sex and national origin in the areas of employment, housing, credit, public accommodations and union membership. The Campaign for Human Rights, organized by a member of the local chapter of Parents, Families and Friends of Lesbians and Gays, called for the ballot measure and organized community support. Several progressive organizations across the state endorsed the proposal. The Christian Coalition of New Mexico (see p. 353) led the opposition effort. The group's executive director, Mark Burton, said, "It's not a behavior that we want to have a non-discrimination policy for... It's a health hazard. It spreads AIDS, sexually transmitted diseases, so there's no reason to endorse a behavior that's dangerous and hazardous." The Christian Coalition distributed voter guides about the initiative to 300 local churches.

Burton's group had the support of many in the community. In the Daily Lobo, columnist Mark Wilson urged citizens to vote against the proposal. "City officials shouldn't spend taxpayers' dollars promoting morals they disagree with," Wilson wrote. "Many citizens believe, through theology, biology, or even bigotry, that homosexuality is wrong." "If the YMCA or the Boy Scouts find homosexuality morally repugnant, the government should not force them to accept it." The Albuquerque Journal also came out against the proposed addition, arguing that the federal and state governments already provide protections against discrimination.

The initiative was rejected 55 percent to 45 percent in October. Turnout was estimated at only 20 percent of registered voters.

Las Cruces: University rejects domestic partner benefits

In March, the Board of Regents of New Mexico State University rejected a proposal to extend domestic partner benefits to university employees. In December 1998, the Faculty Senate had endorsed the proposal, but two regents announced their opposition that same month, citing moral grounds. Calling the proposal a "special privilege" for gay and lesbian employees, John Van Sweden, said, "I think everyone should be entitled to the same thing under the law, but I think this country was built on Christian principles, and they [gay men and lesbians] are leading a deviant lifestyle." Board president Larry Sheffield said that he was personally opposed to the proposal. "You're opening up a Pandora's box. Who's going to define [relationship]? Where's it going to stop?" he asked.

Van Sweden was the only regent to speak publicly during the board meeting at which the issue was decided: "I feel marital status is the most appropriate and reasonable standard for determining the eligibility of benefits... There is no compelling reason for the university to absorb the extra cost of this program." The university estimated the cost of the proposal at $140,000 per year. Fernando Cadena, a professor opposed to the proposal, said it was an "affront to the religious and ethical values of wide segments of our taxpayer population" and might inhibit donations from conservatives.

The board voted unanimously to reject the benefits proposal. After the vote, newly elected board President Del Archuleta said, "It comes down to the simplest way for the university to administer its benefits policy is through the marriage criteria... I don't mean to make this sound like a cop-out, but we don't make rules about marriage. That's an issue for people who write laws." A group of graduate students announced they would withhold financial contributions to the university as alumni to protest the board's decision. "We obviously aren't afraid of being affected or infected by diversity," one student said.

During the fall semester, a gay male student, Aaron Shubert, ran for Homecoming Queen to make a public statement about the regents' decision and about homophobia on campus. "[W]hen people are discriminated against, it's important to bring it to the light," said Shubert. Illustrating that climate, he said, "A friend told me he overheard someone talking in class about 'the faggot running for Queen.' " Shubert won third place in the contest. In response, the student government adopted a policy requiring that Homecoming King and Queen be male and female, respectively, and that those running for the titles should not do so out of a personal political agenda. Critics said they would consider asking the student Supreme Court to invalidate the law because they felt it violated the U.S. Constitution's protection of free speech. Others said they would call for a student referendum on the issue.

Rio Rancho: Hell house

Grace Outreach Center sponsored a Hell House in October depicting the death of a young man from AIDS. The church's Hell House was based on a model developed by the Rev. Keenan Roberts in Denver, Colorado, to depict life in Hell. Grace Outreach's adaptation also included an abortion and the aftermath of a teen suicide. Members distributed more than 12,000 fliers advertising the production that promised attendees they would "get rocked" by the "sin-sational" tour. The church's pastor, Rev. Kent Barnard, said Hell House depicts "sinful choices, according to the word of God, that lead to hell." He said it also would give young people the opportunity to commit themselves to Jesus Christ. The AIDS funeral scene portrayed "Jason," a young, blond man who had recently died. A fog covers the area around the casket and two demons emerge, saying, "I love funerals, especially when it's for one of ours! My close, personal friend, AIDS, got Jason. We told him he was born gay. What kind of idiot would actually believe that?... And AIDS got you, Jason. That would make tonight's score Demons 1, God nothin'." The scene took place in the church's sanctuary.

Critics of Hell House called it a stereotypical and demoralizing way of addressing pressing social issues. Jody Huckaby, the executive director of New Mexico AIDS Services, said, "AIDS is not a moral issue. It's a public health issue." Rev. Pat Langlois said that AIDS is not God's judgment: "Portraying a gay man's funeral who died from AIDS with the accompanying dialogue denigrating the man for his lifestyle only plays into the continuous stereotypes that are perpetrated by misinformation." Officials at Planned Parenthood also objected to Hell House. A group of protesters gathered across the street from the church to condemn the production.

NEW YORK

Statewide: Hate crimes bills opposed

For the tenth year in a row, the New York state Senate failed to pass a bill outlawing hate crimes, including those based on sexual orientation. The Assembly, which is controlled by Democrats, passed two versions of a hate crimes bill in the beginning of the year, one of which was supported by Gov. George Pataki (R), and sent them to the Senate. The Pataki bill would have increased penalties for crimes motivated by hate and would have required police to report them to the state's Division of Criminal Justice. The other bill would have created a new category of crimes motivated by hate, with its own specific penalties. The Republican-controlled Senate failed to act on either bill even though the enhanced penalty bill had Pataki's endorsement. New York's only openly gay state senator, Tom Duane (D), pleaded with Senate Majority Leader Joseph Bruno (R) to allow a floor vote on the Pataki-endorsed bill. Bruno agreed to debate only after expressing his reservations. "I personally have trouble understanding why, if somebody gets their skull fractured by an assailant, that the assailant should get more jail time because a [victim] is gay, or because that person is of a particular race or religion," he said. A majority in the Senate apparently felt the same and took no action for the rest of the year. State Sen. Frank Padavan (R) dismissed as a Democratic "political rally" a November forum in which hate crimes bill supporters from across the state urged the legislature to pass the bill.

The bill was carried over to the 2000 legislative session and the state Senate passed it in June 2000. Gov. Pataki signed it into law a month later.

Averill Park: School district sued over alleged harassment

A high school student who allegedly suffered from the anti-gay harassment of his classmates said he became so distraught that he withdrew from school in April. In December, his mother filed a notice of claim in state court, indicating her intention to sue the school district and board of education for failing to protect her son. Her son said he suffered physical and verbal attacks that administrators failed to stop. His attorney, Richard DiMaggio, said his client had "been hit in the back of the head, kicked, has had his hands held behind his back by other students while receiving beatings and kicks… he has been grabbed by the back of the neck and grabbed by the throat while his fellow students tell him they will kill him." In a letter to school Superintendent Michael Johnson, DiMaggio wrote, "The viciousness of the student body is no worse than the deaf ear your faculty has turned on [him]." DiMaggio claimed several teachers witnessed the harassment and chose not to act. The lawsuit alleges, among other things, that the school district denied the student equal protection from harassment and gender discrimination. "Victims of sexual orientation crimes must be treated with the same force and effect as members outside that [distinct] class," DiMaggio said. At press time, the lawsuit was pending.

Clifton Park: School harassment

School officials suspended a high school student who decided to fight back against classmates whom he says repeatedly taunted him with anti-gay epithets. In September, the student struck a fellow classmate from Shenendehowa High School with a stick after a group of students allegedly cornered him and called him "faggot" and other derisive names. The student in question claims the others also pushed him into a truck and that several classmates later threatened him with violence if he returned to school. At a hearing on the matter, school officials suspended the student for two marking periods and denied him a school-funded tutor. Superintendent Robert McClure later overruled that decision and provided a tutor. The students alleged to have committed the attack, however, were never punished, though one received counseling. The boy's mother told the school board, "To suspend my son and let the others go live their lives sends the wrong message." She maintains her son acted in self-defense after school officials rebuffed his attempts to get them to intercede in the harassment. The boy's mother later announced that her son would be attending private school, as would her daughter.

The suspension angered local gay and lesbian advocates. A student senate representative at Shenendehowa High told the school board that efforts by the Respect Club, a student group promoting diversity and tolerance, to sponsor a seminar on gay and lesbian issues in response to the alleged attack was "met with some trepidation" by the faculty who said those issues had no place in school.

In December, Shenendehowa High School officials implemented new policies prohibiting anti-gay, racial, ethnic, sexual, religion, and other forms of harassment. Principal Robert Melia noted a provision in the new guidelines that encourages students to report harassment to adults in the school. Mitch Hahn, local chair of the Gay, Lesbian, and Straight Education Network, heralded the new policy but said he wished it had been implemented throughout the school system. "I absolutely congratulate the high school on their efforts," Hahn said. "But I feel that a policy such as that should be a district wide policy."

The parents of the suspended student filed a notice of claim in December, signaling their intention to sue the school district for failing to protect their son from anti-gay harassment. They claim the school was deliberately indifferent toward their son and also unfairly singled him out for punishment in the matter. The parents want the school district to pay for their son's education in private school and for other damages.

Dobbs Ferry: Presbyterian conflict over "holy unions"

Right-wing ministers in the Hudson River Presbytery objected to the church's resolution permitting pastors to bless same-sex "holy unions." Rev. Marc Benton, an evangelical pastor of a Presbyterian church in New Windsor, discovered in August 1998 that Rev. Joseph Gilmore of Dobbs Ferry had blessed a same-sex union when he read a newspaper article featuring the "holy union" ceremony of Jeff Halvorsen and George Cisneros. Benton immediately called on his presbytery to investigate whether this violated church doctrine. The Presbyterian Book of Order, the church's code, allows ministers to bless same-sex unions as long as they are not "the same as marriages." The presbytery, which oversees 95 churches, investigated and also voted 105-35 in January to permit the blessings.

Benton and other conservatives appealed that vote to the Synod of the Northeast, the governing entity for New York, New Jersey, and New England churches. "I think that the people who are pushing for gay marriage are in a clear minority," Benton said. "They have pushed the agenda far enough that it has become a very divisive issue." Julius Poppinga, a Presbyterian elder, echoed his concerns: "By playing a semantic game with the language, you can continue to do what the church says is in violation of [church code]."

In November, the Synod affirmed the right of pastors to bless same-sex unions. The Synod's court ruled that the Book of Order's prohibition on same-sex marriage "does not apply to ceremonies of same-sex union." Poppinga vowed to appeal to the national Judicial Commission, introduce legislation at the 2001 General Assembly to ban same-sex conjugal unions, or declare a "constitutional crisis" and ultimately a schism.

Nassau County: Employment bias alleged

In October, a state court dismissed a lawsuit by a man who claimed his former employer fired him because he is gay. Judge Herbert Posner dismissed Jeffrey Mandel's lawsuit charging that his former employer, Computer Associates, violated its own policy against anti-gay discrimination when it fired him. The suit was filed in December 1998 in the New York State Supreme Court. Because Nassau and Suffolk Counties, where Mandel worked and where the company is located, do not prohibit employment discrimination based on sexual orientation, Mandel filed the lawsuit in Queens County, where he lives and where New York City law does prohibition sexual orientation discrimination in employment.

Mandel's lawsuit maintained that the company's firing of him was unlawful because Computer Associates' employee handbook states that the company prohibits discrimination based on sexual orientation. Mandel argued that his dismissal followed an outstanding performance evaluation and that his supervisors unofficially told him he was fired because he was gay. He also alleged that a former supervisor told him to remove a picture of himself and his partner from his desk. Mandel said that Lucy Vieco, another former supervisor, told him that his partner should not drop him off at work, unless he could be dropped off 100 yards away from the company's entrance. He said Vieco told him it appeared improper for a man to drive him to work. "In plain English, we don't want any homosexuals at the new company," she reportedly told him. Firing him in this context, the suit maintained, was a breach of contract. The company, however, claimed that it fired Mandel because of his work performance.

Judge Posner dismissed Mandel's claim of discrimination because the counties where the alleged discrimination took place do not prohibit sexual orientation discrimination in employment. Judge Posner ruled that, absent any laws prohibiting sexual orientation discrimination in employment, Computer Associates was under no legal obligation to follow its own policy against anti-gay harassment. He also ruled that the company's policies exist at its own behest and are not legally binding, writing in the decision, "A general statement of equal opportunity and nondiscrimination in an employee handbook does not serve as a basis for a breach of contract claim." The employee handbook had a provision disclaiming any contractual obligation to uphold the company's non-discrimination statement. The court did not rule on whether Computer Associates fired Mandel because he is gay.

Mandel's attorney criticized the decision, declaring it "a shame that a company is allowed to advertise that they don't discriminate, but then they don't have to live up to those standards." Doni Gewirtzman, an attorney with Lambda Legal Defense and Education Fund, added, "This case really underscores why it is essential for the state to pass a bill that includes protection from sexual orientation discrimination in the workplace."

New York:
Complaints about United Nations travel policies

In August, gay and lesbian employees at the United Nations filed a grievance seeking benefits for their registered domestic partners comparable to spousal benefits currently offered to married, heterosexual employees. Gay, Lesbian, or Bisexual Employees (GLOBE) asserts that frequent dispatches of UN personnel to posts all over the world seldom include provisions allowing domestic partners to accompany them. That forces gay and lesbian UN employees to choose between their careers and their families, the complaint contends. UN policies allow the legal spouses of employees to obtain visas to countries where the employees are stationed so that those couples are not split up. Opposite-sex couples, therefore, are not placed in the same position as gay and lesbian couples because their relationships are not legally valid. GLOBE's grievance statement read, "GLOBE encourages the U.N. to acknowledge this simple fact and to take appropriate action to ensure equal treatment for all its staff."

The United Nations had previously awarded the domestic partners of UN employees the right to travel on a case-by-case basis if the employees' relationships were legally recognized in their home countries. But in recent years, GLOBE members said, gay and lesbian employees were told that if their relationships were not legal marriages in the countries where they were working, they would not be allowed to take their partners on assignment. Susan Allee, vice-president of GLOBE, said that one Swedish employee, whose "civil marriage" is legally recognized in Sweden, secured a Belgian visa for his partner only to have the U.N. later revoke it. "What is clear is that if you were from on[e] of the countries that recognizes domestic partners and you walked in and said that you wanted to give your partner spousal benefits, they would say no," Allee said. GLOBE contended the right of their partners to travel with them is the most crucial employee benefit offered.

New York: Controversial news article

The Metropolitan Gender Network organized a protest in front of the offices of the Village Voice to denounce a November edition featuring a front-page picture a group it claimed mocked transgendered people. The November 23 edition of that newspaper featured the story of a female-to-male transgendered man. The activists said that the incorrect gender pronouns in the story, headlined "Suddenly Not Susan," and the picture of a Barbie doll with sewn-on breasts and a penis on the front page were offensive. They also resented the "constant implication that a person is more real before gender transition than after transition." The protesters asked the editorial staff to, in the future, use language that is consistent with people's gender identity. A letter to the editor amplified these sentiments. "I found the use of a sutured Barbie doll to represent the FTM [female-to-male] on your cover completely offensive," Jack Griffin wrote. "As a female-to-male transsexual, I can attest that image is our worst nightmare. It is exactly what we pray not to become when we begin the process of transition: a feminine woman with male body parts sewn on, haphazard and incongruous."

In an apology, Voice editor-in-chief Don Forst said, "No malice was intended in the piece nor was any malice rendered." He added, "If we were insensitive in our language, we will certainly endeavor to avoid that in the future." He still defended the front-page graphic illustration, saying, "While the cover image was a strong graphic illustration, it was not inappropriate."

New York: Foster children sue city

Attorneys for several gay and lesbian youths in foster care filed a federal class-action lawsuit in January against several New York City agencies charged with child care. The Urban Justice Institute and a private law firm represented the children. Their suit charged the foster care system with neglecting to provide protections needed by gay and lesbian youth and allowing reported abuse to continue. The lead plaintiff was a 13-year-old boy, identified as Joel A., who maintained that the staff at several foster care group homes failed to intervene when other children taunted and abused him because he is effeminate. A day before the suit was filed, Joel A. said that youths at a city playground broke his jaw in two places after demanding to know if he was gay. Another plaintiff, Eric R., tried to hang himself from a baseball backstop after enduring, he claimed, nine years of humiliation for his feminine mannerisms. Eric also said that a city-appointed therapist had told him that all gay people get AIDS.

Jonathan Cole, a provost at Columbia University and legal aide to Joel A., said, "These are youngsters who are at great risk and who in effect are being put out on the street because the city simply doesn't have any mechanism for handling gay and lesbian kids."

The trial judge ruled against the plaintiffs, citing an earlier class action settlement, the Marisol settlement, in which the court imposed a 2-year moratorium on class-action lawsuits against the Administration for Children's Services, one of the agencies named in the suit. Attorneys for the plaintiffs filed an appeal. Although oral arguments in that case were heard in July 1999, a ruling has not yet been issued.

New York: Gay school board candidate targeted

Right-wing politicians attacked an openly gay candidate for a seat on a Queens school board. Wayne Mahlke ran for a position on the Community School District 24 school board in the New York Borough of Queens, known for electing conservative members. District 24 still prohibits teachers from using the words "homosexuality, abortion, masturbation, or contraception" in class. The district is also well-known for rejecting "Children of the Rainbow," a multicultural curriculum designed to teach tolerance. Among the 15 candidates for nine board seats, incumbent Frank Borzellieri, who had previously tried to have an openly gay teacher fired, led the attack.

> "His views are an abomination to this district... He is sick. He is what can only be called allegedly brainwashing for perversion."
>
> — Frank Borzellieri, incumbent member of a Queens school board, on the attack against openly gay challenger Wayne Mahlke.

Borzellieri predicted a nasty campaign, saying, "What I envision is me fighting him tooth and nail." He made sure that vision came true, claiming that Mahlke was running "for one purpose and one purpose only: to further the radical homosexual agenda." Borzellieri added, "His views are an abomination to this district, to this community... He is sick. He is what can only be called allegedly brainwashing for perversion." Mahlke, an official at a nonprofit agency serving autistic children and their families, responded to those attacks: "[F]or too long, the school board has been focused on personal political issues, not the issues of what the children need... I'd add that Mr. Borzellieri is running for his own purpose: to give voice to a handful of bigots."

Steve Dunleavy, a columnist for the New York Post, wrote a scathing piece about Mahlke's candidacy, saying that it "worries the living hell out of me." Focusing on Mahlke's support for a multicultural curriculum, Dunleavy claimed that Mahlke advocated books "about how a father takes off with a gay lover." He called Heather Has Two Mommies "a blatant pitch to celebrate lesbianism." When Mahlke suggested that these books teach tolerance of racial, ethnic, and sexual minorities, Dunleavy responded, "The hell it does."

Mahlke was not elected to the school board.

New York: Gays barred from Bronx Irish parade

Responding to a tide of criticism, organizers of the St. Patrick's Day parade in the Bronx rescinded an invitation extended to the Lavender and Green Alliance, an organization of Irish gay men and lesbians. Parade co-chairman Patrick Devine had initially told the group it would be able to march with its banner. Ads for the first Bronx St. Patrick's Day parade since 1929 said that it was open to "all groups." However, after numerous church groups and the Ancient Order of the Hibernians of Bronx County reportedly threatened to pull out of the parade if the Irish gay group marched, Devine withdrew that invitation. Bronx Borough President Fernando Ferrer was angered when he learned about the Alliance's exclusion and quickly announced that he would not march in the parade. Other local and state politicians followed suit.

State Sen. Tom Duane and City Council member Christine Quinn, both of whom are openly gay and Irish, did march in the parade. They were among six people arrested and charged with disorderly conduct for joining the parade despite being uninvited. They were reportedly met with jeers of "Go home" when they entered the parade route. After those arrests, the crowd reportedly cheered. One spectator said, "It's an immoral lifestyle," while another said, "I have best friends who are gay, but the parade is not about sexual orientation. It's about being proud to be Irish." Parade organizer Karin O'Connor noted, "We're celebrating a Catholic Holy day. We're marching for St. Patrick, and people who march should be in line with what we're celebrating — Irish pride and Irish Catholic pride." She added that Irish gays do not fit that vision. "

New York: Judge upholds university housing policy

Justice Franklin Weissberg of the New York Supreme Court ruled in April that colleges may discriminate between married and unmarried couples in granting housing to their students. In 1998, Sara Levin and Maggie Jones, represented by the American Civil Liberties Union (ACLU), filed suit in the State Supreme Court challenging the housing policy at the Albert Einstein College of Medicine at Yeshiva University that denies requests for married student housing from non-married couples. Levin and Jones are lesbians, each involved in long-term partnerships with other women. They applied for married university housing and were turned down. Their lawsuit contended that the university had discriminated against them on the basis of marital status and sexual orientation.

In his ruling that dismissed their lawsuit, Weissberg wrote, "The plaintiffs' real complaint lies not with the defendants, but, rather, with the refusal of the New York State Legislature to sanction same-sex marriages." He reasoned that the law does not prohibit the university from distinguishing between married and unmarried couples in providing housing. The ruling also rejected the plaintiffs' claim that Yeshiva's housing policy disparately impacts them because they are lesbians, since they were each offered individual housing though they were not offered housing with their partners. Michael Adams of the ACLU's Lesbian and Gay Rights Project called that ruling "disappointing."

Levin and Jones appealed the lower court's ruling, and in April 2000, an appeals court heard oral arguments. The night before those arguments were schedule to be given, several Yeshiva University students set up a "tent city" outside a campus housing facility to call attention to the lawsuit and the school's anti-gay policy.

New York: Lesbian officer sues over alleged harassment

A lesbian police officer sued the city of New York and its Police Department in federal court alleging that she endured two years of harassment based on her sexual orientation. Elizabeth Bryant charged that the harassment began after her much-publicized marriage ceremony in Central Park to fellow officer Marilyn Trapanotto. Bryant claims that obscene pictures of women with her face pasted on them were hung in her Bronx precinct house, that other officers refused to ride with her on patrols, and that she was assigned to cleaning duties in the precinct. Her lawsuit also claimed that one co-worker assaulted her and that officers repeatedly taunted her with derogatory names. "When I complained, everyone turned their backs on me," Bryant said, adding that her commanding officer told her, "No one wants to ride with a dyke." Bryant maintained that the abuse, which continued for over a year, worsened after it was reported.

Trapanotto, however, said she received a completely different response from her precinct. She said fellow officers at the Manhattan North scooter task force asked her, "Gee, Trap, back so soon?" "How was the honeymoon?" and "You're married? That's great." Trapanotto said, "It was very, very special to show you're proud to be a gay police officer, not only a gay couple."

Bryant has since been reassigned to another location. She is suing for $5 million. At press time, the case was pending.

New York: Protesters sue police

Four men sued the New York City Police Department in federal court alleging that the department denied them "life-saving" medication following a vigil protesting the murder of Wyoming college student Matthew Shepard. The Gay Men's Health Crisis and the New York City Gay and Lesbian Anti-Violence Project filed the suit on the men's behalf. They specifically challenged the department's policy of denying detainees access to medication and allowing hospital visits only if deemed medically necessary. Three of the men are HIV-positive and require a variety of medications throughout the day; the fourth suffers from asthma.

All four plaintiffs argued that police enforcement of policy in question caused them emotional distress and placed them at physical risk. Two of the men said they have a fear of civil protests because of this experience with the police. The plaintiffs said that police discouraged them from visiting the hospital, because it would delay their release from jail. The asthmatic maintained that he suffered a severe attack during the arrest, exacerbating his condition. He also said that when he finally got to Bellevue Hospital, the staff informed him they were out of his medication.

> "No one wants to ride with a dyke."
>
> — Elizabeth Bryant, a New York City police officer who sued the police department for harassment, said her commanding officer told her this.

The plaintiffs sought a court-mandated change in the policy and unspecified damages. Ronald Johnson, managing director of community relations at the Gay Men's Health Crisis, said he hoped the lawsuit would "send a clear message to the city of New York that they cannot shirk their responsibility by denying access to life-saving medication for people in their custody."

The Police Department said it was already changing the policy when the suit was filed in October. "We will ensure that future detainees receive their drugs," said Michael Collins, a police spokesperson. As of press time, the lawsuit was pending.

New York: St. Patrick's Day demonstration still prohibited

For the fifth year in a row, the New York City Police Department denied the Irish Lesbian and Gay Organization (ILGO) permission to demonstrate against an annual St. Patrick's Day Parade in Manhattan. That parade is sponsored by the Ancient Order of Hibernians. Leaders of ILGO said the police department's rejection of their application for a permit to demonstrate violated their civil liberties. Ignoring that rejection, members of ILGO tried to stage a counter march against the St. Patrick's Day Parade starting at the New York Public Library's main office, by which the parade was scheduled to pass. Police arrested 17 of the demonstrators and charged them with disorderly conduct. Among those arrested was openly lesbian City Council member Christine Quinn.

In years past, ILGO has gone to court in an effort to win the right to stage a countermarch, without much success. The U.S. Supreme Court ruled several years ago that a private organization sponsoring a parade has a First Amendment right to exclude organizations promoting a message that the sponsor does not want to endorse. In addition, U.S. District Judge John Keenan, in 1998, accepted the city's argument that it did not have enough resources to allow both ILGO and the Ancient Order of the Hibernians to conduct a demonstration and a parade during rush hour. Judge Keenan issued that ruling in response to a lawsuit ILGO had filed after having been denied a permit to hold a demonstration at the same time that the Ancient Order of the Hibernians were to have staged the St. Patrick's Day Parade. Members of ILGO said that action pointed to the spuriousness of the City's argument because in 1999, the event was not held during rush hour, but on a Saturday and that they were still unable to persuade police to allow them to demonstrate.

In yet another lawsuit, a federal jury found that the city did not violate ILGO's First Amendment rights by prohibiting it from demonstrating during St. Patrick's Day. ILGO's attorneys had argued that the city used a "backroom political process" to exclude the group. City attorneys disagreed, having argued that traffic problems and a 1993 court order prohibiting ILGO from marching in the Hibernians' parade were the reasons why the city denied the group a permit to demonstrate. City attorneys also said that ILGO was offered a permit to ILGO march elsewhere in Manhattan.

Rochester: Call to revoke lesbian minister's award

Anti-gay Presbyterian officials tried to revoke an award given to a lesbian minister. The denomination's Women's Ministries Program selected Jane Adams Spahr, who works for a program for gay men and lesbians at the Downtown Presbyterian Church, as one of three recipients of the Women of Faith Awards for 1999. Critics said she was a poor selection because she is an outspoken critic of the denomination's prohibition against ordaining openly gay ministers. Spahr, a lesbian, was ordained before the prohibition was adopted, but was later removed from pastoring a church because she is a lesbian. The Layman, a conservative Presbyterian publication, called Spahr's selection "a study in denomination-al dysfunction." After expressing concerns to the selection committee, which refused to withdraw Spahr as an award recipient, the steering committee of the National Ministries Division of the Presbyterian Church (U.S.A.) voted in April to overturn Spahr's selection. Rev. Curtis Kearns Jr., national ministries director, said, "To recognize her would appear to endorse the position for which she's been advocating." The Beaver-Butler Presbytery, located near Pittsburgh, Pa., considered asking its governing body to disassociate those congregations that favor ordaining gay men and lesbians. It also narrowly rejected a proposal to withhold its contribution toward denominational administration. The presbytery instead issued a statement of "disappointment over the lack of discernment" in selecting Spahr, a Pittsburgh native.

However, the General Assembly Council, a committee within the denomination's governing body, narrowly overruled the National Ministries Division by a 41-40 vote in June. Spahr was given the award at a ceremony later that month, where she was greeted with a standing ovation.

Rochester: Catholics excommunicate congregation

In February, the Catholic Diocese of Rochester excommunicated a priest and members of his parish who organized a separate congregation that welcomed gay men and lesbians, women, and non-Catholics. Rev. James Callan had been a priest at Corpus Christi Church for 22 years and led its growth from 200 to a racially mixed congregation of more than 3,000. In December 1998, church officials suspended Callan for violating the church's prohibitions on blessing same-sex unions and for enlarging women's roles in Mass. Since that time, Callan has used space provided by several Rochester Protestant churches for religious services for the more than 1,000 members of his parish who left Corpus Christi with him. The Rochester Diocese later changed Callan's punishment to excommunication and said that those who choose to stay with him were excommunicated as well. "By starting this new church, a schism has occurred," the diocese said in a statement. "Father Callan has effectively excommunicated himself. Catholics who have joined the new church are not in full communion with the Church and have incurred the same penalty."

Callan responded to the decree with mixed emotions. "I'm not worried about excommunication or defrocking or whatever they want to do. I know who I am. I'm still a Catholic priest, and I will continue to do things that I'm excited about." However, he added, "It hurts me to know that the church that I've been a part of is acting in such an exclusionary way."

Church doctrine maintains that any member of Callan's congregation may rejoin the Church if he or she confess to any priest in the diocese. As a priest, Callan would have to appeal to the bishop.

Saratoga Springs:
Theft and vandalism on college campus

The theft of a gay and lesbian rainbow flag was the first of a series of anti-gay controversies during the fall semester at Skidmore College. In October, thieves stole the rainbow flag from the porch of the Sexuality Awareness House, a residence for gay and lesbian students. Days later, junior Helen Yanolatos wrote a letter in the campus newspaper denouncing the theft. The day after the letter was published, which was the Saturday of Parent's Weekend, residents of the dormitory awoke to find feces and toilet paper in the bed of a truck which had a rainbow sticker on the bumper. They also found soiled toilet paper under the driver's side door handle. "We're all angry, but we're somewhat scared too," Yanolatos said. "We've gotten some slurs yelled at us, but this is a little coincidental. That they brought toilet paper makes me think there was some malice involved."

School officials were quick to respond. Along with four administrators, Skidmore President Jamienne Studley wrote an open letter to the campus community condemning the incident and likening it to a hate crime. The student Senate also condemned the "aggressive acts of harassment." When a November issue of the campus newspaper featured an in-depth story on the incident including graphic pictures of the truck and blunt language, the director of admissions, Mary Lou Bates, and several of her staff removed over 1,000 copies from around the campus. Bates said she removed the copies because they were distributed on the same day the campus hosted a massive recruitment effort. Studley called Bates' action "a serious lapse of judgment" and said the college would pay to reprint the issue. Bates was fined and agreed to address parents and alumni who have questions about her actions. She also agreed to undertake a study of free speech issues.

Police with Saratoga Springs and Skidmore have not apprehended any suspects in the stolen flag incident or the truck vandalism.

Suffolk County: Gay politician targeted

Just before the general election in November, Jon Cooper, an openly gay candidate for the state legislature's 18th District, endured harsh anti-gay criticism from his opponents. The clash started the day before the election when Virginia Riekert, local chair of the Conservative Party, mailed a letter to Conservative Party members asking them to vote for the GOP candidate, Ken Stubbolo. Gay activists said that Riekert pandered to anti-gay sentiments within the voting district when she wrote that Cooper lived "with a same-sex 'domestic partner'... Ken Stubbolo's domestic partner is his wife of 41 years."

> "I don't condone that lifestyle, but in a democracy, can you prevent it?... As long as they keep their hands to themselves, fine."
>
> — State Rep. Michael D'Andre, after openly gay Jon Cooper won election and joined him in the New York legislature.

Richard Thury, who ran on the Conservative and Right-to-Life Party tickets, threw his support to Stubbolo, saying that Cooper's "lifestyle" was "opposite of the Judeo-Christian family values." Cooper and his partner of 18 years have raised five adopted children. "I have gay people in my family and I love them dearly," Thury said. "But I wish they weren't gay." Stubbolo denied he and Thury conspired to defeat Cooper. "That is so utterly ridiculous. [Cooper] must be in a panic... Does he feel guilty about his lifestyle? I'm saying in a positive vein that I support conventional, traditional family values," Stubbolo said. Michael O'Donohoe, County Commissioner of Jurors and the only Conservative elected official in the county legislature, said that he was personally "uncomfortable" with Cooper's homosexuality. He also expressed serious reservations about Cooper's ability to meet with various constituent groups. "A local legislator goes to a lot of firemen's and American Legion dinners, and you bring your partner with you," O'Donohoe said. "If Cooper is going to do that for the next two years, it may be very upsetting to people. You don't have to jump up and down and say it is something that makes people uncomfortable. They will be uncomfortable."

After the election, Stubbolo and Thury declined Cooper's request that they apologize. Reikert defended that decision. "We had a right to tell our people... He is a public figure. When we stress our family values, it's gay-bashing. But they want to go everywhere and push their values. And when you come out with your principles, it's gay-bashing. And I don't believe it is at all," Reikert said.

Cooper won 52.8 percent of the vote. Sloan Wiesen of the Gay and Lesbian Victory Fund said that the anti-gay tactics actually backfired in Cooper's favor. She called those campaign tactics "un-American appeals to personal prejudice."

In discussing how he would respond to Cooper as a fellow legislator, state Rep. Michael D'Andre (R) said, "I don't condone that lifestyle, but in a democracy, can you prevent it?... As long as they keep their hands to themselves, fine."

Suffolk County: Partner benefits proposal opposed

In December, the Suffolk County legislature refused to vote on a proposal extending health benefits to the domestic partners of county employees. In addition, County Executive Robert Gaffney, who must sign all bills passed by the legislature for them to become law, objected to the proposed bill reportedly because it included unmarried heterosexuals, who have the option to legally marry. Without his support, the proposal was tabled; supporters of the measure cited many reasons why it remained so. Some speculated that a majority of the Republican-controlled legislature supported the bill but feared retaliation from "knuckle draggers" in the Conservative Party. Other supporters, like the bill's sponsor, George O. Guldi, said "They were chicken... This was a way for them to avoid a vote on the bill itself." Local gay activist Sandy Rapp said he was not surprised that the bill was tabled — even though Republicans said they were waiting until after the elections to bring it up, and the elections had come and gone. Rapp said, "The lame ducks are still in there... There's a Republican majority and they're homophobes."

Supporters said they would have a better chance during the legislature's next session. Jon Cooper, an openly gay Democrat who won a seat in November, joined the county legislature in 2000.

Westchester County: Battle over proposed human rights commission

Westchester County's effort to establish a human rights commission and adopt an anti-discrimination law covering gay men and lesbians was attacked by right-wing and religious activists. Part of the proposal would prohibit discrimination based on sex, age, national origin, race, marital status and sexual orientation in housing, employment, public accommodations and credit, and create a commission authorized to hear complaints of discrimination in those areas. The other part would create a commission authorized to levy fines of up to $10,000 for violating the proposed anti-discrimination ordinance. When County Council member Andrea Stewart-Cousins introduced the measure in February, right-wing religious groups led most of the opposition.

Opponents decried the proposal on religious, moral and fiscal grounds. The Archdiocese of New York and the Catholic Coalition, a lay group advocating right-wing positions on many social issues, said the measure conflicted with their religious values. Stanley Tompkiel, III, the group's Westchester president, said, "We feel that this legislation will establish public policy that will promote various types of sexual behavior that we consider to be inappropriate." He added, "The real motive is to impose a new sexual agenda and create a new arm of government, a very powerful branch of government." Edward Mechmann, who works for the New York Archdiocese, told the county Board of Legislators during its February meeting that the bill "will be seen as implying that homosexual or bisexual conduct is morally equivalent to heterosexual activity, in contradiction of the beliefs of the vast majority of religious traditions and the great majority of your constituents." Other members of the Catholic Coalition echoed that sentiment. Opponents also focused on the legislation's cost to taxpayers and businesses, claiming that it would become a burden to county residents.

Other Catholic officials joined the fray. A letter denouncing a "homosexual agenda" was circulated among the county's priests. Although the letter claimed to be sent at the behest of Bishop Patrick Sheridan, the New York Archdiocese later disavowed it. At least one priest read it to his congregation before that announcement was made. The Archdiocese did, however, ask the county's priests to speak out against the proposed ordinance. Father John Bonnici, with the New York Archdiocese, issued a letter reiterating Edward Mechmann's earlier claim that the proposal implied that "same-sex relationships have the same value as marriage." Mechmann addressed the board again at a November meeting, suggesting the bill "would undermine marriage and family." Opponents led by the Catholic Church also fought the measure with ads in local newspapers and within its churches. One ad claimed the legislation imposed "a New Sexual Morality and Promotes Homosexuality and Bisexuality of Our Children."

Support from other religious leaders proved that Westchester County's spiritual community was divided on the issue. Rabbi Jacobs of the Westchester Reform Temple said, "It seems a perfect example of where even people of faith who might disapprove of the gay and lesbian way of being should agree there is no possible religious justification for the abuse of human rights." Methodist Minister William Shillady agreed. Rev. Raynor Hesse Jr., a local Episcopal priest, said he was offended by the racial and ethnic slurs he heard in the hallway outside the meeting where the proposal was introduced. "I thought that type of language had died in Westchester," he said.

In September, the Westchester Coalition for Human Rights released the results of a survey showing that 71 percent of the county's residents supported the proposal. In December, the County Council enacted the proposal by a 12-5 vote. The county's Conservative Party, which exercises considerable influence in several of New York's voting districts, vowed to make the measure a "litmus test" for future Republican Party candidates.

NORTH CAROLINA

Statewide: Hate crimes bill defeated

Both houses of the state legislature rejected a bill that would have added sexual orientation, gender and disability to the state's existing hate crimes law. Right-wing activists from around the state, including the North Carolina Family Policy Council, an affiliate of Focus on the Family (see p. 355), urged the legislature to reject the bill. Bill Brooks, the Council's director, said the organization opposed the bill because existing laws already punished violent acts and because the bill would open a Pandora's box.

Early support indicated passage might have been possible. In January, the Episcopal Diocese of North Carolina approved a resolution urging the state legislature to adopt the measure. In March, gay and lesbian activists held a rally at the state Capitol to push for the bill and to demand that the legislature repeal the state's sodomy laws. The activists were met by a protester who claimed that gay men and lesbians would "burn in hell." Capitol police escorted the heckler away. The Equality North Carolina Political Action Committee, a statewide gay rights group, had organized much of the grassroots support behind the bill.

The House Judiciary Committee heard from the bill's supporters and opponents. During a committee hearing on the bill, John Rustin, an official with the Policy Council, claimed that the bill was "attempting to legitimize the homosexual lifestyle by legally recognizing 'sexual orientation' as a protected classification under the law." Rustin asked the committee, "The obvious question raised by such legislation is: Should not all the citizens of our state be provided equal protection under the law?" Rustin argued that the homosexual sex acts that would be covered by the hate crimes law are illegal in North Carolina. Johnny Henderson of the Christian Action League (see p. 353) said that individual gay men and lesbians are already protected under the law as regular citizens, making the bill unnecessary. But Janet Joyner, a retired teacher and lesbian, said that reasoning was a dangerous oversimplification. She told the committee to send a message that attacking someone because he or she is a member of a special category of people is unacceptable.

A day after the committee approved the bill, the full House defeated it by a 58-48 vote. Rep. Zeno Edwards told the house, "You do realize that many of us could support 90 percent of this bill… You do realize that sexual orientation is a deep-founded conviction of many of us who cannot support the bill." M.K. Cullen, head of Equality NC, said, "This just shows the level of homophobia and ignorance we still fight in North Carolina."

A day after it rejected the hate crimes bill, the House also rejected a bill that would have allowed Orange County to adopt its own anti-discrimination ordinance that would have included sexual orientation. Without comment, members voted 67-36.

Chapel Hill: Refusal to broadcast "It's Elementary"

In November, public television station UNC-TV refused to broadcast the film "It's Elementary: Talking about Gay Issues in School." Directed by Oscar-winner Debra Chasnoff, the documentary depicts age-appropriate ways adults and educators can discuss homosexuality with children. Diane Lucas, director of programming at UNC-TV, said she made the decision after watching the film and listening to both its supporters and detractors. Instead of broadcasting the film, Lucas said the station would broaden its race initiative program and create more local explorations of tolerance. The station denied that the decision had been made out of fear of a public backlash.

Tom Howe, the station's director and vice president, said, "Just because our mission is diversity doesn't mean we should show every program that's made on every issue... This film advocates and promotes rather than analyzes. You create more of a flame than a solution when you have one side." Steve Volstad, UNC-TV's communications and marketing director, said the film violated the station's principles of airing programs "based on principles of editorial integrity to guarantee objectivity, fair and balanced presentation of the issues."

The station's actions upset many gay and lesbian North Carolinians. The Gay, Lesbian, and Straight Education Network (GLSEN) called on viewers to send a voided check to the station in protest along with a letter asking the station to reconsider its decision. Mark Slattery, co-chair of the group's Triangle chapter, claimed that the station was making excuses in defending the decision not to air. "We showed [the film] three years ago at UNC [Chapel Hill's] campus. We had about 300 people, and it was well-received," he said. "Public television should be cutting edge. It should be willing to take chances and make people think." GLSEN planned to show the film on Duke University's campus early in 2000.

Chasnoff and a station official squared off in letters to the Raleigh News and Observer. She said that by not broadcasting her film, UNC-TV "missed an opportunity to inspire open, honest dialogue about how teachers can best create classroom climes in which children with gay parents, friends, or relatives feel included and affirmed." Chasnoff said that public television was an appropriate venue in which those discussions should take place. In her response to Chasnoff, Linda Haynes, chair of UNC-TV's board of trustees, reiterated the station's intention to produce a program about North Carolina's grappling with tolerance in public schools and assured readers that plans for that film were already under way. Referring to people who objected to the station's decision not to broadcast the film, Haynes asked readers, "Are you upset because you perceive that UNC-TV has not taken 'your side' in this debate? If your answer... is 'yes,' I would respectfully suggest that you ask yourself if you are contributing more to the problem than the solution in this case."

Debra Chasnoff contributed an essay about the campaign against "It's Elementary" to the 1999 edition of Hostile Climate.

Chapel Hill and Carrboro:
Domestic partners benefits policies targeted

After receiving a $15,000 grant from the anti-gay Alliance Defense Fund (see p. 352) in March, a right-wing activist renewed his lawsuit against the cities of Chapel Hill and Carrboro. A state judge had dismissed Jack Daly's 1998 lawsuit against the domestic partner policies for city employees of Chapel Hill and Carrboro, saying it could not be filed anonymously. In June 1999, Daly filed another legal challenge to the towns' policies, claiming that the cities had overstepped their authority in defining "dependent." North Carolina law, however, does not define what constitutes a "dependent." Chapel Hill and Carrboro allow city employees to classify domestic partners as dependents eligible for employee health benefits, but the lawsuit contends that domestic partners are not dependents under state law. Daly, head of the conservative North Carolina Foundation for Individual Rights and then a candidate for state auditor, said, "Both towns, in our judgment, are in violation of state law." Daly called domestic partnerships "a trendy creation of the militant homosexual activists." Carrboro's openly gay mayor, Mike Nelson, vowed to fight the lawsuit, saying, "Pursuing civil rights, for any group, is always a challenge."

Daly said the residents who were plaintiffs in the suit were defending the taxpayers. Of them, Daly said, "Even in Chapel Hill and Carrboro, there are still some moral people, although evidently they are in the minority." He added, "As someone who is concerned with what I see to be an erosion of character and integrity and morality in public and private life in America, it is not lost on me that... homosexual rights ordinances are a steppingstone for encouraging that behavior."

Carrboro police chief Carolyn Hutchinson spoke out publicly against Daly's suit. "Mr. Daly is not putting a real face on the people who may be negatively impacted by his lawsuit," she said. "If he were to do that, if he is humanitarian at all, he'd lose a little bit of interest in this." Hutchinson and one other couple in town have taken advantage of the benefits package, amounting to 0.6 percent of the town's $295,000 health benefits budget. The cost of the four employees' use of the program in Chapel Hill amounts to 0.27 percent of that city's health benefits budget.

In November, a superior court judge rejected a motion by the towns to dismiss the lawsuit. The cities had argued that the plaintiffs could not justify their case simply because they were taxpayers who disliked a city policy. Nate Pendley, an attorney representing the plaintiffs, said, "It's pretty clear this judge would have given us an injunction [to stop payment of benefits] if we had sought it."

The court, however, ruled in the towns' favor, dismissing the lawsuit in May 2000.

Charlotte: Lesbian-themed play not staged

After an openly lesbian student won a young playwrights contest, the sponsors chose to break with their own custom and not to stage a performance of her play because of its lesbian content. "Life Versus the Paperback Romance," Samantha Gellar's play about a visually impaired woman who meets and falls in love with another woman, was one of five winners out of 200 entrants in the Charlotte Young Playwrights Festival in February. The contest had been jointly sponsored by Children's Theater of Charlotte and the Charlotte-Mecklenburg school system.

Gellar had been warned in advance by contest officials that her play's content would prevent it from being staged, should it win. Although the Children's Theater said it "would never make a play ineligible for a contest based on content," the school system has a policy of determining "what would be appropriate for a school audience." School officials maintained that discussions of sexual orientation were inappropriate for middle and high school audiences. The editorial board at The Charlotte Observer agreed with that decision. Gellar did not, saying, "I understand their reasons. But I still consider it a form of discrimination." She said the play contained only a short kiss and involved no sexual activity.

Some people supportive of the area's arts community were disturbed by the refusal to stage the play. Tonda Taylor, director of Time Out Youth, a gay and lesbian youth support group, said, "There are a lot of well-meaning people who are looking the other way, allowing this discrimination to take place." She added, "It's the same rationale we hear all the time... .The festival, they say, should continue because it serves the greater good even if one play can't be performed. I don't buy that rationale." Gary Zinter wrote a letter to the editor of The Charlotte Observer saying, "Silencing a homosexual participant in the Young Playwrights Festival sends the message that there is an appropriate time and place for prejudice. I'm surprised and disappointed that other participants and sponsors haven't taken a stand against this. How shortsighted. How Charlotte."

The controversy drew considerable attention to Gellar's play. News reports reached as far away as the United Kingdom. With support from local groups, Gellar was able to have her play staged locally in March. That audience gave Gellar a standing ovation. At a public discussion afterward, Gellar criticized the Children's Theater: "You're pretty much admitting that you're too scared of the loss of money. Is Children's Theater that material?" The play was also performed in New York City by actresses Mary-Louise Parker and Lisa Kron. Openly gay playwrights Tony Kushner ("Angels in America") and Paula Vogel ("How I Learned to Drive") attended. Gellar received two standing ovations from that audience.

A personal essay by Samantha Gellar appears on p. 30.

Wake County: Student newspaper ad rejected

Officials with the Wake County school system refused to run an ad from a gay youth group in a student newspaper. In March, Enloe High School's principal, Lloyd Gardner, rejected the student newspaper's request to run an ad by the North Carolina Lambda Youth Network. That group ran ads in other area high school publications. Gardner claimed that the ad in The Eagle's Eye would be disruptive to the school and might be perceived as an endorsement of the Network by the school. Matt Williams, the student editor, said the ad was neither a political endorsement nor a potential disruption to the school. "First, these organizations are not radical," Williams said. " They're not trying to encourage breaking the law. As far as disrupting the school day [is concerned], neither of the ads or the organizations encourage disruption in the school. Second, just because the paper is running these ads doesn't mean the school is endorsing their views." He filed a formal appeal with the school Superintendent Jim Surratt and the board of education.

Others supported Williams' efforts to publish the ad. In a letter to the Raleigh News and Observer, T. Bayard Williams wrote that Gardner "further marginalizes this segment of our community. This helps give, however unintended, cover for the nuts and fanatics who are inclined to commit violence towards gays and lesbians… he is unwittingly contributing to a climate of hostility that could become (guess what?) disruptive in the school environment." Hez Norton, the executive director of the Youth Network, wrote a letter to the News and Observer clarifying the purpose of her organization and saying that access to information on sexual minorities was crucial because of the high rates of suicide among gay and lesbian youth.

> "This show is 100 times worse than 'Ellen' because they're targeting high school kids with their pro-gay propaganda."
>
> — Protester Robert Hales, at a demonstration near the set of "Dawson's Creek" in Wilmington.

Gardner defended his decision, saying he had historically granted students great leeway in their publications. "Enloe High School and the administration has [sic] had a long history of encouraging students to write about sensitive issues… But this was not student writing. This was an ad," he said. He cited the school board's policy governing student publications. The board's policy directs principals to prohibit the distribution of materials deemed vulgar, indecent or obscene, or that contain libelous or abusive language, or encourage the commission of unlawful acts or the violation of school regulations, or advertise products or services not permitted to minors under the law. The policy also allows administrators to prohibit materials that expose students to information deemed inappropriate for their maturity level or that associates the school with "any position other than neutrality on matters of political controversy."

When Surratt upheld Gardner's decision in March, Williams appealed his decision to the school board. The board upheld Surratt's ruling in April.

Wilmington: Filming of "Dawson's Creek" protested

In March, a local youth group protested the filming of the television show "Dawson's Creek." This season's storyline revealed that Jack, a high school teenager, was gay, and several episodes dealt with the process of his coming out. The show is regularly filmed in and around Wilmington. Youths Against the Promotion of Homosexuality organized the rally to denounce the show's having an openly gay character. The protesters, over 30 in number, most of whom were teens, carried placards reading, "Jack and Jill, Not Jack and Bill" and "Hollywood: No More Gay Promo." Seventeen-year-old Robert Hales said, "We're sick and tired of Hollywood trying to force its pro-homosexual values down teenagers' throats on shows like 'Dawson's Creek'... This show is 100 times worse than 'Ellen' because they're targeting high school kids with their pro-gay propaganda." (Hales referred to the canceled show, "Ellen," starring openly lesbian actress Ellen DeGeneres, which in 1997 became the first network television show with a gay leading character.) The crowd of protesters shared Hale's sentiments. They shouted "Don't Holly-weird me!" at employees who were driving onto the lot where "Dawson's Creek" is filmed.

Winston-Salem: University chapel controversy

Wake Forest University was embroiled in a controversy surrounding the use of its chapel for a same-sex wedding ceremony. The dispute began when Wake Forest Baptist Church, which has used the chapel for services for nearly 50 years, asked the university for permission to use the chapel for a same-sex wedding for two of its members in 1997. One of the women was a university Divinity School student. While university officials and trustees deliberated, the couple placed their ceremony on hold for several months. Wake Forest University has historically been affiliated with, but is no longer governed by, the Baptist State Convention of North Carolina. In August 1999, the university chaplain, Rev. Ed Christman, denied the church's request, saying the school did not have a policy regarding same-sex weddings.

An ad hoc committee of the university's Board of Trustees recommended that the chapel not allow same-sex marriage ceremonies. The committee said it based its decision on historical ties to the Baptist State Convention, not out of its own opinions about homosexuality. "Since the university is not prepared to render an ecclesiastical judgment, there is no compelling reason not to respect the prevailing collective wisdom of the Christian church regarding this question... The University does not want to become an involuntary participant or be perceived to have approved such practice, by having its facilities used for this purpose," the committee said. The ad hoc committee's report did not, however, establish a formal university policy on same-sex ceremonies in campus facilities. Kevin Cox, the university's director of media relations, said the committee had deliberated independently from the board of trustees.

Wake Forest Baptist Church's pastor, Rev. Richard Groves, expressed disappointment, saying that when he read the section about "the prevailing collective wisdom" of the church, he was reminded of the exclusion of blacks from white churches in the 1950s and '60s and how instrumental the university had been in desegregating its own campus. Wake Forest's student newspaper criticized the report as being inconsistent with the recent history of university and the Baptist Church. It called the report "hypocritical" and "cowardly."

In September, University administrators told the campus public radio station to confine its reporting of the controversy to the official statement it had issued. Reporters at WFDD, who are university employees, said they feared being fired in the wake of that directive. Sandra Boyette, the university's vice president of public affairs, said that no jobs were threatened. Boyette did not make the same request of the student newspaper, she said, because its staff is not employed by the university. The station's reporters said they planned to air a program looking at the controversy from a national context, but confined the story mostly to the prepared statement. The station's program director, Paul Brown, announced that he would resign in October. Brown said that Boyette had initially planned to eliminate his news supervisory duties. Although Boyette said the plan was never implemented, she did apologize for interjecting herself into the station's editorial processes.

In October, Rev. Christman changed his position to allow same-sex ceremonies in the chapel after statements from the University's president that the school did not prohibit such ceremonies.

NORTH DAKOTA

Statewide: Broadcast of "It's Elementary" attacked

Right-wing activists from around the state criticized the broadcast of Debra Chasnoff's educational documentary "It's Elementary: Talking About Gay Issues in School" on North Dakota's PBS affiliate. The film is a guide for teachers, parents and other adults on addressing gay and lesbian issues with youngsters. The controversy began weeks before the film was scheduled to air on the state's public television network, Prairie Public Broadcasting. Lutheran pastor Harold Reitz said, "I've read my Bible many times. I've found 60 different passages regarding homosexuality and every one is negative." Ralph Muecke led a public campaign criticizing the station, saying "This gay and lesbianism thing is totally abnormal." He claimed that Christians condemning the film are being attacked for their religious beliefs. Muecke wrote a letter that was published in The Bismarck Tribune warning readers that "It's Elementary" was "designed to convey to children as young as three and four years old that homosexuality is normal, acceptable, and 'just another lifestyle.' " The station said it received about 260 calls regarding its broadcast of the film, 225 of which were negative. After the film's September broadcast, Valeria Miller, a teacher from Fargo, wrote a letter to the editor linking the North American Man/Boy Love Association (NAMBLA) with local and national gay and lesbian organizations. She appeared to link pedophilia with homosexuality: "How do we protect our children from such pedophiles when they are being taught in school not only tolerance, but acceptance, of the homosexual lifestyle?"

Among the film's supporters was former Fargo mayor John Lindgren, who said, "We need to wake up and realize [gay] people are our sons and daughters, our friends and neighbors." Kathleen Pavelko, president of Prairie Public Television, said "It's Elementary" was not intended for children and that it would likely bore them. She was undeterred by the opposition.

Debra Chasnoff contributed an essay about "It's Elementary" to the 1999 edition of Hostile Climate.

Garrison: Lesbian-themed play censored

The director of a one-act student play censored its lesbian content because of the community's objections. When the students performed a dress rehearsal of Christopher Durang's "For Whom the Southern Belle Tolls" in school, local residents in the audience reportedly cringed when they heard "dyke" and "lesbian." One asked if bringing the lesbian aspect of the drama to light was necessary. The director, Terry Vandal, eliminated the words "lesbian" and "dyke" from the script. In place of "lesbian," he substituted "that kind of girl," and in place of "dyke," he substituted "swizzle stick stirrer." Vandal defended the changes, saying, "It's about community standards and living within the makeup of the community." He said that many directors change scripts to fit local conditions. Some students, like Kayla Vandal, were upset with the changes. Kayla, who portrayed the play's lesbian character, said, "We changed it so people would back off. People have a problem with high school kids saying that, because they think we don't know what's going on." Nevertheless, the director said, "I think I did the right thing even though they [the students] disagreed with it."

Statewide: Executive order deletes sexual orientation

Gov. Bob Taft deleted the words "sexual orientation" when he revised an executive order prohibiting various forms of discrimination in government employment. Ohio had prohibited sexual orientation discrimination in state employment since 1984, when then-Gov. Richard Celeste issued an executive order containing such a provision. That order expired when former Gov. George Voinovich, who upheld the sexual orientation provision by renewing the order, left office. Taft's revised executive order states that "there are many other groups and classifications of persons that could be subject to discrimination," without naming them. While Taft retained many specifically named categories of discrimination that were prohibited under the previous order, including race, color, religion, sex, national origin, handicap, age and ancestry, he deleted sexual orientation. The executive order was signed in August 1999, although it was not publicly reported until January 2000.

Gov. Taft, his staff, and right-wing members of the legal community defended the order, saying it was part of the administration's policy of ensuring "that all Ohio citizens have equal employment opportunity." Taft's spokesman, Scott Milburn, said the governor did not want to favor any group. "We're not going to go down a laundry list of groups. Is he going to list specific groups? That's really a Pandora's box," he said. Maintaining that the new order covers gay men and lesbians, Milburn called it "a better document." Chris Finney, an attorney who organized support for Cincinnati's anti-gay ballot initiative, Issue 3, applauded the governor's actions. "I certainly think it's a bold and courageous move on the part of the governor," he said. Case Western Reserve University law professor Sharona Hoffman praised Taft for bringing state policy in line with federal civil rights law, which does not prohibit sexual orientation discrimination.

Taft's critics disagreed. Professors at several state universities said his order was a clear reversal of prior state policy. Ruth Colker, an Ohio State University law professor, said, "They [gay men and lesbians] lost something they had, which was the full force of the governor's office behind them... Voluntary rescinding? I've never heard of that before." Ronna Greff Schneider, a law professor at the University of Cincinnati, asked, "If the policy is no different that what it was, then the question to the governor is: 'Why did you need to change it?' " Doreen Cudnik, head of Stonewall Cincinnati, said the revision was "a broadly worded, say-nothing policy. By going out of his way to remove sexual orientation from his order, Taft was sending a message." Jeff Redfield, executive director of Stonewall Columbus, called the new policy diluted and urged residents who disagreed with it to contact the governor and other elected officials.

Cincinnati: Hate crimes proposal rejected

The City Council rejected a proposal to include sexual orientation and disability in Cincinnati's hate crimes law based on opposition from right-wing members of the council and community. Council member Todd Portune had introduced the measure as part of a slate of proposals that also included a resolution urging the state legislature to adopt a hate crimes bill that included sexual orientation and guidelines for city police to collect data on hate crimes.

Opponents cited religious and other grounds as a basis for criticizing the proposal. Equal Rights Not Special Rights, an ad hoc group formed to defeat the hate crimes measure, said the bill would validate lifestyles to which Christians object. Council member Charlie

Winburn said he objected to the proposal because it would give sexual orientation the same status as race, but unlike race, homosexuality is chosen. Phil Burress, head of Citizens for Community Values (see p. 354), said the proposal would punish thought. "Are there any other laws in Cincinnati where people can be arrested for what they're thinking?" he asked. David Langdon, an attorney for the local chapter of the Christian Coalition (see p. 353), claimed that the proposal would "legitimize behavior that many people

> "Studies show that homosexuality begins in the womb, making homosexuality, in actuality, a birth defect... . Hetero is Bettero."
>
> — Ohio State University student Chris Alexander, writing in a campus newspaper.

believe is morally wrong." By testifying before the council in opposition to the proposal, Burress and Langdon continued their long-term efforts to defeat gay rights measures across the state. Both had been active in the campaign to have voters adopt Issue 3, a 1993 anti-gay rights initiative in Cincinnati. Editorials in the Cincinnati Enquirer also opposed the proposal, some of which said the proposal "would actually be a setback for minorities" because, they argued, it punished thought and not actual crimes and would "have serious constitutional problems."

Supporters said the climate of intolerance in the city demonstrated the need for a hate crimes measure that covers gay men, lesbians and the disabled. Michael Blankenship, the victim of a widely publicized hate crime in the city, asserted that Issue 3 had caused a rise in intimidation against gay men and lesbians. That measure effectively prohibited the city from adopting non-discrimination laws that include sexual orientation.

In May, the council rejected the hate crimes proposal by a vote of 6-3.

Columbus: College newspaper's anti-gay column

In January, Ohio State University's student newspaper, The Lantern, ran a column critical of homosexuality and gay and lesbian rights. In the column headlined, "Gay awareness week glorifies perversity," Chris Alexander, a sophomore, called hate crimes laws unnecessary and unconstitutional and said, "The hate crimes laws endorsed by many are a prime example of pro-gay propaganda. Why should it matter if someone is killed over their sexuality or over their wallet?... Why should certain groups have special protections?" He continued, "I really don't understand the concept of 'Gay Pride.' Studies show that homosexuality begins in the womb, making homosexuality, in actuality, a birth defect. How can anyone be proud of a birth defect?" He said same-sex marriage was wrong because it "cheapens the whole concept of marriage, which is two people joining in holy matrimony to, let's be real, procreate." He then specifically attacked lesbians: "The male gay always seems fairly harmless. The female gay, however, DOES scare me. How come lesbians in real life are never like those nice ladies you see in late-night Cinemax movies? The real ones are all hell-bent on filling the world with crappy music… and killing all the men." He ended with "Hetero is Bettero."

OSU students and readers from around the country roundly criticized Alexander in several letters to the editor of the newspaper. A Lantern editorial said that although the paper had distanced itself from Alexander's remarks, hate speech is best refuted by being "exposed as just that."

Columbus: Gay flag at state Capitol

The state's decision to allow the gay and lesbian rainbow flag to be flown over the state Capitol commemorating Gay Pride Week in June ignited a controversy that did not end until February 2000. Stonewall Columbus, the gay group coordinating Gay Pride Week, had originally requested permission from the governor's office to fly the flag but were told that the governor did not have the authority to give such permission. The Capital Square Review and Advisory Board determined that there were no guidelines as to which flags could be flown, although Ron Keller, executive director of the board, said the governor's office had previously made those decisions. The board approved Columbus Stonewall's request, and on June 27, Ohio became the second state to fly a rainbow flag over its state Capitol. That angered state Sen. Eugene Watts, who, in response to the flying of the flag, said he wanted to expand the board's authority and revise its guidelines so that it would permit only government flags to be flown over the Capitol. "Under the current policy, the Ku Klux Klan can fly their flag at the state Capitol," he said.

The controversy escalated when Charles Spingola, an evangelical minister from Newark, Ohio, climbed a statue next to the flagpole and tore down the rainbow flag after a gay pride parade had passed by the area. A crowd of about 30, many reportedly from High Street Baptist Church, cheered as the flag was torn down. A small skirmish ensued when parade marchers returned to the Capitol grounds, in the midst of which Toni Peters, another protester, reportedly burned the flag. Donald Richardson, an itinerant preacher from London, Ohio, was arrested for allegedly slapping the hands of officers as they arrested Spingola. Charles Mainous, pastor of High Street Baptist Church, said, "We knew the flag would be flying today, but we didn't want to burn it until we came down here… But if they put it up again, we'll burn it again." Spingola, Richardson and Peters were all charged with misdemeanor offenses related to their activities.

After Spingola's arraignment, he said, "I'm the one who climbed up the flagpole." He then reportedly gave an interview on a local television station during which he elaborated on his anti-gay views. He allegedly told a reporter that it was his duty to tear the flag down because he did not want to explain to his children why Ohio sanctions what the Bible says is immoral.

The commission's decision to allow the gay flag came under heavy criticism. Delaware County Commissioner James Ward attacked the decision at a commission meeting held the day after the flag-burning incident. Ward called the movement for gay and lesbian rights "a religion, a lifestyle, and a belief" that should be kept separate from the state. He urged the commission to ban all non-government flags from state property, saying that the gay flag controversy was a particular concern even though, "probably in all actuality, they do have the legal right to fly a flag." After Rep. Rex Damschroder introduced a bill requiring the governor's approval for the flying of any non-government flag, the commission voted 5-1 to bring its policies in line with his request, making the bill unnecessary.

In August, Fred Phelps and members of his Westboro Baptist Church (see p. 356) led protests at several local churches and the state Capitol. They targeted local churches that, in their view, were sympathetic to gay men and lesbians and protested at the Capitol during a weekday rush hour. Phelps said they were there to protest the gay flag having been flown over the building. He said the flying of the flag was a "hand-engraved invitation" to him to come and express his views. He had the support of Rev. David Diyanni, a local preacher.

When Spingola was tried in February 2000 for ethnic intimidation under a hate crimes law and criminal damaging, his trial became something of a public spectacle. Spingola claimed that he had been trying to stop Columbus from becoming "worse than San Francisco." His attorney, Thomas Condit, told reporters outside the courtroom, "The greater evil is the promotion of the homosexual agenda from the Statehouse flagpole... Flying that flag is like a punch in the mouth to Christians who believe as Mr. Spingola does." Spingola said, "I just went up and took down the symbol of Sodomites." He added, "but when they [gay men and lesbians] start pushing it [homosexuality] in a culture and vilifying people who oppose them... we'll have a war." During jury deliberations, Spingola allegedly took two dolls and placed them in a sexual position beside a sign that read, "the Bible intimidates Sodomites," and gays "have committed an abomination." Reportedly, he took a rock labeled, "God's righteous judgment" and smashed the dolls. The jury was deadlocked on the hate crime charge, but found Spingola guilty of criminal damaging. Spingola vowed to appeal.

Dayton: Non-discrimination ordinance defeated

Organized opposition led by right-wing religious leaders helped defeat a proposal to expand Dayton's non-discrimination ordinance to include sexual orientation and "source of income" — the latter designed to protect people who receive their income partly from public assistance. Over the summer, it became publicly know that the proposal's chief sponsor, Commissioner Mary Wiseman, was working on language for the measure, and residents flooded City Hall with faxes, calls, e-mail, and letters denouncing it. Wiseman said that opposition to the proposal had come from the "far-right faith-based community," many of whom supported Mayor Mike Turner. She said that many religious leaders had encouraged members of their congregations to "flood us with calls." Wiseman, however, said she quickly gained the support of enough fellow commissioners to assure passage after she formally introduced the proposal in December.

The proposal needed to be passed at two public readings in order to be adopted. Saying that he did not support including gay men and lesbians in the anti-discrimination ordinance, Mayor Turner used a parliamentary maneuver to push the first reading back to December 22. He did so reportedly to allow churches more time to organize an opposition campaign. Mayor Turner also objected to the lack of any exemption for churches or religious organizations. Ken Owens, a local resident, said, "Homosexuals are riding the coattails of those truly disfranchised minorities." Others objected to the proposal on religious grounds and vowed to repeal the ordinance through a citywide referendum should it pass. Opponents continued to fax and call City Hall after the meeting. At that point, Wiseman said she still had commitments from three other commissioners that they would vote for her proposal.

However, Wiseman also had the support of some progressive black ministers. Soon after Wiseman introduced the proposal, Rev. Steve Camp, senior pastor at Faith United Church of Christ, said, "It's not all the black ministers in this town that oppose the resolution." Rev. Darrell Ward, head of Omega Baptist Church, said he supported the need to protect gay men and lesbians from discrimination, but felt that the proposal was too broad. He said, "We instructed our members not to sign some of the other petitions [circulating before the council took its final vote] that contained hateful language and not to applaud the people who spoke against the ordinance for biblical reasons at the commission meeting."

> "If they put it up again, we'll burn it again."
>
> — Rev. Charles Mainous, a minister accompanying a man who reportedly admitted climbing up a flagpole at the state Capitol and ripping down a rainbow flag.

In the weeks leading up to the City Commission's December 22 scheduled vote on the proposal, many commissioners had changed their positions. Wiseman said that vigorous lobbying from local ministers had changed their minds. Commissioner Dean Lovelace said a group of ministers told him they opposed the proposed ordinance because it sanctioned behavior they considered immoral. The ministers reportedly vowed to organize a repeal effort should the commission pass the ordinance. Phil Burress, head of Citizens for Community Values (see p. 354), also lobbied against the proposal. Don McMurray, head of the Greater Dayton Association of Baptists, said, "I would be opposed to any change in the law that would create any special classification for homosexuality."

As a compromise, Wiseman had planned to offer a religious exemption so that some form of her ordinance would pass, but, according to her, that was to no avail. Wiseman said, "What's ironic here is that my colleagues were willing to support my amendment when the opposition was coming from the mostly white churches in the suburbs. Now that mostly African-American churches in the city have been mobilized, they changed their minds. Those churches are perceived to be very powerful." The Dayton Daily News ran a story on the influence that local black ministers had demonstrated in the campaign to defeat the proposal.

Opposition from right-wing forces within the area's religious community helped to turn the tide against the proposal. At the December 22 meeting, the vote was 4-1 against the proposal, thereby removing it from the calendar indefinitely. Commissioner Lloyd Lewis said vote was driven by "fear of referendum and other things." In lieu of adopting the proposal, the commission unanimously voted in favor of a non-binding resolution affirming the rights of gay men, lesbians and the poor to "the same basic rights as other citizens" and opposing "any attempt to deny them such rights." Wiseman later called that vote "a hollow gesture."

Greenville: Anti-Disney protesters

A group claiming that it was affiliated with several right-wing organizations protested the Disney "Mickey's Hometown Parade" when it came to Greenville in July. More than 20 members of "Rock 4 Life," a Wisconsin-based organization aligned with the American Family Association, Southern Baptist Convention, Concerned Women of America and Focus on the Family (see p. 352-355) passed out literature asserting that Disney was pro-homosexuality and anti-family. "In recent years, Disney has established a record of products, policies, and practices that insult the very families to whom it has traditionally catered," it read. The group also sponsored a plane to fly above the parade with a sign reading, "Boycott Disney's pro-gay agenda." The group said it planned to protest all of Disney's "Hometown Parades." The protesters were jeered by crowds that gathered to watch the parade. Several spectators said they disagreed with Rock 4 Life's tactics. Jeanine Whitaker said, "They shouldn't let the protesters in there. If they don't like it, they should stay home." Amber Strawser said, "If you have a statement to make, make it at an appropriate time, not in front of a bunch of kids."

Lakewood: Domestic partner benefits opposed

The City Council ultimately rejected an ordinance that would have made Lakewood the first city in Ohio to extend benefits to the domestic partners of city workers. The proposed ordinance, introduced by council members Michael Skindell and Nancy Roth, needed approval at three public hearings in order for it to be adopted. Early support for the proposal suggested that passage was likely. To increase support among his fellow council members, Skindell attached an amendment that would have limited the benefits to same-sex couples. Another proposed amendment would have provided that the ordinance "by no means" redefined "the state of marriage in Ohio." Skindell and Roth's measure was approved at the first reading by a 5-2 vote and at the second reading by a 6-1 vote. But between the last two hearings, opponents mounted a successful campaign to defeat the proposal.

During a December Rules and Ordinance Committee meeting, 18 out of 45 people permitted to testify about the proposal were opposed to it. While some opponents said they feared the program would be ripe for abuse, others claimed the Council had deliberated behind the public's back. "I wasn't aware of any publicity for the public meetings. I think if people knew what was going on, they would be very concerned," said resident Judy Gillespie. Skindell denied that charge, saying, "[N]othing could be further from the truth. This ordinance has been put under greater scrutiny than most ordinances that come before the council." Another resident, Ellen Malonis, said, "This ordinance redefines marriage. I am concerned about the message it gives to children. This ordinance will only make marriage weaker."

The third and final public hearing, held in January 2000, turned into a heated debate about homosexuality. With more than 400 people in attendance, Skindell had a difficult time keeping the comments focused on the proposed ordinance. One resident was heckled after she announced that she is a lesbian. However, when she asserted that the issue was about fairness, an opponent, Don O'Neal, said, to cheers, "Don't ram your immorality down my throat and I won't force my morality on you."

During that meeting, the council voted 5-2 against the ordinance. Council President Robert M. Seelie said, "I don't feel this should have been handled at a municipal level." Council member Pamela Smith, another opponent, said, "I have voted against symbolic legislation in the past, because it just doesn't feel right to me, and this falls into the category of symbolic legislation." An editorial in The Plain Dealer said the vote "clearly reflected the will of a majority of the residents" and "was probably the right [decision]."

Statewide: Hate crimes bill defeated

Despite early support, the Oklahoma House reversed course in February and defeated a bill that would have added sexual orientation to the state's existing hate crimes law. Introduced by state Rep. Don Ross (D) in response to the widely publicized murder of gay Wyoming college student Matthew Shepard, the bill was approved by the House Judiciary Committee on a 5-3 vote.

Ross had vowed to secure bipartisan support for the bill as it went before the full House, but debate before the committee was at times harsh and partisan. "This is more about having a homosexual lifestyle as a normal lifestyle in contravention of 6,000 years of history. It goes against the Christian religion," said Rep. Bill Graves (R), who had introduced an amendment to a 1998 bill to prohibit "known homosexuals" from teaching in public schools. Graves criticized the state attorney general's support for the bill, suggesting he was trying to legitimize homosexuality. State Rep. Ray Vaughn (R), said, "It seems to me that we're creating a special class of Oklahoma citizens. We're all entitled to the same respect."

The House Judicial Committee approved the bill in mid-February, after which Ken Wood, executive director of the state's Christian Coalition (see p. 353) said, "I think we're going in the wrong direction... I think it creates an inequality of justice. This elevates particular groups to a higher status."

Debate on the House floor mirrored the rhetoric in the Judicial Committee, where opponents objected to including sexual orientation. Because he could not garner Republican support for a bill that included sexual orientation, Ross removed that provision. "The Christian Coalition successfully campaigned against the bill and ended any possibility of bipartisan support" he said. "I said from the beginning I would not allow this issue to become a partisan wedge issue used exclusively against Democrats in the next election." Despite Ross's move, House members rejected the revised version of the bill as well, with opponents using many of the same justifications.

The House did pass a bill that would have prohibited adoptions by gay men and lesbians and that would also have prevented them from serving as foster parents. That bill died in a Senate committee.

Norman: College vandalism

In October, a vandal defaced chalkings and a poster put up by a gay and lesbian student group. Members of the University of Oklahoma's Gay, Lesbian, and Bisexual Alliance said that within a two-hour window, a vandal had written "FAG" and "FAGS SUCK" on chalkings the group drew to celebrate National Coming Out Day and that the word "GAY" had a large X through it. A 40-foot vinyl banner was also torn down and slashed with a knife. University President David Boren denounced the acts as "completely contrary to the values of our university... When the rights of free speech and free expression for any members of our community are violated, we are all diminished."

Tulsa: Methodist minister resigns under scrutiny

A Methodist minister resigned amid a controversy involving same-sex "holy union" ceremonies. Lay member Jake Barker complained in a letter to the state bishop that Rev. Leslie Penrose of the Community of Hope United Methodist Church and Rev. Susan Ross of Perkins, Oklahoma, had presided at a lesbian wedding in Sacramento, California in January. Barker also posted his complaints on a conservative website for a group affiliated with the Methodist Church. Both ministers have publicly attested to their support for including gay men and lesbians as full members of the church, including their support for the church's blessing of same-sex unions. Barker wrote that Penrose and Ross "defiantly and un-repentantly violated their vows of ordination." Barker later said, "A lot of people want to hide their head in the sand and pretend this did not exist." His complaints prompted church officials to begin an investigation. Penrose's church had long welcomed people marginalized by more conservative congregations. She said she has performed many same-sex marriage ceremonies.

When news of Penrose's actions reached the local media in March, she tendered her resignation. The Tulsa World and local television station OETA-Channel 11 ran stories about the allegations and investigation. Penrose faxed a letter to her bishop withdrawing from the United Methodist Church the night that the television station was to broadcast a story on a same-sex commitment ceremony she had performed for two of her lesbian church members in Tulsa. "We've always said we won't lie and we won't hide... We won't turn it [performing holy unions] into a circus, but we won't lie," she said. "It felt right... to take that opportunity, with dignity, to say goodbye."

Rev. Penrose wrote a personal essay describing her experience for the 1999 edition of Hostile Climate.

OREGON

Statewide: Anti-gay ballot initiative on schools

The Oregon Citizens Alliance (OCA) sponsored a ballot initiative to prohibit discussion of homosexuality or bisexuality "in a manner which encourages, promotes, or sanctions such behaviors" in public schools. During a June meeting closed to the press and public, the state Republican Party endorsed the initiative. State Rep. Kevin Mannix said the initiative "pretty closely" tracks the party's platform, which states, "We [the party] oppose governments' efforts to validate or sanction homosexual activity." Though the meeting marked the first time the party had ever entirely closed its doors to the press, Lee Coleman, head of Oregon's Log Cabin Republicans affiliate, attended the meeting and said the debate over the endorsement was "heated and viciously anti-gay." Political analyst Jim Moore said he was surprised the party would endorse an initiative sponsored by a group he said was "on life support." To get on the November 2000 ballot, organizers needed to obtain approximately 70,000 valid signatures by July 2000. By June 1999, the OCA had only obtained 10,000. Lon Mabon, OCA's founder, said the Republican Party was helping to gather signatures. Although the process of collecting signatures was off to what some considered a slow start, the Republican endorsement gave the campaign a tremendous boost.

> Schools can't make you gay, they can't make you straight, but they can make you miserable."
>
> — Kevin Jennings, head of the Gay, Lesbian and Straight Education Network, opposing a ballot initiative to prohibit the discussion of homosexuality in public schools.

Advocates for gay and lesbian civil rights — including the American Civil Liberties Union, the Gay, Lesbian and Straight Education Network (GLSEN), the Queer Youth Network and Basic Rights Oregon — opposed the initiative. Kevin Jennings, head of GLSEN, argued that supporters of the initiative who claim that schools "promote" homosexuality use that claim as a smoke screen for bigotry. "If our schools promote anything, they promote heterosexuality, but with a remarkable lack of success because people continue to be gay. Schools can't make you gay, they can't make you straight, but they can make you miserable."

Statewide: Proposed same-sex marriage ban

A proposal to prohibit the recognition of same-sex marriage and deny courts the ability to require governments to offer domestic partner benefits made its way through the Oregon legislature in the summer. State Rep. Kevin Mannix introduced a bill to place the proposal on the ballot as a state constitutional amendment. His bill came in response to a December 1998 state appeals court ruling (Tanner, et al., vs. Oregon Health Sciences University, et al.) in which the court held that by using marital status to determine which state employees would be offered spousal benefits, the state government discriminated against gay and lesbian employees, whose same-sex relationships are not recognized by the state. Mannix said he feared the ruling would pave the way for the legal recognition of same-sex marriage.

At a legislative hearing on the bill, right-wing activists from around the state including members of the Religious Right spoke in favor of the bill. Mannix said, "We are drawing a firm line in protecting a traditional family unit: marriage." He described the appeals court ruling as a "warning shot" of "perverse reasoning" by the courts. According to Mannix, if same-sex marriage were approved, "We are going to see society turned upside down in terms of the relationship of marriage." A representative from the Oregon Center for Family Policy, an affiliate of Focus on the Family (see p. 355) testified against the bill.

Gay and lesbian rights advocates denounced Mannix's proposal. Laura Dellinger, head of Basic Rights Oregon, said, "It's just another tremendous waste of resources if we end up having to fight this on the ballot... It's unfortunate they're using the marriage issue as a red herring to what's really at stake — making sure people can get insurance for partners." Jean Harris, also with the group, told a legislative committee, "We already can't get married, so why push this out? It's about keeping us from benefits." The Oregon American Civil Liberties Union also opposed the bill.

The bill seemed doomed when the state House defeated it in June. A week later, however, supporters resurrected the measure as a proposed ballot initiative but without the provision prohibiting state courts from requiring that unmarried partners of government employees be provided the same benefits as married employees. The revised bill would still have authorized a ballot initiative that would prevent city and county governments from recognizing same-sex marriages performed in states where the government recognized them, although none have to date. Mannix said, "This innoculates us against the spread of the Tanner theology," referring to the aforementioned court case requiring local governments to offer domestic partner benefits to unmarried employees. The House

Judiciary-Civil Law committee approved it by a 5-4 vote. The full House later passed the revised bill. In July, the Senate took up the measure, but voted it down, 16-13.

Ashland: Domestic partners registry

Right-wing activists opposed a plan by the city of Ashland create a domestic partners registry. Advocates of the proposal modeled it after registries in other U.S. cities. Under the proposal, which was supported by the mayor and several city staffers, registering as domestic partners would grant no legal rights or privileges, but advocates hoped the registry created by the proposal would serve as a guideline for employers seeking to offer domestic partner benefits for their employees. Opponents quickly seized on the proposal to denounce gay men and lesbians. City Council member Cameron Hanson said, "The city shouldn't be in the business of advocating the homosexual lifestyle." He said he hoped that his speaking out against the proposal would create more opposition. "The homosexual community has a reputation for being very loud and overbearing and some people don't want to go against them... I would hope that people who do not go along with the city on this will stand up and be recognized," Hanson said. Terri Mensch, a local entrepreneur, said, "I don't consider myself a member of the Moral Majority, or someone out there shaking my Bible telling them they will all go to hell, but I personally feel like this is a step towards marriage for gays and lesbians."

During the Council's October meeting, several community members again spoke out against the measure. "To weaken this greatest form of human commitment [marriage] is to weaken all other healthy forms; wound the vine and you harm the branches," said Dan Prince, a local minister. John Dezell, a retired attorney, claimed that the city had more important issues to face than creating a domestic partners registry. "Don't you have enough to do as Council members with water and fixing streets? You are digging your political graves," he told the Council. At the end of that meeting, the Council voted in favor of the proposal, with only Hanson voting against it. That vote made Ashland the first city in the state to offer such a registry. The first couple registered in November.

Eugene: Gay dormitory rejected

In February, housing officials at the University of Oregon, Eugene, rejected a proposal to create an on-campus dormitory catering primarily to gay, lesbian, bisexual, and transgendered students. The push for this type of dormitory began in March 1998, when openly lesbian undergraduate Nina Thompson presented a proposal to the Residence Hall Association, which endorsed the idea. Thompson said, "I see creating a safer space for people who are having issues with roommates, issues with homophobia, issues with harassment. Creating a safer place for them is really what this is about." In 1996, an institute at the University of Oregon had conducted a survey showing that between 31 and 41 percent of gay, lesbian, bisexual, and transgendered students feared for their safety on campuses.

The university's director of housing, however, deliberated over the dormitory proposal for several months before rejecting it. This upset many supporters who pointed to a "cyber-dorm," catering to computer-related issues that was proposed around the same time and had since been up and running. In discussing the decision to reject the dormitory, Dan Williams, vice president for administration, said, "Diversity is one of the University of Oregon's greatest strengths. By segregating students in residence halls in this way we run the risk of breaking down rather than enhancing that diversity." He added that students' concerns over safety in the dormitories would be addressed. Jason Wicklund, cochair of the PRIDE Hall Committee, the student group that pushed for the dormitory, said, "We're all kind of refocusing on getting over the fact that we lost this one."

Portland: Diversity curriculum opposed

Six teachers at Cleveland High School criticized a districtwide diversity curriculum for addressing homosexuality and a variety of other topics to which they objected. The diversity curriculum is composed of a series of workshops and recommended books on homosexuality and students. It aims to help schools stop hate speech directed at gay and lesbian students. A group of teachers who found the program objectionable sent a memo to Principal Bruce Plato saying, "We are concerned that an entirely one-sided perspective on the issue of homosexuality is being disseminated to students by the school district through its sexual diversity committee... Its effort has been solely to condone, affirm, and encourage homosexual practices among students and adults."

John Ditmore, one of the teachers who wrote the memo, said he and the other teachers objected to the program after they looked at the recommended readings. They wanted books that included views critical of homosexuality and asked the school to purchase 10 copies of "Homosexuality and the Politics of Truth," by Jeffrey Satinover. Satinover is a psychiatrist who speaks out against homosexuality, claiming that it is not an innate condition and that gay men and lesbians can change their sexual orientation. The teachers wanted the Satinover's book to be made available for teachers, counselors and students in the library. Ditmore added, "I just don't think [homosexuality] is a good thing."

The Oregon Citizens Alliance (see p. 356) cited the teachers' complaints in a notice to its members claiming that gay and lesbian issues had penetrated the state's public schools. Referring to a media story on the controversy, one of the group's direct-mail letters claimed, "What the newspaper failed to report is just how far the 'gay' agenda has already penetrated Oregon schools... .The school safety theme is a ruse for getting a foothold in schools. It is the brainchild of homosexual activist Kevin Jennings, whose Gay, Lesbian, and Straight Education Network (GLSEN) first infiltrated public schools in Massachusetts in the early 1990s." The letter enclosed a petition that OCA was circulating to enlist support for a statewide ballot initiative to prohibit discussion of homosexuality and bisexuality in public schools.

Several school officials defended the Portland Public School system's diversity curriculum. Stevie Newcomer, who heads the district's diversity committee, said the books in question are only suggested readings for teachers and students to become better acquainted with homosexuality. "The district has been working on the issue for several years, so it's not something new. We have tried to do all we can to make schools safe for all kids," she said. The curriculum is needed, she maintained, because "I've heard from teachers [that] when they stand up for gay kids or gay parents, they will be assumed to be gay themselves." Pat Burke, a district administrator, called the teachers' allegations "absolutely untrue." He added, "That training always emphasizes that we're not asking anyone to do anything counter to their personal or religious values, but to recognize that we do have gay and lesbian students."

> "Want a hate-free millennium? Get rid of all the homos!"
>
> — Chanted by protesters at a showing of "Edge of 17," a gay-themed movie, in Portland.

At least a couple of students were upset by the demands of Ditmore and the other teachers who authored the letter of complaint. Dajah Kilgore, who is openly lesbian, said the teachers' complaints would make gay and lesbian students feel uncomfortable in their classes. Ilse Corson agreed, saying, "If they have a problem with people being gay, then they shouldn't be teachers."

Portland: Protesters target theater

In September, a crowd of protesters gathered at a Portland theater to denounce a showing of the movie "Edge of 17," a coming-of-age and coming-out story of a gay teenager. The protesters targeted the Cinema 21 Theater with chants and placards reading, "Jesus Saves From Hell." The crowd grew so large that local police were called in to disperse it. Ed Segel, a history professor caught in the middle of the protests, said, "There was lots of shouting... It caught me by surprise. This certainly isn't the first time a gay film has played there, and I don't remember any picketing in the past."

Fearing that the protesters' activities would extend into an October gay film festival at the same theater, Ron Glanville, with the Human Rights Campaign, warned other gay and lesbian community leaders about a possible anti-gay demonstration. Protesters did in fact return during the festival; moviegoers described them as "young, loud and obnoxious." Darrell Dubois, who attended the festival, said the protesters shouted, "Want a hate-free millennium? Get rid of all the homos!" The next night, there were fewer protesters. By the time four protesters arrived at the theater, almost all the audience was inside. A forum on hate crimes followed the screening.

St. Helens: Play criticized for gay content

A parent of a local high school student jeered a gay-themed play performed at St. Helens High School in February. Students from a neighboring school were performing a scene from the Pulitzer Prize-winning Broadway musical "Rent" as part of a local drama competition. Wayne Mayo said he was there with his son and his mother to watch his daughter perform a scene in another play. He said he walked out after seeing scenes in which two male characters simulated sex and two female characters kissed. At the end of that performance, Mayo re-entered and told the audience, "That was the worst piece of trash I have ever seen." He later said, "Some people in the dramatic world feel that just because it's been performed or it's been written, then it's art. I disagree. Pornography is pornography." Mayo wrote a guest column in The Oregonian about his objections and run-ins with local drama coaches. Mayo said he objected when he was told that his attitude and behavior were "out of place."

The local school superintendent, Cliff Tetreault, said he would not allow any more drama competitions unless he could be assured there would be no inappropriate material. "My understanding was that whatever was presented would conform to community standards," Tetreault said. "This certainly violates the standards of St. Helens. It's kind of like guests coming to your house and bringing a pornographic video." The St. Helens police chief said he investigated the "Rent" incident but did not file any charges because the performers were all 18 years old.

PENNSYLVANIA

Statewide: Ban on partner benefits at public colleges

In a two-hour time span, the state legislature pushed through a bill that prohibits municipalities from requiring state-funded universities and colleges to offer health benefits to their employees' domestic partners. In November, Republican senators, using an unscheduled vote, tacked an amendment onto an existing bill about municipal police education and training. They expedited transfer of the bill to the House, where it passed with another unscheduled vote. Republican Gov. Tom Ridge quickly signed it; his spokesperson said, "The governor believes marriage is a heterosexual institution... We see what's happening in Pittsburgh as an [intrusion]... on the institution of marriage." Critics said Republican legislators used the bill to help the University of Pittsburgh win a lawsuit challenging the university's policy of refusing to provide domestic partner benefits to its employees. Democrat state Rep. Thomas Tangretti said, "Obviously, it's a deal someone is trying to negotiate for the University of Pittsburgh... I didn't particularly care for it." This was the third time in 1999 that the legislature had signaled that it was unwilling to approve domestic partner benefits for employees at state universities.

Despite its passage, the bill caused a political firestorm. Seven Democratic senators who voted for the bill said that they were tricked into voting for it and asked the governor to veto the bill. They said the Republican leadership made it appear non-controversial.

Tangretti, the police bill's original sponsor in the House, withdrew his name as a sponsor in protest. The only Republican to vote against it in the House, Lita Indzel, said, "It was mean, it was wrong. It sends a bad message." Rep. Babette Josephs called the vote "a cheap shot." She added, "It lets enough of them go home and beat their chests and say to their constituents, 'I've saved you, I've preserved marriage for you... It's miserable, it's cowardly, it's deceptive, and I think it shows there's a really grave misunderstanding about a profound change in attitude toward lifestyle choices."

> "Whenever they get a chance to vote against lesbian and gay folks, they get worked up into a frenzy."
>
> — Pennsylvania ACLU Director Larry Frankel, remarking on the speedy progress of a bill prohibiting cities from requiring that state colleges offer domestic partner benefits.

Advocates of gay civil rights decried political maneuvering on the matter. Larry Frankel, executive director of the Pennsylvania American Civil Liberties Union, said, "These guys trip over themselves to vote against gays and lesbians." He added, "Whenever they get a chance to vote against lesbian and gay folks, they get worked up into a frenzy." Activists and elected officials pointed out that the bill strips away the power of local government to formulate policies from which non-traditional families may benefit.

Allentown: Candidate flip-flops on gay issues

A candidate for the City Council flip-flopped on gay and lesbian issues as her campaign geared up for a November election. Mary Cramsey told the gay and lesbian political group Pennsylvania Gay and Lesbian Alliance for Political Action (PAGALA) in the spring that she supported civil rights, employment, and housing protections for gay men and lesbians. In the same questionnaire, she indicated her support for reporting anti-gay hate crimes, for special training on gay and lesbian issues for police officers, for additional funding for AIDS awareness programs, and for educational programs advocating safe sex. After winning the Democratic primary, she switched her position on all these issues. On a questionnaire on gay rights from the conservative Citizens for Traditional Values, Cramsey gave responses that contradicted her previous statements. When the League of Women Voters asked what her major concerns were for the election, she listed opposing the addition of sexual orientation to the human rights ordinance as her chief issue. Cramsey said such an addition would encourage more gay rights legislation. Activists charge that she offered support for gay and lesbian equality to gain their support in the tight primary race she had faced in the spring.

In the fall, Cramsey said, during an interview, that gay and lesbian civil rights were illegitimate. "They have chosen a lifestyle... They have to become more responsible for themselves." She added, "I'm vehemently opposed to this lifestyle... I'm against their receiving the same benefits my [late] husband and I received." She had admitted on the primary questionnaire that she opposed domestic partner benefits. Cramsey said, "This is against my belief in the validity of a true spouse." Explaining the change in her positions, she said, "I was unfamiliar with the issue of sexual orientation... I'm in a learning process." She declined to be more specific though she admitted receiving a number of mailings from Citizens for Traditional Values. Cramsey did not fill out a new survey sent to her by PAGALA, claiming she did not remember getting the letter.

Her flip-flop confused political analysts and angered activists. G. Terry Madonna, a political science professor at Millersville University, said, "That's pretty unusual... Most candidates wait until they get into office to break pledges." Madonna added, "I spend my life studying political socialization, and I have not encountered many people who change their core values in the middle of their lives." Elizabeth Bradbury, co-chair of PAGALA, charged that Cramsey used stealth to play both sides of the issues. She said, "I feel particularly betrayed because I voted for her."

Cramsey won the primary by only 616 votes. Bradbury claimed that gay and lesbian voters were a crucial part of that majority. Cramsey lost the November general election.

Erie: Gay men's request for joint custody

A county judged denied a gay male couple's request for joint custody of the children they were raising together. One father had legally adopted the children soon after each was born, but both of them petitioned to have the non-adoptive father designated as an additional legal guardian. Judge Shad Connelly ruled in June that only the parent who had legally adopted the children could serve as a legal parent. He issued the ruling without a scheduled home visit and hearing and despite the fact that other Pennsylvania judges had granted similar adoption requests. The judge wrote, "Because the Legislature has not seen fit to specifically sanction such adoptions as this, the court is not legally empowered to grant the petition for adoption."

The ruling upset the two men, who asked not to be identified in order to protect the privacy of the children. "I don't need anyone to order me to take on a parental role. I do that every time I lay out clothes for my children," the adoptive father said. His partner said he only wanted to assure the children would receive insurance, Social Security, and other benefits should he die before they become adults. He added, "This really is a time in our country when we all aren't traditional families... This doesn't stop the relationship with the children. It just hurts."

They appealed Connelly's verdict in July to the Superior Court. The couple's attorney, Karen Engro, said, "If the adoption is granted, everyone wins. By denying it, everyone loses." The case was still pending as of press time.

Forwardstown: Attack on rural bar

A preacher resumed his two-year campaign to shut down a rural gay bar in August. The minister, Ron McRae, led a group of anti-gay activists who taunted customers of the Casa Nova bar as they entered and exited. They called the customers "sodomites" and "AIDS carriers." In the past, McRae has used video cameras to tape the customers and their license plates, has shined lights in customers' faces, and blocked the path to their cars. Complaints that the bar's owner, Pat Cramer, made to the county's district attorney, Jerry Spangler, never resulted in charges being levied against any of the protesters. Spangler said he had to strike a balance between the free speech rights of anti-gay protesters and Cramer's need for protection against harassment. "The government has to remain neutral and enforce the law in an even-handed manner." Cramer disagreed. "[Spangler's] not neutral... He's taking their side and he's letting them get away with anything they want to do," she said.

One week after the protests resumed, the bar came under attack by two unidentified vandals, who Cramer said threw rocks at the bar, breaking windows. Cramer said she saw two men destroy a door and the roof of her car early in the morning. She said it took the police three hours to arrive after she called them. Cramer reports that since she opened the bar in 1997, she has endured protests from the Ku Klux Klan, a shotgun blast and death threats.

Lancaster County: Judge bars lesbians' adoption

A state appeals court upheld a trial court's ruling that both members of a lesbian couple could not be granted parental custody of their twin boys. In December 1998, Lancaster County Court Judge James Cullen ruled that the biological mother was the only legal parent the children have. Though other county judges have granted adoptions to both members of gay and lesbian couples when one is not the biological parent, Cullen ruled that state law clearly prohibited two women from sharing parental rights when one of them is the biological mother. In rejecting the couple's claim that they share parental responsibilities like opposite-sex married couples, Cullen also pointed to state laws defining marriage as being exclusively between one man and one woman. In 1996, the legislature prohibited the state from recognizing same-sex unions.

Gay and lesbian activists decried the ruling. "The courts must begin to apply a standard that centers around the best interest of the child... It has to expand the narrow vision of family," said Rita Addessa, executive director of the Philadelphia Lesbian and Gay Task Force. Conservative groups disagreed. Michael Greer, president of the Pennsylvania Family Institute, an affiliate of Focus on the Family (see p. 355), said that the "best interest of the child is to be raised in a family with a father and a mother and not just two adults... The general benefit to society is to maintain the definition of family as is... "

The women appealed Cullen's decision to the state Superior Court. Sandra Gray, an attorney for the couple, remained hopeful. She noted that county courts throughout the state have come down on both sides of the issue. "This needs to be clarified," she said. The Superior Court, however, upheld Cullen's ruling. The plaintiffs petitioned for a rehearing, which the Superior Court granted. As of press time, oral arguments had not been scheduled.

Philadelphia: Catholic Archdiocese distributes voter guide

The Catholic Archdiocese of Philadelphia issued a voter guide for the city's primary elections in May that included candidates' positions on gay and lesbian rights issues. Reportedly inspired by opposition to the city's domestic partner benefits package, the voter guides surveyed candidates for city office on many issues about which the church was concerned. Candidates were asked among other things, whether they favored repealing the benefits package or legally recognizing same-sex unions. The survey also included questions on abortion, condom distribution, and free needle exchanges for drug users. Conservative activists welcomed the church's work. Mike McMonagle, president of the Pro-Life Political Action Committee of Southeastern Pennsylvania, said, "the guide clearly had an impact" in past elections. His organization distributed 50,000 copies of the Catholic Church's 1996 Congressional voter's guide to area churches. "It doesn't get people out, but if people are going to vote, it does have an impact."

The guide may have had an influence on the primary victory of John Street, who as a city councilman opposed offering health benefits to the domestic partners of city employees. Though gay and lesbian political leaders opposed Street, he won both the Democratic primary and the mayoral general election in November. Mark Segal, publisher of the Philadelphia Gay News, suggested the church might suffer a backlash. "The church has lost more and more support because they have misread their congregations," Segal said. Rev. Barry Lynn, president of Americans United for Separation of Church and State, threatened to seek an end to the church's tax-exempt status because of the voter guides. One of that group's analysts said the church's voter guides may "not track the sponsoring organization's known agenda," but must show their positions on a wide array of issues. Lynn wrote the Archdiocese that "this entire scheme smacks of Christian Coalition-style tactics, and I am disappointed that the Archdiocese would consider such an ill-conceived and legally dubious project."

A spokesperson for the Archdiocese said, "The only responsible course of action for the Catholic Church is to participate in a debate started by others." The church said it would not be telling people how to vote. Although Catholic organizations have distributed voter guides for federal elections, they have done so less frequently in municipal elections. The church distributed the guides to over 120 parishes.

Philadelphia: Festival ads censored

An electric utility censored an ad announcing a gay and lesbian pride festival. PECO Energy told Diversity of Pride, a group that sponsors Philadelphia's June gay pride festival and National Coming Out Day in October, that it would not include the words "gay" or "coming out" in an ad atop its Philadelphia skyscraper. Gay and lesbian activists were outraged. "We think their policy is homophobic," said Malcolm Lazin, executive director of PrideFest America, another gay pride festival in Philadelphia. He also requested that PECO cancel an agreement to run an ad for PrideFest, which Lazin's organization sponsors. The company's spokesperson, Neil McDermott, said PECO would honor that request. McDermott also noted that the company makes its electronic bulletin board available to a variety of community groups but reserves the right to edit messages on its sign. He said, "We are not in the business of being enmeshed in social issues." Andrew Park, director of the Philadelphia Center for Gay and Lesbian Civil Rights, said that Diversity of Pride and PECO had been negotiating the ad's wording for some time, but he was still disappointed in the company's decision. "Their saying they'll cover gay events but not use the word gay is plantation politics," he observed. Meanwhile, Lazin urged people to follow his lead and switch to another utility.

In a deal worked out between PECO and state Sen. Vincent Fumo, the utility announced in April 2000 that it would allow the word "gay" to be used in the group's announcement of the Pride Day celebration.

Philadelphia: Vandals destroy rainbow flags

Residents of the Powelton Village neighborhood were disturbed by a challenge to a gay neighbor's effort to fly a rainbow flag outside his home. Vandals repeatedly stole the flags at Kurt Conklin's home. He had to replace his flag three times between February and October because it was repeatedly stolen. Conklin believed students at nearby Drexel University were responsible. "Flying a rainbow flag is like waving a red shirt in front of a bull around here... Some male students have a high level of homophobia," he said. He also reported having college-age males yell epithets like "homo" at him. Conklin said one student urinated on his property in front of him and another threatened to pour beer on a nearby car. He complained to university officials and local police, but the harassment continued. Fortunately, Conklin had his neighbors' support.

In October, Rev. Patricia Pearce, pastor of the Tabernacle United Church in West Philadelphia and Conklin's neighbor, urged all neighborhood residents to hang rainbow flags outside their homes. She said, "Historically, Powelton Village has valued diversity and tolerance as good things. We want to communicate that." A local gay and lesbian bookstore helped supply the flags and Pearce's church helped distribute them. Many residents heeded her call.

By November, several residents reported that their rainbow flags had been vandalized as well. Many residents believed that Drexel students were responsible for the thefts. They stepped up their complaints to university officials. Resident Shan Holt said, "The university in general, and [Drexel president] Papadakis in particular, need to proactively address the whole range of challenges, and not simply wait until something bad happens, and then deplore it." Although university officials denounced discriminatory acts based on sexual orientation and promised to punish students caught committing them, the harassment continued. One resident claimed Drexel students chanted "homo-homo" in front of his house, vandalized a community garden, and littered the neighborhood. He and his neighbors vowed to keep their flags flying. Longtime resident Betty Bauman said, "No, I'm not backing down [from flying the flag]."

Pike County: Anti-gay campaign

An openly gay candidate faced harsh opposition when he ran for a seat on the county commission. When local entrepreneur and former president of the local Chamber of Commerce Gerry Hansen ran in the Democratic primary in May, opponents posted a sign across the street from a polling place saying, "Just Say No to Queers." After complaints, the sign was taken down. Hansen won the primary.

Opposition continued during the general election. Activist and Hansen supporter Sean Strub said that signs for Hansen that Strub placed in his yard had been defaced in October with "Fag" and "Homo" spray painted on them. Strub said that a bus shelter had been vandalized around the same time, with "Hansen is a Homo" sprayed on it. He also noted that a local newspaper ran an exposé on his own background as a gay activist the week of the general election in November. In that election, Hansen, running on a slate with council candidate Karl Wagner, defeated the eight-year incumbent. Although Strub said that many predicted Wagner would distance himself from Hansen, the two remained closely aligned and won the election.

Pittsburgh:
University refuses to provide domestic partner benefits

The University of Pittsburgh (Pitt) challenged the validity of the city's gay rights ordinance as part of its response to a complaint brought by current and former employees. The university argued in February that Pittsburgh's ordinance outlawing sexual orientation discrimination cannot compel it to offer domestic partner benefits to gay and lesbian employees. Deborah Henson, a former professor, filed a complaint with the City Human Relations Commission in 1996, alleging that the university's refusal to provide domestic partner benefits was based on her sexual orientation and came from an "openly hostile attitude" by some university trustees. Pitt filed a motion to dismiss the case, arguing that the Human Relations Commission has no legal authority to enforce the city's ordinance because doing so would exceed the state human rights law, which outlaws various types of discrimination but not sexual orientation discrimination. The commission rejected that motion in June.

Gay and lesbian rights activists fear that a ruling in Pitt's favor would overturn local gay rights ordinances across the state. Christine Biancheria, an attorney for the Henson and other employees who joined her complaint, said, "It's like pointing a nuclear warhead at the gay community in order to avoid paying a few people benefits." She added, "If you remove the ordinance, it would be perfectly legal to discriminate against gay people in Pittsburgh." Leslie Cooper, an ACLU attorney, called Pitt's legal strategy "offensive" because it "is challenging the sovereignty of the cities of Pennsylvania."

In rallies across the state, protesters denounced Pitt's legal challenge to the city ordinance. Almost 250 protesters rallied at Pitt during a February meeting of the Board of Trustees. Shawn Collington, a Pittsburgh teenager and participant, said, "Without this law, I could lose my job. I could be tossed out of my apartment... This is my life. This is all I have." Other protesters carried signs reading "Stop the Hate" and "Trustees, who do you sleep with?" Trustee Chair J. Wray Connolly said, "If these people would like to have these benefits, why don't they get on a bus and go to Harrisburg?" The Graduate and Professional Students Association denounced Pitt's motion. A professor joined 17 students in a 17-day hunger strike protesting the administration's position. The faculty assembly adopted a resolution supporting gay and lesbian rights. Students at Pennsylvania State University collected signatures for a petition presented to the state legislature, calling on it to extend health benefits to domestic partners.

> "It's like pointing a nuclear warhead at the gay community in order to avoid paying a few people benefits."
>
> — Attorney Christine Biancheria, on the University of Pittsburgh's protracted battle against offering domestic partner benefits to university employees.

Pitt Chancellor Mark Nordenberg cited "public relations mistakes" in the school's handling of the lawsuit. He said, "What I think is unfortunate are the risks that are almost always there when someone takes a weak case and tries to use it as a vehicle for social change." During a July deposition in the case, Trustee Connolly said that he would have a problem with gay and lesbian child care workers. "My problem is the gay and lesbian lifestyle is a different lifestyle. And it may be a different lifestyle than the parents of the children under their care are teaching their children or exposing their children to." He expressed concern that gay and lesbian child-care givers would "convince them [the children] that the lifestyle was one they may want to follow." He also said that he opposed same-sex marriage. Attorneys for the university asked the City Human Relations Commission to seal depositions and other discovery material in the case.

Many of the arguments for and against the benefits package revolved around the cost to the university. Pitt claimed that the potentially enormous costs would amount to an undue financial burden. The university claimed its major insurance carrier, Highmark Blue Cross/Blue Shield, might add a surcharge on their policies if Pitt added domestic partners to those eligible for coverage. Another insurance carrier later stipulated that it would not add any extra cost to the university or its employees for the added coverage. The ACLU argued that the costs would amount to no more than $25,000 a year out of an $800 million budget. Kevin Vaughan, with the Philadelphia Commission on Human Relations said, "It's amazing to me that the University of Pittsburgh would try to deny domestic partner and sexual orientation protections to a class of people rather than provide benefits that are becoming a standard part of benefit packages of Fortune 500 companies."

University officials were pleased when the state legislature passed a bill in November prohibiting municipalities from requiring state-funded universities and colleges to offer health benefits to the domestic partners of their employees. According to gay rights activists, Republican legislators passed the bill on behalf of the university (see incident , p. 278). University attorneys then asked the City Human Relations Commission to dismiss the lawsuit. A month later, the commission said the new law did not eliminate its jurisdiction to determine whether or not Pitt's policies are discriminatory. Attorneys for the employees vowed to continue their case.

In December, the university asked the Common Pleas Court to prohibit the city from further litigating the case, arguing that the city had not authority to proceed in the case. Citing the new law passed in November 1999, Judge Robert Gallo ordered the city's Commission on Human Relations to cease its investigation in April 2000. His ruling said that Pitt would "continue to suffer immediate and irreparable injury" should the administrative action proceed.

Troy: Hospital "outs" patient

A high school football player endured homophobic taunts from teammates and fellow students when they discovered he is gay. The player, Greg Congdon, said that when he returned to school after a hospital stay, several classmates yelled anti-gay epithets at him. "Everybody just stared at me... I'd get approached by several students and they would say, 'We heard you're a faggot, is that true?'" he said. Congdon said he feared a physical assault. His fears grew to the point where he skipped classes and eventually left school to be taught at home. He said, "At that time, I was also very stressed out with me being gay and coming to grips with it. It was very overwhelming; it just happened all at once."

Before returning to school, Congdon had been in Troy Community Hospital seeking treatment after a suicide attempt. Congdon told his doctor that he attempted suicide because he was gay. He alleges that hospital employee Cindy Smith, the mother of one his teammates, checked his medical records, discovered he was gay, and then reported that to "third persons." He sued the hospital in local court, claiming that a staff member had revealed his sexual orientation. In his lawsuit, Congdon claims the hospital breached his right to patient confidentiality, interfered with his privacy rights, and caused him "extreme shame, embarrassment, and humiliation." The hospital denied these charges and vowed to fight them in court. He is seeking at least $100,000 in compensation. At press time, the parties were still in the discovery phase of litigation, and no trial date had been set.

Upper Southampton: Hell house

The Episcopal Church of the Redemption sponsored a Hell House in October featuring the death of a young man from AIDS. The church's Hell House was based on a model developed by the Abundant Life Christian Church in Arvada, Colorado, to depict life in Hell. The Church of the Redemption also featured a reenactment of the 1999 school shootings at Columbine High School in Colorado, with young men wearing trench coats walking through the hallway firing guns. The church's pastor, Chris Hanley Jr., said they needed hard-hitting scenes "because I don't think that people in today's society really face the issues head-on." He added, "We don't hate people... We're not bigots. We want to help them."

One official in the Episcopal Church criticized Hanley's production. Bishop Charles Bennison of the Episcopal Diocese of Pennsylvania said he was "unalterably opposed" to the Hell House. He said depicting evil "simply incites evil in others. And what is even more disappointing in this program is that it is labeling certain groups of people, in particular homosexuals, as evil." Despite such criticism, Hell House ran for two days, ending on Halloween night.

RHODE ISLAND

Statewide: Boy Scouts controversies

Two controversies prompted public criticism of the Narragansett Council of the Boy Scouts of America. In August, a 16-year-old Eagle Scout requested to return to full-time summer employment at Camp Yawgoog in Hopkinton, having been cut back to one day per week. His request was denied, and days later, he filed a complaint with the state's Human Rights Commission alleging that he was asked about his sexual orientation during a review of his request. Rhode Island's anti-discrimination law prohibits anti-gay employment discrimination and prohibits employers from asking their employees about their sexual orientation. The scout immediately won the support of 90 camp staffers, who had staged a sit-in in support of him two days after the complaint was filed. The Narragansett Council promptly apologized to the Scout and offered him a full-time position; the Scout then agreed to drop the discrimination complaint and eventually returned to full-time employment.

A day after those agreements were reached, Gregg Shields, a national spokesperson for the Boy Scouts of America, told reporters that any scout who acknowledged that he is gay would be dismissed. The Narragansett Council and the national group then consulted each other and issued a new policy for the council stating they would not ask about a prospective member's sexual orientation, but that "homosexual conduct" ran counter to the Boy Scouts' principles. Jay Sekulow, chief counsel at Pat Robertson's American Center for Law and Justice (see p. 352), said that the national and local policies appeared to contradict each other. Roger Pilon, an official with the Cato Institute, said, "People across the country will be pulling boys from the Scouts, if for nothing more than as a protest."

In the second controversy, a Scoutmaster allegedly pinned a newspaper photo of Eagle Scout James Dale up to a target at the Camp Yawgoog rifle range and fired at it. Dale had just won a New Jersey Supreme Court decision in which the court held that the Boy Scouts of America's prohibition on gay Scouts violated the state's law against discrimination on the basis of sexual orientation. The Scoutmaster was later dismissed.

The Narragansett Council faced further criticism for its ban on openly gay members. In October, The Providence Journal announced that it was withdrawing its support for the Council's annual fundraiser until the prohibition on gay Scouts was eliminated. The Rhode Island Council of Churches, the United Way, and the National Conference for Community and Justice all pressed the Council to end its policy of prohibiting openly gay Scouts. They all urged the Council to pressure the Scouts' national body to end its policy prohibiting openly gay Scouts as well.

> "This place is so infested with fags, you couldn't swing a dead cat without hitting one."
>
> — Timothy Phelps, part of Rev. Fred Phelps' entourage, at Brown University in Providence.

In November, the Narragansett Council bowed to one of those requests and formally asked the national Boy Scouts of America to end its policy prohibiting openly gay members. The Council also asked the national body to form a commission to examine the "relevance and appropriateness" of its membership standards. Those actions drew members of Fred Phelps' Westboro Baptist Church (see p. 356). Carrying their "AIDS Cures Fags" placards, the group of 15 said they were protesting the hiring of an openly gay Scout and the council's request for the national body to end its anti-gay policy. Thirteen-year-old Megan Phelps-Roper reportedly said, "What they [gay men and lesbians] do is wrong and for that, they are going to be sent to hell," as she stood on a gay rainbow flag. Abigail Phelps said, "For [the Narragansett Council] to buckle like this is disgraceful, it's sad, of course. They need to hear a little truth." Several members of the local religious community staged a counter-rally.

While in Providence, the Phelps protesters also went to Brown University and several area churches they deemed too supportive of homosexuality. "This place is so infested with fags, you couldn't swing a dead cat without hitting one," said Timothy Phelps. His wife, Abigail, said that Brown was not a true university because it did not have lively, robust debate, but only shared ideas she called "incestuous." Protesters carried placards reading, "Fags Doom Nations" and "Fags Die/God Laughs."

SOUTH CAROLINA

Statewide: Hate crimes bill defeated

The South Carolina House defeated a hate crimes bill that would have included sexual orientation. In January, state Rep. Doug Jennings Jr. and Sen. Darrell Jackson introduced versions of the bill in their respective chambers. Though he said he did not oppose the legislation, state Attorney General Charlie Condon maintained the bill was unnecessary. That prompted Tony Snell, head of the South Carolina Gay and Lesbian Pride Movement, to claim that Condon was not serious about protecting the victims of hate crimes: "All he intends to do is kill the bill." However, the editorial board at The Herald, a Rock Hill newspaper, took Condon's statements to mean he opposed the bill and praised him and the American Civil Liberties Union of South Carolina for their opposition to the measure. The Senate Judiciary Committee approved the bill in February. State Sen. Mark Fair tried to attach a last-minute amendment that would have excluded any group of people that engaged in "illegal behavior," reportedly referring to gay men and lesbians. Sodomy is still a crime in South Carolina. In a debate in the Senate, Fair said that anyone who labeled him a gay-basher was "dead wrong." State Sen. Larry Martin, who also opposed the bill, said, "There should be no second-class victims. When it comes to crime, all people are victimized." The Senate passed the bill by a voice vote.

The bill moved to the House, where supporters faced considerable opposition. State Rep. John Graham Altman III called his constituents' opinions on the bill "drivel" and referred to the legislation as the "pedophile protection" bill. Altman said the bill would make heterosexuals second-class citizens. "I hear this drivel: Equal protection, but protect us more," he said to several constituents who drove across the state to speak in favor of the bill. Altman also claimed that under the bill, he would receive a stiffer penalty for his revenge against a pedophile who tried to molest his granddaughter if he called the molester a pervert while hitting him. State Rep. Fletcher Smith disagreed, saying, "We don't need that kind of narrow, Ku Klux Klan outlook." Rep. Jennings, the House sponsor of the bill, said, "I hope that Rep. Altman's extremist remarks are not indicative of the Republican Party as a whole."

The House Judiciary Committee voted 14-8 to table the bill, killing its chance for passage during the 1999 session. Jacque Metz of the South Carolina Hate Crimes Coalition said, "It's not over. We'll rise again. We'll raise the issue again."

Greenville: Controversy over parents' letter

After a Baptist magazine published a letter positively depicting homosexuality, its readers called for the editor's resignation. The Baptist Courier published a July letter from Larry and Margie Candler, Baptist parents of a gay son, in which they pleaded for compassion for gay youth. Their letter was marked as a guest viewpoint, though some readers complained it appeared to be the Courier's veiwpoint. "It had more to do with the format and the way the viewpoint was presented than it had to do with the viewpoint... The other concern was there was not any biblical foundation offered for the opinion," said magazine trustee Tony Beam. Editor Don Kirkland said he would not resign. He did, however, apologize for not making it clear whose viewpoint the letter expressed. Kirkland also agreed to publish six letters on the subject and a counterpoint article in the following issue. "It was not at all an attempt to justify homosexuality, but to say these are fellow human beings who have rights and feelings and we need to be compassionate," he said. Jim Goodroe, chairman of the magazine's board of trustees, said Kirkland had assured him that he believed homosexuality was a sin and had made the mistake of not including a counterpoint or disclaimer with the Candlers' letter.

TENNESSEE

Statewide: Hate crimes bill dies in committee

A bill to add sexual orientation to an existing hate crimes law died in a House committee. State Sen. Steve Cohen and Rep. Tommie Brown introduced the bill in the Senate and House, respectively. Both were motivated by the widely publicized bias-motivated murders of Wyoming college student Matthew Shepard and Texas resident James Byrd Jr. The bill would have authorized judges to impose longer sentences on people convicted of specified bias-motivated crimes, including crimes motivated by bias on the basis of sexual orientation. The bill enjoyed the support of the American Civil Liberties Union, the Anti-Defamation League, the National Organization for Women, and Tennessee's Lesbian and Gay Coalition for Justice. About 300 gay and lesbian activists held a rally in March calling on the legislature to pass the bill. The House Judiciary Committee narrowly passed the bill in May. The Senate Judiciary Committee approved it along party lines, with Republicans opposing it. "We have laws in place and in effect, and I don't think we need to add laws for specific groups," said Republican state Sen. Marsha Blackburn. The bill, however, died in the House Finance Committee, from which it also needed approval because of the financial impact it would have on the state's prison system. One Senate sponsor, Robert Rochelle, said he would bring it back up for consideration in the next session.

> "I felt so manipulated because I thought no one else could help me... It's taken me so long since leaving to get back in touch with reality."
>
> — Scott Hobbs, on his experience as a member of Love In Action, one of two "ex-gay" groups that held conferences in Memphis.

Memphis: "Ex-gay" conferences

Memphis hosted two conferences celebrating so-called "ex-gay" ministries. In March, James Dobson's Focus on the Family (see p. 355) held one of its "Love Won Out" conferences featuring self-proclaimed ex-gay speakers John Paulk and his wife, Ann. John Paulk, an analyst with Focus on the Family, said, "We think that today's youth are being taught that homosexuality is biological, and we don't support that myth." Nathan Bell, who said her father is gay, told a reporter, "I don't condemn him for it, but in the eyes of the Lord, he is a sinner, and sin is sin." Bell attended the conference, held at the city's Central Church. The conference taught parents and youth that homosexuality can be prevented.

In response, local critics of the ex-gay movement held their own conference across town. The Memphis Lesbian and Gay Coalition for Justice sponsored "Focus on All Families: A Forum for Gay and Lesbian Quality." Margaret Henkle, with the Coalition, said the Religious Right uses "so-called ex-gay ministries to oppose civil rights protections for gays and lesbians." Openly gay David Hepburn, who attended the Coalition's conference, said, "The Religious Right has a right to believe whatever they want to believe about homosexuality. But parents will take this information [from ex-gays] as being the only truth about homosexuals."

In November, a local ex-gay organization, Love In Action, sponsored its second annual banquet designed in part to drum up financial support. Love In Action charges members $950 per month to go through a "cleansing" program designed to renew their relationships with God and make them heterosexual. John Smid, the group's director, said, "We're here to help lead people to the right way of life." Some speakers used passages from the Bible to justify their condemnation of gay men and lesbians, while others equated homosexuality with pedophilia, depression, and promiscuity. Paulk also spoke at their banquet. One participant claimed he became gay because his father left him at an early age.

Speaking to the press, Scott Hobbs, a former Love In Action member, called the group "a cult." He said, "I felt so manipulated because I thought no one else could help me... I was suicidal... It's taken me so long since leaving to get back in touch with reality."

TEXAS

Statewide: Hate crimes bill rejected

The state legislature rejected a bill that would have outlawed hate crimes in which the victim was targeted because of his or her sexual orientation. The bill was named after James Byrd Jr., a black man who had been viciously dragged to death behind a pickup truck by a group of white men. The bill faced a tougher fight in the Senate than in the House, where it passed 83-61. Despite some bipartisan support, the bill ultimately stalled in the Senate Criminal Justice Committee.

Supporters around the state urged state legislators to pass the bill. Lesbian activist Robin Tyler said, "We have people afraid to come out because of escalating violence. Is it a special right not to get murdered?" The Cathedral of Hope, the world's largest predominantly gay and lesbian congregation, held a "Rally Against Hate," in which members called on Gov. George W. Bush to push for passage of the bill. Mike Piazza, the church's pastor, sent an open letter to Gov. Bush accusing him of pandering to the Religious Right in his failure to show leadership on the issue and push for passage of the bill. "The relentless attacks by the Religious Right broadcasters have created an atmosphere in this country where hating lesbian and gay people is morally justifiable," he said. Referring to Bush's lack of support for the bill, Piazza added, "Our community hopes that the governor will recognize the importance of how even symbolic stands against hate are critical."

> "This nation was not built and given our great Constitution to protect the sodomites' right to adopt children, teach school or hold a public office."
>
> — Rev. W.N. Otwell, voicing his support for bills in the state legislature to prohibit gay and lesbian couples from adopting children or being foster parents.

It was obvious to some that the sexual orientation provision was the source of contention over the bill. State Sen. John Whitmire (D) said, "Sexual orientation was the problem in 1993, and it is still the problem now... The only thing that has changed [since then] is that we have documented more hate crimes in this state and we have a presidential campaign." Whitemire said that the 1993 hate crimes bill had passed only because no specific minority groups were named, leaving law enforcement and prosecutors with what they deemed an unenforceable statute. Whitmire added, "You could take sexual orientation out, and, in my judgment, [the bill] could come flying out of the committees and onto the floor to be debated — and it would pass." After several hours of closed-door negotiations, a majority of committee members still refused to send the bill to the full Senate. The Criminal Justice Committee voted 3-4 to reject sending the bill to the floor, killing its chance for passage. The vote broke down largely along party lines and Republicans said they objected to the bill because it named specific groups to be protected.

Many observers said presidential politics had killed the bill. Senate Democrats argued that Republicans had stalled the bill in order to give the governor, then a likely Republican presidential candidate, political cover to avoid being tied to a bill protecting gay men and lesbians. Gov. Bush seemed to want to have it both ways, saying that he opposed adding sexual orientation to the bill, while maintaining throughout the May deliberations on the bill that he would consider the bill if the legislature passed it.

The Dallas City Council passed a resolution calling on state legislators to pass the bill. Council member John Loza said, "We are just not going to tolerate this type of behavior here in Texas. As we are looking forward to going into the 21st century, there isn't any reason why anybody should be victimized as a result of who they are or what group they belong to." Donna Blumer, the only council member opposing the resolution, characterized the effort as a push for special rights for gay men and lesbians: "It doesn't matter who the person is who is victimized. It doesn't matter what the motivation is."

Many in the religious community joined longtime advocates in urging the state Senate and Gov. Bush to pass the bill. Bush's own pastor, Rev. James Mayfield of Tarrytown United Methodist Church, said, "The James Byrd Jr. Memorial Hate Crimes Act would protect all Texans from the tragedy of hate-based crimes. As religious leaders, we must send the message that Texas is not a hate state. We need to pray that our senators will have the moral courage to pass it."

Dissatisfied with Gov. Bush's inaction, supporters of the bill, including James Byrd's family, held a prayer vigil at the Capitol. They called on the governor to bring the legislature into special session to enact a hate crimes bill. "I promise you had we not received a tax break, [Bush] would have called a special session to make sure a tax break bill would have been passed... What we're asking for him to do is to do the exact same thing he would do with taxes or with education reform or with any of those issues he is extremely compassionate about," said Kyev Tatum, a spokesperson for the National Coalition of African-Americans United for Self- Empowerment.

Statewide: Proposed ban on gay adoptions

State lawmakers introduced two bills that would have prohibited adoptions and foster care by gay men and lesbians. A bill introduced by state Rep. Warren Chisum (R) would have prohibited the state from authorizing foster care and adoptive placements "in homes where homosexual activity is happening or is likely to happen." A separate bill introduced by state Rep. Robert Talton (R) would have prohibited placing foster children in the homes of gay men, lesbians and bisexuals, and would have removed children currently placed with such families. Talton's bill would have required state social workers to ask prospective foster parents about their sexual orientation. He had no public comments on his bill, but Chisum claimed that gay and lesbian households were "not conducive to Judeo-Christian beliefs and... destructive for the children." Chisum also denied that his bill was designed to hurt gay men and lesbians. "The public policy I'm proposing is not about denying gays and lesbians certain rights... .We want to create a situation that is best for the child. I feel that the state can make better choices when it comes to placing children in foster homes and adopting."

The bills became a divisive political issue. State Rep. Debra Danburg (D) said, "[Talton's] bill was intended to be a retaliatory slap against personal lifestyles... It is about making a political statement to right-wing hatemongers in this state." When reporters asked Gov. George W. Bush what he thought about gay and lesbian adoption, he responded, "I would prefer heterosexual married couples to adopt children." When asked why, he said simply, "That's what I believe. That's it." He later expanded on that position by saying, "I'm against gay adoptions." He was less clear about whether foster children already in the care of gay men and lesbians should be removed, as Talton's bill would have mandated. "I have no idea whether the children ought to be removed or not removed. The question is whether I'm for gay adoption. And the answer is, I'm not." State Rep. John Longoria (D) said, "When someone can show me why these bills are necessary, then I would consider voting for them."

Child care experts, economists and gay rights advocates faulted the bills on a variety of grounds. Carol T.F. Bennett, an economics consultant, said the ban would cost about $10 million per year to implement. "For the same additional expenditure as the ban would cost, the state could protect thousands of helpless Texas children and find them safe places to live and grow," Bennett said. Ron Wilkerson, spokesman for the National Association of Social Workers, said, "People who deem gays and lesbians unfit parents do so out of ignorance and personal prejudice." Diane Hardy-Garcia, director of the Lesbian and Gay Rights Lobby of Texas said, "The legislation out there is driven by hate. It shouldn't be tolerated."

When that group staged a rally with more than 6,000 people at the state Capitol in March to denounce these and other anti-gay bills, they faced off with anti-gay counterprotesters. Rev. W. N. Otwell from Mount Enterprise led a group of his fellow church members and other opponents of gay rights. Otwell is well known for his activism in support of a variety of right-wing separatist groups, including the Branch Davidians. He said, "This nation was not built and given our great Constitution to protect the sodomites' right to adopt children, teach school or hold a public office."

Debate on Chisum's bill in May was heated. The majority of those in the packed committee room testified in favor of the proposed ban. Chisum said, "We have a lot of children that we have to care for in Texas. We should be about placing them where it's best for them, with a father and a mother." Austin attorney Jerald Finney said, "I believe children would be far better off living in orphanages than with people who practice homosexual conduct." Among the opponents of the bills were adults and children raised in gay and lesbian homes.

The same day of the hearing on Chisum's bill, a former state social worker requested an emergency injunction banning adoptions and foster care by gay men and lesbians as part of an ongoing lawsuit. Rebecca Bledsoe, a former supervisor at the state's agency that oversees foster care and adoption, had sued the state in 1998 after she was demoted for ordering that a foster child be removed from the home of a lesbian couple who had already been approved as foster parents. Bledsoe had asked the court to prohibit the placement of foster children and adoptive children with gay and lesbian families and to reinstate her as a supervisor. She had sought the injunction in a state court while the case was pending but was turned down by the judge in June. While a final ruling has not yet been issued, Bledsoe's case inspired both Chisum and Talton to introduce their bills prohibiting gay men and lesbians from serving as foster and adoptive parents.

No further action was taken on Chisum's bill after the May hearing, and it died in committee. Rep. Talton's bill met the same fate in February 2000.

Statewide: Proposed partners registries criticized

In December, the state attorney general ruled that county clerks were not required to record domestic partner agreements for unmarried couples. Prompted by questions from gay men and lesbians from San Antonio in July, Bexar County Clerk Gerald Rickoff asked Attorney General John Cornyn whether he was required to recognize domestic partnerships. Cornyn answered with a resounding "no." Domestic partnerships, he wrote, were not "required or permitted by law to be recorded. Accordingly, county clerks are not required to accept them for recording." He said that even if the state law changed to authorize county clerks to record them, the partnerships would not "create a marital relation under Texas law."

That ruling disappointed gay men and lesbians across the state. Travis County, which includes the state capital, Austin, is the only county in the state to maintain a registry for domestic partners. Many of those who have registered are city employees in Austin who have registered in order to obtain benefits for their same-sex partners. County Clerk Dana DeBeauvoir said she did not expect to change that county's registry. However, Beverly Kaufman, clerk of Harris County, which includes Houston, said the ruling would not change anything because no one has ever petitioned for a certificate of domestic partnership in that county.

Cornyn's spokesperson said that the attorney general's decision was not legally binding. Heather Browne said, "Opinions issued from this office are nonbinding legal documents. They're not something someone has to follow by law and put into statute." However, Michael McGowan, chairman of the San Antonio Gay and Lesbian Community Center and one of the original petitioners, was still upset by the ruling. "Naturally, I'm disappointed. In the broad view of things, this is an example of just how far behind the times Texas is." He added that "Texas is going in the wrong direction."

Austin: Refusal to broadcast "It's Elementary"

Austin public television station KSMQ bowed to public pressure and chose not to broadcast Debra Chasnoff's award-winning educational documentary "It's Elementary: Talking About Gay Issues in School." The film features discussions from schools across the country about how to teach elementary school children age-appropriate ways of discussing homosexuality. KSMQ's station's producer-director, Rodd Boyken, said, "We got more 'no' calls than 'yes' calls about this." The station manager, Rick Sailors, added, "The decision not to show it ourselves was a fairly long and complex one. It came down to [that the film] is an advocacy piece." The station chose instead to air a roundtable discussion of the film that included clips from "It's Elementary."

The panel discussion featured Austin High School Assistant Principal Royce Helmbrecht, who believes homosexuality should not be presented in school. He said, "It seems to me very clear that if we were to send home a permission slip saying that for the next two weeks we are going to talk about sexual orientation in class, 99 percent of parents are going to send back the slip and say, 'I don't want my kids doing that.' " He said discussion of such issues belongs only in the home.

> "Go back to San Francisco where you belong... We just don't deal with people with AIDS here."
>
> — Alan Farr alleges that a pharmacist in Corpus Christi said this and refused to fill a prescription for his AIDS medication.

KSMQ's decision to run promotional spots for a broadcast of "It's Elementary" on another PBS affiliate did not satisfy gay and lesbian advocates. "To me, it seems as though when a television station chooses to air a panel debate about a program they chose not to broadcast, it shows a certain bias," said Joe Nix, a member of the local chapter of Parents, Families and Friends of Lesbians and Gays. He said the film teaches adults how to discuss homophobia with children without discussing sex.

An editorial in the Austin American-Statesman newspaper criticizing KSMQ's decision not to broadcast the film drew its own criticism. One local resident wrote, "What's shocking to me is that the American-Statesman apparently doesn't think homosexual behavior is 'perverse and disgusting.' If it isn't, I don't know what is, and the fact that children in grade school are being taught anything about it confirms to me how low we have sunk as a society."

Debra Chasnoff contributed an essay about the campaign against "It's Elementary" to the 1999 edition of Hostile Climate.

College Station: A&M rejects anti-discrimination proposal

Texas A&M University rejected a proposal endorsed by faculty and student groups to add sexual orientation to all of the school's anti-discrimination policies. During the spring semester, the student Senate passed a bill endorsing a proposal to amend the student handbook to include sexual orientation among the list of prohibited categories of discrimination. The Faculty Senate and the Graduate Student Council also endorsed the measure, but university President Ray Bowen rejected it in August, just a few weeks before students returned for fall classes. He said the addition would create an "enormous liability" for the university because it exceeded the protections guaranteed under federal law. A spokesperson for the university said, "The reason this can't be approved is because federal and state laws don't protect against sexual orientation, so this could put us in legal jeopardy."

Many students were unimpressed when Bowen later reiterated his support for diversity in the student body. Bowen said the university would not tolerate discrimination based on sexual orientation in employment and student housing, areas he said the university could control. David Kessler, author of the student Senate bill, pointed out that the University of Texas at Austin and Southern Methodist University prohibited discrimination based on sexual orientation. In August, the Princeton Review Guide ranked A&M among the least gay-friendly campus nationwide. "Alternative lifestyle is not an alternative" at Texas A&M, it said.

The assault on a lesbian student near campus in October while the campus was celebrating Coming Out Week raised greater concerns about campus safety and the climate created by Bowen's rejection of the anti-discrimination proposal. Megan Wright, vice president of the Gay, Lesbian, Bisexual, and Transgendered Aggies, said of the incident, "It's just one more piece of evidence of how hostile the climate here is for gays and lesbians." She said that Bowen's rejection of the sexual orientation proposal sent a negative message to gay and lesbian students: "They can't just *say* the university is inclusive; they should take concrete steps to make it inclusive."

Corpus Christi: Alleged pharmacy discrimination

A California man filed a lawsuit in federal court alleging that a Walgreens pharmacy in Corpus Christi refused to fill a prescription because he is gay and living with AIDS. Alan Farr, who was visiting Texas relatives at the time, said that the Corpus Christi pharmacist told him "to go back to San Francisco where you belong" if he wanted to get his prescription filled. Farr's medical therapy requires that he not miss any doses of his medication. His San Francisco pharmacist had told him that the Corpus Christi Walgreens could fill the prescription. When he went to the Corpus Christi location to pick it up, Farr claimed the pharmacist gasped loudly and backed away from the counter. Farr said the only way he could speak to her was from a distance of almost 20 feet. The pharmacist claimed she could not get payment authorization from the San Francisco location Farr usually used, but Farr said the pharmacist refused to let him pay out of pocket. According to Farr, she said, "We just don't deal with people with AIDS here." According to Farr, even after he explained that missing a few doses would jeopardize his health, she refused to fill his prescription and he had to return immediately to San Francisco to get the prescription filled.

Farr's attorney expressed shock over what had allegedly transpired. "I think it's astonishing that a person trained to provide medications to people would take actions that could impact someone's health, and we're talking about life-saving drugs... The pharmacist's refusal to provide even a couple of days of drugs to give the pharmacy in San Francisco time to mail an additional supply is outrageous," he said. Farr seeks $1 million in damages.

Although Walgreens did not publicly respond to the allegations, it did issue a letter in response to an individual complaint about the incident. In it, the company touted its record in delivering HIV and AIDS drugs to needy people, awards it has received for those efforts, and its AIDS training programs for pharmacists nationwide.

At press time, the lawsuit was pending.

Dallas: Controversy over SMU's anti-discrimination policy

During the spring 1999 semester, a dispute erupted at Southern Methodist University over whether the university would include sexual orientation in its overall non-discrimination policy. Student senator Heather Del Bosco urged the Student Senate to place a referendum on a student ballot requesting that the university add sexual orientation to the policy. Student Scott Langely, who formed Sexual Orientation Movement for Equality, also supported the ballot initiative proposal. Others within the campus community opposed that proposal, however. Eric Roberts, director of the Baptist Student Ministry, said the majority of his group opposed the proposal, fearing that it would eliminate the group's decision-making powers. He claimed that the proposed policy would deprive student organizations of any say in who could apply for leadership positions. "When we sit down and talk about students who are going to be on leadership committees, they need to meet certain qualifications... and we should have some freedom to determine" who leads, he said. The Baptist Student Union's president cited other concerns when he asked, "Are people going to start asking us this question on applications? Will there be quotas? This is none of anyone's business."

Early in the semester, opponents of the policy change remained in the minority. At a February meeting, the Student Senate voted 19-4 in favor the ballot initiative proposal, sending the question to the student body for a vote. Shortly thereafter, the Faculty Senate unanimously endorsed the addition of sexual orientation to the non-discrimination policy. Students voted nearly 3 to 2 in favor of the referendum (59 percent in favor) in the largest student voter turnout in five years. The recommendation was forwarded to the president, who, in turn, put the matter before the Board of Trustees.

Actions by the Board of Trustees during the spring and fall temporarily tempered the wave of student activism. The board voted in May to add sexual orientation to the university's overall non-discrimination policy. But it added a provisions allowing campus religious organizations to establish their own criteria for selecting student leaders and exempted from the non-discrimination policy organizations affiliated with but not governed by the university. The board's policy change also stipulated that damages awarded under the new regulations could not exceed those already in place under the university's other non-discrimination policies.

The trustees also rejected a proposal to extend domestic partner benefits to university employees. President Gerald Turner said that the board was concerned about a possible onslaught of requests for benefit packages from other minority groups on campus, which, he claimed, would be a financial burden. Members of the Faculty Senate, which had recommended in April that the domestic partner benefits be offered, were disappointed. "I'm very disappointed that [the benefits proposal did not pass], but I'm not surprised," said Dennis Foster. "This was a chance to let the country see that we are an open-minded campus. We lost a great opportunity." Faculty members hoped to revisit the issue in the near future, but President Turner said the board would not reconsider the proposal until the state changed the laws governing domestic partner benefits.

Student activists dissatisfied with the board's actions returned for the fall semester and continued their campaign for a more inclusive non-discrimination policy. The Student Senate, prompted by the student activists, drafted a proposal recommending that the university revise the non-discrimination clause so that it would cover leadership positions in campus organizations that receive funds from student fees, including religious groups. Religious and civil libertarian students objected to the proposal, claiming it infringed on religious freedoms. Michael Water, a student senator, quoted Bible verses while defending his claim that the proposal was unnecessary. He said, "If you think Christianity is a discriminating body, in essence you are right. You are saying you want us to go against God, and that is not going to happen." Supporters disagreed. Steven Urban, a gay student activist, said, "I want to be able to have the same equal opportunity as everyone else." After more than five hours of debate, the Student Senate voted 11-9 in favor of the proposal. The university later adopted the Student Senate recommendation as university policy.

> "This was a chance to let the country see that we are an open-minded campus. We lost a great opportunity."
>
> — Southern Methodist University professor Dennis Foster, on the defeat of a proposal to include sexual orientation in the university's non-discrimination policy.

Dallas: Radio station's anti-gay joke

KDGE-FM listeners condemned a gay joke aired in October on the morning show "The Edge." Radio personalities Jagger, Ryan and Julie, who host the show, created a list of "top things that would be different if there were an all-gay team in the World Series." The list included: 1) When a relief pitcher took the field, instead of coming out of the bullpen, he would come out of the closet. 2) Less spitting and more swallowing. 3) Instead of "runs batted in," RBI would stand for "rectums batted in." 4) Whenever a player slid into first base, he'd stand up and ask, "Did that make me look silly?" 5) the term "switch hitter" would take on a whole new meaning. 6) Manager of the year: Nathan Lane.

Many listeners found little humor in this. Judith Yates, a lesbian listener, complained that the list was objectionable because it couched homophobia in humor. "There's no reason anyone needs to be making those kinds of comments about any minority," she told The Dallas Voice. Yates later said that for young listeners questioning their sexuality, that type of humor might be a devastating blow to their self-image. "Kids are already looking for a scapegoat to blame things on, and they [the DJ's] just gave them a scapegoat and a reason to blame them," she said. Yates circulated an e-mail urging recipients to complain to the station. Among those who received Yates' e-mail was Dallas City Council member

Craig McDaniel. McDaniel wrote to the station's program director, "Your station's actions are inexcusable. You owe your listeners, many of whom were offended by the morning show skit, an apology." He urged the director to institute diversity training for the station's staff. The director, Duane Doherty, called hosts' comments "a stupid mistake that they've been reprimanded for."

Jagger resented the criticism, complaining that he and his co-hosts got "hauled into [General Manager Brian Ongaro's] office and yelled at." Jagger claimed that Ongaro did not understand the tone of response after he listened to a tape of the program. He said, "I've been compared to Hitler. I've had people say I am as bad as the guys who killed Matthew Shepard." He also said, "If people think this list is so horrible, they should listen to [KEGL 97.1 The Eagle], where every other word out of their mouths is 'fag.' Or even worse, one of the Christian radio stations. You hear gay-bashing to no end there." He claimed that he was inundated with hate mail as a result of the October show. Yates and the president of Dallas's chapter of Parents, Families and Friends of Lesbians and Gays declined Jagger's invitation to debate on his radio show.

Dallas: Right-wing attack on airline

Religious Right organizations denounced a major airline for its plans to offer employees domestic partner benefits. The leaders of Americans for Truth About Homosexuality (see p. 352) and Kerusso Ministries (see p. 355) issued a joint letter to shareholders at American Airlines' annual meeting, claiming that Chairman and CEO Don Carty had failed to honor a 1998 pledge by the airline's former CEO to "refrain from open advocacy or endorsements of organizations with active political agendas." The letter was distributed in air sickness bags labeled "What American Airlines is doing will make you SICK." The bags contained a list of the airline's actions that Peter LaBarbera of Americans for Truth and Michael Johnson of Kerusso Ministries claim supported the "homosexual lobby." The two hoped the letter would "encourage him [Carty] to abandon policies that promote homosexuality." LaBarbera and Johnson accused Carty of being "committed to becoming 'America's Homosexual Airline' at the risk of offending and alienating millions of American families and loyal customers." A press release touting their activities at the shareholders meeting claimed that organizations such as the Gay and Lesbian Alliance Against Defamation and the Human Rights Campaign engaged in "anti-Christian bigotry and hateful smear tactics."

Other right-wing activists denounced the airline. Allen Wildmon of the American Family Association (see p. 352) said, "They made it clear that they felt there were big dollars at stake because of the size and power of the homosexual community." He added, "I don't think they care one way or the other about the issue of homosexuality… it's a bottom-line, dollar bills issue to them." The decision also angered Rev. Fred Phelps (see p. 356) of Kansas' Westboro Baptist Church. "This is another attack for lucre," Phelps claimed. "American Airlines has spit in the face of God. This is not a business matter. This is not a political matter. This is a religious matter."

Despite such anti-gay pressure, American Airlines began to offer domestic partner benefits in August. Gay rights groups hailed the decision. American spokesperson Tim Kincaid said, "We're always recognizing that not everybody is happy with every decision we make, but we're trying to be fair to our employees, our customers and stockholders." The Human Rights Campaign said the decision was "firmly establishing an airline industry trend to treat all employees with dignity and respect."

Fort Worth: Presbyterians reject proposal to ordain gays

At its June conference, the Presbyterian Church's governing body rejected a proposal to end its ban on the ordination of gay men. The Church Orders and Ministry Committee, which advises the General Assembly on policy decisions, had recommended striking one of two clauses in the church's constitution that prohibit the ordination of gay men. That committee voted 24-14 to recommend that the church strike the "fidelity and chastity" clause. Opponents said homosexuality goes against biblical teachings. Rev. Stephen Moss, a committee member from North Carolina, said, "It is scandalous to the gospel the way these people [gay men] behave... I know of no other behavior that the Scripture forbids that is upheld by the church as proper." The committee made two other recommendations. One urged presbyteries to conduct "unity and diversity conferences" to educate members on the issue of gay ordination. The other referred members to a policy that prohibits the categorical denial of any group from ordination and said decisions should be made on an individual basis. Three days later, the General Assembly voted 293 to 243 against eliminating the ban on ordaining gay men. It chose instead to impose what amounts to a two-year moratorium on the issue, which many delegates welcomed. Rev. Moss said, "... [W]e can choose the way of the majority [to strike the clause] report: we can have ongoing, in-your-face dissension all across the church for the next couple of years... It's a clear choice [to vote for the moratorium]: don't lower the bar on behavior, and don't lower the bar on civil discussion."

Galveston: Gay resort picketed

The opening of a gay and lesbian resort hotel was met by protests organized by a fundamentalist minister. Ken Barber, pastor of Galveston's Grace Baptist Church, organized a group of about eight people to picket the grand opening in April of the Hollywood at Galveston. Barber led a campaign that included publication of a virulently anti-gay guest opinion column in The Galveston Daily News. He also tried drumming up early support from among the area's churches and said that he and other religious leaders had examined legal options in order to prevent the hotel from opening. Hotel owners Bob Wilkins and Sherman Houck did not let Barber's actions deter them, however.

In the opinion piece, Barber wrote, "To begin with, homosexuality is not a natural alternate lifestyle... [People] would be utterly appalled at the idea that anyone would even think of adopting a child to these perverts, let alone defend it. They are all child molesters." Barber called the Hollywood at Galveston a "sodomite hotel," which he said would harm the community. "Everybody better grab your little boys off the beach. These guys love fresh meat. They will molest your children. No matter how much they would like you to think they are normal, they are not," he wrote. Barber concluded with a Bible verse (Romans 1:32) suggesting that the owners and other gay men and lesbians were worthy of death, though he maintained he never called for violence against gay men and lesbians. He did note that "God will kill them... AIDS will kill them. Their own sin will kill them."

> "Everybody better grab your little boys off the beach. These guys love fresh meat. They will molest your children. No matter how much they would like you to think they are normal, they are not."
>
> — From an op-ed in the Galveston Daily News by Rev. Ken Barber, who picketed the opening of a gay and lesbian resort hotel.

Wilkins and Houck were flabbergasted at Barber's allegations, all of which they denied. Houck added, "I'm a grandfather, not a child molester... We're not bringing homosexuality to Galveston. Gay people have lived here for a long time." The two refused to believe most island residents would follow Barber, and the community support they received proved them right.

They were not surprised, then, by the support the community gave them. Letters to the editor of The Galveston Daily News denounced Barber's message. Janet Cohen, president of the local chapter of Parents, Families and Friends of Lesbians and Gays (PFLAG), said, "Do you think they have the right to do business? Sure. So does the Hilton." She said that Barber was "taking the Bible out of context to grandstand on sex." Wilkins said, "It warmed our hearts. Not only have people called but have made a point to go out of their way and stopped by."

Facing an uphill battle to garner support, Barber's three-hour protest attracted only eight people, most of whom, the hotel manager said, came from out of town.

Harris County: Transgender name changes challenged

A Baptist minister challenged the legal right of transgendered people to change their names to reflect their appropriate gender. Rev. Rick Scarborough, pastor of the First Baptist Church in Pearland and founder of Vision America (see p. 357), complained to a state district judge that pre-operative transgendered people might be able to legally marry if judges allow them to change the names listed on their driver's licenses. That might allow two people of the same biological sex to marry, he claimed, though no evidence exists that this had ever occurred in Harris County. According to Scarborough, his attention was initially drawn to the matter by an anonymous fax and e-mail. When he alerted Judge John Devine to his concern, the judge, in turn, brought the issue up at a meeting of the county's civil judges. Scarborough named specific judges who granted name changes for transgendered people in which the petitioners were represented by transgendered attorney Phyllis Frye. Much of Frye's work involves providing legal aid to other transgendered people who seek to change the names on their birth certificates.

Frye disagreed with Scarborough's contentions. "Such a marriage without a change in birth certificate would be fraudulent and illegal," Frye said. "If the marriage was challenged — like in a divorce or something — it would probably not stand up." The state requires a marriage license applicant to present a driver's license or other state-issued identification, leaving room for possible fraud, but Frye said, "[Scarborough] completely misunderstood what's going on."

According to Frye, Scarborough's efforts have hindered her work. Frye reported that since Scarborough complained, she has had difficulty getting cases assigned to judges formerly inclined to allow the name changes. "Now, they are scared to death, so they won't transfer cases." Previously, she would ask that cases be reassigned to the judges she believed to be more tolerant when they wound up before a judge she perceived to be intolerant. Frye said she has since had to have her clients sign affidavits addressing the issue directly. "Since the religious bigots raised the stink, I changed my [proposed] order to specifically state that this [name change] order will not allow them to go off and get a marriage license and get married to someone of the sex my clients began as, until such time as they get a court order changing their gender on their birth certificate," she said. Nevertheless, her work in Harris County has almost ceased. "The bigots closed down Harris County," she said.

Connie Moore, a Houston attorney who also handles name change cases for transgendered people, disagreed with Scarborough's charges. 'Marriage is a goal for the gay and lesbian community, but not so much that you're going to go out and change your sex so that you can get it," she said. "They're more interested in changing the law than their sex."

Houston: Parade protests and police "inspections"

Houston's gay and lesbian pride week in June was almost soured by the actions of anti-gay activists and city police. Picketers demonstrated at pride parade, and days later, police conducted what officials eventually labeled "bar raids." The protesters carried signs calling the parade and its participants sinful. The pastor of Heritage Baptist Church in Mt. Enterprise, Rocky Otwell, said, "We believe homosexuality is wrong." He added, "These people are out of the closet now, but they are going to pay the ultimate price when they are thrown in hell." Their protest did little to disrupt the more than 120 organizations that participated in the parade, including several churches.

Days later, Houston police conducted inspections of several gay bars and clubs which gay activists claimed were not routine. Several patrons at JR's claimed that police ordered the music turned off and the lights turned up while patrons were prevented from leaving. Vice officers visited that bar twice in one evening. Complaints to council member Annise Parker and Police Chief C. O. Bradford prompted an investigation into the inspections.

According to press reports, Bradford's characterization of the vice visits changed over the course of an August meeting he attended with the Gay/Lesbian Political Caucus. At the beginning of the meeting, Bradford reportedly labeled the visits as "inspections," prompted by anonymous complaints. However, after several gay and lesbian citizens complained about the visits to JR's and detailed their observations of police conduct, Bradford reportedly said that the events were "inexcusable" and possibly amounted to a "raid." Although he reportedly labeled the rest of the investigations "routine," he vowed to conduct a follow-up investigation to determine whether police misconduct was involved. "I'm going to go back and do a follow-up, and see why I got a different report." Bradford still maintained that he found no evidence that the number of gay bars targeted exceeded straight clubs.

Kilgore: Backlash against "Angels in America"

Protests against a gay-themed play eventually created a groundswell of support at a community college. Tony Kushner's prize-winning play "Angels in America, Part I: Millennium Approaches" was the target of religious and civic protests when the theater department at Kilgore College staged a production in October. Gregg County commissioners and local officials threatened to revoke a $50,000 grant and a $15,000 donation to the college's Shakespeare festival if Kilgore went ahead with "Angels in America." Kilgore's mayor, Joe Parker, asked the college's board of trustees to meet to address the production. "As Christians, our freedoms are being infringed upon" through the staging of the play, he said. Those actions worried members of the American Civil Liberties Union of Texas. Jay Jacobson, the state director, said, "It's unnerving to think that because the government doesn't agree with a position or idea, they can attempt to shut off expression."

Local religious leaders also tried to stop the play. Several ministers distributed a petition signed by hundreds of local residents denouncing the play. It read, "This play is absolutely full with vulgar and explicit scenes, including one with two men embracing and kissing." The First Baptist Church in Kilgore marquee read, "We too say 'no' to the play at KC." Its pastor, Rev. Mark McClelland, said, "I've read the thing and find it's dirty. I felt like taking a bath after I'd read it." He added, "We've taken a stand against... [the production] because we strongly disagree with it." McClelland insisted that he and other religious leaders were not motivated by antipathy toward gay men and lesbians. "We are not gay-bashers. As Christians, we do not believe that homosexuality is an alternate lifestyle. We believe it is a sinful one that hurts people." Several members of Heritage Baptist Church in Mount Enterprise vowed to demonstrate at each performance. Other ministers denounced the play from their pulpits.

An unidentified local businessman purchased 150 of the 264 seats for the opening night's performance. He planned not to use them and to let the seats remain empty. Instead of seeing them go unused, Kilgore theater director Raymond Caldwell gave them to patrons on a waiting list. "What he has done is donate $750 to finance the production of this play," Caldwell said.

Kilgore officials remained optimistic in the face of fundraising setbacks due to the negative response the play had generated. "Some money that was pledged has been canceled and we have heard others who had planned to pledge and decided not to," the development director, David Wylie, said. He also noted that at least one fundraising staffer resigned because of the controversy. However, Kilgore President William Holda said, "I would rather them not give and have a clear conscience, and we not take the money with strings attached and have a clear conscience ourselves." Wylie noted the many e-mails and letters of support they had received in the face of protests.

Despite the threats of funding cuts, Holda said the play should go on, saying, "I do not want the legacy of this institution to be that we sacrificed principle for dollars." He added that he would not back down on academic freedom. Caldwell carried that sentiment further, saying that advocates of revoking the college's funding who did so "out of their own fear and anger simply because of the play are guilty of political blackmail and emotional hostage-holding." The college's board of trustees voted to back Holda's decision, even though a few members were less than enthusiastic about the play.

Kushner himself threw his support to those involved with the production of his play while denouncing its opponents. He said he was "immensely impressed by Dr. Holda's holding his ground." On staging the play despite the protests, he added, "I think it takes tremendous courage to do so."

Opponents were undeterred. About 30 protesters stood outside the theater on opening night carrying signs that read, "God hates fags." They issued a press release saying, "We are protesting the fact that this country and especially Texas would give any place to these filthy sodomites... It would be better to give honor to a maggot than a faggot. At least maggots are natural and serve a worthwhile purpose, while faggots are filthy, ungodly, perverts who hate God, His Word, and His people." President Holda said that most of those who gathered outside were "professional protesters" from out of town. A contingent of counter-protesters sought to challenge their message.

"Angels in America" sold out on opening night. The remaining performances came close to selling out. Caldwell said, "So the negative response that we initially received seems to have turned into a positive box-office response [for "Angels in America"].

The financial outcome for the college's other theatrical production was mixed. The county commission followed through on its threat to rescind $50,000 in funding for the Shakespeare festival. Kilgore also established a college "committee on controversial works" to review plays deemed contentious. However, the college did receive $8,000 in personal donations, a $10,000 grant from the state's dramatist guild, and other grants for the Shakespeare festival that more than covered the amount lost as a result of the county's decision.

A personal essay by Tony Kushner appears on p. 18.

Mesquite: Proposed counseling workshop canceled

After religious conservatives complained, school officials canceled a planned workshop designed to instruct teachers on how to deal with gay and lesbian issues. Featuring speakers from Oak Lawn Community Services and the Dallas Gay and Lesbian Alliance, the workshop was to be part of a monthly series for Mesquite middle school counselors dealing with issues ranging from academic scheduling to eating disorders. This particular workshop was canceled because school superintendent Dr. John Horn felt the Dallas and Oaklawn groups were "too political," according to district spokesperson Katherine Cernosek.

In early February, a story about the planned training in the Dallas Voice, a gay and lesbian newspaper, caught the attention of the local Christian Coalition (see p. 353). Bruce Bishop, a Texas Republican Party official and Mesquite resident, alerted ministers throughout the area and urged them to complain to the school board and request that religious perspectives be included in the training. He said, "I would not recommend having counselors trained by a gay advocacy group... If it's going to happen, I feel it needs to be balanced." Bishop went on to say that a balanced approach would also teach the view that homosexuality is a sin and that people can change their sexual orientation from gay to straight. Rev. William Sipes, of the North Mesquite Assembly of God, agreed. "To me, homosexuality is in the Bible as a sin... I do not hate homosexuals. I abhor their lifestyle as I would with any sin." He added that religious conservatives have a duty to stand against homosexuality and to counsel that people can change their orientation.

The decision to cancel the workshop disappointed advocates of the training. "This is an issue many, many kids face," Gary Swisher, president of Oak Lawn Community Services, said. David Gleason, president of the local chapter of Parents, Families and Friends of Lesbians and Gays (PFLAG), said, "The fact that they feel there are no gay children is part of the district's not being a safe place for kids to be honest about who they are."

Dr. Horn's spokesperson did say that a revised workshop would be created. "This is still a priority for our counselors, to get training on this issue," she said.

Pearland: Falwell speech

Rev. Jerry Falwell (see p. 356) denounced gay and lesbian civil rights in a fundraising speech at a local church. Falwell said that he wanted to expose the "gay agenda," using the recent attention he garnered by claiming that the children's television show "Teletubbies" featured a gay character. He told a crowd at the First Baptist Church of Pearland, "The average American has no idea what the issues are. They do not understand what the gay and lesbian agenda is all about." He warned the crowd that in two years, the "homosexual lifestyle" will gain acceptance, providing gay men and lesbians with "quotas" and "special rights." Attempting to put a compassionate face on these comments, Falwell went on to instruct the crowd, "They don't understand that we don't hate anyone... We love the sinner, but hate the sin." He charged, "God has given to preachers the responsibility to sound an alarm. We do, in fact, have a responsibility to reclaim America."

Outside the church, a crowd of almost two dozen protesters gathered to counter Falwell's message. "I wanted to add the pro-gay, anti-Falwell sentiment. It is important to be out there and be seen to contradict this person who has some kind of bizarre power in this country," Michael Migura said. The protesters said they were pleasantly surprised by the support they received from passers-by who honked their horns and gave thumbs-up signs in support of the demonstration.

San Antonio: Anti-transgender ruling

In October, a Texas appeals court affirmed a lower court's decision refusing to recognize a marriage between a man and a male-to-female transsexual. The case began in 1996, when Christie Lee Littleton, a male-to-female transsexual, sued her late husband's doctor for malpractice, alleging that his negligence had caused her husband's death. In 1998, a district court judge ruled in favor of the doctor, Mark Prange, holding that Littleton was still biologically a man despite sex reassignment surgery. The court also held that Littleton had no standing to bring the suit because her marriage was void since the state does not recognize same-sex marriages. The American Family Association (see p. 352) applauded the district court's ruling. "An acorn doesn't become a maple tree. You can try as you might but it will become an oak tree," said Brian Fahling, an attorney for the group. He added, "People who want to quarrel with that are quarreling not only with reason and science but the thousands of pages in our life experience."

Littleton appealed that ruling to the Fourth District Court of Appeals of Texas, but in October 1999, that court upheld the district court's ruling in a 2-1 decision. In doing so, it ignored Littleton's amended birth certificate and her current anatomy. The court majority wrote that Littleton "wants and believes herself to be a woman... [but that] male chromosomes do not change with either hormonal treatment or sex reassignment surgery. Biologically, a post-operative female transsexual is still a male." They added, "Some physicians would consider Christie a female; other physicians would consider her still a male. Her female anatomy, however, is all man-made."

The dissenting judge argued that the amended birth certificate nullified the original birth certificate. "As a result, summary judgment was issued based on a nullified document. How then can the majority conclude that Christie is a male?"

San Antonio: Broadcast of "It's Elementary" protested

In June, nearly 200 people protested a local broadcast of a documentary designed to educate parents and educators about gay and lesbian families. The protesters, some carrying placards, picketed public television station KLRN for broadcasting Debra Chasnoff's award-winning documentary "It's Elementary: Talking About Gay Issues in School." Christian radio talk show host Adam McManus urged listeners to participate in the demonstration though he had not yet seen the film. He said, "What is particularly offensive to me is they are using tax dollars to target our children. The point is to go younger and younger and attempt to reach the next generation with a perverted message... This video will further desensitize our kids to traditional boundaries of right or wrong." He was also upset by the station's refusal to broadcast "Suffer the Children," a video produced by the American Family Association (see p. 352) claiming to refute the messages in "It's Elementary." Carole Deffenbaugh, who carried a sign reading "KLRN: Protect our kids, don't harm 'em," told a reporter, "I have children, and this is about the only station I let them watch. When I heard about this, I decided to boycott the station." Another protester celebrating his birthday at the demonstration said, "Homosexuality is wrong and disgusting and filthy. I'd like to take a stand against it and stop them from showing it." Some opponents of the broadcast had previously vowed to withdraw future contributions if KLRN broadcast "It's Elementary."

Charles Vaughn, a vice president at KLRN, defended the broadcast, noting the viewers' positive feedback for "It's Elementary." Vaughn also said that "Suffer the Children" takes much of "It's Elementary" out of context. "I have a problem with its editorial integrity, and I have a problem with the extent they use material from 'It's Elementary.' " Byron Trott, with the Gay and Lesbian Community Center of San Antonio, said, "This video ["It's Elementary"] is trying to find a fair, reasonable way for adults to answer these questions [about homosexuality], without trying to influence them one way or another."

Wichita Falls: Church expels PFLAG chapter

An Episcopal bishop forced a church to expel a support group for family and friends of gay men and lesbians that had been meeting in a church because he felt the group was "too controversial." Bishop Jack Iker told the members of St. Stephen's Episcopal Church in June that the local chapter of Parents, Families and Friends of Lesbians and Gays (PFLAG) would no longer be able to use the church as its meeting place. The group, which had been meeting there since January, received notice just days before its monthly meeting. After reviewing a copy of the group's mission statement, Bishop Iker's spokesperson, Rev. Charles Huff, said that although the bishop did not object to their providing aid to the families of gay men and lesbians, he did oppose its larger effort to make society more accepting of gays. Huff said, "[P]art of that purpose, I can't remember the exact wording, had to do with 'promoting the enlightenment of society' or the 'transformation of society' in regards to gays and lesbians." That objective, Huff said, "was simply too controversial for the church." The Metropolitan Community Church of Wichita Falls and two nonprofit agencies offered the PFLAG chapter meeting space.

Wichita Falls:
Judge upholds father's veto of lesbian mother's church

Interpreting a final decree of divorce as agreed to by the divorcing couple, a district judge ruled that a lesbian mother could not take her daughter to worship at a predominantly gay and lesbian church. When the divorcing parents entered into a divorce decree, they agreed that the father would instruct the child on Judaism and that the mother would provide "informal Christian training in her home," but also that the father had "[t]he right to direct the moral and religious training of the child." The father subsequently objected to the mother's taking the daughter to the Metropolitan Community Church (MCC), a Protestant denomination wholly accepting gay men and lesbians. When the mother sought to modify the divorce decree as being unworkable, Judge Keith Nelson denied the mother's motion. In so ruling, he also held that "[I]t was the intent of the parties... that mainline churches would be utilized by the parties for the religious training of the child... and that such mainline churches would include the Catholic Church, churches of the Protestant church such as Presbyterian, Methodist, Baptist... and the like, as well as the Jewish synagogue would be included." He continued, "The Court finds that the Metropolitan Community Church at Wichita Falls does not fall within this category."

Lay and religious gay and lesbian leaders were outraged. MCC's founder, Troy Perry, said, "Because we're gay or lesbian, this homophobic, sexist judge feels he can decide by official government decree which churches or synagogues are 'acceptable' and which are not." Rich Tafel, head of the Log Cabin Republicans, a gay political group, said, "This ruling is an appalling and unconstitutional overreach of the government, and a clear violation of the separation of church and state." He added, "It is time for anti-gay organizations like the Christian Coalition, the Family Research Council and the Traditional Values Coalition, all whom have claimed that they are only concerned with religious freedom, to immediately join in condemning this ruling and demanding it be reversed."

The judge's ruling also dismayed legal experts. Michael Adams, an attorney with the American Civil Liberties Union, argued, "Every mother — gay or straight — has the right to share her faith with her child without interference from the government." Adams pointed out how several churches now considered mainline in America historically have been ostracized. He also noted that several Protestant denominations have increasingly welcomed gay men and lesbians in recent years. Kate Kendell, head of the National Center for Lesbian Rights, noted, "It is extraordinary for a judge to issue a ruling restricting a parent's right to provide a religious education to a child as they see fit."

Kendell went on to say, "The precedent, if extended to its logical conclusion, would be that a liberal, progressive gay judge would allow a parent to object to an ex-spouse taking a child to a fundamentalist Baptist service or a Seventh-day Adventist service."

With the help the National Center for Lesbian Rights, the mother filed an appeal in September. In March 2000, the Texas Court of Appeals upheld the trial court's ruling. An attorney for the mother said that the mother had no plans for further appeals.

People For the American Way Foundation, the American Civil Liberties Union, and others had filed an *amicus curiae* brief in the Court of Appeals in support of the mother.

UTAH

Statewide: Hate crimes bill defeated

In February, the Utah legislature defeated a hate crimes bill that included sexual orientation. Introduced by state Sen. Pete Suazo, the bill would have upgraded misdemeanor assault, harassment, and vandalism charges motivated by hate to felonies and would have allowed judges to impose longer sentences on other bias-motivated crimes committed against groups of people or institutions, including churches and abortion clinics. The state's prosecutors said that the existing hate crimes bill was too weak to enforce, and that because it does not stand up well against legal challenges, they rarely charge criminals with violating it.

Introduction of the new bill was met with quick criticism from right-wing activists. Gayle Ruzicka, head of the Utah chapter of Phyllis Schafly's Eagle Forum (see p. 354), asked, "Why are we even considering something like this?" She claimed that Utah should not protect "illegal and immoral behavior" and that the bill was "biased and it should not pass." Attorney Frank Myler, with the Utah Leadership Council, also opposed the bill, saying it would elevate one class of people above others. Committee Chairman Terry Spencer echoed that sentiment, saying, "We cannot treat groups differently," and called the bill "a great step backwards." He compared the disparity in treatment he said would exist under the bill to the "Separate but Equal" doctrine adopted by the Supreme Court at the turn of the century. After hearing public testimony, the Senate Judiciary Committee voted 4-2 against the measure.

Suazo was disturbed by the vote, saying, "I am concerned about the message this sent. I think we may have cheated the public" by not forwarding the bill to the full Senate. Supporters hoped to introduce a similar measure in the legislature's next session.

Statewide:
Utah bans adoptions by gay men and lesbians

A year-long controversy over the right of gay and lesbians couples to adopt and serve as foster parents ended with a statewide prohibition. In January, Scott Clark, chairman of the Board of Trustees of the state's Division of Child and Family Services (DCFS), proposed a statewide prohibition on adoptions by unmarried couples or polygamists. He said, "I don't believe that given all the alternatives, it is a reasonable choice to permit people who are not married — be they man-woman, woman-woman, or man-man or living together in a clan but not legally married — to be an appropriate adoption choice." The proposed policy would have required social workers to verify that all adults in the households of prospective parents be related by blood, a legally recognized marriage, or adoption.

> "The end result is a whole category of competent, caring, and loving parents are left out of adopting children who need desperately to be adopted."
>
> — Doug Wortham, head of Salt Lake's Gay and Lesbian Community Center, referring to a state policy prohibiting gay and lesbian couples from adopting children.

Clark's proposal faced significant opposition from within the state agency itself and from gay and lesbian advocates. DCFS Director Ken Patterson said that "the division did not seek to put this on the agenda of the board. We think, in fact, there are more pressing issues for the division to deal with." The division's own advisory panels opposed the proposal. Roz McGee, head of the child advocacy group Utah Children, said, "I would be really disappointed to see this board take this kind of narrow position." Doug Wortham, head of the Gay and Lesbian Community Center of Salt Lake City, said, "This is just another one of those policies based on ignorance. The end result is a whole category of competent, caring, and loving parents are left out of adopting children who need desperately to be adopted." Even some of Clark's fellow board members disagreed with his proposal.

Clark, however, defended his position, saying, "[Children] have to learn about commitment of one person to another. And they have to learn what their sex role is... Gay parents are handicapped in that regard. They can't model the behavior of the missing parent."

The board held a public hearing in late January before voting on the proposed policy change. Bradley Weischedel, a social worker who had adopted a son with his same-sex partner, said, "[W]e are completely dumbfounded that anyone on the board of DCFS would even consider reducing the number of potential parents for at-risk children in the state's custody." Right-wing activists disagreed. Gayle Ruzicka of Utah's Eagle Forum (see p. 354) said she feared the emotional problems adopted children of gay and lesbian parents would face when they realize they do not have two opposite-sex parents. Lynn Wardle, a Brigham Young University law professor and conservative activist, reportedly told the board that he would help them draft further policy changes. Members of the Eagle Forum were pleased when the board voted 7-2 in favor of Clarke's proposal.

In August, the board took up a separate proposal to prohibit unmarried couples from providing foster care. Under the proposal, caseworkers would have to verify that adults living in prospective parents' homes were related by blood, a legally recognized marriage, or legal adoption. The board adopted the proposal by a 5-2 vote. In response to the board's actions, the Child Welfare League of America ordered the DCFS to remove its endorsement from the agency's policy manual. In September, the governor's office reported that there were 2,308 children in state care and only 1,014 families prepared to care for them.

In October, Utah Children, a statewide child advocacy group, filed a lawsuit in state court challenging the adoption rule. The group contends that the rule violates constitutional guarantees of equal protection by prohibiting an entire class of people from adopting or caring for foster children. The lawsuit also claims the agency ignored the tide of public testimony against the new policies, violating Utah's Administrative Rulemaking Act. The American Civil Liberties Union and the National Center for Lesbian Rights filed a separate lawsuit on behalf of three prospective foster parents in December, and also asked the court that the case be consolidated with the one brought by Utah Children.

In response to the lawsuit, the DCFS board's Clark issued a statement saying, "Best practice requires that children be guaranteed the legal benefits and protections of legally recognized relationships." At press time, the lawsuits were pending.

North Salt Lake: Anti-gay school conference

The Utah Coalition for Freedom in Education sponsored a conference in May to address homosexuality in public education. The Coalition promotes vouchers, tax credits for private schooling, and parents' rights over schooling and curriculum choice. The conference, entitled "Education or Indoctrination? The Homosexual Agenda for Our Schools," promoted the belief that a "militant gay community" subversively influences children in public schools. "Gay Rights, Special Rights," an anti-gay rights video produced by the Traditional Values Coalition (see p. 357), was shown at the conference. Joan Celi, a San Francisco-based lecturer who claims the gay community uses covert tactics to accomplish its goals, told attendees, "The children are being destroyed because they are being encouraged to experiment with homosexuality" and that "homosexuality is a lethal lifestyle." Ruth Lehenbauer, chair of the coalition, claimed that children are being indoctrinated with hedonistic and atheistic beliefs. She also claimed that the gay community wants a one-world government and tries to undermine religious beliefs.

Doug Wortham, head of the Gay and Lesbian Community Center of Utah, disagreed. He said, "It's purely a propaganda lie to make it look like we're trying to push something." An attorney with the state Board of Education noted that board policy forbids "acceptance or advocacy" of homosexuality in public schools.

Salt Lake City: Mormon Church opposes same-sex marriage

In October, the Church of Jesus Christ of Latter-day Saints (the Mormons) reaffirmed its political opposition to same-sex marriage. Gordon Hinkley, the church's president, addressed the General Conference, reminding members of the church's support for the Knight Initiative in California (which passed in March 2000). Backers of that initiative, which defined marriage as being between one man and one woman, claimed it would prevent the state from recognizing same-sex marriages, although California had not previously done so. At issue was a fundraising letter from the church's leaders encouraging California members to "do all you can by donating your means and time" to passing the initiative. Hinkley said, "Some portray legalization of so-called same-sex marriage as a civil right. This issue has nothing to do with civil rights. For men to marry men, or women to marry women, is a moral wrong." Defending the church's political role, he said, "We believe that defending this sacred institution... lies clearly within our religious and constitutional prerogatives... We regard it as not only our right, but our duty... " During Hinkley's address, protesters gathered outside to denounce the church's work against gay and lesbian civil rights.

VERMONT

Statewide: Ruling on same-sex marriage lawsuit

Right-wing organizations mobilized public opposition to a case before the Vermont Supreme Court about marriage rights for same-sex couples. In 1997, three same-sex couples had sued the state after being denied marriage licenses, maintaining that the state constitution gave the couples the right to marry any person they chose. Their lawsuit sought legal recognition for same-sex marriages. The plaintiffs appealed the case to the state Supreme Court in 1998. Anti-gay forces from across the nation mounted an opposition campaign in the months before the state supreme court issued its decision in December 1999.

In April 1999, two organizations opposed to the legal recognition of same-sex marriage sent an open letter to every register voter in Vermont. "We believe that traditional marriage provides the best place to raise and nurture our children... We wish you the same success [in prohibiting same-sex marriage] in Vermont," it read. The letter campaign was funded by a conservative Ohio group, Citizens for Community Values (see p. 354), and organized by Mike Gabbard, an internationally active anti-gay activist. The letter, which was cheered by Take It To the People, a Vermont-based group opposing the plaintiffs in the court case, reportedly sparked its own backlash. In the wake of the letter's distribution, progressive Democrats were named House speaker and lieutenant governor.

Take it To the People organized its own campaign against same-sex marriage in Vermont. It published the Hawaii letter on its website and encouraged Vermonters to adopt a state constitutional amendment prohibiting the legal recognition of same-sex marriages. It also urged support for legislation limiting marriage to unrelated, opposite-sex couples.

Several right-wing organizations and conservative religious institutions, including the Massachusetts Family Institute, Pat Robertson's American Center for Law and Justice (see p. 352), Take it To the People, the Catholic Diocese of Burlington, Vermont, and the Christian Legal Society (see p. 353), filed *amicus* briefs against the plaintiffs. Matthew Daniels, head of the Massachusetts Family Institute, wrote an op-ed piece that appeared in the Wall Street Journal in June. In it, he said that if the court ruled in favor of gay men and lesbians it would "remake the moral, legal, and social landscape of the state by judicial fiat." The ACLJ called the plaintiffs' legal arguments "insulting to the people of Vermont."

> "This decision is the most recent example of imperial and non-elected judges run amok."
>
> — Gary Bauer, former head of the Family Research Council, on the Vermont Supreme Court's ruling that gay men and lesbians were entitled to the benefits and privileges of marriage.

In August, Fred Phelps and members of his Westboro Baptist Church (see p. 356) protested in front of the statehouse. Their announcement said, "When the nation's militant, activist fags brag about a place, watch out!" The protesters, who carried placards reading, "God Hates Fags" and "Fags Doom Nation," were outnumbers by a crowd of about 200 people supporting the plaintiffs.

In December, the state Supreme Court issued a historic ruling in favor of the plaintiffs. Citing the Common Benefits Clause in the state constitution, the court held that gay men and lesbians are entitled to all of the rights and privileges of marriage. The court left it to the state legislature to determine how to implement this ruling, either by legal recognition of same-sex marriage or through other means that would ensure that same-sex couples receive all of the benefits of marriage.

The ruling sparked immediate condemnation from conservative organizations across the country. Family Research Council (see p. 355) spokesperson Janet Parshall said, "The Vermont Supreme Court is still playing with fire by mandating sex-partner subsidies... It was wrong for this court — or any court — to arrogate to itself powers that are wholly legislative by mandating marital benefits for non-marital relationships." James Dobson, head of Focus on the Family (see p. 355), urged Vermont legislators to begin the process of adopting a state constitutional amendment prohibit the state from recognizing same-sex marriage. Doing so would "declare that Vermont marriages have always been, and will always be, between one man and one woman," he said. The ACLJ argued the ruling was "a slap in the face for marriage between a man and a woman." Rev. Lou Sheldon, head of the Traditional Values Coalition (see p. 357) and Beverly LaHaye of Concerned Women for America (see p. 354) offered similar comments. However, the American Family Association (see p. 352) called the ruling a victory because the court stopped short of forcing the state to recognize same-sex marriage.

Republican presidential candidates also criticized the court's decision. Gary Bauer, former head of the Family Research Council, called the ruling "an unmitigated disaster for the American family" and compared it to an act of terrorism. He said, "This decision is the most recent example of imperial and non-elected judges run amok." Malcolm W. "Steve" Forbes Jr. called the ruling "a flagrant example of judicial activism."

Conservative media outlets nationwide ran stories and columns critical of the court. The Conservative News Service reported that the head of the Catholic League for Religious and Civil Rights said, "The Catholic, Protestant, Jewish, and Muslim citizens of Vermont… have just been told to take a walk." The Wall Street Journal ran an op-ed by right-wing legal scholar Robert Bork entitled, "Activist Judges Strike Again," in which he said the Vermont Supreme Court "misused the state constitution." The Washington Times published an editorial called, "Vermont's Unelected Lawmakers." It referred to the ruling as a "radical decree" and went on to cite Bork's assertion that the court had circumvented democratic institutions. Syndicated columnist and radio host Laura Schlessinger also denounced the decision in several columns.

After heated debate among state legislators and passionate testimony from residents on both sides of the issue, the state legislature passed a Civil Unions Law that granted same-sex couples all of the benefits and rights the state confers on lawfully married opposite-sex couples. The governor signed it into law in April 2000.

VIRGINIA

Statewide: Pro-gay bills fail

A slate of bills that would have added sexual orientation provisions to the state's existing hate crimes law failed to advance this legislative session. One would have provided for enhanced criminal and civil penalties for the perpetrators of hate crimes based on sexual orientation. Another would have required state and local police to maintain statistics on bias-motivated crimes, including those motivated by anti-gay bias. A third would have added actual or perceived sexual orientation and gender to the existing hate crimes laws and provided for enhanced criminal and civil penalties. All three bills died in committee.

The first bill, which would have added sexual orientation to the existing hate crimes law, drew support from towns across the state. The Human Rights Commission of Norfolk voted 8-3 to urge the General Assembly to adopt such a law. Though some commissioners worried about offending the City Council, which appoints members of the commission, Rev. J. Scottie Griffin, a commissioner, said the vote was important enough to risk getting fired. The commission said it would notify the Virginia Beach City Council and state representatives about its support for expanding the hate crimes law. Norfolk Mayor Meyera Oberndorf and the Charlottesville City Council both endorsed the bill.

Committee votes on the bills fell along party lines, with Republicans opposing them. Rep. J. Randy Forbes said he feared expanding the hate crimes law would create a "new class of individuals." He said, "I have been against creating any new classes of individuals. Any time you have a violent crime, it's a hate crime." He also expressed concern about the meaning of sexual orientation. He said, "The terms need to be defined. But even if a definition is there, I have a very real concern saying we will protect one group above the other." He said he feared the bill would protect pedophiles. Patrick Heck, head of the gay and lesbian rights group Virginians for Justice, disagreed, saying, "Either they lack the political will or they're homophobic... By not passing the law, they're tacitly supporting gay hate violence."

Two other gay rights bills received similar treatment. One would have prohibited anti-gay discrimination in housing and employment. The other would have removed consensual sexual acts from the state's "crimes against nature" law, effectively ending the state's ban on homosexual sodomy. Both died in committee in February.

Arlington County: Domestic partner benefits struck down

Three Arlington County residents successfully challenged the county's policy extending health insurance benefits to its employees' domestic partners. Jordan Lorence, an attorney with Northstar Legal Services (see p. 356) and counsel to the plaintiffs, argued that the policy created a marriage-like status for unmarried couples. He pointed out that Virginia does not recognize same-sex couples or common law marriages and argued that Arlington County had circumvented Virginia's "Dillon Rule," which gives local governments "only those powers that are expressly granted... or implied" by the state legislature. County attorneys disputed the plaintiff's claims: "The county is not creating a new marital status... We're not creating same-sex marriage," Assistant County Attorney Peter Maier said.

Circuit Judge Benjamin Kendrick ruled in March that the domestic partner benefits policy illegally overstepped the county's authority. "What the county is trying to do, noble as it might be, is illegal," he wrote. He said that the state does not allow the county to define a "dependent" to include married and unmarried domestic partners. When Arlington began offering the benefits in 1997, it became the first county in Virginia to do so.

The judge encouraged county attorneys to appeal the decision to the state Supreme Court. Noting that he had only addressed a legal question and not a moral one, Kendrick stayed his ruling until the county appealed the case.

Nevertheless, right-wing and anti-tax advocates cheered the judge's ruling. Wendell Brown, one of the plaintiffs, said he sued because the policy hurt the family as an institution. "I was concerned that the county was trying to redefine marriage... I care deeply about protecting marriage, which I understand is one man and one woman. This is not a gay rights issue. This is a family issue," he said. Tom Brooke, spokesperson for the Arlington Republican Party, blamed the all-Democratic county board for instituting such a policy without consulting voters and state officials. "It's the typical Arlington way... It's a behind-closed-door deal, and it blew up in their faces," he said.

The ruling disappointed gay rights advocates. Kim Mills, spokesperson for the Human Rights Campaign, the nation's largest gay and lesbian rights organization, said, "The decision continued to illustrate the inequity in our society when it comes to the relationships of gay and lesbian people... .This is certainly out of step with what private industry is doing... .They're simply equal pay for equal work [sic]." Openly gay county board member Jay Fisette, who was elected to the board after the policy had been instituted, said that the county adopted the policy out of fairness to gay and lesbian employees and as a recruiting tool for high-quality employees. He said the lawsuit was backed by "right-wing organizations that want to impose their narrow definition of the family."

When county attorneys filed their appeal with the state Supreme Court in March, they further angered some members of the GOP. Henriette Warfield, a party official, said, "I'm speechless, to be honest." She claimed that county Democrats were eager to waste money on "dead-end lawsuits." Mike Lane, a Republican candidate for the county board, said, "The judge made clear that the Arlington domestic partners is a gross violation of the Dillon rule. No legal appeal is going to change that fact." The state Supreme Court unanimously affirmed the lower court's decision invalidating the domestic partner benefits policy in April 2000.

Arlington: Radio station targeted for broadcast

A Religious Right group filed charges with the Federal Communications Commission (FCC) over comments made by a longtime gay activist on a local radio program. In December 1998, Frank Kameny went on WZHF-AM's "Rainbow Hour" show to denounce the arrests of several men in Roanoke for solicitation of sodomy. His strategy was to solicit, on the air, "the entire adult population of the state of Virginia, with particular emphasis upon all prosecutors, police chiefs, and police officers, and judges in the state," presumably to commit sodomy. He told listeners to "Drop the hang-dog, bowed-head, ashamed reaction to soliciting sodomy and accusations thereof and arrests therefor, and make a vast joke of it. Solicit, solicit, solicit! Publicize!" In January, the Traditional Values Coalition (see p. 357) filed charges with the FCC claiming the station had been a "party to a commission of a felony" when Kameny invited Virginians to engaged in acts of sodomy with him. Virginia outlaws the commission of oral and anal sodomy as well as the solicitation of sodomy.

Coalition spokesperson James Lafferty said, "We support the sodomy statute in Virginia, and we felt this was a new startling use of the media." He added, "The FCC has pretty tough standards for [Don] Imus and [Howard] Stern, and this exceeds anything on the Stern show. It's still a felony in Virginia." The state's attorney for Arlington County said he would not prosecute Kameny for his comments.

Kameny hoped the solicitation would become a test case or show that the law was unenforceable. He maintained that his efforts did "substantially end the arrests" by showing that the law is unenforceable: "With a little determination, planning, organization, and ingenuity, the entire legal structure supporting sodomy and solicitation laws, and prosecutions under them, can be wrecked to the accompaniment of much fun and games."

Although the FCC took no action against Kameny, he followed up on his on-air solicitations with letters to two Virginia judges. He solicited sodomy from each of them and publicized the letters. The judges acknowledged receiving the letters but chose not to respond, citing legal reasons.

Lynchburg: Falwell-White meeting

Anti-gay religious leaders protested and denounced a historic meeting between leaders of the Religious Right and gay rights movements. In October, Rev. Jerry Falwell, founder of the Moral Majority (see p. 356), chancellor of Liberty University and noted televangelist, met with Rev. Mel White, founder of Soulforce, a non-violent interdenominational gay religious group. Protesters launched into their criticism before the meeting actually took place, objecting to the idea of spiritual and civil equality for gay men and lesbians.

Falwell himself made statements in advance of the actual October meeting that undermined White's mission of open-mindedness and reconciliation. Falwell announced well in advance that he would not be convinced that homosexuality is not sinful. "I continue to believe that God has given us unmistakable divine instructions for living — and homosexuality is not a part of it," he said. "The message of God's Word is clear: any sexual activities outside the heterosexual bonds of marriage is — very plainly — sin." Falwell's organizers also canceled plans to have dinner with Mel White's 200 supporters.

Although Falwell said he wanted to tone down the Religious Right's rhetoric about homosexuality, other right-wing groups made no such promises. A day before White and Falwell met, the director of cultural studies for the Family Research Council, Robert Knight, said his group "continues to have concerns about meetings of this nature... News reports may indicate that Rev. Falwell's orthodox Christian views regarding homosexuality are on a moral par with the unbiblical distortions of Mel White and his followers." He added, "Mel White's biblical exegesis has about as much legitimacy as that of Fred Phelps, whose obsession with hatred of homosexuals matches Mr. White's hateful comments toward orthodox evangelical Christians."

Groups of anti-gay protesters demonstrated throughout the weekend's meeting. Rev. Fred Phelps (see p. 356) brought members of his Westboro Baptist Church from Topeka, Kansas. He previously protested at Falwell's Thomas Road Baptist Church in Lynchburg, accusing him of being too soft on gays. "Falwell used to teach the Bible word for word, now he's going off and meeting with these fags and going against everything he's ever taught," Phelps told a reporter. "He always says 'hate the sin, but love the sinner,' but it's impossible to separate the two. Does a judge send the crime or criminal to jail?" Citizens Against Moral Deterioration, made up mostly of followers of Rev. Edward Nelson, associate pastor of Fairmont Baptist Church in Nelson County, also showed up. Members of Heritage Baptist Church of Mount Enterprise, Texas, which threatened to picket a gay-themed college play in Texas earlier that month, joined the crowd. One member said, "We've supported Jerry Falwell over the years... and he has thrown in the towel." Reports on their numbers varied from 24 to 40. Some in the crowd carried signs saying, "Jerry and a Fairy Equal Sin."

> "I continue to believe that God has given us unmistakable Divine instructions for living — and homosexuality is not a part of it."
>
> — Rev. Jerry Falwell, discussing his plans to reaffirm his opposition to gay rights during a meeting with activist Mel White.

Falwell disappointed many who had hoped he might temper his rhetoric at a press conference following a meeting between the two leaders. He made several comments comparing gay men and lesbians to substance abusers. "We oppose alcoholism and drugs... not alcoholics and drug addicts." Falwell said, "I've been a preacher for 47 years, a preacher of the gospel... but in the end homosexuality is wrong. It is my hope that evangelicals might build a bridge of friendship to gays and lesbians as we have to alcoholics and unwed mothers." After a former Liberty University student discussed the anti-gay climate he had endured, Falwell reiterated his policy of prohibiting all types of sexual activity between students at the university.

Perhaps an editorial Falwell ran on an Internet news site was most revealing about the impressions with which he left the meeting. It was designed to explain why he met with Rev. White and what he took from the meeting. He reiterated his opposition to homosexuality, saying, "With 200 homosexuals staring me in the face last Saturday, I accentuated the biblical position that homosexuality is a sin." Although Falwell condemned Fred Phelps for his brand of anti-gay hatred, he also touted the spiritual journey of self-proclaimed "ex-gay" Michael Johnston, of Kerusso Ministries (see p. 355), who also attended the summit.

Martinsville: Religious Right targets brewer

Using the backdrop of an auto racing event, three Religious Right organizations denounced a major brewer's policy of sponsoring gay and lesbian pride celebrations. The Family Policy Network (see p. 354), Americans for Truth About Homosexuality (see p.

352), and the American Family Association (see p. 352) held a press conference before a NASCAR race at a local auto racing arena to denounce Anheuser-Busch's pro-gay advertising campaigns. Joe Glover, president of the Family Policy Network and Virginia state director of the American Family Association, said, "Anheuser-Busch seems to be endorsing sodomy for money," as he called on racing fans to urge the company to change its policies. He claimed that homosexuality led to heartache, disease, and early death from what he called abnormal sexual behavior.

Representing Americans for Truth About Homosexuality, two self-proclaimed "ex-gays," Yvette Cantu and Holt McCormick, spoke at the press conference. Cantu said, "While I was in the lesbian lifestyle, I helplessly watched 15 of my homosexual friends die of AIDS. After seeing that and other damaging effects of homosexual behavior, I know firsthand that it is irresponsible of Anheuser-Busch to promote homosexuality in its ads." McCormick labeled homosexuality a "deathstyle" and not a "lifestyle." He called on Anheuser-Busch to withhold funds from organizations he said promoted a "gay agenda." Glover asked beer drinkers to boycott Anheuser-Busch products until the company changed its policies. "We're asking a corporate giant to put people and principle above profits. We're urging good people to tell Anheuser-Busch that they don't patronize companies who promote homosexuality."

A few weeks later, Glover posted signs at the Martinsville NASCAR raceway saying, "Boycott Bud, Busch, Michelob. They promote homosexuality. Do you?" Anheuser-Busch is a major sponsor of races at that track. Glover hired a plane to fly above the track towing a sign saying, "Anheuser-Busch: Stop promoting homosexuality." The beer company's officials tried unsuccessfully to stop the plane. Thousands of leaflets were also distributed at the track saying, "Tell Anheuser-Busch you know when to say when." The leaflet listed several amusement parks the company owns and directed readers to Glover's website denouncing the company. Glover posted signs along the highway leading to and from the track targeting the company. "Many of Anheuser-Busch's customers are appalled at their promotion of homosexuality," he claimed.

Norfolk: Church tried to convert Jews and gays

Jewish, gay and lesbian residents in the Ghent neighborhood of Norfolk were disturbed by a new church's effort to proselytize in the community. Saying "We didn't just want to be in any part of Norfolk; we wanted to be in Ghent specifically," Rev. Vic Pope, pastor of Bethel Temple-Norfolk, began a campaign to convert Jews and gays in the surrounding area to Christianity. The church rents space from a local high school in a diverse neighborhood with black, Jewish, and gay populations. Pope said, "Maury [the school the church rents] sits right in the middle of a larger Jewish community. We want to make inroads there." He also noted the prominent number of gay men and lesbians who live in Ghent. "There's a huge homosexual population. That's an area that most people don't want to mess with,

but they're just bound-up, hurting people that need to be set free by the power of Jesus."
The campaign drew the ire of many residents.

The church's efforts particularly disturbed members of Norfolk's Jewish and gay and lesbian communities, who said the program was offensive. One rabbi said he was reminded of the Inquisition and the Crusades, in which Jews and other non-Christians were persecuted when they did not convert to Christianity. "Out of love for you, they burned you at the stake. It's nauseating," said Lawrence Forman. Fear of anti-Semitism also provoked their criticism. "How am I supposed to feel? How is my congregation supposed to feel?" asked Rabbi Arthur Ruberg, whose synagogue sits across from the school. "But in an age in which we need mutual understanding and respect, it's unfortunate that here is a group saying, 'We need to change you in order for you to be a whole person.' "

> "They're just bound-up, hurting people that need to be set free by the power of Jesus."
>
> — Bethel Temple's Rev. Vic Pope, remarking on his church's plans (since dropped) to proselytize among gays, lesbians and Jews in Norfolk's Ghent neighborhood.

The attention the criticism received caused a backlash against Bethel Temple. By the end of October, the church had backed off its plan to proselytize.

Richmond: Baptists withdraw university funding

When the University of Richmond incorporated sexual orientation into its non-discrimination policies, the Baptist General Association of Virginia announced it would phase out its financial support of the university. In March, university officials said they were bringing the school in line with top-ranked colleges across the nation by adding the language to their policies. Although the school did not publicize the breakdown of the trustee board's vote, it did acknowledge a significant amount of resistance from conservative trustees. The university's chaplain, Dr. David Burhans, said, "Some persons expressed concern that inclusion of this clause could be misinterpreted as the University of Richmond promoting gay and lesbian relationships... But the university is, by making this statement, neutral on that."

In November, the Baptist General Association approved recommendations from its Mission Board, phasing out $246,500 in funding and student scholarships. Frank Cain, a Mission Board member, said the board did not want to give the appearance that it supported gay rights. "[A]s for gay rights, we have a statement that [says] we don't feel it is an acceptable lifestyle," he said. By withdrawing its funding, the group relinquished its power to nominate four of the 40 university trustees. Reginald McDonough, executive director of the General Association, claimed that the university's decision gave "tacit approval" to homosexual behavior. In 1993, the association passed a resolution declaring homosexual behavior "sinful and unacceptable for Christians." The relationship between the Virginia Baptists and the university has diminished over the last 25 years in part because of the school's stand on social issues.

The Virginia Baptists did not sever all ties, however, with the University of Richmond. The school will still house the Virginia Baptists' archives and will host the Center for Baptist Heritage and Studies.

Roanoke: Transgendered inmate denied medicine

Medical professionals at the Roanoke City Jail denied a transgendered inmate hormones necessary for him to continue gender reassignment. For three years prior to his incarceration, "Jay" McCulley had taken hormones as part of his sex reassignment process. Corrections officials said his gender transformation was a choice, not a medical necessity. Sheriff George McMillan said that withholding McCulley's hormones did not endanger his life or cause him serious injury, which the sheriff claimed were the requirements for providing medication to inmates. "Our doctors ruled it wasn't a medical necessity, and our psychiatrist gave him an antidepressant because he said he was depressed," McMillan said. He added that McCulley was being confined to an isolated cell because of his "unique" situation.

In January, McCulley brought suit in federal court against Correctional Medical Services, which provides medical care for the jail, for denying him hormones while he was incarcerated. Right before his suit was filed, corrections officials transferred McCulley to a state jail partly because, according to McMillan, it was better equipped to handle his "special condition." Because McCulley was moved to another correctional facility, the case was dismissed as moot within weeks of its being filed.

WASHINGTON

Statewide: Safe schools bill dies

A bill to require public schools to address, discuss, and discipline anti-gay harassment met stiff opposition from leaders in the state House of Representatives during the spring legislative session. The bill would have directed the state superintendent of schools to develop a model policy against harassment based on a variety of categories, including sexual orientation. Public schools would then be required to develop similar policies. State Rep. Gigi Talcott held up the bill in committee through March, claiming it was not needed. She finally scheduled a public hearing on the bill, but the date was more than a week after the deadline for bills to be approved by committees and sent to the full House. She said, "I believe local school boards are the ones capable of handling this issue." The state chapter of the Christian Coalition (see p. 353) and several Republican legislators also opposed the bill. A newspaper's advance poll of House members revealed that the bill was supported by 49 Democrats and 16 Republicans. Gay and lesbian activists called on legislators to pass the bill a March rally at the state Capitol. The bill, however, languished in committee and died at the close of the session.

Cheney: Schools sued over alleged harassment

In December, the parents of two brothers who say they endured anti-gay harassment from fellow students sued the Cheney public schools in state court. In their lawsuit, the parents assert that both boys were targeted because one of them was perceived to be gay. The parents contend that school personnel failed to follow the district's anti-harassment policies and took actions that actually increased the harassment. The parents further allege that their sons suffered humiliation, embarrassment, degradation and mental and physical harm. They are seeking an unspecified amount of compensation for their sons. The plaintiffs' attorney, Sheryl Phillabaum, said that neither of the boys is gay, "but it doesn't matter if you're homosexual or heterosexual. It's still not OK to be called those derogatory names." School Superintendent Phil Snowdon said school officials actively enforced anti-harassment policies. At press time, the case was pending.

Everett: Gay youth conference criticized

Two state legislators criticized a gay youth conference as age-inappropriate. The conference, Links and Alliances '99, was a free all-day conference held at Everett Community College designed to promote the prevention of HIV transmission and healthy behavior among teens. Frank Busichio, one of the event's sponsors and a public health educator, said the event would be well-chaperoned. At issue was a social mixer to which youth between the ages of 14 and 20 were invited. State Sen. Val Stevens and state Rep. John Koster wrote the college's president a letter urging him to cancel the conference. "I am very troubled that the sponsors of this event are inviting children and youth as young as 14 years old to engage in social intercourse with adult proponents of these questionable and unhealthy 'lifestyles,' " the letter read. Koster said, "It's a disaster waiting to happen." Stevens claimed that "sex and coercion and the possible use of non-inhibiting drugs could be part of the evening's unintended consequences." Organizers said that adult speakers had been fully screened and had undergone criminal background checks. No problems had been reported in connection with the two previous conferences. The Everett conference took place as planned, attended by about 20 youths and 15 adults. One local student, Vanessa Wharton, 19, said, "It boggles my mind that people think there's an orgy here," and challenged Stevens and Koster to attend next year's conference.

Seattle: Candidate's anti-gay remarks

A City Council candidate made several anti-gay comments during an interview with the city's gay and lesbian political group. According to Michael Andrew, the facilitator for the meeting between City Council candidate Lenora Jones and the Seattle Metropolitan Elections Committee for Gays, Lesbians, Bisexuals, and Transgenders, Jones interrupted a brief introduction Andrew gave to her about his group and told them about how to "overcome" homosexuality though Christianity. Andrew said Jones called all gay people sinners and said she would do everything within her power to stop gay men and lesbians from gaining power. Andrew also reported that after her speech, Jones told the committee that there was no point in continuing the interview. "Often candidates are unintentionally hostile out of ignorance, but she came deliberately to be hostile," he claimed.

Days after interview, the committee received Jones' response to a questionnaire the group had sent her. In her responses, Jones reiterated her position that her top priority in office would be opposing gay men and lesbians. One question asked Jones to discuss the difference between her constituents' wishes and those of the city's gay and lesbian residents, to which Jones responded, "You are not an ethnicity or a culture. You are living a sin. You don't have to live this lifestyle, God loves you... Repent, turn from your ways to God's way." However, Jones said that the gay community should still vote for her because she is an honest person. The committee gave her a zero rating. Jones lost the general election, garnering less than 22 percent of the vote.

Seattle: Church rejects gay ceremony

A church that had allowed gay community groups to use its space for some time rejected a gay couple's request to use it for their commitment ceremony. The First United Methodist Church allowed the Seattle Gay Men's Chorus to practice in its sanctuary and allowed the group to use its space to hold a benefit auction as well. One item offered for sale during that auction was a "one-day use of the Sanctuary." The description did not suggest any limitations. Richard Manoli, the father of a chorus member, bid on the item and won. According to Manoli, when he called the church to schedule his son's commitment ceremony, the church's staff director, Heidi Thompson, told him the ceremony did not fit the church's expectations. Jane Manoli, the mother, said they did not ask the church for pastoral services — just the space to provide for a gathering of family and friends. Richard Manoli said he was shocked and that finding an alternative location was a considerable expense. John Hierholzer, the church's pastor, said he was following the United Methodists' guidelines, which prevent the blessing of gay unions or the provision of member churches for such events. The church now says that only a church function or public event would be an acceptable use of the sanctuary. The church's development director said that the Manolis' money would be refunded.

Seattle: Gay book removed from school libraries

The acting superintendent of schools for Seattle removed a gay and lesbian book from several school libraries in February. The book, "One Teenager in Ten, edited by Ann Heron, is a collection of essays from gay and lesbian teenagers dealing with their sexuality. Acting Superintendent Joseph Olchefske reportedly heard local anti-gay activist Linda Jordan on a local radio show discussing the book and her earlier attempts to remove it from school libraries and subsequently ordered that the books be taken off the shelves of one middle school and two high schools. On the radio program, Jordan claimed the book described acts of pedophilia. The essay she targeted was actually written by a young woman who described an intimate encounter with an older female teacher as part of her coming out experience. Olchefske's spokesperson, Trevor Neilson, said the books would stay off the shelves pending review by a select committee composed of a teacher, student, principal and community leader. "It's being reviewed because a graphic portion of the book was brought to the acting superintendent's attention," Neilson said.

Liz Burbank, from the bookstore Red and Black Books, said, "It is just more homophobic censorship. Doing this sends the message that the school district thinks teenagers are idiots and cannot make their own decisions."

Weeks later, Olchefske, with the select committee's approval, permanently removed the book from the three schools libraries but replaced it with an updated edition, "Two Teenagers in Twenty", in which the publisher removed the essay Jordan found objectionable. Nielson said, "We are resolute in our commitment to diversity and are in no way bowing to anti-gay people like Linda Jordan." Jordan headed a group called Parents and Teachers for Responsible Schools and led unsuccessful campaigns in 1998 to have" One Teenager in Ten" removed and to fight unfiltered Internet access in libraries.

Seattle: Radio stations pull ads

Two local radio stations pulled an ad dealing with lesbian health care in January. The ad was designed to encourage lesbians to get annual pap smears for early detection of cervical cancer. It was funded in part by grants from the city, developed by the Lesbian Health Matters campaign, and supported by the Seattle City Council, Seattle-King County Health Department and Seattle Commission for Sexual Minorities. Mark Richards, program director at KMPS-FM, said he pulled the ad after receiving 10 to 20 complaints about use of the word "lesbian" each time the ad ran. He said, "My children were listening to this campaign and I'm not ready to talk to them about sexual orientation," was the typical comment callers made to the station's officials. Another radio station, KMTT-FM, pulled the ad as well. Both stations aired the ad several times before it was pulled.

These decisions to pull the ad angered lesbian activists and public health officials. "We think it was a violation of our contract. It saddened me realizing those kinds of biases keep us from getting lifesaving messages to people," said Dr. Alonzo Plough, head of Seattle's Department of Public Health. Kathleen Stine, head of the Commission on Sexual Minorities, said, "I'm witnessing the genesis of a hatred. It's painful to me as a lesbian and it hurts my feelings."

In February, KMTT revised the ad and placed it back on the air, paying for it in part. That station had claimed its that objections were to "Pap smear" in the original ad, so the wording was changed to "annual exam." The station kept "lesbian" in the revised ad. Chris Mays, the station's vice president, said they still received complaints.

Seattle: "Suffer the Children" broadcast

Gay rights advocates criticized a Seattle public television station for its decision to broadcast the anti-gay video "Suffer the Children" along with Debra Chasnoff's award-winning documentary "It's Elementary: Talking About Gay Issues in School." The American Family Association (see p. 352), which produced "Suffer the Children," claims that its video is a rebuttal of "It's Elementary" because it shows the part of the "gay agenda" that involves recruiting children. "It's Elementary" seeks to guide parents, teachers and and school administrators through age-appropriate ways to discuss homosexuality with schoolchildren. "Suffer the Children" has been subject to allegations of copyright infringement for its use of clips from "It's Elementary." KCTS broadcast "Suffer the Children" immediately after it showed "It's Elementary" in July. Kay Ingram, a programming executive, said, "In looking at this issue, we're trying to bring the diverse perspectives to the table to talk about it."

> "Get real... This is a propaganda piece... of name-calling, omissions, and lies."
>
> — Seattle City Council member Tina Podlodowski on the American Family Association's "Suffer the Children," which was produced as a counterpoint to "It's Elementary" and broadcast on KCTS.

Gay and lesbian advocates criticized the station's decisions. Mike Balasa, board member of the Seattle chapter of Parents, Families and Friends of Lesbians and Gays, said, "KCTS is showing an incredible lack of sensitivity." More than 100 people staged a protest at the station's offices the day the programs aired. Among the protesters were long-term contributors, gay and lesbian activists, and elected officials. Referring to the messages in "Suffer the Children," John Gelert, a past contributor, said, "It causes a lot of pain and a lot of hurt for children." Openly gay City Council member Tina Podlodowski said, "Get real... This is a propaganda piece... of name-calling, omissions, and lies."

Debra Chasnoff contributed an essay about the campaign against "It's Elementary" to the 1999 edition of Hostile Climate.

Spokane: Bid to repeal non-discrimination ordinance

In a year-long campaign, right-wing activists sought to stop the city from expanding an existing non-discrimination ordinance to include gay men and lesbians. The proposal added sexual orientation to the city's existing non-discrimination ordinance, which prohibits discrimination in employment, housing and public accommodations. Opponents formed a group called Equal Rights, Not Special Rights to work for the proposal's defeat. Penny Lancaster, the group's researcher, claimed that the proposal was unnecessary, would place a financial burden on the city and would restrict free speech. Rev. Ron Johnson, the group's executive director, said, "This ordinance is really a Trojan horse for homosexuals, transsexuals and bisexuals," and claimed it would be a step toward incorporating gay and lesbian subject matter into the public school curriculum. Other opponents said the proposal was an unnecessary government intrusion and gave special rights to gay men and lesbians. Johnson warned, "This issue will not go away regardless of how the council will vote." To better its chance at being passed, council members amended the original proposal to omit provisions covering transgendered people and those receiving public assistance.

Soon after the City Council approved the proposal in January by a 4-3 vote, Equal Rights, Not Special Rights began a petition drive to put the new measure to the voters as a November ballot referendum. By July, the group had gathered 2,000 more signatures than were required. Although Johnson said, "I feel confident that section [dealing with sexual orientation] will be repealed," he characterized the fight as David versus Goliath: "The homosexual community clearly has much more financial resources than we do... We're local people with families to raise and schedules to keep." Opponents of the referendum organized under the name No! On Discrimination and were confident they could defeat the referendum. Dean Lynch, a member, said, "We're raising families, holding jobs, paying taxes, and we are organizing to advance and protect equal rights for all in the city of Spokane." He added, "I personally believe that if they put out a call to the Christian Coalition, they will have all the money and support they could use."

Voters defeated the ballot measure with 52 percent of the vote, thus keeping the new provision in the anti-discrimination ordinance. The vote disappointed Johnson, who said, "Clearly, the narrow margin of victory... was by no means a mandate by voters... Whether the ordinance is challenged again in the future, I alone cannot say."

Vancouver: Challenge to partners benefits policy

A right-wing resident backed by national anti-gay organizations filed a lawsuit challenging the city's domestic partners benefits package for city employees. The package was first offered in 1998, after the City Council passed a proposal sponsored by openly gay City Council member Jim Moeller. The policy defines a domestic partnership as two people who "have an intimate, committed relationship of mutual caring and are responsible for each other's common welfare." Roni Heinsma, who filed the suit as a taxpayer, contended that the city has no authority under state law to offer the benefits. The lawsuit seeks an end to the domestic partner benefits program. The Alliance Defense Fund (see p. 352) has funded the lawsuit and retained Jordan Lorence, an attorney with Northstar Legal Services (see p. 356), to handle the case. Lorence called Heinsma "a concerned citizen who started asking around to see who could do something about this." The ADF has claimed that domestic partner benefits are "bad public policy" and run contrary to the "millennia of consensus from every major culture in the world." Lorence added that "It's dragging marriage down to the level of unmarried cohabitation" and "It's tinkering with a social institution, and we mess around with it at our peril." Oral arguments were heard in May 2000, and a ruling had not been issued at press time.

WEST VIRGINIA

Statewide: Hate crimes bill dies

Although a bill to add sexual orientation to the state's existing hate crimes law died in a committee of the legislature in January, its detractors and supporters continued their campaigns well into the rest of the year. During its annual conference in June, the West Virginia United Methodist Church announced support for the bill. Not all churches were as supportive. The Charleston Gazette published an anti-gay op-ed by Rev. Randy Wilson, pastor of Esta Memorial Baptist Church. He called gay men and lesbians "wicked sinners before God." He said the bill would forbid him from preaching "against these awful sins" and that "[The bill] would put the righteous in jail, while leaving the Sodomite to prey on the unsuspecting youth of our society." He ended by saying, "As common people, let us all tell the Sodomites and all that support them: You are not welcome in our state of West Virginia, let alone protected to do your ungodly deeds." On the page opposite the column, the editors placed the warning: "Today's opposite page contains one of the cruelest commentaries we've ever printed." The following day, they published an editorial criticizing the Boy Scouts' policy of excluding openly gay members and employees.

House Judiciary Committee Chairman Rick Staton, who opposed the bill, criticized the Methodists for announcing their support for the bill. "It sounds more like the Christian Coalition or a PAC than a church," he said, while doubting the measure had enough support for passage. Hilary Chiz, head of the West Virginia American Civil Liberties Union, disagreed, saying, "The decision by the United Methodist Church is in keeping with the best liberal tradition of social action, especially for an established church."

Statewide: Proposed same-sex marriage prohibition

Lawmakers tried to pass a bill to prohibit the state from recognizing same-sex marriages. Rick Staton, chair of the House Judiciary Committee, said, "We contemplate marriage to be between a man and a woman." Del. Steve Harrison had previously introduced similar bills, but they had all failed. He continued his efforts, however, saying, "Homosexuality is an immoral and unhealthy lifestyle. It's not something our government should encourage or endorse… Until we pass this law, we are not going to be safe." He added, "Let's not let another state force this on us. I don't think everyone really realizes the urgency."

Conservatives outside the legislature also drummed up support for the bill. The West Virginia Conservative Coalition commissioned a poll showing that 97 percent of state residents opposed legal recognition of same-sex marriage. James Dobson's Focus on the Family (see p. 355) urged residents to petition their legislators in favor of the bill. Posted on its website was an alert: "If the state does not enact DOMA [Defense of Marriage Act] legislation this session, it could be forced to recognize homosexual 'marriages' if they are legalized in Vermont or any other state." It urged readers to contact the chairmen of the Senate and House Judiciary Committees and support the bill.

Bills in both houses died in committee.

Statewide: Dueling domestic partner bills

Anti-gay state legislators introduced bills that would prohibit state and municipal governments from extending domestic partner benefits to their unmarried employees. Successes in advancing such legislation sparked a backlash resulting in a slate of bills affirming the rights of gay men and lesbians.

State Rep. Stephen Nass (R) denounced the few cities that had recently adopted domestic partner benefits policies and a proposal to introduce such benefits statewide. Nass said, "There is not widespread support in the state of Wisconsin for that kind of [domestic partner] coverage... I am simply following the will of the people." He claimed that granting domestic partner benefits "tears away at the bonds of marriage." Nass added, "Heterosexuals can freely go and get married. Now, the gays and lesbians will come back and say 'We can't get married.' Well, that's right. That's just the way the law is." Nass introduced two bills: -one that would have allowed the state and its municipalities to deny domestic partner benefits to government employees and another that would have given municipal governments the option of refusing to discuss the issue with employee unions. He had proposed similar measures in 1997.

Nass' bills faced considerable opposition. Demian, who goes by one name and is co-director of the Partners Task Force for Gay and Lesbian Couples, criticized Nass' bills, saying, "That's like going out of your way to legislate exclusion and hate... More than 800 workplaces offer domestic partner benefits... It creates mostly good will at next to no cost. Any workplace that is exclusionary and hateful will not produce well." Officials with the state employees union called the bills' "part of the right-wing 'culture war' on domestic partner agreements." At a hearing on the bills, Nass was the only person to speak in their favor. The Assembly Committee on Family Law approved the bills in late October, but they never went to a floor vote before the full House and were carried over into the 2000 legislative session.

In contrast, state Rep. Mark Pocan (D) introduced two pro-gay bills, one that would have created a statewide registry for same-sex couples and granted them most of the legal benefits of marriage, and another that would have broadened the scope of the state insurance pool to include the domestic partners of state government employees. Gay and lesbian advocates hoped that both bills would erase any doubt that municipalities could extend partner benefits to government employees. In early October, elected officials in Madison wanted to offer domestic partner benefits but were concerned about whether they had the legal authority to do so. Instead, they chose to reimburse city employees for the cost of extra insurance for their partners. Both of Pocan's bills were carried over into the 2000 legislative session.

Madison: Religious group protests governor's letter

Religious activists denounced Gov. Tommy Thompson's welcome letter to a gay, lesbian, bisexual and transgendered conference held in February. Ralph Ovadal, head of Wisconsin Christians United (see p. 357), organized a call-in campaign to criticize Thompson's welcome to the Midwest Lesbian, Bisexual, Gay, Transgendered College Conference, which was held at the Madison convention center and attended by 1,200 students from 20 states. Ovadal claimed the governor's office received telephone calls protesting the letter and that the office said the welcome letter was fabricated. Jason Rasmussen, chair of the conference, denied that, noting that it was a form letter encouraging participants to tour the city. He said there was nothing "pro-gay" in the letter.

Milwaukee: Domestic partners registry opposed

A local Religious Right group opposed Milwaukee's creation of a domestic partners registry for gay and lesbian couples. The registry, open only to same-sex couples, conveys no legal rights but does give gay men and lesbians a certificate attesting to their relationships. Gay men and lesbians hoped the registry will also make it easier for couples to visit each other in hospitals and guide their employers in offering domestic partner benefits. The text of the law creating the registry states that Milwaukee has an interest in recognizing same-sex relationships.

Ralph Ovadal, head of Wisconsin Christians United (see p. 357), led the opposition campaign. The group distributed fliers throughout the city denouncing supporters of the registry. The group claimed the registry would burden the city with heavy expenses and that taxes would have to be increased to compensate. The flier listed the names and phone numbers of members of the Milwaukee Common Council. Ovadal's group attached to the flier a three-page document attacking the city's gay and lesbian community that included claims that gay men and lesbians were responsible for the Holocaust. The organization followed up with door-to-door visits and phone calls to residents to drum up opposition to the registry.

At a June public hearing on the issue, opponents voiced their fears that the registry would lead to the recognition of same-sex marriage. They claimed the registry would threaten "family values" and would tear the community apart.

Supporters of the registry were outraged. The registry's sponsor, Alderman Mike D'Amato, said, "It's tragic to see that much hatred in the city and fear-mongering by those types of people. I am confident this is just a small group of people that don't represent the fair-minded people of Milwaukee." He denied charges that the registry would pose an expense to the city, saying, "This doesn't cost the city of Milwaukee a penny, while it does provide many Milwaukeeans with the ability to register and receive benefits from other organizations." Patrick Flaherty, co-chair of Milwaukee's Domestic Partners Task Force, denounced the "despicable tactics" of Wisconsin Christians United and urged residents to contact their aldermen and urge their support. He said, "The Common Council needs to decide who it will side with: hate-filled, out-of-town extremists or same-sex couples committed to each other and Milwaukee."

The council adopted the registry in July by a 10-7 vote. Disappointed opponents carried signs denouncing the measure. One group of opponents vowed to challenge it in court. Nevertheless, on September 1, 20 same-sex couples registered their relationships with the city. About 200 people gathered at city hall for a privately sponsored celebration.

Sussex: Teacher alleges harassment

A gay teacher sued the Hamilton School District in federal court, claiming the district had failed to enforce its policies protecting students and faculty from anti-gay harassment. Tommy Schroeder claimed that though the school district has a policy against anti-gay discrimination, harassment from the students and faculty caused him such emotional stress that he had to seek professional help. In his lawsuit, Schroeder claimed that "he has been subjected to students chanting 'queer' and 'faggot' at him." He also asserted that rumors circulated that he had AIDS, that he received harassing, vulgar phone calls at home and work, and that school staff members also "verbally abused" him. Schroeder said the harassment started soon after began working at Templeton Middle School. He claimed that one parent called him at home and said, "We just want you to know, you [expletive] queer, that when we pull out all of our kids you will have no job."

The lawsuit contends that school administrators failed to respond appropriately to Schroeder's complaints of harassment. Schroeder alleged that on two occasions, sexually explicit graffiti that included Schroeder's name was written in the boy's bathroom. Students were punished for defacing school property but not for the graffiti's anti-gay content. Schroeder also maintained that school officials repeatedly denied his requests to be transferred to another school. Finally, Schroeder said one student actually threatened his life. Schroeder claimed the student had targeted him because he is gay and that he had made the threat in front of another teacher. Schroeder said that although he made repeated complaints to school officials, the school's associate principal ignored the problem and told him "we can't stop middle school students from talking. Boys will be boys."

Schroeder was finally reassigned to a local elementary school. At press time, his suit was pending.

Verona: Gay student group targeted

Rev. Ron Greer, who had lost an earlier campaign to become the Republican challenger to openly lesbian U.S. Rep. Tammy Baldwin, organized a campaign to ban the Student Alliance for Acceptance, a gay-straight student group at Verona High School. Greer, pastor of Trinity Evangelical Fellowship, was fired in 1998 from the Madison Fire Department for his anti-gay campaigning on the job. Greer said a student upset with the high school group had alerted him to its existence.

Using church stationery, Greer and his congregation mailed 3,000 information packages to area residents. The cover letter attacked the student group and the superintendent for accepting and affirming "dangerous sexual behavior." In it, Greer said, "Verona schools have decided that a dangerous sexual behavior is important for your children to accept and affirm, then call that 'tolerance.' " He claimed that students were being "endangered" because, he said, the group promotes homosexuality. "By their own admissions, GLSEN [the Gay, Lesbian, and Straight Education Network] leaders and other radical groups advocate teaching homosexual affirming lessons even to elementary school children, including kindergartners. And yes, you're paying for it!" he wrote. Greer continued, "Countless children will unnecessarily suffer physically, emotionally and some will even die as a result of this deception." Included in the mailing were what Greer called fliers but what were actually excerpted minutes for an Alliance meeting that included the names of some students and a "Safe Zone" poster that school social workers could display showing their support for gay and lesbian students.

> "Countless children will unnecessarily suffer physically, emotionally and some will even die as a result of this deception."
>
> — Anti-gay activist Rev. Ron Greer, in a letter to 3,000 area residents protesting the formation of a gay-straight alliance at Verona High School.

The school was deluged with calls from outraged parents. Superintendent Bob Gilpatrick said, "In this time when schools are trying so hard to build an atmosphere of safety, acceptance, and tolerance for the kids, we get an adult who does something like this to undermine the entire effort." He noted that parents who both supported and opposed the group denounced Greer's tactics. Gilpatrick contended that Greer had intruded on the students' privacy when he published the names of students attending the Student Alliance for Acceptance's meeting. "What he did is immoral. He owes each and every one of those kids and their families a sincere apology," he said.

Greer remained steadfast in the wake of this criticism. "According to the phone calls and e-mail I've been getting, there are lots of people who are enraged by what the district is doing... The whole idea of addressing homosexuality in schools is inappropriate to me," he said. He called the district's attention to the harassment of gay and lesbian students "disingenuous" and defended publicizing the names of students in the group.

Whitefish Bay: Gay/lesbian student group targeted

Members of Pride and Respect for Youth in Sexual Minorities (PRYSM) at Whitefish Bay High School witnessed vandalism and claimed they were verbally harassed during their campaign to start an alliance of gay and straight students, despite having secured permission from the principal.

When an adult gay man was reportedly beaten near the school, Ruth Eglsaer, one of the founders of PRYSM, said she heard several students make remarks supporting the attackers. In response, she and other club members put up signs around the school, only to later find that they had been torn down. Club members put them back up in a locked display case. Other students wrote anti-gay comments on the hallway walls. Finally a group of students put up a sign advertising a new group, People Against Queers. A student using school computers to advertise that group by e-mail was punished and later apologized to PRYSM members. Eglsaer said that many of her friends distanced themselves from her when they discovered she was involved with PRYSM. One straight student confided in a teacher that her parents feared membership in PRYSM would hinder her chance of being accepted into college.

Teachers who supported PRYSM also said they suffered from anti-gay sentiment among their co-workers. The group's faculty adviser, Judie Born, said, "One staff member approached me and said, 'I always respected you before this but you can't be a Christian and do this.' This was a colleague with whom I had shared literature from my church!" Born also said messages had been left on her answering machine saying, "fag lover."

Eglsaer and Principal Neil Codell said the school's climate improved because of PRYSM's work. "People who wouldn't think of using an ethnic slur wouldn't think twice about using the term 'faggot'... People had no idea how hurtful that was to some kids," Eglsaer said. The students have addressed a faculty meeting and are helping to plan a longer in-service program. Codell said, "They have raised the level of consciousness to the issues and made people stop and think." Eglsaer added, "I've taken the attitude that if we help even a few people, it's been worthwhile."

WYOMING

Statewide: Hate crimes bills killed

The state legislature defeated several hate crimes bills that would have included sexual orientation. Calls for passage of a hate crimes bill increased after the murder of gay University of Wyoming student Matthew Shepard in October 1998. Despite Gov. Jim Geringer's support for a hate crimes law, the bills all died in their respective legislative houses. All but one would have increased the penalties imposed on those convicted of crimes motivated by bias. The other would have created a task force to study bias crimes and make recommendations for developing public awareness of bias crimes. A straw poll taken in January suggested support for the bills was insufficient. Some state senators, including John Hanes, objected to the bills, saying they were the wrong way to address the issue. Hanes said, "What we need is a massive reorientation of attitude" and that adopting a hate crimes law would further divide people. Among the bills' few supporters, state Sen. Rae Lynn Job said, "I think laws have gone a long way toward changing attitudes. Certainly civil rights laws did, even seat belt laws." State Sen. Steven Youngbauer countered, "I just believe the laws currently in place have to be equally enforced. We don't need any new laws." The task force bill passed the House, but the Senate Majority Leader later killed it by preventing a floor debate. State Sen. John Shiffer said, "This legislation as written does not fit with what the state wishes to have in a bias crimes bill." Only one of the other three bills that would have increased penalties for bias-motivated crimes received a floor vote. That bill died in a tie vote.

Casper: Anti-gay college program

A photography instructor at Casper College developed a program to counter the school's "Safe Zone" program, which provides support, information, and a "safe haven" for gay, lesbian, bisexual, and transgendered students. Mike Keogh's "Anchor" program consists of campus presentations, one of which characterizes gay men and lesbians as "sexual deviants" who may try to seduce others into a homosexual lifestyle. The Anchor program was presented to the college's president, Leroy Strausner, in 1998, and approved in December 1999. The college did not endorse the program, as it did for the Safe Zone Program. However, Keogh can still use college facilities and e-mail to promote and produce it. Keogh said the Safe Zone program was offensive to those who oppose homosexuality and that two other professors, Jay Graham and Bob Carlson, have also complained about the program. Keogh said the word "homophobe" offended him and claimed that gay men and lesbians lie when they say their lifestyle does not affect others. "It is very divisive, very painful, and very damning to families, and I take exception to people trying to promote that lifestyle," he said.

The Northwest Coalition for Human Dignity criticized Keogh's anti-gay message. "A college should be a place of academic freedom, but it also needs to be a place where all students feel safe and free. That is especially true in the wake of the gruesome murder of Matthew Shepard," said Marlene Hines, director of the Coalition.

Lander: Tolerance resolution opposed

A local gay and lesbian group petitioned the Lander City Council for a resolution seeking tolerance based on sexual orientation. The resolution stated that the city would "foster a community that respects and celebrates the diversity of human expression and identity" and called for all citizens, including gay men and lesbians, to receive equal treatment under the law. The Wyoming group of Equality Begins at Home, a national grassroots campaign started by the National Gay and Lesbian Task Force, made the request in March. Its spokesperson, Debbie East, said that the resolution would "make a statement in this time that intolerance is not acceptable in Lander." A couple of residents spoke against the proposal, saying it was not needed or that it favored some groups over others. Lander Public Works Director Dave Koch objected to the resolution: "The only reason for any crime is hate... Whoever does anything against his neighbor does it because he hates him."

The council narrowly defeated the proposal 4-3, at a meeting held a week later. At that meeting, opponents claimed that the proposal was part of a national "gay agenda" seeking "special rights" for gay men and lesbians. East said she was disappointed with the vote but glad the issue had come up publicly.

Laramie: Hate crimes measure rejected

The City Council in Laramie, where gay University of Wyoming student Matthew Shepard was murdered, declined to debate or hear public testimony on a proposed local hate crimes law. A loosely organized citizens group proposed an ordinance that would have enhanced penalties for crimes motivated by bias. "One would think, if only for public relations purposes, the state and city would have enacted a hate crimes ordinance," said Rev. Stephen Johnson, pastor of a local Unitarian church. Mayor David Williams claimed that there were sufficient laws to punish perpetrators of hate crimes. He added, "We don't want this to become a focus of the City Council and the media. This is an internal thing for the citizens of Laramie." Many local residents said it was absurd to hold the community responsible for the death of Shepard. University of Wyoming President Philip Dubois said, "Who can explain these things? I'm not any more responsible for their [the suspects'] behavior than yours."

> "The city doesn't want to deal with it. The city is still in denial."
>
> — Laramie Rev. Stephen Johnson, on the Laramie City Council's refusal to debate a proposed hate crimes ordinance after the murder of resident Matthew Shepard.

Rev. Johnson said, "Fair or unfair, Laramie will always be remembered as the town where Matthew Shepard was murdered... The city doesn't want to deal with it. The city is still in denial."

A personal essay by Walt Boulden, a friend of Matthew Shepard's, appears on p. 42.

Laramie: Phelps protest

Rev. Fred Phelps and members of his Kansas Westboro Baptist Church (see p. 356) protested outside the trial of Aaron McKinney, one of the murderers of gay University of Wyoming student Matthew Shepard, in October. Phelps' crew has carried placards saying

"Matthew in Hell" since they protested at Shepard's funeral in October 1998. "The everlasting word of God says what they [gay men and lesbians] do is filthy," Phelps said. "This conduct is being described by the Almighty as dogs eating their own vomit." The demonstrators were met by another group, Angel Action, whose members wore angel costumes and silently protested Phelps. A jury found McKinney guilty of Shepard's murder, and under a sentencing agreement between McKinney, the prosecutor and Shepard's parents, McKinney will serve two life jail terms without the possibility of parole.

APPENDIX Incidents Indexed by Category

The 364 incidents described in this edition of *Hostile Climate* are grouped into the states where they took place. To give a sense for how the incidents occurred within certain types, we have indexed them according to the eight categories outlined below. Some incidents could be accurately classed within more than one category (for example, a student play that was censored could be classed both as Censorship or as Education/Academic). In those instances, the incident is marked with an asterisk. In each category, the incidents are listed alphabetically by state, as they appear in the report.

CATEGORIES:

Anti-Discrimination Ordinances: 33 incidents

These are incidents at the national, state, or local levels involving efforts to pass or repeal laws, ordinances or policies prohibiting various forms of discrimination based on sexual orientation.

Censorship: 19 incidents

These are incidents in which the freedom of expression for individuals or institutions is challenged due to anti-gay bias.

Culture War: 87 incidents

These are incidents of general intolerance that demonstrate the larger cultural and societal attack on the interests of gay men and lesbians.

Education/Academic: 75 incidents

These are incidents occurring in an academic or educational setting or incidents involving the services of academic professionals.

Employment: 20 incidents

These are incidents involving discrimination based on sexual orientation in the workplace. They include several disputes over proposals to offer domestic partner benefits.

Hate Crimes Bills: 23 incidents

These are incidents where governments (federal, state or local) debated legislation providing penalties for hate crimes based on sexual orientation. Often, these bills would expand existing hate crime laws to protect gay men, lesbians, bisexuals or transgendered people.

Marriage and Family: 62 incidents

These are incidents in which the status of gay and lesbian relationships and family come under attack, in areas such as marriage, adoption, child custody and foster parenting.

Politics/Government: 57 incidents

These are incidents in which elected officials use anti-gay rhetoric to further their political power or to diminish their opponents, and incidents where officials create or uphold governmental policies that are hostile to the interests of gay men and lesbians.

Religion: 51 incidents

These are incidents in which religious leaders or institutions marginalize the status or interests of gay men and lesbians within their congregations and denominations.

INDEX:

Anti-Discrimination Ordinances   Page

	Page
California	89
Colorado	117
Boulder, CO	119
Colorado Springs, CO	119
Greely, CO	124
Delaware	133
Dade County, FL	137
Hawaii	154
Illinois	164
Iowa	182
Cedar Rapids, IA	184
Dubuque, IA	186
Bowling Green, KY	188
Henderson, KY	190
Jefferson County, KY	192
Lexington, KY	193
Louisville, KY	194
Falmouth, ME	198
Maryland	200
Frederick County, MD	202
Michigan	211
Ferndale, MI	213
Jackson, MI	215
Royal Oak, MI	217
Montana	227
Nevada	234
New Mexico	239
Albuquerque, NM	241
Westchester County, NY	255
Dayton, OH	268
Lakewood, OH	270
College Station, TX*	296
Spokane, WA	326

Censorship

	City or State	Page
"It's Elementary" denounced*	National	60
Proposed "Gay Content" TV label	National	67
Gay book ban*	Anchorage, AK	75
Gay display removed	Oakland, CA	98
"It's Elementary" targeted	Idaho	157
Ban on gay-themed book	Boise, ID	160

Ban on gay-themed book . . . . .Nampa, ID .162
"After Stonewall" not aired . . . . .Ft. Wayne, IN 179
Gay-themed book ban . . . . .Fairfield, IA .187
Gay displays dismantled* . . . . .Plymouth, MI 215
Interview cancelled .Omaha, NE 234
"It's Elementary" not aired . . . . .Chapel Hill, NC 258
Gay-themed play banned . . . . .Charlotte, NC 260
Wake County Schools censor* . . . . .Wake County, NC 261
Controversy over Pridefest ads . . . . .Philadelphia, PA 282
"Angels in America" controversy* . . . . .Kilgore, TX 304
Sodomy comments targeted* . . . . .Arlington, VA 317
Gay-themed book banned . . . . .Seattle, WA .324
Lesbian health radio ads pulled . . . . .Seattle, WA .325

Culture War

Culture War	City or State	Page

Dr. Laura's anti-gay series	National	59
"It's Elementary" denounced*	National	60
Falwell and Teletubby	National	62
John Rocker's anti-gay comments	National	66
Wrestling characters	National	70
Kia commercial	National	70
AOL Dictionary	National	71
Gaither memorial protested	Birmingham, AL	72
Veterans Day parade controversy	Phoenix, AZ	82
Steve May controversy*	Phoenix, AZ	83
Pride parade targeted	Phoenix, AZ	85
Knight Initiative*	California	87
Anti-gay store employee	Cabazon, CA	92
Rich Agonino Show	Costa Mesa, CA	93
Anti-gay billboards	Los Angeles, CA	96
Lesbian denied medical treatment	Mission Viejo, CA	98
Attack at "Creating Change"	Oakland, CA	99
Proposed scout troop rejected	Petaluma, CA	102
Right wing sues San Francisco*	San Francisco, CA	108
Gay-themed books defaced	San Francisco, CA	110
Mass wedding protested	San Francisco, CA	110
Sisters of Indulgence controversy*	San Francisco, CA	111
Simi Valley cops taunt*	Simi Valley, CA	113
Simi Valley Pride targeted	Simi Valley, CA	114
Lesbians sue Denny's	Turlock, CA	114
Religious Right condemns council	Colorado Springs, CO	121
"Corpus Christi" protested	Denver, CO	121
Phelps protests hospital	Trinidad, CO	126

Anti-gay health worker . . . . .Branford, CT 128
"Gay Day" cancelled . . . . .Bristol, CT 129
Gay flag condemned . . . . .Hartford, CT 129
Gay pro-life group barred . . . . .Washington, DC 134
Anti-gay fireman promoted* . . . . .Washington, DC 134
Conference protested . . . . .Washington, DC 135
Ft. Lauderdale Scouts controversy . . . . .Ft. Lauderdale, FL 138
Bally's discounts controversy . . . . .Ft. Lauderdale, FL 140
Anti-gay Lee County Sheriff* . . . . .Ft. Myers, FL 140
Gay neighbor harassed . . . . .Lakeland, FL 141
Gay Days . . . . .Orlando, FL 143
Controversy about gay in the Holocaust . . . . . .Atlanta, GA 148
Transgender canoer . . . . .Honolulu, HI 156
Diversity conference opposed . . . . .Boise, ID 160
Community center opposed . . . . .Elk City, ID 161
Controversy over airing gay program . . . . .Chicago, IL 167
Slurs from bus . . . . .Chicago, IL 168
Response to anti-gay attack . . . . .Chicago, IL 170
"It's Elementary" targeted . . . . .Urbana, IL 173
AAUW Anti-lesbian allegation . . . . .Western Springs, IL 174
"It's Elementary" targeted . . . . .Kentucky 188
Anti-gay murder at Fort Campbell . . . . .Fort Campbell, KY 190
"Corpus Christi" targeted . . . . .Louisville, KY 195
Pro-gay billboard not displayed . . . . .New Orleans, LA 197
"It's Elementary" targeted . . . . .Maine 197
Theater rejects gay group . . . . .Boston, MA 207
Alleged bank discrimination . . . . .Holyoke, MA 208
Anti-gay pamphlets . . . . .Sherborn, MA 210
Anti-gay radio show . . . . .Detroit, MI 213
Alleged stink bomb . . . . .Royal Oak, MI 217
Anti-gay cab driver . . . . .St. Louis, MO 225
Beer boycott . . . . .St. Louis, MO 226
Village Voice anti-transgendered article . . . . . .New York City, NY 247
St. Patrick's Day Parade controversy . . . . .Bronx, NY 249
Police harassment alleged . . . . .New York City, NY 250
St. Patrick's Day Parade controversy . . . . .New York City, NY 251
"Dawson's Creek" protested . . . . .Wilmington, NC .262
"It's Elementary" targeted . . . . .North Dakota 263
Gay flag controversy* . . . . .Columbus, OH 267
Disney protest . . . . .Greenville, OH 270
Gay-themed movie protested . . . . .Portland, OR 277
Attack on rural bar . . . . .Forwardstown, PA 281
Rainbow flags vandalized . . . . .Philadelphia, PA .283

Hospital outs patient . . . . .Troy, PA 286
Scouts controversy . . . . .Rhode Island 287
"It's Elementary" targeted . . . . .Austin, TX .295
Alleged pharmacy discrimination . . . . .Corpus Christi, TX 297
Anti-gay radio jokes . . . . .Dallas, TX .299
Gay resort picketed . . . . .Galveston, TX 301
Transgender name change denied . . . . .Harris County, TX 302
Anti-gay Falwell speech . . . . .Pearland, TX 307
"It's Elementary" targeted . . . . .San Antonio, TX 308
Sodomy comments targeted* . . . . .Arlington, VA 317
Falwell-White meeting* . . . . .Lynchburg, VA 318
Anti-gay boycott of brewer . . . . .Martinsville, VA 319
Transgendered inmate denied medicine . . . . . . .Roanoke, VA 322
Youth conference targeted . . . . .Everett, WA 323
"Suffer the Children" aired . . . . .Seattle, WA 326
Phelps protest trial . . . . .Laramie, WY 335

Education   City or State   Page

"Just the Facts" denounced . . . . .National 63
Gay book ban* . . . . .Anchorage, AK 75
Gay mural defaced . . . . .Palmer, AK .76
Women's studies targeted . . . . .Arizona 80
Gilbert gay club opposed . . . . .Gilbert, AZ .81
State safe schools* . . . . .California 90
Transgender teacher ousted* . . . . .Antelope, CA 91
Grossmont safe schools . . . . .Grossmont, CA 95
Lesbian teacher comes out . . . . .Hemet, CA .96
UCLA program protested . . . . .Los Angeles, CA 97
Alleged harassment in schools . . . . .Menifee, CA 97
Gay-Straight Alliance Club opposed . . . . .Orange, CA .99
Controversy in health class . . . . .Redlands, CA 104
"Ex-Gay" youth conference . . . . .Sacramento, CA 105
Gay mural defaced . . . . .San Francisco, CA 110
"Just the Facts" criticized* . . . . .San Francisco, CA 111
Gay student club . . . . .Colorado Springs, CO 120
Denver safe schools .Denver, CO 123
Gay-themed skit targeted . . . . .Grand Junction, CO 124
Gay allegation made in Columbine massacre . . .Littleton, CO 126
U-Conn. hate preacher* . . . . .Storrs, CT 130
U-Conn. anti-gay graffiti . . . . .Storrs, CT 131
University system benefits derailed* . . . . .Florida 137
Palm Beach County rejects protections . . . . . . .Palm Beach County, FL 144
Dress code at prom .Pierson, FL .145

Pinellas County discrimination controversy .....Pinellas County, FL 146
Transgendered Homecoming competitor ....Tampa, FL 147
Anti-gay school amendment ....Georgia 147
Transgender name change denied ....Cobb County, GA 151
"It's Elementary" controversy ....Chicago, IL 168
Notre Dame non-discrimination controversy ...South Bend, IN 180
Gay-themed textbook targeted ....Terre Haute, IN 181
Anti-gay graffiti in dorm ....Portland, ME 191
Harassment policy opposed ....Maryland 201
Schools conference denounced ....Montgomery County, MD 204
Anti-gay vandals ....Amherst, MA 207
Vandalism at Harvard ....Cambridge, MA 208
Hope College speaker* ....Holland, MI 214
Gay displays dismantled* ....Plymouth, MI 215
Anti-gay school harassment alleged ....Duluth, MN 219
Non-discrimination proposal rejected ......Missouri 222
Non-discrimination for schools criticized .....Columbia, MO 223
Anti-gay school harassment alleged ....Pleasant Hill, MO 224
Pride Week targeted ....St. Louis, MO 225
Coach's anti-gay remarks ....Lincoln, NE 231
Women's Studies targeted ....Lincoln, NE 233
Controversy over university benefits* ....Durham, NH 236
Gay-Straight Alliance Club opposed ....Manchester, NH 237
Controversy over university benefits* ....Las Cruces, NM 241
Anti-gay school harassment alleged ....Averill Park, NY 243
Controversy over school harassment policy ....Clifton Park, NY 244
Yeshiva Housing suit ....New York City, NY 249
Controversy at Skidmore College ....Saratoga Springs, NY 253
Wake County Schools Censor* ....Wake County, NC 261
University Chapel controversy* ....Winston-Salem, NC 262
Lesbian-themed play targeted ....Garrison, ND 264
Anti-gay OSU column ....Columbus, OH 266
Anti-gay vandalism at OSU ....Norman, OK 272
Anti-gay schools initiative* ....Oregon 273
Gay dorm rejected ....Eugene, OR 275
Anti-gay teachers at Cleveland High School ...Portland, OR 276
Play criticized for gay content ....St. Helens, OR 278
No domestic partner benefits at U-Pitt. * ......Pittsburgh, PA 284
Texas A&M rejects non-discrimination proposal* .College Station, TX 296
Controversy over SMU benefits* ....Dallas, TX 298
"Angels in America" controversy* ....Kilgore, TX 304
Gay-themed workshop canceled ....Mesquite, TX 306
Anti-gay school conference ....North Salt Lake City, UT 312

Baptists break with university of Richmond* . . . . . Richmond, VA .321
Safe schools proposal . . . . .Washington .322
Safe schools proposal opposed . . . . .Chaney, WA .323
Gay teacher alleges harassment* . . . . .Sussex, WI 331
Verona Schools . . . . .Verona, WI 332
Whitefish students . . . . .Whitefish Bay, WI 333
Casper College's anti-gay program . . . . .Casper, WY 334

Employment · City or State · Page

ExxonMobil anti-gay controversy* . . . . .National 57
Jesse Helms bill* . . . . .National 68
Lesbian cop sues . . . . .Phoenix, AZ 83
Transgendered teacher ousted* . . . . .Antelope, CA .91
Alleged Wal-Mart discrimination . . . . .Modesto, CA .98
Alleged music store harassment . . . . .Pleasant Hill, CA 103
Scouts fire gay employee . . . . .Sacramento, CA 105
Alleged discrimination at Westek . . . . .Scotts Valley, CA 112
Simi Valley cops taunt* . . . . .Simi Valley, CA 113
Hotel's alleged anti-gay firing . . . . .Miami Beach, FL 143
Alleged harassment at Ford factory . . . . .Hapeville, GA 152
Transgender resignation . . . . .Union, IL 174
Lesbian cop alleges discrimination . . . . .Caroll County, IN 179
Alleged discrimination at Wells Fargo . . . . .Las Vegas, NV 235
Pilots' lawsuit . . . . .Pomona, NJ .238
Harassment suit dismissed . . . . .Nassau County, NY 245
UN Benefits . . . . .New York City, NY 246
Lesbian cop alleges discrimination . . . . .New York City, NY 250
Governor's order excludes gays* . . . . .Ohio 264
Gay teacher alleges harassment* . . . . .Sussex, WI 331

Hate Crimes Bill · Page

Federal Hate Crimes Prevention Act 55
Alabama 72
Arkansas 85
Colorado 118
Idaho 159
Champaign County, IL 165
Indiana 178
Michigan 212
Missouri 222
Montana 228
New Mexico 239
New York 243
North Carolina 257

Cincinnati, OH 265
Oklahoma 271
South Carolina 289
Tennessee 290
Texas 291
Utah 310
Virginia 315
West Virginia 328
Wyoming 333
Laramie, WY 335

Marriage/Family	City or State	Page
ExxonMobil anti-gay controversy*	National	57
Domestic partner lawsuit*	Alaska	73
Gay foster parent ban*	Arizona	76
Anti-domestic partners bill*	Arizona	78
Same-sex marriage denounced*	Arizona	79
Domestic partner benefits*	California	87
Petaluma benefits opposed*	Petaluma, CA	102
San Bernardino domestic partnership*	San Bernardino County, CA	107
Santa Barbara domestic partnership*	Santa Barbara County, CA	112
Same-sex marriage bill	Statewide, CO	115
Same-sex marriage initiative	Colorado	115
Challenge to adoptions by gays*	Colorado	116
Denver domestic partner registry opposed	Denver, CO	122
Joint custody ruling denounced	Jefferson County, CO	125
Anti-gay custody ruling*	Connecticut	127
Adoption by gays assailed	Connecticut	127
State employee benefits controversy	Connecticut	128
Pool rules exclude gays	West Hartford, CT	132
Anti-gay adoption rider*	Washington, DC	135
Challenge to adoptions by gays	Florida	136
University system benefits derailed*	Florida	137
Broward County benefits ordinance	Broward County, FL	138
Atlanta domestic partners challenged	Atlanta, GA	147
Domestic partner benefits expire	Hawaii	155
Same-sex marriage case dismissed	Hawaii	155
Renegade judge	Chicago, IL	166
Controversy over lesbian corrections officer	Chicago, IL	169
Lesbian adoption targeted	Chicago, IL	169
Domestic partner benefits targeted	Cook County, IL	170
Ban on adoptions by gays	Indiana	176
Domestic partner benefits targeted	Bar Harbor, ME	198

Domestic partner benefits targeted . . . . .Portland, ME 199
Domestic partner benefits targeted . . . . .Montgomery County, MD 203
Same-sex marriage bill . . . . .Massachusetts 206
Anti-gay adoption ruling . . . . .Mississippi 220
Same-sex marriage bill . . . . .Nebraska 229
Repeal of adoption ban opposed . . . . .New Hampshire .236
Controversy over university benefits* . . . . .Durham, NH 236
Same-sex marriage bill . . . . .New Mexico 240
Controversy over university benefits* . . . . .Las Cruces, NM .241
Yeshiva Housing suit . . . . .New York City, NY 249
Domestic partner benefits opposed . . . . .Suffolk County, NY 255
Domestic partners policy challenged . . . . .Chapel Hill/Carrboro, NC 259
Same-sex marriage bill* . . . . .Oregon 274
Ashland registry opposed . . . . .Ashland, OR 275
No to domestic partners benefits* . . . . .Pennsylvania 278
Gay men's adoption rejected . . . . .Erie, PA 280
Lesbian adoption rejected . . . . .Lancaster County, PA 281
No domestic partner benefits at U-Pitt.* . . . . . . .Pittsburgh, PA 284
Proposed adoption ban . . . . .Texas 293
No state partners registry . . . . .Texas 295
Controversy over SMU benefits* . . . . .Dallas, TX 298
American Airlines targeted . . . . .Dallas, TX 300
Harsh custody ruling for lesbian mother* . . . . . .Wichita Falls, TX 309
Ban on adoptions by gays . . . . .Utah 311
Mormons denounce same-sex marriage* . . . . . .Salt Lake City, UT 313
Supreme Court ruling denounced . . . . .Vermont 313
Domestic partner benefits challenged . . . . .Arlington County, VA 316
Domestic partner benefits targeted . . . . .Vancouver, WA .327
Same-sex marriage bill . . . . .West Virginia 328
Domestic partners bills* . . . . .Wisconsin 329
Domestic partner benefits challenged . . . . .Milwaukee, WI .330

Politics   City or State   Page

Anti-gay Presidential campaigns . . . . .National 61
Log Cabin controversy . . . . .National 65
Congressman criticized for meeting . . . . .National 66
Jesse Helms bill* . . . . .National 68
Congressman panders to anti-gay group . . . . . .National 70
Domestic partner lawsuit* . . . . .Alaska 73
Housing Discrimination* . . . . .Alaska 74
Gay foster parent ban* . . . . .Arizona 76
Anti-domestic partners bill* . . . . .Arizona 78

Same-sex marriage denounced* . . . . .Arizona .79
Failed sodomy repeal . . . . .Arizona .80
Steve May controversy* . . . . .Phoenix, AZ 83
Sodomy repeal challenged . . . . .Arkansas 86
Domestic partner benefits* . . . . .California 87
Knight Initiative* . . . . .California 87
State safe schools* . . . . .California 90
Rally against legislator . . . . .El Monte, CA 94
Petaluma benefits opposed* . . . . .Petaluma, CA 102
Anti-gay prayer for legislator* . . . . .Sacramento, CA 106
San Bernardino domestic partnership* . . . . . . .San Bernardino County, CA 107
Santa Barbara domestic partnership* . . . . .Santa Barbara County, CA 112
Challenge to adoptions by gays* . . . . .Colorado 116
Anti-gay custody ruling* . . . . .Connecticut 127
Anti-gay fireman promoted* . . . . .Washington, DC 134
Anti-gay adoption rider* . . . . .Washington, DC 135
Anti-gay Lee County Sheriff* . . . . .Ft. Myers, FL 140
Anti-gay state official . . . . .Tallahassee, FL 146
Prosecutor continues to target gays . . . . .Gwinnett County, GA 152
Anti-gay campaign . . . . .Chicago, IL 166
Anti-gay alderman . . . . .Chicago, IL 167
Anti-gay presidential pledge . . . . .Des Moines, IA 185
Councilman leaves diversity training . . . . .Baton Rouge, LA 196
Anti-gay campaign . . . . .Washington/Frederick County, MD 205
Anti-gay campaign . . . . .Newton, MA 209
Sodomy repeal challenged . . . . .Missouri 221
Jury discrimination . . . . .Kansas City, MO 224
Failure to repeal sodomy statute . . . . .Montana 227
Bauer chides teens on marriage . . . . .Manchester, NH 237
Gay foster children's suit . . . . .New York City, NY 247
Anti-gay school board campaign . . . . .New York City, NY 248
Gay Rep. denounced . . . . .Suffolk County, NY 254
Governor's order excludes gays* . . . . .Ohio .264
Gay flag controversy* . . . . .Columbus, OH 267
Anti-gay schools initiative* . . . . .Oregon 273
Same-sex marriage bill* . . . . .Oregon 274
No to domestic partners benefits* . . . . .Pennsylvania 278
Anti-gay campaign . . . . .Allentown, PA 279
Anti-gay Catholic voters guide* . . . . .Philadelphia, PA 282
Anti-gay campaign . . . . .Pike County, PA 284
Police inspections before Pride parade . . . . . . .Houston, TX 303
Anti-transgendered ruling . . . . .San Antonio, TX 307

Harsh custody ruling for lesbian mother* . . . . . . .Wichita Falls, TX 309
Anti-gay council candidate . . . . .Seattle, WA 323
Same-sex marriage bill . . . . .West Virginia 328
Domestic partners bills* . . . . .Wisconsin 329
Governor's declaration targeted . . . . .Madison, WI 330
Proposed tolerance resolution rejected . . . . . . .Lander, WY .334

Religion City or State Page

Lutherans on gays .National 69
Anti-gay Baptist lesson . . . . .National 69
Housing Discrimination* . . . . .Alaska 74
Catholic outreach assailed . . . . .Contra Costa County, CA 93
Commission's diversity controversial . . . . .Redlands, CA 103
Lesbian wedding targeted . . . . .Sacramento, CA 106
Anti-gay prayer for legislator* . . . . .Sacramento, CA 106
Catholic priest defrocked . . . . .San Francisco, CA 107
Right wing sues San Francisco* . . . . .San Francisco, CA 108
"Ex-gay" Conference . . . . .San Francisco, CA 109
Pro-gay churches ousted . . . . .San Francisco, CA 109
"Just the Facts" criticized* . . . . .San Francisco, CA 111
Sisters of Indulgence controversy* . . . . .San Francisco, CA 111
Anti-gay Arvada Hell House . . . . .Arvada, CO .118
Lesbian minister fired . . . . .Boulder, CO .118
Methodist Bishop charged . . . . .Denver, CO .122
UCONN hate preacher* . . . . .Storrs, CT 130
Gay minister charged . . . . .Stamford, CT 131
Church ousts pro-gay minister . . . . .Washington, DC 133
Anti-gay Conference . . . . .Ft. Lauderdale, FL 137
"Ex-gay" Church . . . . .Lakeland, FL .141
Baptists ousts pro-gay churches . . . . .Atlanta/Decatur, GA 149
Anti-gay Hell House . . . . .Champaign, IL 165
Gays and supporters ousted from camp . . . . . . .Des Plaines, IL 171
Rev. Dell convicted .Downers Grove, IL 173
Exodus Conference .Wheaton, IL .175
Conversion proposal . . . . .Ames, IA 184
Pro-gay Catholics criticized . . . . .Des Moines, IA 186
Phelps-White Meeting . . . . .Topeka, KS .187
Gay ministry stopped . . . . .Baltimore, MD 201
Hope College speaker* . . . . .Holland, MI .214
Methodists anti-gay policies . . . . .Nebraska 229
Rev. Jimmy Creech's trial . . . . .Grand Island, NE 230
Anti-gay Hell House . . . . .Rio Rancho, NM 242

Presbyterians on same-sex marriage . . . . .Dobbs Ferry, NY 245
Lesbian cleric's award challenged . . . . .Rochester, NY 252
Pro-gay Catholics excommunicated . . . . .Rochester, NY 252
University Chapel controversy* . . . . .Winston-Salem, NC 262
Methodist resigns amid controversy . . . . .Tulsa, OK 272
Anti-gay Catholic voters guide* . . . . .Philadelphia, PA 282
Anti-gay Hell House .Upper Southampton, PA 287
Baptist Magazine . . . . .Greenville, SC 289
"Ex-gay" Conference . . . . .Memphis, TN 291
Anti-gay Presbyterians votes . . . . .Fort Worth, TX 301
PFLAG Expulsion . . . . .Wichita Falls, TX 308
Harsh custody ruling for lesbian mother* . . . . . .Wichita Falls, TX 309
Mormons denounce same-sex marriage* . . . . . .Salt Lake City, UT 313
Falwell-White meeting* . . . . .Lynchburg, VA .318
Church's conversion program . . . . .Norfolk, VA 320
Baptists break with University of Richmond* . . . .Richmond, VA .321
Church rejects gays .Seattle, WA 324

APPENDIX II Glossary of Organizations

Alliance Defense Fund

Based in Scottsdale, AZ, this group funds legal cases relating to perceived attacks on Christians and "pro-family" causes. It participates directly through litigation and by funding lawsuits for right-wing Christian legal causes throughout the nation. It has challenged domestic partner benefit programs across the nation and was head legal counsel in the Supreme Court case that led to the prohibiting of Irish gay and lesbian activists from participating in Boston's St. Patrick's Day Parade. D. James Kennedy of the Coral Ridge Ministries, Don Wildmon of the American Family Association and James Dobson are three of its founders.

American Center for Law and Justice

Based in Virginia Beach, VA and founded by Pat Robertson, this public interest law firm is devoted to promoting anti-abortion and what it terms "pro-family" lawsuits. It has been instrumental in the campaign to dismantle anti-discrimination laws that include sexual orientation and gender identity and domestic partner policies across the nation. Jay Sekulow, the ACLJ's chief counsel, has argued six cases before the U.S. Supreme Court.

American Conservative Union

Based in Alexandria, VA, this group describes itself as the "oldest right-wing lobbying organization." It rates political candidates on right-wing social issues including homosexuality. It organized the defeat of national health care proposals and is a co-sponsor of CPAC, the Conservative Political Action Conference.

American Enterprise Institute

Based in Washington, DC, this think tank is widely regarded as one of the major organizations dedicated to right-wing policy making. Its resident scholars exert significant influence over how Congress and the states deal with social, budgetary, and civil rights issues.

American Family Association

Based in Tupelo, MS, this group monitors the media and entertainment industries "to promote the Biblical ethic of decency in American society." Its legal arm, the Center for Law and Policy, crticizes the media's depiction of homosexuality and other issues to which it objects. The AFA is also known for its calls to boycott what it claims are liberal media outlets. The AFA has affiliates in Alabama, Alaska, Arkansas, California, Colorado, Georgia, Indiana, Iowa, Kentucky, Michigan, Minnesota (called the Family Assoc. of Minnesota), Mississippi, Missouri, New Jersey, New York, North Carolina (called the Christian Action League), Ohio, Oregon, Pennsylvania, Texas and Virginia (called the Family Policy Network).

Americans for Truth About Homosexuality

Based in Washington, D.C., this group publishes the "Lambda Report" and is "dedicated to opposing the homosexual movement." Its members are also known for attending gay and lesbian pride celebrations across the nation and portraying their most outrageous elements as the norm. Its members have testified before state legislatures opposing gay and lesbian rights. Its president, Peter LaBarbera, speaks nationwide about opposing gay and lesbian rights, and is also an editor at the Family Research Council, producing a variety of publications for that group.

Capitol Resource Institute

Based in Sacramento, CA, this group is dedicated to seeing "Judeo-Christian values conveyed into spheres of American Society" and is closely aligned with Focus on the Family. It helps fund various right-wing causes throughout California.

Center for Individual Rights

Based in Washington, D.C., this legal group backs conservative causes from a free-speech perspective. It has litigated against domestic violence laws, affirmative actions programs, and supported California's Proposition 209, which eliminated government-run affirmative action programs. Its recent legal work included challenging universities' affirmative action programs and advocating on behalf of religious student groups on college campuses.

Center for Law and Religious Freedom

Based in Annandale, VA, this is the religious advocacy and information arm of the Christian Legal Society, operating as a nationwide network of evangelical attorneys. The CLS website and its CLRF portion provide attorneys in up-to-date information about cases involving alleged threats to religious freedom, including right-wing challenges to anti-discrimination ordinances that include sexual orientation.

Center for Reclaiming America

Based in Fort Lauderdale, FL, the Center is an outreach of Coral Ridge Ministries (founded by D. James Kennedy) and is headed by Janet Folger. She was the coordinator of the "Truth in Love" campaign advocating that gay men and lesbian should change their sexual orientation through religious devotion. Folger does a weekly national radio broadcast.

Chalcedon Foundation

Based in Vallecito, CA, this think tank promotes "Christian Reconstructionism," the belief that all laws should be based on biblical law. Among the past accomplishments it touts are the conversion of influential Jewish leaders to Christianity and regular financing of right-wing causes. Its founder, Rousas John Rushdoony, reportedly advocated the death penalty for "practicing homosexuals."

Christian Action Network

Based in Forest, VA, this group is dedicated to teaching Christian activists to lobby local, stat, and federal government against gay rights and public funding of the arts. It also lobbies for prayer in schools and for what it terms "pro-family" issues.

Christian Anti-Defamation League

Based in Rue, CA, this group frequents college campuses and public events across the country to preach the gospel of Jesus Christ and has been known incite heated debates on what it claims are attacks against Christians. Its organizers publish the "Virgin Pride" newsletter. The group's title is the same as a pro-Aryan organization that surfaced during the last days of the Weimar Republic in Germany.

Christian Coalition

Founded by Pat Robertson and based in Chesapeake, VA, this group is perhaps the most nationally prominent Christian lobbying group. It is dedicated to making government more responsive to Christian and "pro-family" concerns. It has state and local affiliates in all 50 states.

Christian Family Network

Based in Dayton, OH, this group is dedicated to advancing "Christ-centered" values and to restoring morality to the community. It believes "The truth about homosexuality is that it is unnatural, abnormal, unhealthy, and behavioral — not genetic." It "actively opposes the Homosexual Agenda."

Citizens for Community Values

Based in Cincinnati, OH, this group is dedicated to promoting what it claims are "Judeo-Christian moral values" and to reducing the "destructive behaviors contrary to those values" through grassroots organizing and community partnerships. It has reached out to right-wing grassroots organizers from Hawaii to Vermont.

Colorado for Family Values

Based in Colorado Springs, CO, this group is dedicated to the "education of the public concerning the homosexual agenda in government, schools, and communities." It gained national prominence after it spearheaded Amendment 2, which barred state and local governments from adopting laws protecting gay men and lesbians from discrimination.

Concerned Women for America

Based in Washington, DC, the CWA is a legal and educational foundation that says it works to "restore the family to its traditional purpose." Founded by Beverly LaHaye, wife of former televangelist Tim LaHaye, CWA claims to be the largest national conservative women's organization and conducts media campaigns against gay and lesbian rights. CWA also awards grants for right-wing causes and builds coalitions with other right-wing groups to carry out its ends.

Coral Ridge Ministries

Based in Fort Lauderdale, FL, this media outreach center is dedicated to promoting "ex-gay" ministries. Its founder, D. James Kennedy, hosts a radio and television program focusing on right-wing Christian issues, and encourages his audience to oppose policies that accept homosexuality as valid in public and religious life. Coral Ridge Ministries also includes the Center for Reclaiming America, which Kennedy also founded.

Eagle Forum

Based in Alton, IL, this group is dedicated to lobbying for right-wing and so-called "pro-family" issues. It was instrumental in defeating the Equal Rights Amendment and supporting the military buildup in the 1980s. Its president, Phyllis Schafly, speaks out across the country on right-wing issues, including opposition to homosexuality. It conducts research and educational work through its affiliates in Nevada (Nevada Families Eagle Forum), Illinois, Idaho, Washington and 24 other states.

Exodus International

Based in Seattle, WA, this group is, perhaps, the most widely recognized "ex-gay" group in the nation. It maintains that gay men and lesbians can change their sexual orientation through Christian devotion. Exodus has been active in the "Truth in Love" campaign in print and broadcast media and sponsors an annual conference discussing the "ex-gay" movement.

Family Policy Network

Based in Forest, VA, this group is the Virginia affiliate of the American Family Association. It specializes in educating religious groups about morality and faith-based issues in public policy, primarily through its fax newsletter distributed nationwide.

Family Protection Lobby

Based in Annapolis, MD, this affiliate of Focus on the Family seeks to stop the "erosion of family values" in society and protect Judeo-Christian heritage through opposition to "laws protecting perverse practices that will impact [the] family such as... homosexuality."

Family Research Council

Based in Washington, DC, this group is one of the most high-profile right-wing organizations in the country whose former head, Gary Bauer, made an unsuccessful run for the 2000 Republican presidential nomination. Its policy work, which includes opposition to gay and lesbian rights and media campaigns, has made it one of the top so-called "pro-family" lobbying groups and think tanks in the nation's capital. The FRC also awards grants to a variety of right-wing causes and was originally launched as the political wing of James Dobson's Focus on the Family.

Family Research Institute

Based in Colorado Springs, CO, this group publishes so-called "scientific" reports on homosexuality, which are largely the work of discredited psychologist Paul Cameron. Its publications have claimed that gay and lesbian parenting is harmful to children and that the average lifespans of gay men and women are shorter than the general population because of their sexual behavior.

Florida Family Association

Based in Tampa, FL, this former state affiliate of the American Family Association is dedicated to educating the public about what it can do to "protect and promote traditional biblical values" and oppose progressive causes like "the homosexual agenda... which have a negative influence on families." It has opposed gay rights ordinances and policies statewide. FFA President David Caton and the AFA continue to lead the right-wing boycott of Disney for its policy of providing domestic partner benefits to gay and lesbian employees.

Focus on the Family

Based in Colorado Springs, CO, this group claims to be the largest right Religious Right organization in America. Its media outreach includes a nationally distributed magazine and an internationally syndicated radio program hosted by the group's founder and president, James Dobson, which is heard on almost 3,000 stations in over 70 countries. FOTF works with state affiliates and local religious leaders to coordinate so-called "pro-family" campaigns against progressive laws and policies, especially those favoring gay men and lesbians. Among its affiliates are the Alabama Family Alliance, Capitol Resource Institute, Rocky Mountain Family Council, Family First of Florida, Idaho Family Forum, Illinois Family Institute, Kentucky Family Foundation, Christian Civic League of Maine, Family Protection Lobby of Maryland, Massachusetts Family Institute, Michigan Family Forum, North Carolina Family Policy Council, Oregon Center for Family Policy, Pennsylvania Family Institute, and the Family Foundation of Virginia, along with others throughout the country.

Kerusso Ministries

Based in Newport News, VA, this group promotes an "ex-gay" event called National Coming Out of Homosexuality Day every October. During celebrations for that event, members of the group distribute literature denouncing gay rights and encourage gay men and lesbians to change their sexual orientation through Christian devotion. Its president, Michael Johnston, speaks around the nation about how he renounced his homosexuality and "became straight."

Media Research Center

Based in Alexandria, VA, this group serves as a media watchdog against leftist bias in news reporting and television programming. Its online news division, the Conservative News Service, reports on news that "the liberal media fail to air."

Moral Majority

Based in Lynchburg, VA, and founded by Rev. Jerry Falwell in the 1970s, the Moral Majority was dedicated to promoting right-wing values in public life. It was the largest Religious Right group in the 1980s but later disbanded and was replaced by the Liberty Federation.

National Association for Research and Therapy of Homosexuality

Based in Encino, CA, this group is dedicated to research and prevention of homosexuality. Founded by Drs. Charles Socarides, Benjamin Kaufman, and Joseph Nicolosi, NARTH is staffed mostly by right-wing "scientists" who claim that "homosexuality distorts the natural bonds of friendship that would naturally unite persons of the same sex." It also distributes a variety of anti-gay "scientific" publications.

Northstar Legal Center

Based in Minneapolis, MN, this is the legal arm of the Minnesota Family Council and Institute, which, itself, is an affiliate of the American Family Association. Its general counsel, Jordan Lorence, a Washington, D.C.-area attorney, has filed numerous lawsuits challenging domestic partner benefit programs that state and local governments across the nation offer their employees. The center has also been active in supporting the legal challenges to college policies that various college students claim infringe upon their religious rights.

Northwest Legal Foundation

Based in Tacoma, WA, this group is a right-wing public interest law firm dedicated to what it argues is the protection of individual rights, private enterprise, and limited government. It also rates nominees to the Washington state judiciary.

Oregon Citizens Alliance

Based in Brooks, OR, this group is dedicated to right-wing Christian activism in politics and the promotion of what it claims are "pro-family" public policies. It has sought to introduce ballot initiatives that would prohibit public schools from discussing homosexuality in an affirmative way and define marriage as being between a man and a woman, among others. Its alliance with the state Christian Coalition has placed a host of anti-gay initiatives and other measures on the ballot since 1988.

Pacific Justice Institute

Based in Citrus Heights, CA, this group has been an advocate for right-wing Christians in California. Its legal activities included fighting against the rights of gay, lesbian, and transgendered teachers and funding anti-gay ballot initiatives, among other right-wing causes.

Rev. Fred Phelps/Westboro Baptist Church

Based in Topeka, KS, Phelps has picketed all forms of gay and gay-affirming activity. He gained national attention for picketing the funeral of murdered Wyoming college student Matthew Shepard. Members of his church, many of whom are his family members, have picketed in other countries and even protested some leaders of the Religious Right for not condemning homosexuality sufficiently.

Parents and Families of Ex-Gays

Based in Alexandria, VA, this group takes its name from the gay-friendly Parents, Families and Friends of Gays and Lesbians (PFLAG). It is a clearinghouse for the "ex-gay" movement, advocating that gay men and lesbians should change their sexual orientation through religious devotion. It operates through local chapters across the nation. In 2000, PFOX sponsored its annual conference during the Millennium March on Washington.

Pro-Family Network

Based in Massachusetts, this group's work focuses on grassroots organizing in Massachusetts for a variety of right-wing causes, including opposition to gay and lesbian rights. Among the groups it claims are "not friends of the family" are the National Education Association, the American Civil Liberties Union and Planned Parenthood. It also plans to begin functioning as a clearinghouse of information for right-wing activists.

Southeastern Legal Foundation

Based in Atlanta, GA, this public interest law firm advocates limited government and a right-wing approach to individual rights. It has challenged Atlanta's minority set-aside program, several local non-discrimination ordinances that included sexual orientation, and domestic partner benefit programs throughout the nation.

Traditional Values Coalition

Based in Anaheim, CA, this group is dedicated to opposing gay and lesbian rights and advocates "pro-family" issues. Its founder and chairman, Rev. Lou Sheldon, has been instrumental in developing grassroots opposition in California to laws and public policy favorable to gay men and lesbians. Sheldon and the TVC have developed an increasing network of affiliated churches throughout the country, notably through outreach to predominantly African-American and Latino congregations. Sheldon travels nationwide, speaking out against gay and lesbian rights.

Transforming Congregations

Affiliated with the United Methodist Church, this group is a coalition of Protestant congregations that maintain gay men and lesbians can and should change their sexual orientation through Christian devotion. As a coalition, it coordinates the otherwise disparate activities of congregations' "ex-gay" programs, most notably through its annual conference.

Vision America

This organization seeks to use the Internet to motivate likely Republican voters to vote party candidates into office. Among the many groups and individuals to which it refers people are Pat Robertson's Christian Broadcasting Network, right-wing news outlets such as Worldnet Daily and the American Spectator, and right-wing pundits Matt Drudge, G. Gordon Liddy, and Michael Reagan.

Wisconsin Christians United

Based in Monroe, WI, this group's activities are largely the work of its head, Ralph Ovadal. It has sought to obstruct many of the state's programs and laws favorable to gay men and lesbians. In 1998, it put up billboards in Madison claiming that homosexuality was a sin.

People For the American Way Foundation's
2000 Hostile Climate Team

Lead Researcher
Kareem Murphy

Director of Research
Carol Keys

Editor/Essays Coordinator
Will Heyniger

Additional Editing
Nancy Coleman
Peter Montgomery
Judith Schaeffer

Research Assistance
Kyle Mantyla

Designer
Diahann Hill

Printer
Harris Lithographic

To order additional copies of this book, visit:
www.HostileClimate.org

Or contact:
People For the American Way Foundation
2000 M Street N.W., Suite 400
Washington, D.C. 20036
800/326-PFAW
pfaw@pfaw.org ▌ www.pfaw.org

NOTES